D0848693

Middle Atlantic Prehistory

Middle Atlantic Prehistory

Foundations and Practice

Heather A. Wholey
and Carole L. Nash

ROWMAN & LITTLEFIELD
Lanham • Boulder • New York • London

Published by Rowman & Littlefield
A wholly owned subsidiary of The Rowman & Littlefield Publishing Group, Inc.
4501 Forbes Boulevard, Suite 200, Lanham, Maryland 20706
www.rowman.com

Unit A, Whitacre Mews, 26-34 Stannary Street, London SE11 4AB

British Library Cataloguing in Publication Information Available

Library of Congress Cataloging-in-Publication Data
Names: Wholey, Heather A., editor, author. | Nash, Carole L., editor, author.
Title: Middle Atlantic prehistory : foundations and practice / Heather A. Wholey
    and Carole L. Nash.
Description: Lanham : Rowman & Littlefield, 2018. | Includes bibliographical
    references and index.
Identifiers: LCCN 2017024843 (print) | LCCN 2017039736 (ebook) | ISBN
    9781442228764 (Electronic) | ISBN 9781442228757 (cloth : alk. paper) | ISBN
    9781442228764 (electronic : alk. paper)
Subjects: LCSH: Indians of North America—Middle Atlantic States—Antiquities.
    | Antiquities, Prehistoric—Middle Atlantic States. | Middle Atlantic States—
    Antiquities.
Classification: LCC E78.M65 (ebook) | LCC E78.M65 M53 2017 (print) | DDC
    974.004/97—dc23
LC record available at https://lccn.loc.gov/2017024843

♾™ The paper used in this publication meets the minimum requirements of
American National Standard for Information Sciences—Permanence of Paper
for Printed Library Materials, ANSI/NISO Z39.48-1992.

Printed in the United States of America

Contents

Contents

1

✛

Introduction

Heather A. Wholey and Carole L. Nash

The Middle Atlantic is a relatively spatially compressed, yet highly diverse region whose archaeology has defied simple characterization. Ecologically, it is in the temperate zone, and thus since the onset of the Holocene has been typified by seasonal fluctuations. Within roughly 250 miles, the region encompasses six principal physiographic provinces (Coastal Plain, Piedmont, New England, Ridge and Valley, Blue Ridge, and Appalachian Plateau) with an approximate 3,500 foot elevation gain. It includes five major river basins (James, Potomac, Delaware, Susquehanna, and Ohio), large coastal embayments (Delaware and Chesapeake Bays), marshes (e.g., Dismal Swamp), and mountain ranges (Blue Ridge, Massanutten, Catoctin, Appalachian, Catskill, Pocono, Taconic). The region has some of the earliest evidence for people in the Americas (e.g., Meadowcroft Rockshelter, Cactus Hill, Miles Point) as well as some of the earliest instances of indigenous contact with European colonizers, and has been home to Algonquian (e.g., Delaware, Powatan) and Iroquoian (e.g., Susquehanock) groups. It is due to this ecological and cultural mosaic that the Middle Atlantic has been difficult to define as a research unit. Archaeologists tend to focus their work within specific river drainages, within a certain physiographic province, or on a particular culture group. Small groups of researchers may also form around a specific research problem such as identifying early cultures or defining certain technological industries. It can thus be challenging to see the unity in Middle Atlantic archaeology or to see the Middle Atlantic as a cohesive culture area. This volume provides some historical perspective on the Middle Atlantic as a research entity in prehistoric archaeology, provides some testimony on its unique nature, and its strengths and its contributions to big picture topics and issues. Chapters in the volume also provide some considerations for future and continued work in the region.

The chapters in this volume are organized into two sections. The first part, Archaeological Practice in the Middle Atlantic, consists of seven chapters concerned with the development, growth and contributions of foundational practices in archaeology. Dennis C. Curry's chapter situates the Middle Atlantic region historically and provides a comprehensive account of the role of universities, museums, state archaeology societies, State Historic Preservation Offices, the Middle Atlantic Archaeological Conference, and individual personalities in shaping the practice of archaeology in the Middle Atlantic region. His chapter provides an interesting review of research trends in the region over a roughly forty year period of practice (since the publication of the *Journal of Middle Atlantic Archaeology*), notes hurdles to the present conduct of archaeology in the region, and provides sound direction for capitalizing on what the region has and does best. Chris Espenshade's chapter focuses on the role, contributions, and obligations of cultural resources management in the region and outlines how cultural resources managers in the region must learn to deal with relatively poor preservation conditions, yet also be prepared to encounter a range of circumstances. Elizabeth Crowell's chapter outlines the long history and sustained practice of collaboration between government, professional, and avocational organizations and points to several positive models for public archaeology and outreach programming.

In chapter 5, Greg Lattanzi and Jessie Cohen write about the research potential of museum collections, providing case studies from the Middle Atlantic, with particular focus on collections and programs at the New Jersey state museums. They call for a proactive approach on the part of museums that bring public attention to the role of museums as stewards and educators, and propose that museums have a responsibility to educate and engage the public and are thus in a position to promote the value of archaeology. Chapter 6 reviews technological applications to Middle Atlantic archaeology. In this chapter, Bernard Means examines how technology has been applied for the purposes of developing chronology, making and documenting discoveries, identifying origins and sources, and analyzing and presenting findings. He demonstrates that Middle Atlantic archaeology has applied and developed and advanced certain technologies specifically to overcome challenging circumstances or analyze unique or distinctive data sets. In chapter 7, Marshall Becker writes on the significance of ethnohistoric research in Middle Atlantic archaeology. He reveals the depth and wealth of information available through ethnohistoric sources and demonstrates the value of applying this information to research involving the contact period legacy. Bill Schindler's chapter on experimental research in Middle Atlantic archaeology makes the case the Middle Atlantic region has been the vanguard for experimental archaeology in the Americas and that experimental archaeology researchers in the region have made global scale contributions in their work.

The second part of this volume, Topics in Middle Atlantic Prehistory, consists of nine chapters organized around foundational problems in regional research. The first chapter in this section, written by Roger Moeller, is concerned with the uses, misuses, and abuses of typology. He contends that typologies should only be used to describe large data sets to facilitate analysis, but that Middle Atlantic archaeologists have been guilty of misusing or even abusing the practice of typology by extending it to relative dating and ultimately to build chronologies and culture histories. He builds his argument with reference to several problematic pottery types that yield localized chronometric dates, have long use life or recur through time, or are part of a frequent site revisitation practice. He also challenges the long held assumption of one type-style per time period and argues for a much more complex material record. The following chapter by Dan Griffith works as a companion to Moeller's chapter, outlining the contributions of culture history in Middle Atlantic prehistory. Griffith asserts that culture histories in the region have tended to be overly broad, lacking in fine-scale chronological sequences, and failing to provide a sense of people living in a real time and in a real place. He argues that, to be meaningful, Middle Atlantic culture histories must be considered a *method* of research, rather than a product of research, and the approach must entail methodical context control, site specific research and studies of specific artifact classes, and embrace the participation of descendant communities.

Chapter 11 provides a review of Paleoindian research in the Middle Atlantic. In this chapter, Kurt Carr asserts that research in the Middle Atlantic region has significantly informed big-picture models on when and how people first entered the Americas as well as their cultural adaptations after entering the New World. This chapter gives an overview of the early, sustained, and groundbreaking work on questions regarding the peopling of the New World in Middle Atlantic archaeology. The review includes what is currently known regarding paleo-environments for the region, subsistence and adaptive strategies, settlement patterns, social organization and the Clovis lithic tradition, and evaluates pre-Clovis evidence for the region. Chapter 12, written by Mike Barber, is a chronicle of the evolution of subsistence studies in the Middle Atlantic region from a primarily descriptive endeavor to one more concerned with social and environmental issues. He documents methodological trends in the shift from a focus on *food remains* to *foodways*, which ranged from not collecting subsistence remains at all in the field, materials being collected but only crudely identified in the lab, to tedious but unanalyzed remain and trait lists. Barber argues that the major shifts in perspective and methodological breakthroughs emerged in the 1990s with the integration and synthesis of ethnohistory, archaeobotany, ethnographic models and a focus on detailed, context-specific analysis. Chapter 13 is Carole Nash's contribution on environment in Middle Atlantic prehistory. Middle Atlantic prehistoric archaeologists arguably excel at the integration of environmental sciences into their work and a large cohort are reputed to have a profound ecological perspective to their work. Chapter 14 is Bob Wall's review of settlement pattern studies in Middle Atlantic prehistoric archaeology. In this chapter, he addresses (1) the role of cultural ecology as a perspective for investigating the relationships of humans to the landscape and constructing predictive models for archaeological settlement; (2) the role of cultural resources management in generating large volumes of archaeological survey data, including under or unexplored areas that may fall outside of high probability location; and (3) the role of spatial and geophysical technologies for visualizing, analyzing, and presenting vast amounts of settlement data. In all, the spatial and temporal scale of resolution of Middle Atlantic prehistoric settlement pattern research has greatly broadened and become more encompassing of multiple social and environmental factors. In chapter 15, Heather A. Wholey provides a review of population studies in Middle Atlantic prehistoric archaeology. She outlines the approaches and perspectives, ranging from ethnohistory to floor area estimates to studies grounded in the concept of carrying capacity. The chapter points to the complex factors that must be accounted for in doing population studies in the absence of permanent structures and under circumstances of high or relatively high mobility and makes. It makes the case that there is no one right approach to doing population studies in prehistory because the methods must fit the available data and particular circumstances. Rather than contributing to models of overshoot and collapse, population studies in Middle Atlantic prehistory help to model resiliency through collective agency in adaptation of and response to a dynamic landscape.

In chapter 16, Jay Custer presents the history of Susquehannock studies to argue that archaeologists in the Middle Atlantic are guilty of not confronting the impact of colonialism on indigenous peoples, and of not candidly engaging in postcolonial dialogue to identify the legacies of colonialism for the indigenous peoples and for the practice of archaeology. Instead, he proposes, archaeologists more comfortably engage in an "archaeology of colonialism" that is, in part, based on the "tyranny" of "colonial truths." In his case study, this includes using the archaeological record to affirm that the Susquehannock were violent "intruders" from some outside location, that Susquehannock "authenticity"

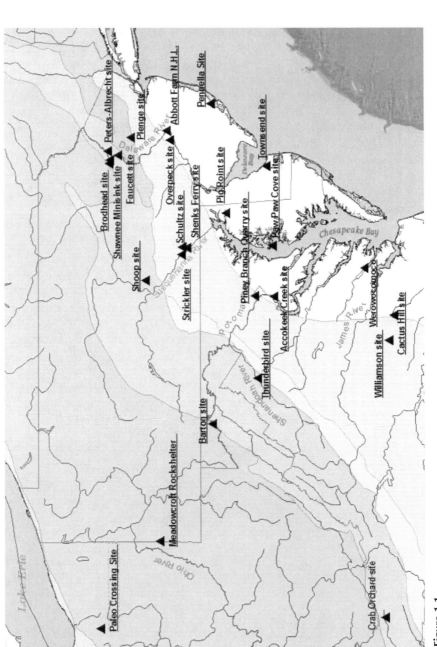

Figure 1.1.

was early on destroyed through acculturation with Europeans, and that the Susquehannock "vanished" after the last known community was massacred. Custer goes on to cite some promising recent work that uses detailed, context specific analysis to challenge these colonial tropes. These studies share in common that they reject a strict adherence to a linear direct historical approach in favor of a more nuanced, anthropological understanding of cultural identity. Richard J. Dent's chapter is the final piece in the second part of the volume. In it he writes in defense of the Middle Atlantic as a region, pointing out that the Middle Atlantic has been treated as an archaeological research area since the late nineteenth century. He argues that rigid fixed boundaries are an impediment to culture area research, but instead can be recognized through sustained interest by a community of scholars who recognize the area as a cohesive research entity.

Chapters in this volume collectively demonstrate that the region operates as a cohesive culture area not despite but because of the physical and cultural mosaic that characterizes the region. They reveal a shared concern for a highly contextualized problem orientation. What several of the chapters in this volume share in common is that they challenge some of the long-standing conventions in archaeology, such as rigid typologies, broad, sweeping regional synthesis, and the direct historic approach. All of the chapters in the volume share in common an historical grounding that reveal the depth and breadth of research and practice in Middle Atlantic prehistoric archaeology. They are also forward-looking and propose paths and objectives to innovate practices and perspectives that will form the modern archaeological landscape.

Part 1

ARCHAEOLOGICAL PRACTICE IN THE MIDDLE ATLANTIC

2

+

A Chronicle of Prehistoric Archaeology in the Middle Atlantic Region

Dennis C. Curry

The study of prehistoric archaeology in the Middle Atlantic region—now entering its second century—is examined here from a historical perspective. The influence of individual personalities and institutions, the changing motivations for undertaking archaeological investigations, and trends in the foci of archaeological research are all discussed, as is the role of the Middle Atlantic Archaeological Conference over the course of its forty-plus years. And lastly, the very concept of a Middle Atlantic culture area is considered.

The vague notion of a "Middle Atlantic province" began at the turn of the last century when Smithsonian archaeologist William Henry Holmes used it to encompass the Potomac–Chesapeake region and surrounding environs. Later, in the 1950s and 1960s, Karl Schmitt and Robert L. Stephenson revived the use of the term for the area including various portions of Virginia, Maryland, Pennsylvania, Delaware, New Jersey, and New York (see Figure 2.1). With the creation of the Middle Atlantic Archaeological Conference in 1970, the Middle Atlantic—though still formally undefined—came to mean the area stretching from Virginia to coastal New York; at various times, portions of North Carolina, West Virginia, and Connecticut have been included as "fringe areas." Essentially, it is the greater Chesapeake Bay–Delaware Bay region carved out of the interface of the more traditional Northeast and Southeast culture areas.

This narrative reviews the history of prehistoric archaeological research in what has become known as the Middle Atlantic region. It traces the transformation from antiquarian roots to early professionalism in the field, and examines the roles of local archaeological societies, various

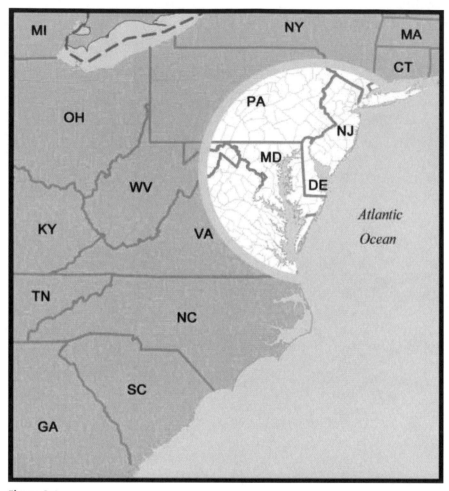

Figure 2.1.

academic institutions, and, after 1970, the Middle Atlantic Archaeological Conference in the quest for archaeological knowledge. Early archaeological programs at the state level—largely established in response to federal historic preservation legislation in the 1960s—are reviewed, but subsequent evolution of these programs is not examined. Likewise, the vast post-1960s universe of cultural resources management is not discussed except in general and for examples to provide context to the overall archaeological research in the region. The development and role of cultural resources management in the Middle Atlantic is covered in-depth in Espenshade's chapter in this volume.

As will be seen, the archaeological record of prehistory in the Middle Atlantic region is a rich one that archaeologists have spent more than a century attempting to explicate. Although much has been learned, many questions remain, all but guaranteeing a challenging next hundred years.

THE EARLY PURSUIT OF ARCHAEOLOGY IN THE MIDDLE ATLANTIC REGION:[1] FROM ANTIQUARIANISM TO STATE HISTORIC PRESERVATION OFFICE

Interest in ancient relics may be ingrained in human nature, and it seems that all cultures look to the past for answers and inspiration. No one knows when the first archaeological endeavor took place in the Middle Atlantic region, but it was likely far earlier than most would think. In a modern-day artifact collection from the Hagerstown Valley of Maryland there is evidence of a surface collector who was active millennia ago. At some point in Archaic times, this ancient surface collector found a beauti-fully made, deeply fluted Clovis point fashioned from high-quality chert. Apparently, however, the fluted point was not collected out of curiosity but rather for expediency, because this collector then pressure-flaked two deep, well-formed notches into the sides of the Paleoindian relic, trans-forming it into a serviceable Archaic side-notched spearpoint.

This anecdote aside, the first recorded formal study of Middle Atlantic prehistory occurred more than two centuries ago. In the 1780s, Thomas Jef-ferson set out to respond to a questionnaire concerning the thirteen origi-nal states. The result was Jefferson's (1787) *Notes on the State of Virginia*, which includes a section characterizing the Indian tribes of Virginia. Em-bedded within his descriptions of the various tribes, Jefferson (1787:104) examines the notion of an "Indian Monument," stating that he knows of none "unless indeed it be the Barrows, of which many are to be found all over this country." Mounds, or "barrows," were—and would continue to be—features of curiosity in North America, and the scientifically minded Jefferson set out to elucidate their meaning. Even in Jefferson's time, the mounds had long been known to be burial places, but opinions varied as to what instigated the burial ceremony. In his (Jefferson 1787:104) words, "There being one of these [barrows] in my neighborhood, I wished to satisfy myself whether any, and which of these opinions were just. For this purpose I determined to open and examine it thoroughly." The result was the first published report of an archaeological excavation in North America, in which Jefferson ably describes a "spheroidical" mound 40 feet in diameter and 7½ feet high (estimated to have been 12 feet high originally). Throughout the mound, Jefferson found deposits of human bone and noted their stratigraphic differences, leading to his accurate description of an accretional burial mound that formed over a time span of periodic reuse. Although Jefferson did not discern "whatever occasion they may have been made" (he did conclude that the mounds were not the burial place of lost warriors, and refuted the local lore that it served as a "common sepulchre of a town, in which the bodies were placed upright, and touching each other"), he did note the mounds' importance to then-living Indians, whom Jefferson had observed solemnly visiting the mound near his property some thirty years prior. As a result of this work, many consider Jefferson to be the father of American archaeology.

Despite Jefferson's surprisingly modern scientific approach to the study of mounds and Indians, an age of (sometimes wild) speculation followed for nearly the next hundred years. Emblematic of this trend was Ira Hill's (1831) *Antiquities of America Explained*, in which he attempted to shed light on the first peopling of America. His review of North American mounds and "characters engraved on rocks" (e.g., Dighton Rock in Massachusetts) is cast in a biblically oriented post-Flood perspective, and concludes that American Indians were descended from "ancient Jews and Tyrians" (i.e., the Ten Lost Tribes of Israel). Such notions were commonplace at the time and, in the case of the "moundbuilders," it would require the masterful surveying work of Ephraim Squire and Edwin Davis (1847) to begin to lay the foundations for reassertion of a Native American origin. Nonetheless, old notions die hard, and certain stakeholders would resort to anything to prove their point. The result was a series of well-known hoaxes that muddied the waters: the *Walam Olum*, a reputed historical narrative of the Lenape (1830s), West Virginia's Grave Creek Stone (1838), Delaware's Holly Oak Pendant (1864), New York's Cardiff Giant (1869), and Pennsylvania's Lenape Stone (1872), to name some of the more notorious. It would take a concerted scientific approach to set matters straight.

While American scholars continued to seek the origins of American Indians, events in Europe would have a profound influence on the direction of such inquiry. In 1859, the discovery in Britain and France of stone tools in association with Pleistocene fossils opened the doors to prehistory—the Paleolithic Age was revealed. As news of the European finds reached America, those seeking the first Americans now had to consider a much greater time-depth—could North American remains date back to Paleolithic times? At the forefront of this quest was Charles Conrad Abbott. Abbott, a New Jersey physician turned naturalist, had collected stone artifacts from his farm, Three Beeches (now Abbott Farm National Historic Landmark), for years and recognized their resemblance to the hand-axes being found in Europe. Abbott's "rude implements" were found deep in gravels that he considered to be glacial outwash of the Pleistocene Age, thereby demonstrating the great antiquity of man in the Delaware Valley (Abbott 1872, 1881). Understandably, these finds created quite a scientific stir, prompting Frederick Ward Putnam (Peabody Museum of Archaeology and Ethnology at Harvard) to sponsor a more concentrated investigation of the Trenton Gravels. This work was directed by Abbott's friend, Ernest Volk, over the next two decades, resulting in the discovery of many more "rude implements" in the gravels and eventually, in 1899, a human femur and skull bones (Volk 1911:117–18). Abbott had demonstrated that the antiquity of man reached back to the New Jersey Ice Age—the "American Paleolithic."

Whatever sense of accomplishment Abbott may have felt must have been short-lived, for there was dissension on the horizon, and it came chiefly from Washington, DC—the Smithsonian's Bureau of American Ethnology, spearheaded by archaeologist William Henry Holmes. Holmes doubted the antiquity of Abbott's "rude implements" and set about to accumulate data on stone tool production. From 1889 to 1894, Holmes carried out archaeological investigations at the prehistoric quartzite quarries along Piney Branch and other stream valleys in Washington, DC. His meticulous study—illustrated by his own exquisite artwork—demonstrated a staged process of tool manufacture and proved conclusively that "the rudely flaked stones of the province are rejects of manufacture" (Holmes 1897:14). Furthermore, Holmes personally inspected the various purported Paleolithic sites—beginning with the Trenton Gravels—and (relying on the support and interpretations of the USGS's head glacial geologist, Thomas C. Chamberlin) concluded that not only were the artifacts not ancient, but even the gravels did not date to the Pleistocene. The final blow may have come from Smithsonian physical anthropologist Aleš Hrdlička. Hrdlička examined the femur Volk found in the Trenton Gravels—and subsequently examined human bone from a number of purported Pleistocene deposits from throughout the United States—and declared that these bones exhibited "close affinity to or identity with those of the modern Indian" (Hrdlička 1907:98). The American Paleolithic was nothing more than the debris and remains of recent Native American groups!

Eventually, former supporters and friends (including Putnam and Henry Mercer) were no longer able to endorse Abbott's Paleolithic claims. Ultimately, of course, Abbott was correct about the Pleistocene origin of man in North America, but for the wrong reasons (the deposits at Three Beeches were later shown to be Middle Woodland in age). And, ultimately, Holmes and his cohorts from the Smithsonian were wrong about the antiquity of man—but not about the contemporary examples touted as Pleistocene sites. Each of those has been shown—using the modern systematic techniques and approaches promoted by the Smithsonian scientists—to be Holocene in nature.

The next fifty years in the Middle Atlantic would see refinement of the archaeological method and burgeoning archaeological investigation throughout the region. At the forefront of this progress were local archaeological societies and early state-sponsored archaeological programs. With the advent of federal historic preservation laws in the mid-1960s, formal state archaeological programs and State Historic Preservation Offices (SHPOs) came to dominate the archaeological scene. A selective review of the development of archaeology in the Middle Atlantic region's core states is presented below.

New Jersey

Charles Abbott, who went on to become the first curator of the University of Pennsylvania's newly established (1890) Department of American Archaeology, is considered by many to be the father of New Jersey archaeology. And while the fascination of Abbott and his associates with the American Paleolithic may have served to spotlight New Jersey archaeology, it certainly did not represent the range of archaeological interests in the state. As with other coastal states, New Jersey witnessed an early curiosity in ancient shell middens. Prior to his association with the Smithsonian, archaeologist Charles Rau (1865) reported on New Jersey middens, as later did Fountain (1897) and Jordan (1906). In the early twentieth century, Max Schrabisch carried out extensive surveys and excavations in the Passaic River Valley—especially at cave and rockshelter sites. In 1912, the New Jersey legislature funded the first statewide archaeological survey, carried out by Skinner and Schrabisch (1913), in which more than a thousand camp and village sites, shell heaps, cemeteries, rockshelters, quarries, caches, and trails were cataloged. The year 1931 witnessed two watershed events in New Jersey archaeology: Dorothy Cross began working with the New Jersey State Museum (she was one of a handful of women employed as a professional archaeologist at that time, and would eventually become curator of the Museum's Bureau of Archaeology in 1936), and the Archaeological Society of New Jersey (ASNJ) was organized. Working together, Cross and the ASNJ compiled the results of the 1936–1942 Works Progress Administration's Indian Sites Survey project and undertook extensive controlled excavations at the Abbott Farm site; the results of these efforts were published in the massive two-volume set *The Archaeology of New Jersey* (Cross 1941, 1956). Cross set the standard for professional involvement with the ASNJ. Later, in 1948—when the society's journal, *Bulletin of the Archaeological Society of New Jersey*, was founded—J. Alden Mason served as its founding editor. In 1960, Herbert C. Kraft first joined the society and would go on to a fifty-year career in New Jersey, excavating throughout the Delaware River Valley, teaching at Seton Hall University, and providing a mainstay to New Jersey archaeology. New Jersey's State Historic Preservation Office is a division of the Department of Environmental Protection. The New Jersey State Museum, founded in 1895, curates extensive archaeological and ethnological collections, and serves as a primary repository for materials generated by state and federal archaeological projects in the state. And, like in many states, the Department of Transportation is one of the largest sponsors of archaeological work, including extensive modern excavations at the Abbott Farm National Historic Landmark (e.g., Wall et al. 1996a, 1996b; Stewart 1998a).

Pennsylvania

In the 1890s, Henry Chapman Mercer involved himself in the American Paleolithic conundrum. A friend of Charles Abbott, Mercer—from Doylestown, Pennsylvania—sought data to support Abbott's premise, focusing on the argillite and jasper quarries of Pennsylvania. To the credit of his powers of observation and his objectivity, Mercer (1897a) concluded—much as did William Henry Holmes—that Abbott's paleoliths were manufacturing rejects. During the early twentieth century, the eastern portions of Pennsylvania were of great interest to a large number of collectors, such as David Landis, Henry Deisher, and Gerald Fenstermaker, to name just a few. These amateur archaeologists amassed enormous artifact collections, and the data from these helped form the basis for some of the earliest professional efforts in the state, including Christopher Wren's (1914) treatise on pottery and Warren K. Moorehead's (1938) Susquehanna River Expedition of 1916. The latter, sponsored by George Heye of the Museum of the American Indian, was an ambitious attempt to survey the Susquehanna River from Ostego Lake in New York to the head of Chesapeake Bay in Maryland, seeking to document the significant sites in the drainage and collect artifacts for the museum. The strong amateur interest in Pennsylvania led in 1929 to the creation of the Society for Pennsylvania Archaeology, with J. Alden Mason serving as president; the first issue of its journal, *Pennsylvania Archaeologist*, was published the following year. Also in 1929, Donald A. Cadzow was hired by the Pennsylvania Historical Commission to study the Safe Harbor petroglyphs threatened by hydroelectric dam projects. Cadzow would later be appointed first state anthropologist of Pennsylvania and would go on to expand the Safe Harbor survey to include historic Susquehannock sites in addition to the petroglyphs (Cadzow 1934, 1936). In 1945, the State Museum of Pennsylvania (founded in 1905) merged with the Pennsylvania Historical Commission (founded in 1913) to create the Pennsylvania Historical and Museum Commission (PHMC) (which now houses the Bureau for Historic Preservation, Pennsylvania's SHPO). This began a period of intense archaeological activity by such notables as Mary Butler (1947) at two rockshelter sites, John Witthoft (1952; Witthoft and Farver 1952) at the

Shoop Paleoindian site and at Shenks Ferry sites (among many others), and Fred Kinsey (1959a, 1959b) at the Late Archaic Kent-Hally site and work on Susquehannock ceramics. This was followed in the late 1960s by work directed by Barry C. Kent (1970, 1984) at Late Archaic sites in the Lower Susquehanna and Susquehannock sites in the Washington Boro area. Today, the archaeological staff at the PHMC continues this legacy of archaeological research with projects like their recent investigations at the King's Jasper Quarry (Carr and McLearen 2005).

Delaware

In 1865, Joseph Leidy (1865:95, 1866:290–91) reported on his observations at the extensive shell middens near Lewes, Delaware. Leidy mentioned projectile points, shell-tempered ceramics (including a decorated elbow pipe), and a partial human skeleton recovered from the "kitchen refuse heap." Although the middens Leidy observed no longer survive, his descriptions match extant middens in the National Register's Cape Henlopen Archaeological District—a series of shell heaps often visited by Middle Atlantic Archaeological Conference attendees when the meetings were held in Rehoboth Beach. In 1882, a cache of some sixty argillite bifaces was uncovered along the Christina River near the Crane Hook site. This was the first of a series of caches—including one found at the Kiunk Ditch site on the lower St. Jones River, which contained 190 argillite bifaces—that would be found in the state, and hinting at an Adena presence in the region. Eventually, a number of Delmarva Adena mortuary sites would come to light in Delaware, including Killens Pond, St. Jones, and Frederica (Thomas 1970). Interest in these and other finds throughout the state had long been keen, and in 1933 a group of avocational archaeologists—led by H. Geiger Omwake—joined to form the Archaeological Society of Delaware. The society teamed with professionals to undertake a number of early excavations, including the Slaughter Creek site, which contained numerous shell-filled pits, ossuary-like burials, and extensive faunal deposits (including an antler carving of men in a canoe). Such finds were reported in the society's newly established *Bulletin of the Archaeological Society of Delaware* (e.g., Davidson 1935, 1936). In later years, other local archaeological societies were formed in the state. In 1948, the Sussex Society of Archaeology and History was formed, and carried out excavations at the Townsend site; results were reported in its journal, *The Archeolog* (Omwake and Stewart 1963). And in 1965, the Kent County Archaeological Society was created, largely in response to the discovery of the Island Field site. Today, only the ASD survives. The year 1965 also witnessed the hiring of Delaware's first (and only) state archaeologist, Ronald A. Thomas, at the Delaware Section of Archaeology (now the

Division of Historical and Cultural Affairs). Thomas worked closely with ASD members to expand the state's archaeological registry, and undertook extensive excavations at the Island Field site in South Bowers—a Middle Woodland mortuary complex (Thomas 1974). The Island Field site was later developed as a state museum and curation facility; the human remains were reburied in 1988, the museum was closed, and some of the state collections were relocated to a facility near Dover (the University of Delaware Center for Archaeological Research also serves as a state-mandated collection repository). As of this writing, Jay Custer is currently completing a major re-analysis of the Island Field site and preparing his report for publication.

Maryland

Shell mounds had long been of interest in Maryland, dating back to at least the 1830s when Maryland's first state geologist, J. T. Ducatel, mapped and reported on the shell middens of the Chesapeake Bay (although his interest in shell was economic rather than archaeological). Later, William Henry Holmes (1907) would carry out investigations at the vast shell mounds at Popes Creek in southern Maryland. Smithsonian collaborators and others (Reynolds 1884, 1889a; Jordan 1906) contributed to the study of Maryland shell middens, bringing them to international attention. Other early interests in the state included burial sites, especially tidewater ossuaries (Reynolds 1889b; Mercer 1897b; Graham 1935; Weslager 1942) and the ritual burial site at Sandy Hill on the Eastern Shore (Ford 1976). In search of data relevant to the "American Paleolithic" controversy, Smithsonian archaeologists Frank H. Cushing (in 1877) and J. D. McGuire (in 1903) conducted preliminary investigations at Busheys Cavern in Washington County. Later, in 1905, Warren K. Moorehead and Charles Peabody carried out extensive excavations at the site, which yielded an array of stone and bone tools along with (often exotic) pottery (Peabody 1908). In the 1920s and 1930s, William B. Marye undertook wide-ranging historical and archaeological research into the Indians of Maryland; topics included Indian paths, Piscataway villages, burial methods, and shell heaps. Marye (1938) also prepared the most complete description of the Bald Friar petroglyphs found on a series of islands in the Susquehanna River (unfortunately, attempts by the Maryland Academy of Sciences to salvage the glyphs prior to their inundation by the Conowingo Dam project involved the use of dynamite; most surviving glyphs are fragmentary, and can be found at the Harford County Courthouse, the Cecil County Public Library in Elkton, and the Maryland Archaeological Conservation Laboratory). In the late 1930s and early 1940s, Alice L. L. Ferguson carried out extensive excavations at her farm and adjacent properties nestled at the confluence of

Piscataway Creek and the Potomac River. Her investigations, carried out with the assistance of various professionals (most notably T. Dale Stewart of the Smithsonian), documented a major palisaded village of the Piscataway Indians, numerous ossuaries, and the historic 1675 Susquehannock Fort, among other sites (Stephenson et al. 1963). In the 1930s and 1940s, Richard E. Stearns directed the Natural History Society of Maryland's Department of Archaeology, during which he produced an impressive list of publications on Indian village sites, pottery, and other artifact types. In 1954, the Archeological Society of Maryland was founded as part of the Maryland Academy of Sciences; in 1964 a splinter group formed the Archeological Society of Maryland, Inc.; both groups merged under the latter name in 1975. The society has published a journal, *Maryland Archeology*, since 1965, as well as special publications. In the 1950s, the society undertook a number of excavations, most notably at Late Woodland sites along the Potomac River (MacCord et al. 1957; Slattery and Woodward 1992). Subsequently, the society has teamed up with the state archaeology office to run an Annual Field Session in Maryland Archeology, now in its forty-second year. In the late 1950s and early 1960s, a young society member carried out excavations at a series of Woodland sites in the Severn–South River region. Based on this work, Henry T. Wright (1973) published an archaeological sequence that still stands today (Wright is currently the Albert C. Spaulding Distinguished University Professor of Anthropology at the University of Michigan). In 1961, the Maryland Historical Trust (MHT) was created to encourage historic preservation in the state; it became the SHPO in 1967, and added its first staff archaeologist, Leland Gilsen, in 1976. The trust sponsored a number of regional surveys (Stewart 1980a; Hughes 1980; Wanser 1982; Steponaitis 1983) and later developed a major archaeological property in Calvert County as the Jefferson Patterson Park and Museum, which includes the Maryland Archaeological Conservation Laboratory. In 1969, Tyler Bastian was appointed Maryland's first state archaeologist, housed within the Maryland Geological Survey's (MGS's) newly created Division of Archeology. Bastian, in addition to establishing an inventory for sites in the state, oversaw several regional surveys (Wall 1981; Kavanagh 1982) and built a strong highway archaeology program (now at the Maryland State Highway Administration) that conducted scores of surveys as well as in-depth excavations (e.g., Ebright 1992). In 1990, the MHT and MGS archaeology offices merged at the trust.

Virginia

As with Maryland, the Smithsonian's interest in Virginia was extensive. From 1891 to 1893, Gerard Fowke (1894) undertook a survey of a vast section of Virginia (and lesser portions of Maryland and West Virginia) in order to identify the Indian tribes that once inhabited the region; the result is an encyclopedia of the archaeological character of the James and Potomac valleys. In the 1920s and 1930s, David I. Bushnell Jr. undertook numerous excavations in the James and Rappahannock valleys, in addition to investigations of soapstone quarries (Bushnell 1926). From 1935 to 1940, T. Dale Stewart (1992) teamed with Judge William J. Graham to excavate the ca. 1608 Indian town of Patawomeke. The result of this work exposed a palisaded village containing numerous houses, features, and ossuaries, and provided the data for Karl Schmitt (1952) to define the Potomac Creek Focus. In 1950, Clifford Evans (1955) undertook a statewide survey and analysis of Virginia pottery types (which was supplemented by a study of Virginia projectile points by C. G. Holland). Holland (1960) would later undertake an archaeological survey of five counties in northwestern Virginia. Perhaps the intense professional interest in Virginia prehistory helped instigate avocational attention, and in 1940 the Archeological Society of Virginia (ASV) was organized. The ASV has long had a strong publication program, publishing a journal, *Quarterly Bulletin*, since the society's inception, as well as a long list of special publications. Premier among the latter are a series of synthetic volumes resulting from public symposia on Virginia archaeology co-sponsored by the Council of Virginia Archaeologists in the late 1980s and early 1990s (Wittkofski and Reinhart 1989; Reinhart and Hodges 1990, 1991, 1992; Reinhart and Pogue 1993). The ASV has also sponsored studies such as the "Survey of Virginia Fluted Points." Begun by Ben C. McCary fifty years ago (and now maintained by Wm. Jack Hranicky), this project has documented more than a thousand fluted points from Virginia. In 1963, the Chesopiean Archaeological Association (later the Chesopiean Library of Archaeology)—based out of Virginia and long associated with amateur archaeologist Floyd Painter—began publishing its journal, *The Chesopiean* ("A Journal of Atlantic Coast Archaeology"). Also in 1963, Howard A. MacCord Sr. was hired by the Virginia State Library as what might be called the unofficial state archaeologist. MacCord—a stalwart of Virginia and Middle Atlantic archaeology—had earlier collaborated with Carl P. Manson and James B. Griffin on the Keyser Farm site in Page County (Manson et al. 1943). While at the Virginia State Library, MacCord enlisted the assistance of ASV members to investigate nearly two hundred sites across the state, dutifully reporting the results in the *Quarterly Bulletin* and elsewhere. In 1975, the Virginia Research Center for Archaeology (VRCA) was created as part of Virginia Historic Landmarks Commission. MacCord retired from the library, and its archaeological functions were transferred to the VRCA. Virginia's archaeological and SHPO functions are now housed at the Virginia Department of Historic Resources.

THE INFLUENCE OF CULTURAL
RESOURCES MANAGEMENT

The Antiquities Act of 1906 outlined the first national preservation policy in the United States and instigated the management of archaeological sites on federal lands. With the National Historic Preservation Act of 1966, the scope of historic preservation was broadened into a federal–state–local partnership to guide comprehensive historic preservation, largely through the establishment of State Historic Preservation Offices. And in 1974, the Archeological and Historic Preservation Act expanded cultural resources management (CRM) responsibilities beyond those of mere salvage archaeology. The result was a transformation of the archaeological profession—a transformation witnessed in the Middle Atlantic as well as elsewhere throughout the country. The need for archaeologists went from that of a few federal agencies and academia to the need for thousands of archaeologists in a variety of programs and institutions. In addition to a greater need for archaeologists, the new federal legislation also opened a wealth of funding sources. The result was an explosion of opportunity for the field of archaeology.

While space limitations here prevent a detailed history of the development of cultural resources management archaeology in the Middle Atlantic (see Espenshade, this volume), rest assured that CRM's role in the archaeology of the region is fundamental. Every federal agency (think National Park Service alone) required archaeological expertise and staffing to oversee their archaeological programs. Likewise, every State Historic Preservation Office—as well as other state agencies like highway and parks departments—would require the services of archaeologists. Soon, local jurisdictions would enact historic preservation laws, and city and county programs would hire their own archaeologists. Each of these governmental agencies served, for the most part, to *oversee* archaeological programs and to monitor archaeological work. The task of actually carrying out archaeological investigations fell to an entirely new creation—private archaeology-for-profit firms (and for each government archaeologist monitoring a project, CRM firms might require scores of archaeologists). Universities—once confined to the ivory towers of pure research—also soon saw financial opportunity in CRM, and brought in archaeologists (sometimes for the first time) to tap those opportunities. In some cases, anthropology departments were established on the backs of CRM initiatives. In turn, university programs with CRM arms expanded, and were soon able to offer funding opportunities, CRM-related research projects, and wide-ranging field experiences for students.

So the influence of CRM on archaeology in the Middle Atlantic region was—and is—pervasive. Virtually every aspect of modern archaeology in the region owes a debt to cultural resources management and historic preservation legislation. It is now the responsibility of professional archaeologists—at all levels and in all arenas—to fulfill the hopes and goals of cultural resources management.

THE ROLE OF UNIVERSITY PROGRAMS
IN THE MIDDLE ATLANTIC REGION

A number of colleges and universities in the Middle Atlantic region have offered programs in prehistoric archaeology. The foci of such programs, however, often seems more tied to the interests of individual personalities than to any university or departmental objectives. Furthermore, the "local" programs lack the time-depth of prehistoric archaeological research found at some universities (e.g., Michigan and North Carolina), and seem more vulnerable to the waxing and waning interest in the subject over time. A review of some of the more prominent programs since the late 1960s is illustrative.

In Virginia, the College of William & Mary—long known for its ties to Williamsburg and historic archaeology—initiated a survey of Native American sites along the Chickahominy River in the late 1960s. Directed by Norman Barka and Ben McCary, this multi-year initiative located an array of sites—from villages to burial grounds—associated with the Chickahominy tribe. Although they never published the results of their survey, the project has been resuscitated by Martin Gallivan, who is re-examining the artifacts and remains preserved in the college's collections. Gallivan has also directed a multi-year investigation of Powhatan's village, Werowocomoco. In both instances, Gallivan has included students in the projects, using the studies as hands-on educational opportunities. Also in both cases, Gallivan has sought the input and advice of modern Native American tribes—first to build and ensure a cooperative venture, but also to affirm those groups as rightful stakeholders. Similarly, Jeffrey Hantman at the University of Virginia has spent several decades studying the history of the Monacan Indian people of Virginia, a program that has contributed to the revitalization of the Monacan Indian Nation. At James Madison University, lithic specialist Clarence Geier and prehistorian William Boyer proved anchors to the anthropology section, but currently it is Carole Nash (in the Department of Integrated Science and Technology) at the forefront of the school's study of Middle Atlantic prehistory. As director of the Shenandoah National Park Environmental Archaeology Program, Nash and her students focus on long-term climate change and its impact on people. At Virginia Commonwealth University, L. Daniel Mouer (joined early on by Stephen Perlman and Gordon Bronitsky) directed an active program partially supported by CRM activities, which produced a number of stimulating prehistoric studies (e.g., Mouer et al. 1980). Following Mouer's departure, the VCU archaeology program went dormant until Bernard Means arrived as a professor of archaeology in 2004. Means, who specializes in Native American village spatial and social organization (especially at Monongahela sites), has reinvigorated archaeology at VCU, as evidenced by a recent string of student competition papers presented at the Middle Atlantic Archaeological Conference, and by the creation of the Virtual Curation Laboratory. And in far southwestern Virginia, C. Clifford Boyd and Donna C. Boyd have spent a quarter century teaching archaeology and bioarchaeology at Radford University, where they have established the University's Forensic Science Institute.

In the late 1960s, three archaeologists were hired by universities in Washington, DC: Robert Humphrey (George Washington University), Charles W. McNett Jr. (American University), and William M. Gardner (Catholic University of America). Each arrived about the same time, and each shared similar interests, and early on they created a collaborative program, the Potomac River Archaeology Survey (which continues to this day). Humphrey published a booklet on the Native American cultures of the Potomac Valley (Humphrey and Chambers 1977), but later went on to specialize in Arctic and Mesoamerican sites. McNett and Gardner continued to collaborate, but each eventually focused on multi-year investigations at major Paleoindian sites. McNett directed excavations at the Shawnee-Minisink site, on the Delaware River in Pennsylvania, where some of the first evidence for Paleoindian use of seeds and fish was recovered from hearth features. Gardner studied the Flint Run Complex in Virginia (the core of which was the Thunderbird site) where he employed a multidisciplinary approach then new to archaeology—including such varied tactics as studies of soils and geology, environmental reconstruction, piece plotting of artifacts, and core reconstruction—to re-create the physical and cultural landscapes present during Paleoindian times. The archaeology program at American University continues under the direction of Richard J. Dent, a veteran of the Shawnee-Minisink project who lately has focused his research on Late Woodland villages of the Potomac Valley. At Catholic University, however, Gardner's position was not filled following his retirement in 2001, and only adjunct professor David Clark offers courses immediately relevant to Middle Atlantic prehistory. Nonetheless, the archaeological legacy of both American and Catholic University lives on in the numerous former students who now teach at universities, staff State Historic Preservation Offices and the like, and serve as principal investigators at CRM firms throughout the Middle Atlantic region.

Maryland's longest-lived prehistoric archaeology program is at Towson University, where Robert D. Wall leans on his three decades of experience in western Maryland along the north branch of the Potomac River to introduce his students to the region's prehistory. On the Eastern Shore at Washington College, John Seidel has dealt with predictive models for prehistoric site location, and William Schindler has established a presence based on experimental archaeology. In southern Maryland at St. Mary's College of Maryland, Julia A. King—long known in historic archaeology circles—has recently involved her students in a multi-year project that ultimately located the ca. 1680 Zekiah Fort of the Piscataway Indians. A major shortcoming in the state, however, exists at the flagship of its university system—the University of Maryland at College Park; no program for the study of prehistoric archaeology has ever taken hold there despite several attempts to establish one. This lack is made perhaps more evident by the presence of such a strong long-time program in historic archaeology.

The University of Delaware has the only prehistoric archaeology program in that small state. Led by Jay F. Custer since 1979, archaeological investigations have been carried out throughout the Delmarva Peninsula–Southeastern Pennsylvania region. In the 1980s, the University of Delaware Center for Archaeological Research undertook a number of large regional surveys for the Delaware Department of Transportation, allowing Custer and his students to synthesize mid-Holocene environments and settlement patterns in a series of journal articles, papers at conferences, and books (e.g., Ward and Bachman 1986; Custer 1989a). The university maintains a large archaeology laboratory facility, and Custer continues to provide his students with problem-oriented archaeological opportunities.

Pennsylvania has a number of university programs that have prepared students for archaeological careers. W. Fred Kinsey III established the archaeology programs at Franklin and Marshall College and—relying on his decades of work in the Susquehanna and Delaware valleys and the extensive artifact collections housed at the North Museum (which Kinsey directed)—provided one of the most fertile training grounds for Middle Atlantic archaeology; his former students, like those of Gardner and McNett, are prolific in the profession today. In the late 1990s, Mary Ann Levine—with a background in Northeast archaeology, including the radiocarbon dating of Paleoindian sites and native copper studies—arrived at F&M. Among her more recent projects is the study of the post-Contact village of Otstonwakin in Pennsylvania, where she directed several field schools. Temple University maintains a strong program, largely under the leadership of R. Michael Stewart. Stewart, with a long history of CRM experience, is well known for his trade and exchange and metarhyolite studies, and more recently for work with prehistoric ceramics. He maintains an active fieldwork program, including excavations at a stratified Paleoindian–Late Archaic site in the Lehigh Gorge, and has encouraged his students to undertake innovative studies (including topics such as stable isotope, starch grain, lithic sourcing, and fire-cracked rock analyses). The anthropology department at West Chester University was long led by Marshall J. Becker, who employed archaeological, ethnohistorical, and historical data in a life-long study of the Lenape Indians. Heather Wholey now teaches archaeology at WCU, with a focus on Archaic hunter-gatherers of the Eastern Woodlands. She, too, encourages student innovation as evidenced by recent x-ray fluorescence studies on soapstone deposits in the region. Three other Pennsylvania programs from the western half of the state deserve notice. Pennsylvania State University has a strong archaeology component in its anthropology department. Prior to his death in 1999, James W. Hatch—who had carried out extensive research on Pennsylvania jasper quarries (e.g., Hatch 1994)—cultivated a crop of students who would go on to careers in Middle Atlantic archaeology. And even though two of Penn State's current primary archaeologists' main interests lie outside of the Middle Atlantic region (Dean Snow with the Iroquois of the Northeast, and George Milner with settlement patterns in the Midwest and Southeast), the research of both has direct implications for this region. Similarly, the research of James M. Adovasio (first at the University of Pittsburgh and now at Mercyhurst College) has long affected the study of prehistory in the Middle Atlantic. The meticulous 1970s excavation of Meadowcroft Rockshelter had profound influence on Paleoindian studies, and remains an important component in the pre-Clovis debate. His geoarchaeological study of Paleoindians continues today at the Shoop site in Pennsylvania, and in the search for submerged sites on the continental shelf. And more recently, at Indiana University of Pennsylvania, led by Phillip and Sarah Neusius and Beverly Chiarulli, students have gained practical experience in Middle Atlantic archaeology, including the use of geophysical techniques (e.g., Neusius and Chiarulli 2011), through the university's Archaeological Services cultural resources program.

If these university programs appear personality-dependent, the situation in New Jersey was perhaps even more so. At Seton Hall University, Herbert C. Kraft built a career on the archaeology of the Lenape and Delaware Indians in the Delaware River Valley. In preparation for the construction of the Tock's Island Dam in the Delaware Water Gap, Kraft spent a decade excavating sites that would be flooded in New Jersey (Fred Kinsey directed excavations at sites on the Pennsylvania side of the river). Kraft served as an anthropology professor at Seton Hall for five decades, and also was curator of the Seton Hall University Museum of Anthropology and Archaeology, which amassed thousands of prehistoric artifacts recovered from his fieldwork. Regrettably, Kraft's faculty position was not filled after his death in 2000, and the informal museum is not open to the public (although plans are under way for possible artifact displays, at least online). Similarly, the late John Cavallo tried to establish an archaeological presence at Monmouth College (now University) where he studied Paleoindian sites in New Jersey. Cavallo went on to direct Rutgers University's Center for Public Archaeology (a CRM branch of the university) before moving to Africa to focus on zooarchaeology. Peter Pagoulatos briefly followed Cavallo at Monmouth, and Richard Veit is now on the faculty there and has some interests in prehistoric archaeology (especially the late/Contact period), although his primary focus is on historical archaeology; the Rutgers public archaeology program is now defunct.

Universities from outside the core areas of the Middle Atlantic have also been involved with the archaeology of the region, often through their graduate programs. This was particularly evident at SUNY-Binghamton, as their graduate students presented a wide variety of research at MAAC meetings in the 1970s and 1980s. Subjects included hunter-gatherer exchange systems (Snethkamp 1978), the early practice of CRM (Versaggi 1978), Blue Ridge geography and settlement patterns (Foss 1980), lithic analysis (Andrefsky 1983), and Patuxent River settlement patterns in Maryland (e.g., Steponaitis 1984). Similarly, at SUNY-Cortland Ellie McDowell-Loudan (a graduate of American University) was a frequent contributor at the MAAC meetings, covering topics such as projectile point typology, settlement patterns, the Middle-Late Woodland Glen Haven site on the Potomac in West Virginia (1983), and the parallels between Middle Atlantic and Northeast archaeological sites (1999). In North Carolina, Appalachian State University was represented early on by Burt Purrington (e.g., 1976, 1979) who focused on settlement and subsistence patterns in Appalachia. Later, Cheryl Claassen arrived at ASU and carried out work at shell midden sites including Dogan Point in New York (e.g., 1990), and Thomas R. Whyte created an extensive body of zooarchaeological research in the Middle Atlantic. During the 1980s and 1990s, David Sutton Phelps established an active field archaeology program at East Carolina University, where the Archaeology Laboratory now bears his name. Much of his work was presented at MAAC meetings, covering topics such as coastal Carolina Algonkians (1984), Carolina mortuary practices (1985), and the Contact period Neoheroka Fort (1992). And more recently in West Virginia, Robert F. Maslowski (after retiring from the U.S. Army Corps of Engineers) has joined Marshall University, where he continues his long history of ceramic analysis (e.g., 2006, 2011).

THE ROLE OF THE MIDDLE ATLANTIC
ARCHAEOLOGICAL CONFERENCE

The Middle Atlantic Archaeological Conference (MAAC) was first held on April 17–18, 1970, at the Catholic University of America in Washington,

DC; William M. Gardner (the Catholic University) and Charles W. McNett Jr. (the American University) co-planned the program. This first meeting was organizational—reviewing the state of archaeology throughout the region and determining how the conference would be organized. Representatives from North Carolina, Virginia, Maryland, Delaware, Pennsylvania, New Jersey, and New York convened on the first day to present overviews of their respective region's geography and cultural sequences; on the second day, they laid out research plans for their areas.

The second MAAC was held on March 19–20, 1971, at the American University in Washington, DC, and was organized by McNett. It was here that the first of the MAAC's thematic sessions were born, with themes including shell middens (Brennan 1971; McNett and Gardner 1971), early ceramics from the region (Kraft 1971; Smith 1971; Gardner and McNett 1971), and a session on the vexing notion of typology—particularly projectile point typology—chaired by Gardner and summarized by Melburn D. Thurman (1971). The latter would be a subject often resurrected and hotly discussed, would spawn one of the first MAAC "proposition papers" (Broyles 1974), and would spur June Evans to chair three consecutive MAAC sessions (1984–1986) on Late Archaic projectile point typology.

Proposition papers would come to be an early mainstay of the MAAC, and the champion of this genre was Louis A. Brennan (1974, 1982, 1983) who touched on topics such as the Middle Woodland Fox Creek–Cony–Selby Bay complex, the Middle Atlantic as a culture province, and early cultural resources management. Similarly, McNett (1987, 1991) and Thurman (2010) have presented proposition papers both reminiscing about, and looking into the future of, Middle Atlantic archaeology.

If proposition papers were early hallmarks of the MAAC, synthetic overview papers (and later sessions) came to characterize the mid-history of the conference; at the forefront of this trend was William Gardner (1978, 1980, 1982a, 1982b). Gardner had the knack for retrospectively analyzing the findings from multiple projects—academic, CRM, and even casual examinations of artifact collections—and repackaging the results as broad-sweeping models applicable to large areas of the Middle Atlantic region. Gardner's synopsis papers were intended to be information-packed, thought-provoking, and starting points for discussion; the latter often led to stimulating debates (e.g., Mouer and Ryder 1981). Later, others organized entire sessions aimed at a synthesis of Middle Atlantic data. For instance, in 1989 Jay Custer chaired a session on the Middle-to-Late Woodland transition, organized regionally (Curry and Kavanagh 1989; Fischler and French 1989; Stewart 1989a; Custer 1989b). Similarly, in 1993 Fred Kinsey chaired a review of Middle Atlantic prehistory, organized by time period (Gardner 1993; Carr 1993; Kent 1993; Stewart 1993; Herbstritt 1993; Moeller 1993). Some of Gardner's former students continue this tradition of overviews (Carr 1993; Custer 1987; Curry 1999, 2007; Nash 2006, 2011; Wall 1999; Wholey 2004).

An informal review of old MAAC programs is instructive regarding trends in archaeological topics over time. At the forefront are several subjects that were dealt with at the earliest MAAC meetings—environmental matters, settlement and subsistence patterns, and ceramics. With respect to environmental factors, the initial Middle Atlantic conference began with a review of each state's geography. Later, the topic was treated more regionally. At the 1975 MAAC, Victor A. Carbone (1975) presented his seminal paper "Environment and Prehistory in the Middle Atlantic"; Griffith (1975) and Handsman (1975) presented complementary papers. Carbone (1978, 1980, 1982)—like Gardner—produced a number of far-reaching overviews that provided a sound foundation for environmental studies. These likely influenced the steady stream of environmentally focused papers presented at the MAAC meetings—ranging from broad ecological models to detailed soil studies from individual sites—and prompted an edited volume on the subject (Moeller 1982). Environmental factors continue to serve as the basis for MAAC papers, including Stuart Fiedel's (2006) innovative study linking climate change and shifts in projectile point styles (including connecting the onset of broadspear expansion to widespread drought conditions in the region) and Darrin Lowery's (2008; Lowery and Wagner 2012) studies of sea level rise and the effects of submergence on artifacts. In counterpoint, the concept of an Algonquin migration—based on linguistic studies—was proposed as an alternative explanation to the pervasive notion of cultural change induced by environmental stimuli (Luckenbach et al. 1982).

The first MAAC also included a floor discussion of settlement and subsistence patterns in the region, and virtually every subsequent MAAC included at least one paper on this topic. Ceramic studies were introduced at the second MAAC, with a session on early pottery in the Middle Atlantic, organized by Fred Kinsey; again, most MAAC meetings include at least one presentation on this subject.

Lithic studies vie with environmental studies for the topical lead at MAAC meetings. This is somewhat surprising given its relatively late appearance on conference programs. Aside from a one-page observational paper by Thomas Mayr in 1974, it was not until 1980 that lithics appeared as a titular subject: Michael Stewart's (1980b) paper on Maryland and Pennsylvania metarhyolites and Stephen Perlman's (1980) treatise on lithic procurement systems. Subsequently, lithic studies commonly have been presented, perhaps reaching an acme in 2003 when a dozen lithic papers were given.

In terms of the chronological period dealt with in presentations, the more recent the period, the more papers presented: Woodland–Archaic–

Paleoindian. Similarly, this ordering repeats with sub-periods: Contact–Late Woodland–Middle Woodland–Early Woodland and Late Archaic–Middle Archaic–Early Archaic. Trends are also apparent for some periods. For instance, it was not until 1977 that the first paper dealt with the Contact period—and that was from the northern fringe of the Middle Atlantic region (Williams 1977). The first organized session dealing with the Contact period was organized by Stephen R. Potter in 1984; it was revisited in 1988 in a session chaired by Herbert Kraft, and again in 1995 in a session chaired by James Harmon and Virginia Busby; but it was not until post-1991 that Contact papers began to proliferate.

The study of human remains and burial practices is also deep-seated in the MAAC. At the third MAAC meeting, held in Newark, Delaware, Ronald A. Thomas (1972) chaired a session on mortuary practices. The transcription of this open discussion is rambling and free-flowing, touching on whatever burial topics popped into the audience's minds. There is some good data here, but it is informal and hard to tweeze out. This session was continued at the 1973 MAAC in Penns Grove, New Jersey (where it was chaired by Douglas Ubelaker), but consisted of more formal papers (Feest 1973; Ubelaker 1973; Thurman 1973; Thomas 1973). These papers were split between regional and site-specific discussions, and mirror current treatment of mortuary studies in the Middle Atlantic. In 1987—three years before the formal adoption of the federal NAGPRA law—Paul B. Cissna (1987) broached the Indian–archaeologist–Indian burial conundrum. The next year, he (Cissna 1988) chaired a session on the reburial debate. This included reviews of policies, concerns, and the relationships between archaeologists and Indians on a state-by-state basis, and opened a public debate that continues today. This also introduced a period of MAAC introspection, and saw the first attempts at outreach to modern Native Americans. In 1996, Joseph W. Hopkins III chaired a session entitled "Polyphony: The Many Voices of Native American History." Speakers included Native Americans, archaeologists, and anthropologists. In 2002, Cara Lee Blume chaired a session entitled "Saving the Black Creek Site: Native Americans Take Control of Their Heritage." It included a series of papers (Ridgeway 2002; Gould 2002; Evans 2002; Blume 2002) dealing with the Black Creek site in New Jersey and the Lenape. In 2003, Blume organized a session entitled "Native Americans Take Ownership of their Past," followed by a workshop dealing with Indian–archaeologist partnerships. And in 2004 and 2005, Blume followed up with sessions on "Archaeologists and American Indians" and "Indigenous Issues"; the panels again included both archaeologists and Native Americans.

Historic Native American tribal groups have long been a focus of MAAC study—from archaeological, ethnohistorical, and historical perspectives. Some of the groups have included the Susquehannocks (Kinsey

1987; Handsman 1987; Lauria 2002; East 2007), the Massawomecks and Monongahela (Johnson 1997; Johnson and Means 2007), the Monacan (Hantman 1988), the Westos (Meyers 2002), the Tuscarora (Pietak 2002), and the Cherokee (Whyte 2005). But by far it is the work of Marshall Becker on the Lenape and related groups that stands out. Becker has authored dozens of articles on the Lenape, and it is a rare MAAC meeting that he did not present his research (see for example Becker 1982, 1984, 2003, 2010, 2011).

Floral and faunal studies have displayed a wide array of techniques and approaches. A number of papers dealt with determining seasonality from the analysis of shellfish (Aiken 1977; Dreibelbis 1978; Kent 1981). Blood residue analysis has been carried out on stone tools (Flanagan 1985; Petraglia et al. 1993; Vish and Yeshion 2005). Michael B. Barber (1982, 2004, 2008) has undertaken zooarchaeological studies to better understand subsistence strategies, bone tool production, and shell bead manufacture, while Thomas R. Whyte (1986, 1990) and William Schindler (2005) have examined prehistoric fisheries. Elizabeth A. Moore and Heather Lapham (1995; Moore 1997; Lapham 2002) have successfully determined patterns in the production and trade of deerskin. Floral studies have included numerous ethnobotanical studies (e.g., Moeller 1975; Ameringer 1975; Kauffman and Dent 1987) as well as more specialized studies including that of phytoliths (Piperno 1987), charcoal (McWeeney 1989), and starch grain analysis (Messner and Dickau 2005). Somewhat surprisingly, papers dealing specifically with horticultural and agricultural practices are rather rare (Miller and Gardner 1993; Stewart 1998b; Hart 2003; Gallivan and McKnight 2006). Recently, Justine McKnight and Martin Gallivan have advanced archaeobotanical study in the region by creating an archaeobotanical database for Virginia (2007) and later expanding it to the entire Chesapeake region (2008); the Maryland portion of the database is available online at www.jefpat.org/archeobotany/. And recent work by Sharon Allitt (2007; Allitt et al. 2008) has combined floral and faunal research by using isotope analyses of deer and dog bone to reconstruct patterns of maize consumption.

Some topical trends are apparent over the MAAC's history. Papers dealing with cultural resources management subjects were most prevalent in the 1970s and 1980s. Regional surveys were popular in the early 1980s, and saw a slight resurgence in the early 2000s. The notion of predictive site location models seems to arise every five years or so. And while cultural sequences were a focal point of the first MAAC, close looks at stratigraphy post-date 1990, and papers dealing specifically with critical evaluations of radiocarbon dates and dating are rare. Another of the more uncommon topics was that of gender, represented by a mere three prehistoric papers (Blume 1991; Custer 1991; Sassaman 1991) in a 1991 plenary session on "The Archaeology of Gender," organized by Richard J. Dent and Christine Jirikowic.

Clearly the annual meetings of the Middle Atlantic Archaeological Conference reflect the record of archaeological research in the region. And while sitting and listening to presentations can certainly be interesting and informative, those ideas can be fleeting. Early in the conference's history, many authors distributed paper copies of their presentations. But these now-fading blue mimeographs—if one was lucky enough to snag a copy from a table at the back of the room—are increasingly hard to find. In 1985, a partial remedy to this problem was devised by founding editor Roger W. Moeller—the *Journal of Middle Atlantic Archaeology*. Designed as an outlet for conference papers as well as a forum for all types of archaeological research in the region, the first volume debuted with a Brennanesque proposition paper by Melburn Thurman, "A Cultural Synthesis of the Middle Atlantic Coastal Plain" and a series of papers from a 1984 MAAC symposium on Protohistoric/Contact societies. With that, the *Journal of Middle Atlantic Archaeology* was up and running, and its annual issue has been recording Middle Atlantic archaeology ever since.

THE MIDDLE ATLANTIC AS A CULTURE AREA

William Henry Holmes (1903), in his treatise on aboriginal pottery of the eastern United States, was perhaps the first to use the term "Middle Atlantic province." Centered on the Chesapeake Bay/Potomac River region, it extended south to Cape Hatteras, North Carolina, and north to New Jersey. Holmes did not use "Middle Atlantic province" to delineate a culture area (although he did generally equate it with Algonquin groups), but rather as a means for sorting regional pottery types (he considered net-impressed pottery to be a defining trait for the region). In the 1930s, cultural anthropologist Regina Flannery (1939) recognized a distinct sub-area within the general coastal Algonquian culture area (roughly Virginia, Maryland, and much of Delaware, i.e., the core region of the Middle Atlantic). Karl Schmitt (1952) was one of the first to treat the Middle Atlantic (which he equated with Virginia, Maryland, Pennsylvania, New Jersey, and Delaware) as a culture area. In his attempt to define the archaeological chronology for the region, he described a number of components, sites, and foci representative of the area. Throughout, though, he recognized outside influences from the Southeast (Mississippian weeping eye motifs), the Northeast (Owasco-Iroquois traits from New York), and the Ohio Valley (Fort Ancient, Hopewell, and Adena). Robert L. Stephenson examined the Accokeek Creek site in Maryland as part of a larger "Middle Atlantic Seaboard culture province" (which he defined geographically as extending from the Rappahannock River Valley on the south, north to the Palisades of the Hudson River and Long Island, and west to the foothills of the Blue Ridge Mountains [Stephenson et al. 1963:200–205]). He dismissed influences from the Southeast and Ohio Valley, and, while he recognized ties to the traditions of the Northeast, stated that the Middle Atlantic was not a full participant in that heritage. In essence, Stephenson views the Middle Atlantic as a culture area that developed its own traditions in relative isolation.

In a review of the Accokeek Creek report, Louis Brennan (1969:23) posits that the prevailing sentiment regarding a "Middle Atlantic" province held that it was a "non-descript and heterogenous [sic] acculturation." But Brennan, relying on his years of experience investigating the Taconic Tradition of the Lower Hudson Valley, saw similarities to Accokeek Creek and accepted the notion of a culture area (even agreeing on its northern boundary to within a few miles). Likewise, Fred Kinsey (1971)—in the only formal paper presented at the first Middle Atlantic Archaeological Conference—became a staunch proponent of the Middle Atlantic culture province. However, whereas Stephenson applied the Middle Atlantic province concept to largely Woodland occupations at Accokeek Creek, Kinsey saw its greatest utility in understanding Late Archaic cultures. He (Kinsey 1971:1) considered Paleoindian assemblages "remarkably homogeneous" and felt that non-ceramic Woodland materials were "so basically uniform and conservative" to be of limited use in defining a culture area. Kinsey considers long, slender, narrow-bladed, stemmed points made from locally available lithic materials to be the predominant Archaic form in the Middle Atlantic, and envisions a Piedmont Archaic tradition quite distinct from the Laurentian Archaic and other northern traditions.

A decade later, the validity of a Middle Atlantic culture province was still being debated. In 1979, Cara Wise (1979) reviewed the concept of "Middle Atlantic," discussing its shifting boundaries, and even attempting to relate the concept to the historic period. Archaeologists continued to argue the meaning of "Middle Atlantic" vociferously, to the point that in January 1982 Howard A. MacCord Sr. convened a Middle Atlantic Culture Province Symposium at Old Dominion University in Norfolk, Virginia. Some two dozen representatives from the Middle Atlantic states (North Carolina, Virginia, Maryland, Delaware, Pennsylvania, New Jersey, and New York) met to synthesize data into "regionally-identifiable cultures" and to examine the relationships between Middle Atlantic cultures. The spotlight of the meeting was a position paper by Louis Brennan (1982) on "What is (was) the Middle Atlantic culture province in prehistoric times?" (Brennan presented this same paper three months later to a larger audience at the MAAC meetings in Rehoboth Beach, Delaware.) Once again, Brennan championed the notion of such a culture province,

citing physiographic–environmental unity through time, similar subsistence strategies, and, for the most part, in situ cultural development.
Brennan agrees with Kinsey's narrow-bladed, stemmed Archaic tradition.
The broadspear tradition, however, is seen as the result of diffusion of the
notion of "Savannah River culture" out of the Carolina Piedmont. As for
later cultures, Brennan considered Adena but a temporary intruder—and
Hopewell nearly absent—in the Middle Atlantic region. He sumed up
his argument with this provocative statement, "If there is any clinching
argument that there was a Middle Atlantic Culture Province, it is that no
singular or salient cultural development ever took place within it." Apparently, Brennan considered the Middle Atlantic a mixing bowl—the
result of cultural systems borrowed from surrounding regions.

In the inaugural issue of the *Journal of Middle Atlantic Archaeology*, Melburn Thurman (1985) continued the discussion of the Middle Atlantic as a
culture area. Focusing on the Coastal Plain, he saw three defining factors:
generally uniform pottery (at least until late times); an absence of burial or
temple mounds; and some dependence on riverine/sea resources. During
the Transitional period, Thurman considered the Savannah River cultures
as sources of both narrow and broad spearpoints, with narrow points more
common in coastal areas (along with steatite-tempered pottery) and broadspears more common in the interior (along with steatite bowls). Later, Thurman—based on collaborative work with William Barse (e.g., Thurman and
Barse 1974)—saw Mockley pottery as the *oikoumene* (or "world system")
of the Middle Atlantic Coastal Plain, with its presence documented from
New York City to North Carolina. This generally uniform ceramic tradition
continued uninterrupted except for a brief period during the Webb phase
with its Hell Island pottery; ceramic homogeneity on the Coastal Plain was
once again restored with the appearance of Townsend/Rappahannock
pottery, which stretched from Maryland and Delaware to North Carolina.
Thurman finds little evidence for ranked societies throughout Mockley and
Townsend/Rappahannock times, believing instead that such social ranking did not arise until Contact times (or at least until the introduction of
maize horticulture). In essence, Thurman considered the Middle Atlantic
Coastal Plain to be a distinctive sub-area of the larger Woodlands culture
area, based on the Middle Atlantic's distinctive resource base.[2]

Thus, it seems clear that the notion of a Middle Atlantic culture area
is valid from a variety of perspectives. To these arguments, we can add
perhaps one more. At the first MAAC meeting, Fred Kinsey (1971:2) made
an interesting observation. He noted that one of the factors retarding the
recognition of a Middle Atlantic Culture Province was an absence of concentrated professional archaeological effort. In some ways, the Middle Atlantic was more of a void bounded to the south by the work of Joffre Coe
(1964) in the North Carolina Piedmont, to the west by Bettye Broyles's

(1971) excavations at St. Albans on the Kanawha River in West Virginia, and to the north by the extensive investigations in New York by William Ritchie (1965) and later Robert Funk. Certainly, the nearly half-century existence of the Middle Atlantic Archaeological Conference has changed that, and the mere synergy created among professional archaeologists in the region by the existence of MAAC may be enough to proclaim the reality of Middle Atlantic archaeology. Perhaps Michael Stewart (1989b:48) sums it up best, "The Middle Atlantic region is thought of as both a culture area and a universe of researchers sharing common meetings, conferences, and publication outlets."

LOOKING FORWARD

As we look back on the first hundred years of Middle Atlantic archaeology, we see a rich archaeological record that has been amassed by a variety of individuals and institutions. Though continual, interest in—and support for—Middle Atlantic archaeology has waxed and waned over the last century. Local archaeological societies' rosters swell, then dwindle, then swell again. State and local government archaeological programs flourish or starve at the vagaries of politics and economics. And university departments tend to thrive or decline on the strengths and interests of individual professors. Despite such uncertainties, the overall trending of Middle Atlantic archaeology has been to move forward—sometimes plodding, but sometimes making leaps.

Take, for example, a recent project in Maryland. The Maryland Historical Trust—Maryland's State Historic Preservation Office—has a long history of managing historic preservation projects funded by the Non-Capital Historic Preservation Grant Program, a program financed by the state legislature. Among the projects supported by these funds are archaeological undertakings. In the past, outside archaeologists applied for grant funds by submitting research proposals that were evaluated by trust staff. Successful proposals resulted in a wide variety of research projects, usually lasting one year, and generating sundry results. In 2007, trust staff attempted to focus research by encouraging submittal of proposals for long-term, phased archaeological study of a specific topic. The challenge was accepted by the archaeologists with the Anne Arundel County Trust for Preservation, led by Al Luckenbach. They proposed a survey and assessment of Middle Woodland period sites in Anne Arundel County. Phase 1—undertaken in 2008—consisted of a comprehensive literature review of the subject resulting in an annotated bibliography; a report on the status of current knowledge on Middle Woodland in central Maryland (which resulted in a Master's thesis [Sperling 2009]);

a list of research questions to be addressed by future Middle Woodland studies; and a multi-year plan for revisiting and documenting the nearly two hundred Middle Woodland sites in Anne Arundel County. In 2009, Phase 2 produced updated site survey forms and a summary report detailing the revisitation of known sites, and created a GIS tool incorporating all Middle Woodland data collected to date. Phase 3, to be undertaken in 2010, was to expand the GIS tool, conduct intensive excavations at two selected Middle Woodland sites, and prepare a National Register nomination for Middle Woodland sites in central Maryland. Following submittal of the proposal for this work, however, the Maryland state legislature made substantial cuts to the Non-Capital Grant program. As a result, the project was scaled back 40 percent, and redesigned to carry out intensive archaeological excavations at one Middle Woodland site—Pig Point (more on this incredible site in a minute). In 2011, a planned Phase 4 was to carry out testing at four additional sites, analyze a number of existing Middle Woodland artifact collections, and develop a model for identifying landscapes along the Patuxent River similar to those at Pig Point (which sits on a high hill overlooking the Jug Bay estuary). Once again, however, grant funds were curtailed and the project was scaled back by more than half; the final report on this work is currently being prepared. Subsequently, funding of the Non-Capital Grant program has been eliminated from the budgets for the last two fiscal years. While this has severely hampered the trust's ability to sponsor archaeological research, at least temporarily, it has not stopped the work at Pig Point, where Luckenbach and his team have cobbled together various funding sources to continue excavation at the site—a site that perhaps serves as the poster child for the future potential of Middle Atlantic archaeology.

What started out as shovel-test excavations at Pig Point—a Middle Woodland site known from fifty-year-old surface collections—has grown to massive, deeply stratified block excavations that have turned Middle Atlantic archaeology on its ear. Each shovelful seemed to expose new surprises—rare or unique in Maryland and beyond—including:

- Archaeological deposits buried to depths of more than two meters.
- A series of postmolds representing superimposed structures spanning the Late Woodland–Middle Woodland–Early Woodland/Late Archaic, some with interior pit or hearth features.
- Radiocarbon dates ranging from A.D. 1540 to 7300 B.C.—all in correct vertical sequence. Likewise, the various pottery types and projectile points conform stratigraphically to established cultural sequences (except for a series of triangular points, below).
- At Pig Point, triangle projectile points were found in the Woodland strata, but continue down the profile, well below ceramic-bearing

levels into Archaic levels—an association confirmed by radiocarbon dates. Only at the Abbott Farm site in New Jersey has this anomaly been seen before in the Middle Atlantic (Stewart 1998c; Luckenbach et al. 2010).

- Ceramics at Pig Point include an array of typical Woodland types as well as some more unusual examples, including a Rappahannock pot incised rim to base with a woodpecker design, a zoned-incised sherd with a crenellated rim, and a punctated toy pot measuring only 15 mm in diameter.
- Other exotic materials include Flint Ridge chalcedony and Fuert Hill pipestone from Ohio, copper beads presumably from the Great Lakes region, and green Coxsackie chert from New York.
- Adena-like artifacts include blocked end pipes, platform pipes, Adena blades, copper beads, sharks' teeth, and drilled and incised gorgets. Related to this material is an area containing human bone in seemingly ritual or mortuary processing contexts rather than as interments.

Much is yet to be learned at Pig Point, but it serves as a modern example of Middle Atlantic archaeology. It reflects—in one site—influences from the Northeast, Southeast, and Midwest occasionally seen at sites throughout the Middle Atlantic region. This cooperative venture, initiated by state and local government archaeological programs, has uncovered remains of national significance; it continues despite the loss of state grant funding. Archeological Society of Maryland members have supported the project by serving as a volunteer labor source, and Maryland's Native American community has been consulted on the project. The project has even produced a master's thesis on Middle Woodland archaeology in a department almost totally focused on historic archaeology.

If Pig Point is an example of what Middle Atlantic archaeology holds for the future, then the future is bright. Yes, there are hurdles to be faced. Government agencies need to lobby for sufficient archaeological funding, and need to ensure that existing funding is used in the most effective manner possible. University programs need to recognize the value of programs in prehistoric archaeology—either by adding those programs to their curricula or by strengthening existing programs (and relying on adjunct or part-time professors is not the answer). The Middle Atlantic Archaeological Conference needs to continue to serve as a forum for archaeologists—both professional and student—from throughout the region, and as a pipeline for the *Journal of Middle Atlantic Archaeology*. And local archaeological societies need to become more vocal advocates to help ensure the above needs are met. The reward to meeting these needs is the opening of vast new, unexpected, exhilarating discoveries in Middle Atlantic archaeology.

ACKNOWLEDGMENTS

I thank Carole Nash and Heather Wholey for inviting me to attempt this chapter, and for organizing the 2013 MAAC session, *Foundations of Middle Atlantic Prehistory*. I am grateful for review comments from Maureen Kavanagh, Jay Custer, Al Luckenbach, Orlando Ridout V, and Michael Stewart. Perhaps this chapter should be considered a framework for the history of Middle Atlantic prehistory, for I know it is incomplete, and the important contributions of many people have not been mentioned in this short space. I apologize for such omissions. However, I do hope this framework will be useful to the future of Middle Atlantic prehistory—our understanding of which is constantly being reshaped and redefined.

NOTES

1. For this general overview, I have relied on a number of sources that should be consulted in greater depth for a fuller understanding of early archaeological endeavors in the Middle Atlantic and beyond. These include: nineteenth-century hoaxes (Kraft 1996; Williams 1991; Oestreicher 1994, 1995; Sturtevant and Meltzer 1985; Custer 1989a:82–84; Mercer 1885); the American Paleolithic (Dillehay and Meltzer 1991; Meltzer 1993); C. C. Abbott (Horan 1992; Kraft 1993); W. H. Holmes (Meltzer and Dunnell 1992); H. C. Mercer (Mason 1956; Custer and Doms 1988); early Maryland archaeology (Bastian 1980); early Delaware archaeology (Weslager 1974; Custer 1989a:60–79); early Pennsylvania archaeology (Custer 1996:35–89); the 1916 Susquehanna River Expedition (Custer 1986); and early New Jersey archaeology (Grossman-Bailey 2001; Veit 2001; Mounier 2003).

2. As might be expected, not all Middle Atlantic archaeologists agreed with Thurman's pan-ceramic (see Stewart 1987) and other notions. Unfortunately, the responses to Thurman's article unleashed one of the more public bevies of sniping for which Middle Atlantic archaeologists—and perhaps Thurman in particular—are infamous (see Thurman 1987; Moeller 1987, 1989; Custer 1989c). Such sentiments may have been epitomized by Stephen Potter, who—while observing a heated MAAC debate on projectile point typology—leapt to his feet and exclaimed, "The two most overused words in the Middle Atlantic are 'type' and 'asshole.'"

REFERENCES CITED

Abbott, Charles Conrad
  1872   The Stone Age in New Jersey. *American Naturalist* 6:144–60, 199–229.
  1881   *Primitive Industry: Or Illustrations of the Handiwork, in Stone, Bone and Clay, of the Native Races of the Northern Atlantic Seaboard of America.* George A. Bates, Salem, MA.

Aiken, Larry
 1977 Estimating Seasonality from Shellfish. Paper presented at the Middle
       Atlantic Archaeological Conference, Trenton, NJ.

Allitt, Sharon
 2007 The Mohr Site: In Search of a Proxy—A Preliminary Stable Carbon Isotope
       Study of Deer Bone as an Indicator of Human Dependence on Maize (ZEA
       Mays) Agriculture in a Northeast Prehistoric Village. Paper presented at
       the Middle Atlantic Archaeological Conference, Virginia Beach, VA.

Allitt, Sharon, Timothy Messner, and R. Michael Stewart
 2008 Utility of Dog Bone (Canis familiaris) in Stable Isotope Studies for Inves-
       tigating Prehistoric Maize (Zea mays ssp. mays) Consumption: A Pre-
       liminary Study. Paper presented at the Middle Atlantic Archaeological
       Conference, Ocean City, MD.

Ameringer, Carl
 1975 Susquehannock Plant Utilization. In *Proceedings of the 6th Annual Middle
       Atlantic Archaeological Conference*, edited by W. Fred Kinsey III, pp. 58–62.
       Lancaster, PA.

Andrefsky, William, Jr.
 1983 Experimental Archaeology and Lithic Assemblage Analysis. Paper
       presented at the Middle Atlantic Archaeological Conference, Rehoboth
       Beach, DE.

Barber, Michael B.
 1982 The Vertebrate Faunal Utilization Pattern of the Middle Woodland Mock-
       ley Ceramic Users: The Maycock Point Shell Midden (44PG51), Prince
       Georges County, Virginia. Paper presented at the Middle Atlantic Ar-
       chaeological Conference, Rehoboth Beach, DE.
 2004 An Evolutionary Approach to Bone Tool Production on the Roanoke and
       Adjacent Rivers during the Late Woodland Time Period. Paper presented
       at the Middle Atlantic Archaeological Conference, Rehoboth Beach, DE.
 2008 The Keyser Farm Site (44PA1): Evidence of an Interior Shell Bead Indus-
       try. Paper presented at the Middle Atlantic Archaeological Conference,
       Ocean City, MD.

Bastian, Tyler
 1980 The Early Pursuit of Archaeology in Maryland. *Maryland Historical Maga-
       zine* 75(1):1–7.

Becker, Marshall J.
 1982 Distinctions between the Jersey and the Pennsylvania Lenape: The Eth-
       nohistorical Record as a Reflection of the Archaeological Past. Paper
       presented at the Middle Atlantic Archaeological Conference, Rehoboth
       Beach, DE.
 1984 Silver Trade Goods as Indicators of the Lenape Acculturation Process: The
       Earliest Documented Lenape Examples Prior to 1750. Paper presented at
       the Middle Atlantic Archaeological Conference, Rehoboth Beach, DE.

2003   Susquehannock Living among the Lenape, 1675–ca. 1690. Paper presented at the Middle Atlantic Archaeological Conference, Virginia Beach, VA.

2010   The Lenape after 1675: Changes in Settlement Patterns before the Arrival of William Penn. Paper presented at the Middle Atlantic Archaeological Conference, Ocean City, MD.

2011   Lenape Fishing Revisited: No Salmon in the Delaware, Even During the Little Ice Age. Paper presented at the Middle Atlantic Archaeological Conference, Ocean City, MD.

Blume, Cara Lee

1991   Painting Faces on the Past: The Role of Limited Function Sites in Gender-Informed Archaeology. Paper presented at the Middle Atlantic Archaeological Conference, Ocean City, MD.

2002   Relinquishing Control: The Archaeologist as Consultant to Native Americans. Paper presented at the Middle Atlantic Archaeological Conference, Virginia Beach, VA.

Brennan, Louis A.

1969   Review of the Accokeek Creek Site. *Bulletin of the New York State Archaeological Association* 47:19–23.

1971   The Implications of Two New C-14 Dates from Montrose Point, Lower Hudson, N.Y. In *Proceedings of the Middle Atlantic Archaeology Conference*, edited by Charles W. McNett Jr. and William M. Gardner, pp. 9–20. The Catholic University of America, Washington, DC.

1974   Fox Creek–Cony–Selby Bay. Proposition paper presented at the Middle Atlantic Archaeological Conference, Baltimore, MD.

1982   Statements and Propositions Intended to Initiate Discourse on the Definable Reality of a Prehistoric Middle Atlantic Region Culture Province. Paper presented at the Middle Atlantic Culture Province Symposium, Norfolk, VA.

1983   Sermons in Stone. Paper presented at the Middle Atlantic Archaeological Conference, Rehoboth Beach, DE.

Broyles, Bettye J.

1971   *Second Preliminary Report: The St. Albans Site, Kanawha County, West Virginia.* West Virginia Geological and Economic Survey, Report of Archeological Investigations 3. Morgantown, WV.

1974   Projectile Point Typology. Proposition paper presented at the Middle Atlantic Archaeological Conference, Baltimore, MD.

Bushnell, David I., Jr.

1926   Ancient Soapstone Quarry in Albemarle County, Virginia. *Journal of the Washington Academy of Sciences* 16(19):525–28.

Butler, Mary

1947   Two Lenape Rockshelters near Philadelphia. *American Antiquity* 12:246–55.

Cadzow, Donald A.

1934   *Petroglyphs [Rock Carvings] in the Susquehanna River near Safe Harbor, Pennsylvania.* Pennsylvania Historical Commission, Safe Harbor Report 1, Harrisburg.

1936 *Archaeological Studies of the Susquehannock Indians of Pennsylvania.* Pennsylvania Historical Commission, Safe Harbor Report 2, Harrisburg.

Carbone, Victor A.
1975 Environment and Prehistory in the Middle Atlantic Province. In *Proceedings of the 6th Annual Middle Atlantic Archaeological Conference*, edited by W. Fred Kinsey III, pp. 42–49. Lancaster, PA.
1978 The Paleoecology of the Archaic in Anthropological Perspective. Paper presented at the Middle Atlantic Archaeological Conference, Rehoboth Beach, DE.
1980 Setting the Stage: The Environment of the Middle Atlantic during the Archaic. Paper presented at the Middle Atlantic Archaeological Conference, Dover, DE.
1982 Environment and Society in Middle Woodland Times. Paper presented at the Middle Atlantic Archaeological Conference, Rehoboth Beach, DE.

Carr, Kurt W.
1993 The Early Archaic Period/Phase in the Middle Atlantic Region. Paper presented at the Middle Atlantic Archaeological Conference, Ocean City, MD.

Carr, Kurt W., and Douglas C. McLearen
2005 Recent Testing at the King's Jasper Quarry, Lehigh County, Pennsylvania. Paper presented at the Society for American Archaeology meetings, Salt Lake City, UT.

Cissna, Paul B.
1987 Rocking the Boat: Indians, Archaeologists, and Indian Burials. Paper presented at the Middle Atlantic Archaeological Conference, Lancaster, PA.
1988 Reburial in the Middle Atlantic States: Law, Policy, and Ethics. Session chaired at the Middle Atlantic Archaeological Conference, Rehoboth Beach, DE.

Claassen, Cheryl
1990 Dogan Point, New York. Paper presented at the Middle Atlantic Archaeological Conference, Ocean City, MD.

Coe, Joffre Lanning
1964 The Formative Cultures of the Carolina Piedmont. *Transactions of the American Philosophical Society*, NS, 54(5).

Cross, Dorothy
1941 *The Archaeology of New Jersey, Vol. 1.* The Archaeological Society of New Jersey and New Jersey State Museum, Trenton.
1956 *The Archaeology of New Jersey, Vol. 2, The Abbott Farm.* The Archaeological Society of New Jersey and New Jersey State Museum, Trenton.

Curry, Dennis C.
1999 "Gathering together their dead bones:" Maryland's Aboriginal Ossuaries. Paper presented at the Middle Atlantic Archaeological Conference, Harrisburg, PA.

2007   Ossuary Burials in Middle Atlantic Landscapes: An Archaeological Overview. Paper presented at the Middle Atlantic Archaeological Conference, Virginia Beach, VA.

Curry, Dennis C., and Maureen Kavanagh
1989   The Middle to Late Woodland Transition in Maryland. Paper presented at the Middle Atlantic Archaeological Conference, Rehoboth Beach, DE.

Custer, Jay F.
1986   The Susquehanna River Expedition of 1916. *Pennsylvania Archaeologist* 56(3–4):52–56.
1987   Environmental Change and Cultural Dynamics on the Delmarva Peninsula. Paper presented at the Middle Atlantic Archaeological Conference, Lancaster, PA.
1989a *Prehistoric Cultures of the Delmarva Peninsula: An Archaeological Study.* University of Delaware Press, Newark.
1989b The Woodland I–Woodland II Transition in the Delmarva Peninsula and Southeast Pennsylvania. Paper presented at the Middle Atlantic Archaeological Conference, Rehoboth Beach, DE.
1989c A Personal Note. *Journal of Middle Atlantic Archaeology* 5:147–48.
1991   "Women's Work" in Middle Woodland Times: Tool Kits from the Island Field Site, Kent County, Delaware. Paper presented at the Middle Atlantic Archaeological Conference, Ocean City, MD.
1996   *Prehistoric Cultures of Eastern Pennsylvania.* Pennsylvania Historical and Museum Commission, Anthropological Series No. 7, Harrisburg, PA.

Custer, Jay F., and Keith R. Doms
1988   Henry Chapman Mercer—Technology and Culture. *Pennsylvania Archaeologist* 58(1):71–75.

Davidson, D.S.
1935   Notes on Slaughter Creek. *Bulletin of the Archaeological Society of Delaware* 2(2):1–5.
1936   Notes on Faunal Remains from Slaughter Creek. *Bulletin of the Archaeological Society of Delaware* 2(4):29–34.

Dillehay, Tom D., and David J. Meltzer
1991   *The First Americans: Search and Research.* CRC Press, Boca Raton, FL.

Dreibelbis, Dana
1978   Determining Seasonal Occupation of the Tuckerton Shell Mound Using Clam Shell Growth Patterns. Paper presented at the Middle Atlantic Archaeological Conference, Rehoboth Beach, DE.

East, Thomas C.
2007   The Susquehannock Origin Myth. Paper presented at the Middle Atlantic Archaeological Conference, Virginia Beach, VA.

Ebright, Carol A.
1992   *Early Native American Prehistory on the Maryland Western Shore: Archeological Investigations at the Higgins Site.* Maryland State Highway Administration Archeological Report Number 1.

Evans, Clifford
    1955   A Ceramic Study of Virginia Archeology. *Smithsonian Institution, Bureau of American Ethnology Bulletin* 160. Washington, DC.

Evans, Earl
    2002   Black Creek Site and the Broader Native American Community. Paper presented at the Middle Atlantic Archaeological Conference, Virginia Beach, VA.

Feest, Christian F.
    1973   Southeastern Algonquian Burial Customs: Ethnohistorical Evidence. In *Proceedings of the Fourth Annual Middle Atlantic Archaeological Conference*, edited by Ronald A. Thomas, pp. 1–9, Penns Grove, NJ.

Fiedel, Stuart J.
    2006   Climate Change and Point Style Shifts: A Tentative Correlation. Paper presented at the Middle Atlantic Archaeological Conference, Virginia Beach, VA.

Fischler, Ben, and Jean French
    1989   The Middle to Late Woodland Transition in the Upper Delaware Valley. Paper presented at the Middle Atlantic Archaeological Conference, Rehoboth Beach, DE.

Flanagan, Edward J.
    1985   Identification of Prehistoric Blood Residues and Other Organics on Stone Tools: An Instrument for Determining Function. Paper presented at the Middle Atlantic Archaeological Conference, Rehoboth Beach, DE.

Flannery, Regina
    1939   An Analysis of Coastal Algonquian Culture. Ph.D. dissertation, The Catholic University of America, Washington, DC.

Ford, T. Latimer, Jr.
    1976   Adena Sites on Chesapeake Bay. *Archaeology of Eastern North America* 4:63–89.

Foss, Robert W.
    1980   Geographic Variation in Prehistoric Settlement of the Blue Ridge. Paper presented at the Middle Atlantic Archaeological Conference, Dover, DE.

Fountain, George H.
    1897   Shell Heaps of the Shrewsbury River, N.J. *The Antiquarian* 1(2):48–50.

Fowke, Gerard
    1894   *Archeologic Investigations in James and Potomac Valleys*. Smithsonian Institution, Bureau of Ethnology, Washington, DC.

Gallivan, Martin, and Justine Woodward McKnight
    2006   Archaeobotanical Assessment of Chesapeake Horticulture: The View from Werewocomoco. Paper presented at the Middle Atlantic Archaeological Conference, Virginia Beach, VA.

2008 Emerging Patterns in Chesapeake Archaeobotany: An Update on the Virginia Archaeobotanical Data Base Project. Paper presented at the Middle Atlantic Archaeological Conference, Ocean City, MD.

Gardner, William M.
1978 Comparison of Ridge and Valley, Blue Ridge, Piedmont, and Coastal Plain Archaic Period Site Distribution: An Idealized Transect (Preliminary Model). Paper presented at the Middle Atlantic Archaeological Conference, Rehoboth Beach, DE.
1980 The Archaic. Paper presented at the Middle Atlantic Archaeological Conference, Dover, DE.
1982a Early Woodland in the Middle Atlantic: Review and Overview. Paper presented at the Middle Atlantic Archaeological Conference, Rehoboth Beach, DE.
1982b General Overview of the Middle Woodland Period in the Middle Atlantic Area. Paper presented at the Middle Atlantic Archaeological Conference, Rehoboth Beach, DE.
1993 Paleo-Indian in the Middle Atlantic (One More Time Around). Paper presented at the Middle Atlantic Archaeological Conference, Ocean City, MD.

Gardner, William M., and Charles W. McNett, Jr.
1971 Early Pottery in the Potomac. In *Proceedings of the Middle Atlantic Archaeology Conference*, edited by Charles W. McNett Jr. and William M. Gardner, pp. 42–52. Catholic University of America, Washington, DC.

Gould, Mark
2002 The Black Creek Site and the Lenape Community. Paper presented at the Middle Atlantic Archaeological Conference, Virginia Beach, VA.

Graham, William J.
1935 The Indians of Port Tobacco River, Maryland, and Their Burial Places. Privately printed.

Griffith, Daniel R.
1975 Ecological Studies of Prehistory. In *Proceedings of the 6th Annual Middle Atlantic Archaeological Conference*, edited by W. Fred Kinsey, III, pp. 30–38. Lancaster, PA.

Grossman-Bailey, Ilene
2001 Toward a History of Archaeological Research in the Outer Coastal Plain of New Jersey. *Bulletin of the Archaeological Society of New Jersey* 56:22–31.

Handsman, Russell G.
1975 Paleoecological Models: Efficient Exploitation and Explanation of the Archeological Record. In *Proceedings of the 6th Annual Middle Atlantic Archaeological Conference*, edited by W. Fred Kinsey, III, pp. 64–76. Lancaster, PA.
1987 The Socio-politics of Susquehannock Archaeology. Paper presented at the Middle Atlantic Archaeological Conference, Lancaster, PA.

Hantman, Jeffrey L.
1988 Monocan Prehistory: Results of Recent Excavation and Survey in Central Virginia. Paper presented at the Middle Atlantic Archaeological Conference, Rehoboth Beach, DE.

Hart, John P.
  2003   Rethinking the Three Sisters. Paper presented at the Middle Atlantic
         Archaeological Conference, Virginia Beach, VA.

Hatch, James W.
  1994   The Structure and Antiquity of Prehistoric Jasper Quarries in the Read-
         ing Prong, Pennsylvania. *Journal of Middle Atlantic Archaeology* 10:23–46.

Herbstritt, James
  1993   A Late Prehistoric Social Boundary for the Susquehanna/Potomac Di-
         vide. Paper presented at the Middle Atlantic Archaeological Conference,
         Ocean City, MD.

Hill, Ira
  1831   *Antiquities of America Explained.* William D. Bell, Hagerstown, MD.

Holland, C. G.
  1960   Preceramic and Ceramic Cultural Patterns in Northwest Virginia. *Smithso-
         nian Institution, Bureau of American Ethnology Bulletin* 173. Washington, DC.

Holmes, William Henry
  1897   Stone Implements of the Potomac-Chesapeake Tidewater Province. In
         Fifteenth Annual Report, Bureau of Ethnology, 1893–1894:13–152, Washing-
         ton, DC.
  1903   Aboriginal Pottery of the Eastern United States. In *Twentieth Annual
         Report, Bureau of American Ethnology, 1898–1899*:1–201, Washington,
         DC.
  1907   Aboriginal Shell-Heaps of the Middle Atlantic Tidewater Region. *Ameri-
         can Anthropologist* 9(1):113–128.

Horan, Sharon
  1992   Charles Conrad Abbott: Associations with the Peabody and Museum
         of Archaeology and Paleontology. *Bulletin of the Archaeological Society of
         New Jersey* 47:29–36.

Hrdlička, Aleš
  1907   Skeletal Remains Suggesting or Attributed to Early Man in North Amer-
         ica. *Bureau of American Ethnology Bulletin* 33, Washington, DC.

Hughes, Richard B.
  1980   A Cultural and Environmental Overview of the Prehistory of Maryland's
         Lower Eastern Shore Based Upon a Study of Selected Artifact Collec-
         tions. *Maryland Historical Trust Manuscript Series* 26.

Humphrey, Robert L., and Mary Elizabeth Chambers
  1977   *Ancient Washington: American Indian Cultures of the Potomac Valley.* GW
         Washington Studies 6, Washington DC.

Jefferson, Thomas
  1787   *Notes on the State of Virginia.* Edition of 1853, J. W. Randolph, Rich-
         mond, VA.

Johnson, William C.
  1997 Re-Examining the Massawomeck-Monongahela Connection: Trans-
        Appalachian Trade Axes in the Late 16th and Early 17th Centuries. Pa-
        per presented at the Middle Atlantic Archaeological Conference, Ocean
        City, MD.

Johnson, William C., and Bernard K. Means
  2007 Why Pennsylvania 1607?: Reexamining the Massawomeck-Mononga-
        hela Connection. Paper presented at the Middle Atlantic Archaeological
        Conference, Virginia Beach, VA.

Jordan, Francis, Jr.
  1906 *Aboriginal Fishing Stations on the Coast of the Middle Atlantic States*. The
        New Era Printing Company, Lancaster, PA.

Kauffman, Barbara, and Joseph Dent
  1978 Flora Recovery and Analysis at the Shawnee-Minisink Site. Paper pre-
        sented at the Middle Atlantic Archaeological Conference, Rehoboth
        Beach, DE.

Kavanagh, Maureen
  1982 Archeological Resources of the Monocacy River Region. *Maryland Geo-
        logical Survey, Division of Archeology, File Report* 164.

Kent, Barry C.
  1970 Diffusion Spheres and Band Territoriality among the Archaic Cultures of
        the Northern Piedmont. Ph.D. dissertation, Pennsylvania State University.
  1984 *Susquehanna's Indians*. Pennsylvania Historical and Museum Commis-
        sion, Anthropological Series 6. Harrisburg.
  1993 Late Archaic Society. Paper presented at the Middle Atlantic Archaeo-
        logical Conference, Ocean City, MD.

Kent, Brett
  1981 Making Old Oysters Talk: New Insights on Oyster Use in Colonial Mary-
        land. Paper presented at the Middle Atlantic Archaeological Conference,
        Ocean City, MD.

Kinsey, W. Fred, III
  1959a Recent Excavations on Bare Island in Pennsylvania: The Kent-Hally site.
        Pennsylvania Archaeologist 29(3–4):109–133.
  1959b Historic Susquehannock Pottery. In *Susquehannock Miscellany*, edited by
        John Witthoft and W. Fred Kinsey, pp. 61–98. Pennsylvania Historical
        and Museum Commission, Harrisburg.
  1971 The Middle Atlantic Culture Province: A Point of View. *Pennsylvania
        Archaeologist* 41(1–2):1–8.
  1987 Susquehannock Animal Art and Iconography. Paper presented at the
        Middle Atlantic Archaeological Conference, Lancaster, PA.

Kraft, Herbert C.
  1971 The Earliest Ceramics in the Northeastern Sector of the Middle Atlantic
        States Area. In *Proceedings of the Middle Atlantic Archaeology Conference*,

edited by Charles W. McNett Jr. and William M. Gardner, pp. 34–39. Catholic University of America, Washington, DC.

1988   European/Indian Contact and Trade in the Middle Atlantic Region. Session chaired at the Middle Atlantic Archaeological Conference, Rehoboth Beach, DE.

1993   Dr. Charles Conrad Abbott, New Jersey's Pioneer Archaeologist. *Bulletin of the Archaeological Society of New Jersey* 48:1–12.

1996   Mammoth Frauds in Archaeology. *Bulletin of the Archaeological Society of New Jersey* 52:1–11.

Lapham, Heather
2002   Native American Deer Hunting Strategies and Deerskin Production in a Contact Period Context. Paper presented at the Middle Atlantic Archaeological Conference, Virginia Beach, VA.

Lauria, Lisa
2002   Mythical Giants of the Chesapeake: An Evaluation of the Archaeological Construction of "Susquehannock." Paper presented at the Middle Atlantic Archaeological Conference, Virginia Beach, VA.

Leidy, Joseph
1865   [Observations on a Kjökkenmödding at Cape Henlopen]. *Proceedings of the Academy of Natural Sciences of Philadelphia* 17:95.

1866   [Observations on the Kitchen Middens of Cape Henlopen]. *Proceedings of the Academy of Natural Sciences of Philadelphia* 18:290–91.

Lowery, Darrin L.
2008   Delmarva Archaeology and Sea Level Rise: Geoarchaeological Investigations into Holocene Marine Transgression. Paper presented at the Middle Atlantic Archaeological Conference, Ocean City, MD.

Lowery, Darrin L., and Daniel P. Wagner
2012   Archaeological Deposits in Drowned Coastal Landscapes: The Geochemical Impacts of Sulfidization and Sulfuricization. Paper presented at the Middle Atlantic Archaeological Conference, Virginia Beach, VA.

Luckenbach, Alvin H., Wayne E. Clark, and Richard S. Levy
1982   Rethinking Cultural Stability in Eastern North American Prehistory: Linguistic Evidence from Eastern Algonquian. Paper presented at the Middle Atlantic Archaeological Conference, Rehoboth Beach, DE.

Luckenbach, Al, Jessie Grow, and Shawn Sharpe
2010   Archaic Period Triangular Points from Pig Point, Anne Arundel County, Maryland. *Journal of Middle Atlantic Archaeology* 26:165–79.

MacCord, Howard A., Karl Schmitt, and Richard G. Slattery
1957   The Shepard Site Study (18Mo3), Montgomery Co., Md. *Archeological Society of Maryland Bulletin* 1.

McDowell-Loudan, Ellis E.
1999   Wyns Farm and General Spaulding Farm: Lessons Learned. Paper presented at the Middle Atlantic Archaeological Conference, Harrisburg, PA.

McDowell-Loudan, Ellis E., and Gary L. Loudan
   1983   The Glen Haven Site: 1983 Interim Report. Paper presented at the Middle
          Atlantic Archaeological Conference, Rehoboth Beach, DE.

McKnight, Justine, and Martin Gallivan
   2007   Towards a Synthesis of Archaeobotany: The Virginia Archaeobotanical
          Data Base Project. Paper presented at the Middle Atlantic Archaeological
          Conference, Virginia Beach, VA.

McNett, Charles W., Jr.
   1987   Middle Atlantic Archaeology: Past, Present, and Future. Paper presented
          at the Middle Atlantic Archaeological Conference, Lancaster, PA.
   1991   The Next 20 Years: Diagnosis and Prognosis. Paper presented at the
          Middle Atlantic Archaeological Conference, Ocean City, MD.

McNett, Charles W., Jr., and William M. Gardner
   1971   Shell Middens of the Potomac Coastal Plain. In *Proceedings of the Middle
          Atlantic Archaeology Conference*, edited by Charles W. McNett, Jr., and
          William M. Gardner, pp. 21–31. Catholic University of America, Wash-
          ington, DC.

McWeeney, Lucinda
   1989   What Can Be Said from the Charcoal Remains? Paper presented at the
          Middle Atlantic Archaeological Conference, Rehoboth Beach, DE.

Manson, Carl, Howard A. MacCord Sr., and James B. Griffin
   1943   The Culture of the Keyser Farm Site. *Papers of the Michigan Academy of
          Science, Arts, and Letters* 29:375–418.

Marye, William B.
   1938   Petroglyphs near Bald Friar. In *A Report on the Susquehanna River Expedi-
          tion*, edited by C.A. Parker, pp. 97–121, Andover Press, Andover, MA.

Maslowski, Robert F.
   2006   Cordage Twist Analysis: Cultural Conservatism among Native Ameri-
          cans and Archaeologists. Paper presented at the Middle Atlantic Ar-
          chaeological Conference, Virginia Beach, VA.
   2011   Page Cord-Marked and the Huffman Phase. Paper presented at the
          Middle Atlantic Archaeological Conference, Ocean City, MD.

Mason, J. Alden
   1956   Henry Chapman Mercer, 1856–1930. *Pennsylvania Archaeologist* 26(3–
          4):153–65.

Mayr, Thomas
   1974   Notes on the Occurrence of Green Jasper in the Selby Bay Complex.
          Paper presented at the Middle Atlantic Archaeological Conference, Bal-
          timore, MD.

Meltzer, David J.
   1993   *Search for the First Americans*. San Remy Press and Smithsonian Books,
          Montreal and Washington, DC.

Meltzer, David J., and Robert C. Dunnell
 1992   Introduction. In *The Archaeology of William Henry Holmes*, edited by David
        J. Meltzer and Robert C. Dunnell, pp. vii–l, Smithsonian Institution Press,
        Washington, DC.

Mercer, Henry C.
 1885   *The Lenape Stone, or the Indian and the Mammoth*. Putnam, New York, NY.
 1897a The Antiquity of Man in the Delaware Valley. In *Researches Upon the An-
        tiquity of Man in the Delaware Valley and the Eastern United States*, edited
        by Henry C. Mercer, pp. 1–86. Publications of the University of Pennsyl-
        vania, Series in Philology, Literature, and Archaeology, Volume 6. Ginn
        & Company, Boston, MA.
 1897b Exploration of an Indian Ossuary on the Choptank River, Dorchester
        County, Maryland. In *Researches Upon the Antiquity of Man in the Dela-
        ware Valley and the Eastern United States*, edited by Henry C. Mercer,
        pp. 87–109. Publications of the University of Pennsylvania, Series in
        Philology, Literature, and Archaeology, Volume 6. Ginn & Company,
        Boston, MA.

Messner, Tim, and Ruth Dickau
 2005   New Directions, New Interpretations: Paleoethnobotany in the Upper
        Delaware Valley and the Utility of Starch Grain Research in the Middle
        Atlantic. Paper presented at the Middle Atlantic Archaeological Confer-
        ence, Rehoboth Beach, DE.

Meyers, Maureen S.
 2002   Modeling Westo Movements from Virginia to South Carolina. Paper
        presented at the Middle Atlantic Archaeological Conference, Virginia
        Beach, VA.

Miller, Patricia E., and Paul S. Gardner
 1993   Late Woodland Horticulture Strategies on the Appalachian Plateau of
        Central Pennsylvania. Paper presented at the Middle Atlantic Archaeo-
        logical Conference, Ocean City, MD.

Moeller, Roger W.
 1975   Late Woodland Floral and Faunal Exploitative Patterns in the Upper
        Delaware Valley. In *Proceedings of the 6th Annual Middle Atlantic Archaeo-
        logical Conference*, edited by W. Fred Kinsey, III, pp. 51–56. Lancaster, PA.
 1987   Editor's Comments. *Journal of Middle Atlantic Archaeology* 3:34.
 1989   Mea Culpa: A Reply to Custer and Others. *Journal of Middle Atlantic Ar-
        chaeology* 5:149–50.
 1993   A Model for Understanding Late Woodland Site Formation Processes.
        Paper presented at the Middle Atlantic Archaeological Conference,
        Ocean City, MD.

Moeller, Roger W. (editor)
 1982   *Practicing Environmental Archaeology: Methods and Interpretations*. Ameri-
        can Indian Archaeological Institute Occasional Paper 3, Washington, CT.

Moore, Elizabeth A.
  1997 Skin and Bones: Zooarchaeological Evidence of the Deer Skin Trade. Paper presented at the Middle Atlantic Archaeological Conference, Ocean City, MD.

Moore, Elizabeth A., and Heather Lapham
  1995 Protohistoric Hunting Strategies at the Graham White Site, Salem, Virginia: The Effect of European Contact. Paper presented at the Middle Atlantic Archaeological Conference, Ocean City, MD.

Moorehead, Warren King
  1938 *A Report of the Susquehanna River Expedition Sponsored in 1916 by the Museum of the American Indian, Heye Foundation.* Andover Press, Andover, MA.

Mouer, L. Daniel, and Robin L. Ryder
  1981 Site and Society: A Polite Assault on the "Gardner Method." Paper presented at the Middle Atlantic Archaeological Conference, Ocean City, MD.

Mouer, L. Daniel, Robin L. Ryder, and Elizabeth G. Johnson
  1980 Down to the River in Boats: The Late Archaic/Transitional in the Middle James River Valley, Virginia. Paper presented at the Middle Atlantic Archaeological Conference, Dover, DE.

Mounier, R. Alan
  2003 *Looking Beneath the Surface: The Story of Archaeology in New Jersey.* Rutgers University Press, New Brunswick, NJ.

Nash, Carole
  2006 Scales of Temporality and Social Complexity: Middle Woodland Hunter-Gatherer Societies of the Interior Middle Atlantic. Paper presented at the Middle Atlantic Archaeological Conference, Virginia Beach, VA.
  2011 Middle Atlantic Archaeology and Anthropocene Climate Change. Paper presented at the Middle Atlantic Archaeological Conference, Ocean City, MD.

Neusius, Sarah, and Beverly Chiarulli
  2011 Late Woodland Sites, Sensitivity Models and Geophysical Investigations in Western Pennsylvania. Paper presented at the Middle Atlantic Archaeological Conference, Ocean City, MD.

Oestreicher, David M.
  1994 Unmasking the *Walam Olum*: A 19th-Century Hoax. *Bulletin of the Archaeological Society of New Jersey* 49:1–44.
  1995 Text Out of Context: The Arguments that Created and Sustained the *Walam Olum. Bulletin of the Archaeological Society of New Jersey* 50:31–52.

Omwake, H. Geiger, and T. Dale Stewart
  1963 The Townsend Site near Lewes, Delaware. *The Archeolog* 15(1):1–72.

Peabody, Charles
  1908   *The Exploration of Bushey Cavern, near Cavetown, Maryland.* Phillips Academy, Department of Archaeology, Bulletin IV, Part I, Andover, MA.

Perlman, Stephen
  1980   Hunter-Gatherer Exploitation Systems and Lithic Procurement Systems. Paper presented at the Middle Atlantic Archaeological Conference, Dover, DE.

Petraglia, Michael, Dennis A. Knepper, and Petar Glumac
  1993   Microwear and Immunocological Analysis of Prehistoric Artifacts from Virginia. Paper presented at the Middle Atlantic Archaeological Conference, Ocean City, MD.

Phelps, David Sutton
  1984   Protohistory and the Carolina Algonkians: Decimation and Acculturation. Paper presented at the Middle Atlantic Archaeological Conference, Rehoboth Beach, DE.
  1985   Comparison of Iroquoian/Tuscarora and Algonquin Mortuary Practices. Paper presented at the Middle Atlantic Archaeological Conference, Ocean City, MD.
  1992   Subterranean Structures at the Neoheroka Fort. Paper presented at the Middle Atlantic Archaeological Conference, Ocean City, MD.

Pietak, Lynn Marie
  2002   Body Ornamentation among the Tuscarora. Paper presented at the Middle Atlantic Archaeological Conference, Virginia Beach, VA.

Piperno, Dolores
  1987   The Application of Phytolith Analysis to the Paleoethnobotany of the Middle Atlantic Region. Paper presented at the Middle Atlantic Archaeological Conference, Lancaster, PA.

Potter, Stephen R.
  1984   Protohistoric and Contact Period Societies in the Middle Atlantic Region. Session chaired at the Middle Atlantic Archaeological Conference, Rehoboth Beach, DE.

Purrington, Burt
  1976   Soils and Site Distribution in the Upper Watauga Valley, North Carolina. Paper presented at the Middle Atlantic Archaeological Conference, Front Royal, VA.
  1979   Changing Subsistence and Settlement Patterns in a Southern Appalachian Locality. Paper presented at the Middle Atlantic Archaeological Conference, Rehoboth Beach, DE.

Reinhart, Theodore R., and Mary Ellen N. Hodges (editors)
  1990   Early and Middle Archaic Research in Virginia: A Synthesis. *Archeological Society of Virginia Special Publication* 22.
  1991   Late Archaic and Early Woodland Research in Virginia: A Synthesis. *Archeological Society of Virginia Special Publication* 23.

1992   Middle and Late Woodland Research in Virginia: A Synthesis. *Archeo-
        logical Society of Virginia Special Publication* 29.

Reinhart, Theodore R., and Dennis J. Pogue (editors)
1993   The Archaeology of 17th-Century Virginia. *Archeological Society of Vir-
        ginia Special Publication* 30.

Reynolds, Elmer R.
1884   [Memoir on the] Pre-Columbian Shell-Mounds at Newburg, Shell-Fields
        of the Potomac, [and] The Shell-Fields of the Wicomico River. *Interna-
        tional Congrès des Américanistes Proceedings* 5: 292–314. Imprimerie de
        Thiele, Copenhague.
1889a   The Shell Mounds of Potomac and Wicomico. *The American Anthropolo-
        gist* 2(3):252–59.
1889b   Notes on the Shell-Mounds and Ossuaries of the Choptank River, Mary-
        land, U.S.A. In *Report of the Fifty-Eighth Meeting of the British Association
        for the Advancement of Science Held at Bath in September 1888*, pp. 846–47.
        John Murray, London.

Ridgeway, Urie
2002   Black Creek Site: The Tribal Context. Paper presented at the Middle At-
        lantic Archaeological Conference, Virginia Beach, VA.

Ritchie, William A.
1965   *The Archaeology of New York State*. American Museum of Natural History,
        Natural History Press, Garden City, NY.

Sassaman, Kenneth E.
1991   The Androgenic Nature of Prehistoric Lithic Technology. Paper presented
        at the Middle Atlantic Archaeological Conference, Ocean City, MD.

Schindler, William
2005   No Bones about It: An Experimental Study in Prehistoric Shad Exploi-
        tation in the Delaware Valley. Paper presented at the Middle Atlantic
        Archaeological Conference, Rehoboth Beach, DE.

Schmitt, Karl
1952   Archeological Chronology of the Middle Atlantic States. In *Archeology of
        Eastern United States*, edited by James B. Griffin, pp. 59–70. University of
        Chicago Press, Chicago, IL.

Skinner, Alanson, and Max Schrabisch
1913   A Preliminary Report of the Archaeological Survey of the State of New
        Jersey. *Geological Survey of New Jersey Bulletin* 9.

Slattery, Richard G., and Douglas R. Woodward
1992   The Montgomery Focus: A Late Woodland Potomac River Culture. *Ar-
        cheological Society of Maryland, Inc. Bulletin* 2.

Smith, Ira F., III
1971   Early Pottery of the Lower Susquehanna Valley. In *Proceedings of the
        Middle Atlantic Archaeology Conference*, edited by Charles W. McNett Jr.

and William M. Gardner, pp. 40–41. The Catholic University of America, Washington, DC.

Snethkamp, Pandora
  1978   Hunter-Gatherer Exchange Systems and the Prehistoric Record. Paper presented at the Middle Atlantic Archaeological Conference, Rehoboth Beach, DE.

Sperling, Stephanie Taleff
  2009   Assessment of Middle Woodland Period Research in Anne Arundel County, Maryland. Master in Applied Anthropology thesis, Department of Anthropology, University of Maryland, College Park.

Squire, E. G., and E. H. Davis
  1847   *Ancient Monuments of the Mississippi: Comprising the Results of Extensive Original Surveys and Explorations.* Smithsonian Institution, Washington, DC.

Stephenson, Robert L., Alice L. L. Ferguson, and Henry G. Ferguson
  1963   *The Accokeek Creek Site: A Middle Atlantic Seaboard Culture Sequence.* University of Michigan, Anthropological Papers No. 20, Ann Arbor, MI.

Steponaitis, Laurie C.
  1983   An Archeological Study of the Patuxent Drainage. 2 vols. *Maryland Historical Trust Manuscript Series* 24.
  1984   Diachronic Trends in Prehistoric Settlement in the Lower Patuxent Drainage, Maryland. Paper presented at the Middle Atlantic Archaeological Conference, Rehoboth Beach, DE.

Stewart, R. Michael
  1980a Prehistoric Settlement and Subsistence Patterns and the Testing of Predictive Site Location Models in the Great Valley of Maryland. Ph.D. dissertation, Department of Anthropology, The Catholic University of America, Washington, DC.
  1980b Environment, Settlement Pattern, and the Prehistoric Use of Rhyolite in the Cumberland Valley of Maryland and Pennsylvania. Paper presented at the Middle Atlantic Archaeological Conference, Dover, DE.
  1987   Catharsis: Comments on Thurman's Coastal Plain Synthesis. *Journal of Middle Atlantic Archaeology* 3:111–24.
  1989a The Middle to Late Woodland Transition in the Middle Delaware Valley. Paper presented at the Middle Atlantic Archaeological Conference, Rehoboth Beach, DE.
  1989b Trade and Exchange in Middle Atlantic Region Prehistory. *Archaeology of Eastern North America* 17:47–78.
  1993   Status of Early and Middle Woodland Research in the Middle Atlantic. Paper presented at the Middle Atlantic Archaeological Conference, Ocean City, MD.
  1998a *Ceramics and Delaware Valley Prehistory: Insights from the Abbott Farm.* Trenton Complex Archaeology: Report 14. Report prepared by Louis Berger & Associates, Inc. for the Federal Highway Administration and the New Jersey Department of Transportation, Trenton, NJ.

1998b A Model for the Adoption of Native Agriculture in the Middle Atlantic Region. Paper presented at the Middle Atlantic Archaeological Conference, Cape May, NJ.

1998c Archaic Triangles at the Abbott Farm National Landmark: Typological Implications for Prehistoric Studies in the Middle Atlantic Region. Paper accompanying an exhibit at the Middle Atlantic Archaeological Conference, Cape May, NJ.

Stewart, T. Dale
1992 Archeological Exploration of Patawomeke: The Indian Town Site (44St2) Ancestral to the One (44St1) Visited in 1608 by Captain John Smith. *Smithsonian Contributions to Anthropology* 36. Washington, DC.

Sturtevant, William C., and David J. Meltzer
1985 The Holly Oak Pendant. *Science* 227:242–44.

Thomas, Ronald A.
1970 Adena Influence in the Middle Atlantic Coast. In *Adena: The Seeking of an Identity*, edited by B. K. Swartz, pp. 56–87. Ball State University, Muncie, IN.

1972 Mortuary Practices. In *Proceedings of the Third Annual Middle Atlantic Archaeological Conference*, edited by Ronald A. Thomas, pp. 21–42, Newark, DE.

1973 Prehistoric Mortuary Complexes of the Delmarva Peninsula. In *Proceedings of the Fourth Annual Middle Atlantic Archaeological Conference*, edited by Ronald A. Thomas, pp. 50–72, Penns Grove, NJ.

1974 Webb Phase Mortuary Customs at the Island Field Site. *Transactions of the Annual Meeting of the Delaware Academy of Science* Vol. 5:49–61.

Thurman, Melburn D.
1971 Some Remarks on Typology. In *Proceedings of the Middle Atlantic Archaeology Conference*, edited by Charles W. McNett, Jr., and William M. Gardner, pp. 53–58. Catholic University of America, Washington, DC.

1973 A Short Paper on Ossuaries. In *Proceedings of the Fourth Annual Middle Atlantic Archaeological Conference*, edited by Ronald A. Thomas, pp. 37–43, Penns Grove, NJ.

1985 A Cultural Synthesis of the Middle Atlantic Coastal Plain, Part I: "Culture Area" and Regional Sequence. *Journal of Middle Atlantic Archaeology* 1:7–32.

1987 "A Funny Thing Happened to Archaeological Data Coming Back from Delaware": Some Models for Middle Atlantic Archaeology. *Journal of Middle Atlantic Archaeology* 3:125–41.

2010 Another Interpretation of the Archaeological History of the Middle Atlantic. Paper presented at the Middle Atlantic Archaeological Conference, Ocean City, MD.

Thurman, Melburn D., and William P. Barse
1974 Mockley and Mockley-like Pottery in the Mid-Atlantic Region. Paper presented at the Middle Atlantic Archaeological Conference, Baltimore, MD.

Ubelaker, Douglas
  1973   The Hurley [sic, read "Juhle"] Ossuary at Nanjemoy Creek. In *Proceedings of the Fourth Annual Middle Atlantic Archaeological Conference*, edited by Ronald A. Thomas, pp. 17–29, Penns Grove, NJ.

Veit, Richard
  2001   Turning Points: A Brief History of Archaeology in New Jersey. *Bulletin of the Archaeological Society of New Jersey* 56:74–82.

Versaggi, Nina
  1978   Report Preparation and Content for Cultural Resources Surveys and Preliminary Evaluations. Paper presented at the Middle Atlantic Archaeological Conference, Rehoboth Beach, DE.

Vish, Al, and Ted Yeshion
  2005   Blood Residue Testing. Paper presented at the Middle Atlantic Archaeological Conference, Rehoboth Beach, DE.

Volk, Ernest
  1911   *The Archaeology of the Delaware Valley*. Papers of the Museum of Archaeology and Ethnology, Harvard University, Vol. V, Cambridge, MA.

Wall, Robert D.
  1981   *An Archeological Study of the Western Maryland Coal Region: The Prehistoric Resources*. Maryland Geological Survey, Baltimore, MD.
  1999   Late Woodland Ceramics and Native Populations of the Upper Potomac Valley. Paper presented at the Middle Atlantic Archaeological Conference, Harrisburg, PA.

Wall, Robert D., R. Michael Stewart, and John Cavallo
  1996a *The Lithic Technology of the Trenton Complex*. Trenton Complex Archaeology: Report 13. Report prepared by Louis Berger & Associates, Inc. for the Federal Highway Administration and the New Jersey Department of Transportation, Trenton, NJ.

Wall, Robert D., R. Michael Stewart, John Cavallo, Douglas McLearen, Robert Foss, Philip Perazio, and John Dumont
  1996b *Prehistoric Archaeological Synthesis*. Trenton Complex Archaeology: Report 15. Report prepared by Louis Berger & Associates, Inc. for the Federal Highway Administration and the New Jersey Department of Transportation, Trenton, NJ.

Wanser, Jeffrey C.
  1982   A Survey of Artifact Collections from Central Southern Maryland. *Maryland Historical Trust Manuscript Series* 23.

Ward, H. Henry, and David C. Bachman
  1986   Testing the Xerothermic Model on the Delmarva Peninsula: Buried Sites in Aeolian Contexts. Paper presented at the Middle Atlantic Archaeological Conference, Rehoboth Beach, DE.

Weslager, C.A.
  1942   Ossuaries on the Delmarva Peninsula and Exotic Influences in the Coastal Aspect of the Woodland Period. *American Antiquity* 8(2):142–51.
  1974   A Brief History of Archaeology in Delaware. *Transactions of the Annual Meeting of the Delaware Academy of Science* Vol. 5:11–24.

Wholey, Heather A.
  2004   Modeling Hunter-Gatherer Population Ecology. Paper presented at the Middle Atlantic Archaeological Conference, Rehoboth Beach, DE.

Whyte, Thomas R.
  1986   Zooarchaeology of the Addington Site: A Prehistoric Fishery of the Lower Chesapeake Bay. Paper presented at the Middle Atlantic Archaeological Conference, Rehoboth Beach, DE.
  1990   Fish Remains from the Leggett Site, Halifax County, Virginia. Paper presented at the Middle Atlantic Archaeological Conference, Ocean City, MD.
  2005   Genesis of the Cherokee in the Late Archaic Period of the Southern Appalachian Mountains. Paper presented at the Middle Atlantic Archaeological Conference, Rehoboth Beach, DE.

Williams, Lorraine
  1977   Contact Fortified Village Sites of Coastal New York and Connecticut. Paper presented at the Middle Atlantic Archaeological Conference, Trenton, NJ.

Williams, Stephen
  1991   *Fantastic Archaeology: The Wild Side of North American Prehistory.* University of Pennsylvania Press, Philadelphia, PA.

Wise, Cara L.
  1979   The Middle Atlantic as a Region: A Historical Perspective. Paper presented at the Middle Atlantic Archaeological Conference, Rehoboth Beach, DE.

Witthoft, John
  1952   A Paleo-Indian site in Eastern Pennsylvania: An Early Hunting Culture. *Proceedings of the American Philosophical Society* 96(4):464–95.

Witthoft, John, and Sam S. Farver
  1952   Two Shenks Ferry Sites in Lebanon County, Pennsylvania. *Pennsylvania Archaeologist* 22(1):3–32.

Wittkofski, J. Mark, and Theodore Reinhart (editors)
  1989   Paleoindian Research in Virginia: A Synthesis. *Archeological Society of Virginia Special Publication* 19.

Wren, Christopher
  1914   A Study of North Appalachian Indian Pottery. *Proceedings of the Wyoming Historical and Geological Society* Vol. 13. Wilkes-Barre, PA.

Wright, Henry T.
  1973   An Archeological Sequence in the Middle Chesapeake Region, Maryland. *Maryland Geological Survey, Archeological Studies* 1.

3

＋

CRM in the Mid-Atlantic

Not Quite Like Anywhere Else

Christopher T. Espenshade

Cultural resource management archaeology in the Middle Atlantic is unusual in several respects. A high diversity in physiography, ecology, scholastic traditions, and culture history is packed into a condensed region that can easily be driven across in eight hours. This has led to less territoriality among CRM firms, and greater interaction and cooperation between CRM practitioners. The Middle Atlantic lacks the huge military bases and broad expanses of public land that characterize much of the rest of the nation, and, as a result, transportation archaeology has been a prime mover in the industry. The region lacks reservations of federally recognized Indian tribes, and local CRM archaeologists have instead learned to work with federally recognized tribes now in the western United States and with state- and self-recognized groups. Lastly, due in large part to quality personnel in review positions, the region does not suffer too badly from budget undercutting. Although the Middle Atlantic operates under the broad mandates of the National Historic Preservation Act, our CRM is not quite like that practiced elsewhere.

HISTORY OF CRM

The trajectory of the American CRM industry is fairly consistent, region to region. University programs were often the incubators for CRM, and then engineering or architectural firms recognized a need to develop CRM sections, and then small CRM specialist shops developed, and finally larger CRM firms came to the forefront. Paralleling this development was a concomitant growth in the cultural resource staffs of SHPOs, federal agencies, and state agencies.

In considering the growth of CRM, it is instructive to look at historical data on the archaeological/paleontological expenditures for 1956–1974 (Table 3.1). Not only is the project count low (mean of 3.4/state), but the mean expenditure per project is only $26,157. CRM was clearly in its infancy in the Middle Atlantic through the mid-1970s.

In the mid- to late-1970s, some university programs saw CRM as an opportunity to emphasize practical experience and teach students beyond the field school context. It was not yet clear that CRM was going to revolutionize the career options of archaeologists, but the potential to teach students while paying them was attractive. Key university programs during this time included the College of William & Mary, the University of Delaware, the Catholic University of America, the University of Virginia, and Virginia Commonwealth University. The University of Delaware stands as a successful university-based CRM program. Under the guidance of Dr. Jay Custer, the university was almost the exclusive provider of CRM service to the Delaware Department of Transportation (DelDOT) in the late 1970s through the 1990s. Custer's program provided quality work while providing practical experience to undergraduate students (e.g., Custer and Bachman 1984; Custer et al. 1988, 1989, 1990, 1995, 1996a, 1996b, 1997).

Patrick Garrow experienced much of the growth of CRM in the Middle Atlantic region. When asked for a synopsis, Garrow (personal communication, June 21, 2013) reported:

> I started the Soil Systems Inc. archaeological program in July, 1976. The first year of operation we mainly did 201 facility plan projects (wastewater plants and lines). I wrote close to a hundred of those reports before we did much else. When SSI got started there was very little competition at the private sector level. Much of the work was being done by academic programs, and most

Table 3.1.   Federal Aid Transportation, Archaeology, and Paleontological Projects, 1956–1974

State	Number of Projects	Total Funds Expended
Delaware	1	$26,660
Maryland	1	$14,080
New Jersey	3	$134,262
New York	14	$218,572
Pennsylvania	4	$231,100
Virginia	1	$3100
District of Columbia	0	$0

were not very good at it. They failed mainly in the areas of report quality and timeliness. That enabled the private sector to develop and then dominate the CRM market. SSI expanded to Washington D.C. and Delaware by 1980, and to New York City by 1981. My participation in Maryland archaeology began a little later, with Garrow & Associates in 1984. We did the Oxon Hill Manor project for Maryland SHA (that year), which was the largest data recovery done in Maryland to that time. We subsequently secured a series of IDIQs with Maryland SHA and remained active in the state.

Competition for work built gradually at first and then way too rapidly by the early 1980s. The initial private sector competition came from programs in A&E firms, and began to swing towards stand-alone CR firms by the early 1980s. By 2000 or so the market began to swing back towards large A&Es as it became more and more difficult to execute contracts and meet prevailing safety standards. I believe that, with the recession, the pendulum is now swinging back towards stand-alone CR firms.

I turned to my personal bookshelf for a reminder of what CRM looked like in the early, university-based days. As an undergraduate, I was a co-author (I analyzed the lithic artifacts and helped a day or two in the field) on the June 1977 report on the examination of three tracts in Shenandoah National Park by the Laboratory of Archaeology at the University of Virginia (Troup et al. 1977). The report was accepted by the National Park Service. The report provides an interesting window into how things have changed. The 1977 report does not mention Section 106, the Area of Potential Effects, or the National Register of Historic Places. There are no eligibility recommendations offered. The effort is variously described as a reconnaissance, a survey, and an evaluation. The field and laboratory crew included a mixture of paid and volunteer workers. Although many university programs in this period were calendar-challenged, this project moved quickly from fieldwork in April and May, to a final report in June.

As the demand for consultants increased, and in conjunction with the implementation of state and federal equal opportunity programs and the Small Business Act, the Middle Atlantic saw an increase in small businesses and woman-owned or minority-owned firms. It became common for many agencies to meet their participation goals for small or disadvantaged business enterprises (DBEs) by using a DBE for cultural resource services. The DBE program has significantly increased the number and diversity of CRM firms working in the Middle Atlantic region.

In recent years, a number of universities have entered into cooperative agreements with federal land managers. These agreements are the bases for long-term research relationships that address both "pure" research and Section 106/110 concerns. For example, James Madison University is party to a cooperative agreement with Shenandoah National Park. Similarly, several universities in the Middle Atlantic have developed research interests and expertise in military history/archaeology, and have serviced recipients of National Park Service American Battlefield Preservation Program (ABPP) grants and other friends of battlefields. As in the old days, these programs provide practical training for students in field methods, analysis, and reporting. The work of James Madison University with the Shenandoah Valley campaign is a prime example.

DISTINCTIVE TRAITS OF MIDDLE-ATLANTIC CRM

The purpose of this chapter is to delineate how CRM archaeology in the Mid-Atlantic is different from that in other regions. The chapter is an unabashed endorsement for Middle Atlantic CRM. As such, most of the cited examples are drawn from our region's flagship publication, the *Journal of Middle Atlantic Archaeology*.

Lack of Huge Military Bases

Over much of the country, military bases constitute a large slice of the CRM pie. For example, through the Southeast there is almost a continuous chain of large bases in the Sand Hills–Fort Bragg, Fort Jackson, Fort Benning, and Eglin Air Force Base—and a second string of large bases hugging the coast–Camp Lejeune, Beaufort Naval Air Station, Parris Island, Fort Stewart, and Kings Bay Submarine Base. Military lands are not such an important part of the Middle Atlantic. There are bases, but not of the size seen in other regions. The Middle Atlantic (5 percent of the land area of the United States) contains only 3.2 percent of Department of Defense lands in the nation. If one excludes Fort Drum (on the very fringes of the Middle Atlantic), the percentage of military land in the Middle Atlantic is even less. In many areas of the country, military compliance with Sections 106 and 110 is a mainstay of the CRM industry. In the Middle Atlantic, however, the client mix is different.

Relative Paucity of Federal Land

When one looks at the size of Shenandoah National Park, it might seem strange to talk about a relative paucity of federal land in the Middle Atlantic. The key word is "relative." Unlike Western states where the federal government owns more than one-half of the land (e.g., 81.1 percent in Nevada, 61.8 percent in Alaska, and 61.7 in Idaho), federal land comprises only 0.7 to 9.2 percent of land in Middle Atlantic states (2010 data from Gorte et al. 2012). The region does not see massive surveys for the Bureau of Land Management or National Forest Service, as occur elsewhere.

Resultant Emphasis on Transportation

With a reduced military presence (in terms of acres, not command structure) and limited other federal land, and a relatively high population density, transportation becomes a major force in Middle Atlantic CRM. There are thus a large number of firms focusing on transportation clients, as well as transportation engineering firms developing in-house CRM programs, and the substantial and sophisticated CRM programs within the state Departments of Transportation and the regional offices of the FHWA. As an example of the size of the transportation business sector, in 2012, DelDOT contracted for $3.2 million in archaeological studies (Kevin Cunningham, personal communication, July 18, 2013). The transportation sector of CRM is sufficiently large that DOTs help fund SHPO staff positions in several states (Pennsylvania, West Virginia, New Jersey, and formerly Delaware). In Pennsylvania, the SHPO and DOT implemented a Programmatic Agreement that delegates many minor compliance responsibilities from the SHPO to the PennDOT.

Condensed Region

The compressed area of the Middle Atlantic is composed of several states, and various histories and environments. An archaeologist in Nevada pretty much does Great Basin archaeology. If they go five hours in any direction, they are still in the Great Basin. In contrast, the archaeologist in Richmond is two hours from the crest of the Appalachians, and three hours from the ocean. To CRM archaeologists, who tend to work within a reasonable driving distance of their offices, the condensed environmental and cultural patchwork means there is a lot more to master. While the Nevada archaeologist can specialize in Great Basin prehistory and history, Middle Atlantic archaeologists must be more diverse in their knowledge and expertise.

Geomorphology and geoarchaeology are important to Middle Atlantic archaeology. The relatively short lengths of many rivers from the mountains to the Fall Line and continuing to the lower Coastal Plain often means that these rivers had a high suspended load capacity and the propensity for significant overbank deposition episodes. As well, the severity of historic land clearance, especially during the plantation and logging eras, means there may be more than a meter of historic alluvium capping prehistoric deposits in certain locations. CRM practitioners in the Middle Atlantic have increasingly included geomorphologists at every phase of investigation (e.g., Schulderein 2000; Pendley 2008).

The condensed region also means that there are significantly overlapping areas of academic influence. There may be Temple University–trained archaeologists working in the same drainage as those trained at the University of Pittsburgh. Likewise, the Catholic University graduate program has provided compliance officers, educators, and consultants working throughout the Middle Atlantic.

Lastly, the condensed region almost always means there are multiple consulting firms within an easy drive of a Middle Atlantic project. This fosters a general competitiveness among consultants. I have found that this helps force all consultants to keep current and to be aware of new developments and new literature.

Omnipresence of African Americans and Associated Resources

The Mid-Atlantic captures much of the former Upper South. The early establishment and longevity of plantation-based economies in this area means that there were significant numbers of Africans or African Caribbeans imported as slaves. In certain Virginia counties, as much as 73 percent of the population was black in 1860, and Henrico County alone had 20,041 slaves in that year (UVA Census Browser 2012). This means that the CRM archaeologist in this region must become a student of the African diaspora (e.g., Sanford 2012; Heath 1999).

The archaeology of sites occupied by or created by African Americans presents interesting challenges. Because for much of their history, African Americans were often marginalized, the common parameters of site location (e.g., well-drained soils) may not apply. It was often the case that African Americans—whether owners, renters, sharecroppers, or squatters—chose or were forced onto marginal lands, meaning their site location may not be predicted under common probability models. Also, given an often depauperate material culture and relatively insubstantial dwellings, African American sites can be difficult to recognize during a survey.

The Middle Atlantic archaeologist must also recognize the underrepresentation of African American sites in the archival record (the same applies to other marginalized groups including remnant Native American communities). We cannot expect a detailed archival record for each African American site, and we have to be careful not to use the lack of a related archival record as a reason to dismiss the research potential of African American sites. Middle Atlantic archaeologists must also be aware of the traditions and belief systems of African Americans (e.g., Galke 2003).

Banging Against the Sea

A not too subtle trait of the Middle Atlantic is its eastern border, the Atlantic Ocean. Unlike the Sea Island coast of the Southeast or the rocky shores of New England, the Middle Atlantic meets the ocean in broad beaches, extensive marshes, and large estuary embayments (with the Chesapeake Bay dominating the region). CRM archaeologists in the region must be well versed in the archaeology of shell middens, often exhibiting excellent faunal bone preservation. Middle Atlantic archaeologists have addressed distinctive coastal zone phenomena such as Carolina Bays (e.g., Egghart 2008) and relict dunes (e.g., Custer 1999). The shallowness of the bays and the low elevation of adjacent landforms mean that Middle Atlantic archaeologists have to be aware of sites already inundated and those soon to be lost to sea level rise and storm-enhanced erosion.

One need only attend a MAAC meeting to see another major element of doing CRM in the Middle Atlantic: underwater archaeology (e.g., Austin 2005; Holmes Steinmetz 2008). Such studies are typically handled by specialty firms (e.g., Tidewater Atlantic Research, Dolan Research), but certain CRM firms also have an underwater division (e.g., PanAmerican Maritime, HRA Gray & Pape, Southeastern Archaeological Research, Commonwealth Cultural Resources Group). The long history of the eastern seaboard combined with the relatively shallow continental shelf and estuaries to preserve a lot of shipwrecks and other underwater resources. Battle losses and purposeful scuttling of craft during war added significant resources from the Revolutionary War, War of 1812, and Civil War.

Intensity of Historic and Modern Urbanization and Suburbanization

Almost 19 percent of the U.S. population lives in the Middle Atlantic region, which comprises only 5 percent of the land area of the United States. The Middle Atlantic contains two of the ten largest cities in the country, New York and Philadelphia. Given the history of settlement of the United States, the Middle Atlantic combines a large population, cities that often expanded onto filled wetlands or lowlands, and a significant time depth of Euro-American cities and towns.

For the CRM practitioner of the Middle Atlantic, this means there is a requirement for competency or literacy in urban archaeology. People have been living and expanding key communities since the earliest settlement of the colonies. Much of the early enhancement of cities was done by accrual, building up the land forms for better drainage and for removal of wetlands. This means the deposits and features of earlier houses and industries (including pre-contact living surfaces) are often sealed beneath later deposits (e.g., Yamin 2008; Cantwell and diZerega Wall 2001; Garrow et al. 1992). It also means that sometimes historic deposits or objects were brought in to help "make land," and we end up with things like an eighteenth-century ship preserved beneath New York City (Geismar 1983; AKRF, Inc. 2013).

The intensity of agriculture in the region means that much archaeology is conducted on plowed ground. Middle Atlantic archaeologists have led the effort to address the best means of approaching sites in plowed fields (e.g., Schindler 2004; King et al. 2006; Reith 2008). CRM archaeologists in the region are increasingly calling on geophysical prospection, especially magnetometer and ground penetrating radar, to determine what is present beneath the plowed ground.

Plenty of Dead

The relatively great time depth and density of the Euro-American, Native American, and African American settlement in the Middle Atlantic means there are a lot of human graves. The population data for the eighteenth and nineteenth centuries means that a huge segment of those who died in America in this span are buried in the Middle Atlantic. Historic and modern development often has impacted or now threatens to impact burial grounds and cemeteries. Churches close or move, families move on, and the archival data or oral history of former cemetery locations is too often lost. For example, in 1829, Adam Hamaker instructed his heirs to assure that the family cemetery near Hersey, Pennsylvania, was "kept up and well fenced forever." Within twenty-three years, his heirs had sold the land, the new owners knocked down the headstones, and the cemetery became a part of a corn field (Espenshade 2003).

This translates to a need for CRM practitioners to become familiar with past burial patterns (e.g., LeeDecker 2001), and with appropriate means of finding and delineating unmarked or poorly marked graves (e.g., McKeown and Owsley 2002). It also means that archaeologists need to be aware of the types of sites and features likely to contain prehistoric burials, and the legal and ethical parameters of investigating such sites (e.g., Becker 2008; Powell Kiser 2008). Lastly, Middle Atlantic archaeologists need to become aware of diverse burial traditions to best predict where graves are placed and how they are marked.

Lack of Resident, Federally Recognized Tribes

With the exception of New York State, the Middle Atlantic lacks reservations of federally recognized tribes. The historic processes of Euro-American settlement, expansion, and tribal relocation have led to the situation where there are few reservations and resident tribes remaining in the Middle Atlantic. The CRM practitioners of the region instead must interact with one or more of the following: displaced, federally recognized tribes (e.g., the Delaware Nation and Delaware Tribe of Indians, both now located in Oklahoma); resident tribes with some level of state recognition (e.g., the Mattaponi); and self-recognized remnant communities. As several researchers have noted, there were times when it was illegal to be a Native American in the Middle Atlantic (Heite et al. 2010). Many local communities downplayed their Native American identity, as a survival strategy, and certain Native American remnant populations sought protection by mixing with African American communities. Although archaeologists in many parts of the country can easily identify the appropriate federally recognized tribes with whom to consult, this task is not simple in the Middle Atlantic. The archaeologists of the Middle Atlantic have evolved a much more nuanced approach to consultation and interaction with Native Americans, an approach that reaches beyond the bare-bones requirements of Section 106. Many close partnerships have developed between the CRM industry and local Native American communities.

Ironically, although there is spatial discontinuity between historic tribes and many of their present ancestors, the region benefits from a rich archival/chronicle record of the former native occupants. Such a record informs our approaches to Contact Period sites (e.g., Klein 2004; Rountree 2004; Gallivan 2009; Woodard and Moretti-Langholtz 2009). The records are naturally best for the groups of the Coastal Plain and Fall Line, and the written database diminishes as one enters the mountains and Ohio Valley.

The War Between the States and the Metal Detecting Disciples Thereof

More correctly, the heading should include the French and Indian War, the Revolutionary War, the War of 1812, and the American Civil War. For each of these conflicts, much of the activity occurred in the Middle Atlantic. One need only look at the key battlefields addressed by the ABPP for these wars; the Middle Atlantic has a high density. Although other regions saw their share of action (e.g., the Southeast in the Civil War), you cannot really practice CRM in the Middle Atlantic without having to work with battlefields, camp sites, earthworks, picket posts, field hospitals, and so on (e.g., Starbuck 1996; Espenshade and Balicki 2010; Mandzy et al. 2010; Smith 2010; McBride and McBride 2010; and Geier and Whitehorne 2010). The Middle Atlantic has led in the quest to assure that military resources are being properly identified, interpreted, and evaluated in the Section 106 process (e.g., Espenshade et al. 2002; Wood 2010). For example, Virginia was one of the first states to require metal detecting and consultation with avocational detectorists when working in areas with a high potential for military sites. Alexandria, Virginia, stands out for having a city-level ordinance that similarly requires the use of appropriate methods to find and assess military sites.

This density of military action in the Middle Atlantic can be directly correlated with the high frequency of modern military zealots and relic collectors. These folks have much knowledge of "their own" local battle-field, and they are not bashful about loudly pointing out when they think CRM archaeologists have missed something (e.g., Jolley 2010). The metal detecting community is a mixed blessing. It can be a source of data and assistance from avocational detectorists (those concerned primarily with preservation and history) (Corle and Balicki 2006), or it can be a source of wanton site destruction by relic hunters concerned only with objects for their shelves or for eBay.

Reduced Territoriality

There are traditions and regulations in some areas of the country that serve to geographically limit an archaeologist's service area. California counts only California experience when assessing if you are qualified to work in the state. The BLM has divided many western states into regions, and the archaeologist must hold a permit to work in that region. More anecdotally, it has been said it is difficult to be accepted in Connecticut if you were not born, raised, and trained there, and Florida is another example of a state that is hard to break into.

In the Middle Atlantic, many states are not that large; and state lines do not follow any cultural or physiographic boundaries. Research interests thus frequently cross-cut state lines. We tend to describe ourselves not as a "Pennsylvania archaeologist" or a "Virginia researcher" but rather as a "Middle Atlantic archaeologist." This flexibility means the research-ers have an obligation to do their homework and not go where they are not qualified to work, and the compliance officers have an obligation to review and police the work of a lot of different people and firms.

Less Emphasis on Cost

After I moved from the Southeast to the Middle Atlantic, my new boss took the first budget I wrote and started in with "double this," and "this is not enough," and "they are used to paying more for this." This was about the same time I was handed the Tunkhannock pottery col-lection and was told I had a year of calendar time and a half-year of billable time to do the analysis. I had never heard of such luxury in the Southeast. It is a credit to many of the major clients and compliance re-view personnel at SHPOs and other agencies that it is not always about price in the Middle Atlantic. A focus on transportation, as discussed above, has resulted in many DOTs turning to IDIQ contracts, which are awarded based both on quality and price. The contracts allow the DOTs to identify and lock in quality firms, and limits cost competition once the initial contracts are awarded.

This is not to say that cost is never a factor in the region. In certain market sectors, for example, residential and commercial development, cost often is given primacy in choosing consultants. Furthermore, as noted in Garrow's quote above, the economic downswing of recent years has impacted the industry, and as the work has slowed, the tendency to cut budgets has increased.

Who Are the Players?

In order to characterize the CRM providers that are active in the Middle Atlantic, the consultant list maintained by the American Cultural Resource Association (ACRA) was reviewed for those known to work in the region. It should be noted that the ACRA list comprises only ACRA members, and not all firms choose to join ACRA. As well, no university research programs in the region are members. The ACRA data for each firm is not complete. For the thirty firms known to work in the Middle Atlantic on a regular basis, at least nineteen are small businesses (and at least six of these are woman- or minority-owned firms). The small end of the spectrum includes 1–2-person shops. In contrast, eleven are identified as large businesses, and these include national/international firms such as AECOM, HDR, Mead and Hunt, Versar, URS, and Berger. Seventeen of the thirty firms in the ACRA sample are solely cultural resource firms. The other thirteen companies offer CRM as well as environmental and engineering services.

Despite the generalized trajectory of the development of CRM, as presented above, there continues to be strong contract programs in many of the universities of the Middle Atlantic. William & Mary has a long-lived tradition that continues through the present. Binghamton University, James Madison University, and Indiana University of Pennsylvania are among those that maintain contract research programs. These universities pursue straight contract work (i.e., compete with CRM firms) or service grants (e.g., ABPP battlefield preservation) and enter into cooperative agreements with federal land managers. The Middle Atlantic also has a number of historic sites owned by private organizations. Several of these feature their own archaeological research programs. Although these in-house programs generally do not compete for other CRM work, they are in the business of managing the cultural resources of their host property. The Monticello archaeological program has long been a leader in African American archaeology (Kelso 1997; Heath 1999). Montpelier, Poplar Forest, Stratford Hall Plantation, and Mount Vernon likewise have active research programs (e.g., Collins 2011; Proebsting and Lee 2012; Reeves and

Greer 2012; Breen et al. 2012; Wilkins 2010). These historic sites often have their own, site-specific version of Section 106/110; that is, they are careful to consider potential archaeological resources as part of their broader interpretive mission.

Lastly, there are many CRM practitioners in the federal, state, and local governments of the Middle Atlantic. These agency personnel do their own research and also on occasion contract with outside consultants. National forests, national parks, and military bases commonly have in-house expertise. Likewise, SHPOs/Offices of State Archaeology, state parks programs, and state departments of transportation maintain a cadre of professionals in CRM. We have also seen individual counties and cities in heritage-rich, high-growth areas developing their own CRM programs (the City of Alexandria and Fairfax County, both in Virginia, are two strong examples).

Intimacy

For many of the reasons discussed above, there is an intimacy in the CRM of the Middle Atlantic. Practitioners tend to know their competitors, their research interests, and their approach to staying in business. Although it may just be a product of my aging and maturing (I came to the Middle Atlantic after more than ten years of working in the Southeast), I have found that people are not as distrustful or disdainful of their competitors as seen in other regions. I think much of this is due to the fact that you keep running into the same folks again and again. If you attend the Southeastern Archaeological Conference (the major conference for the Southeast), there are more than ten concurrent sessions, and you might feel a small speck in the sea of people. In contrast, at the Middle Atlantic Archaeological Conference, there are two or three sessions, and it is easy to track down the researcher you want to ask about any given subject.

This closeness also translates into a strong support of students and new graduates. For example, the MAAC has sponsored a student paper competition with undergraduate and graduate categories for many years. This contest provides mentors when requested, and the judges provide direct feedback to each student regarding their written papers and their presentations. More recently, the professional community has begun a program of student sponsorships, whereby the membership and conference registration are paid for students presenting at the conference. This serves to keep the membership young and growing, and to allow students to begin developing a professional network in the Middle Atlantic.

The CRM practitioners of the Middle Atlantic have also benefited from this intimacy by relying on one another for information and assistance. The personification of this broad reach for peer input is Kevin Cunningham at DelDOT. When one of his consultants runs into something unusual, Kevin emails more than three hundred of his closest friends and asks for thoughts, leads, and comments.

SUMMARY

The Middle Atlantic offers a rich environmental and cultural mosaic that brings challenges to CRM practitioners. The very nature of the region argues against over-specialization among CRM archaeologists. The region is relatively small, and there is much communication within the professional community. The rich pre-contact and historic period archaeological record can be demanding, but tends to keep practitioners engaged. CRM archaeology in the Middle Atlantic is distinctive, dynamic, and interesting.

REFERENCES CITED

AKRF, Inc.
    2013   *Final Technical Report, Data Recovery and Analysis of the 18th Century WTC Ship, World Trade Center Memorial and Development Plan, Blocks 54, Lot 1 and Block 56, Lots 15, 20, and 21, New York, New York.* AKRF, Inc., New York, New York. Submitted to the Lower Manhattan Development Corporation, New York.

Austin, Karl
    2005   USS Alligator: The Navy's First Submarine in the Community and in the Classroom. *Journal of Middle Atlantic Archaeology* 21:53–62.

Becker, Marshall Joseph
    2008   "Power Point": Multiple Perspectives on Native American Grave Recovery, Including Those Relating to American Legal Systems. *Journal of Middle Atlantic Archaeology* 24:27–38.

Breen, Eleanor, Esther C. White, and Jeanne Higbee
    2012   Processing Fine Screen Samples from Archaeological Sites: A Case Study from the South Grove Midden at Mount Vernon Plantation. *Journal of Middle Atlantic Archaeology* 28:117–25.

Cantwell, Anne-Marie, and Diana diZerega Wall
    2001   *Unearthing Gotham: The Archaeology of New York City.* Yale University Press, New Haven, CT.

Collins, Crystal E.
    2011   Playing in the Dirt: The Archaeology of Childhood at Thomas Jefferson's Poplar Forest. *Journal of Middle Atlantic Archaeology* 27:89–100.

Corle, Bryan L., and Joseph F. Balicki
 2006 Finding Civil War Sites: What Relic Hunters Know, What Archaeologists Should and Need to Know. In *Huts and History: The Historical Archaeology of Military Encampment During the American Civil War*, edited by Clarence R. Geier, David G. Orr, and Matthew B. Reeves, pp. 55–74. University Press of Florida, Gainesville.

Custer, Jay
 1999 Aeolian Sand Deposition at the Gum Branch Site (7S-E-83C), Sussex County, Delaware. *Journal of Middle Atlantic Archaeology* 15.

Custer, J. F., and D. C. Bachman
 1984 *Phase III Data Recovery of the Prehistoric Components from the Hawthorn Site 7NC-E-46, New Churchman's Road, Christiana, New Castle County, Delaware.* University of Delaware, Department of Anthropology, Center for Archaeological Research, Newark. Submitted to the Delaware Department of Transportation, Dover.

Custer, J. F., W. P. Catts, J. Hodny, and C. DeSantis Leithren
 1990 *Final Archaeological Investigations at the Lewden Green Site (7NC-E-9), Christiana, New Castle County, Delaware.* University of Delaware, Department of Anthropology, Center for Archaeological Research, Newark. Submitted to the Delaware Department of Transportation, Dover.

Custer, J. F., and J. Hodny
 1989 *Final Archaeological Investigations at the Hockessin Valley Site (7NC-A-17), New Castle County, Delaware.* University of Delaware, Department of Anthropology, Center for Archaeological Research, Newark. Submitted to the Delaware Department of Transportation, Dover.

Custer, J. F., A. Hoseth, B. H. Sisler, D. J. Gretner, and G. Mellin
 1997 *Final Archaeological Investigations at the Pollack Prehistoric Site (7K-C-203), State Route 1 Corridor, Kent County, Delaware.* University of Delaware, Department of Anthropology, Center for Archaeological Research, Newark. Submitted to the Delaware Department of Transportation, Dover.

Custer, J. F., D. Kellogg, B. H. Silber, and R. Varisco
 1995 *Final Archaeological Investigations at the Wrangle Hill Prehistoric Site (7NC-G-105), State Route 1 Corridor, Chesapeake and Delaware Canal Section, New Castle County, Delaware.* University of Delaware, Department of Anthropology, Center for Archaeological Research, Newark. Submitted to the Delaware Department of Transportation, Dover.

Custer, J. F., L. Riley, and G. Mellin
 1996a *Final Archaeological Excavations at the Leipsic Site (7K-C-194A), State Route 1 Corridor, Kent County, Delaware.* University of Delaware, Department of Anthropology, Center for Archaeological Research, Newark. Submitted to the Delaware Department of Transportation, Dover.

Custer, J. F., S. C. Watson, A. Hoseth, and E. C. Coleman
 1988 *Final Archaeological Investigations at the Dairy Queen Site (7NC-D-129), New Castle County, Delaware.* University of Delaware, Department of Anthro-

pology, Center for Archaeological Research, Newark. Submitted to the Delaware Department of Transportation, Dover.

Custer, J. F., S. C. Watson, and B. H. Silber
   1996b *Final Archaeological Investigations at the Carey Farm (7K-D-3) and Island Farm (7K-C-13) Sites, State Route 1 Corridor, Kent County, Delaware (Draft Report).* University of Delaware, Department of Anthropology, Center for Archaeological Research, Newark. Submitted to the Delaware Department of Transportation, Dover.

Egghart, Chris
   2008 Carolina Bays of the Atlantic Coastal Plain: An Archaeological Overview. *Journal of Middle Atlantic Archaeology* 24:87–97.

Espenshade, Christopher T.
   2003 *Archaeological Delineation of the Hamaker Cemetery, Hershey, Pennsylvania.* Skelly and Loy, Inc., Monroeville, Pennsylvania. Submitted to Hershey Foods Corporation, Hershey, Pennsylvania.

Espenshade, Christopher, and Joseph Balicki
   2010 Doug Scott Military Archaeology, Eastern Style: Status 2010. *Journal of Middle Atlantic Archaeology* 26:1–6.

Espenshade, Christopher T., Robert L. Jolley, and James B. Legg
   2002 The Value and Treatment of Civil War Military Sites. *North American Archaeologist* 23(1):39–68.

Galke, Laura J.
   2003 Ritual Caches and Ethnicity: How Do We Recognize Them and Who Is Responsible for Their Creation? *Journal of Middle Atlantic Archaeology* 19:55–66.

Gallivan, Martin
   2009 The Chickahominy River Survey: Native Settlement in Tidewater Virginia, AD 200–AD 1600. *Journal of Middle Atlantic Archaeology* 25:73–83.

Garrow, Patrick H., Jana Keller, Amy Friedlander, and James Collins
   1982 *Archaeological Investigations on the Washington, D.C. Civic Center Site.* Soil Systems, Inc., Marietta, Georgia.

Geier, Clarence, and Joseph Whitehorne
   2010 Chaos at Meadow Brook: The 1864 Battle of Cedar Creek: Preliminary Thoughts. *Journal of Middle Atlantic Archaeology* 26:61–74.

Geismar, Joan
   1983 *The Archaeological Investigation of the 175 Water Street Block, New York City.* Prepared for HRO International, New York, by Soil Systems Division, Professional Services Industries, Inc., Marietta, Georgia.

Gorte, Ross W., Carol Hardy Vincent, Laura A. Hanson, and Marc C. Rosenblum
   2012 *Federal Land Ownership: Overview and Data.* Congressional Research Service, Washington, DC.

Heath, Barbara J.
  1999   "Your Humble Servant": Free Artisans in the Monticello Community. *In*
         "I, Too, Am America": Archaeological Studies of African-American Life, edited
         by Theresa A. Singleton, pp. 193–217. University Press of Virginia, Char-
         lottesville.

Heite, Edward F., Cara L. Blume, William Sandy, Edward Otter, and H. J. Heik-
kenen
  2010   *Mitsawokett to Bloomsbury:Archæology and History of an Unrecognized*
         Indigenous Community in Central Delaware. Heite Consulting, Camden,
         Delaware. Submitted to Delaware Department of Transportation, Dover.

Holmes Steinmetz, Joyce
  2008   Middle Atlantic Deepwater Shipwreck Study: Side-Wheel Paddle
         Steamer Admiral DuPont, 1847–1865. *Journal of Middle Atlantic Archae-*
         ology 24:141–52.

Jolley, Robert L.
  2010   Archaeological Survey of Rutherford's Farm: A Multicomponent Civil
         War Site in the Shenandoah Valley, Virginia. *Journal of Middle Atlantic*
         Archaeology 26:7–20.

Kelso, William M.
  1997   *Archaeology at Monticello: Artifacts of Everyday Life in the Plantation Com-*
         munity. Thomas Jefferson Memorial Foundation, Charlottesville.

King, Julia A., James G. Gibb, Philip A. Perazio, Scott Shaffer, R. Michael Stewart,
Sterven McDougal, Matthew B. Reeves, Michael F. Johnson, and Faye L. Slocum
  2006   Issues in Plowzone Archaeology: A Forum Held at the 2006 Middle At-
         lantic Archaeological Conference. *Journal of Middle Atlantic Archaeology*
         22:111–33.

Klein, Michael
  2004   Introduction: An Annales Approach to Contact-Era Archaeology. *Journal*
         of Middle Atlantic Archaeology 20:1–6.

LeeDecker, Charles
  2001   The Coffin Maker's Craft: Treatment of the Dead in Rural Eighteenth
         Century Delaware. *Journal of Middle Atlantic Archaeology* 17.

McBride, W. Stephen, and Kim A. McBride
  2010   Excavations at Three French and Indian War Forts: Insights into Fort
         Design and Construction. *Journal of Middle Atlantic Archaeology* 26:43–60.

McCarthy, John P.
  1999   17th Century Quaker Lifestyles: Philadelphia's Merchant Elite at the
         Front and Dock Streets Site. *Journal of Middle Atlantic Archaeology* 15.

McKeown, Ashley M., and Douglas W. Owsley
  2002   In Situ Documentation of Historic Period Burials for Bioarchaeology.
         Journal of Middle Atlantic Archaeology 18:73–92.

Mandzy, Adrian, Erik Hale, and Joseph Marine
2010   Is a Battlefield Ever Truly Lost? Blue Licks and the Question of Impact. *Journal of Middle Atlantic Archaeology* 26:21–30.

Pendley, Anna
2008   Geomorphology of the New Deal-Excavated Fort Hill Monongahela Village Site and its Surroundings. *Journal of Middle Atlantic Archaeology* 24:13–20.

Powell Kiser, Laura
2008   Last Rights: Maintaining the Dignity and Humanity of the Deceased. *Journal of Middle Atlantic Archaeology* 24:39–43.

Proebsting, Eric, and Lori Lee
2012   Piecing Together the Past: Interpreting Inter-Site Connections at Thomas Jefferson's Poplar Forest. *Journal of Middle Atlantic Archaeology* 28:55–68.

Reeves, Matthew, and Matthew Greer
2012   Within View of the Mansion—Comparing and Contrasting Two Early Nineteenth-Century Slave Households at James Madison's Montpelier. *Journal of Middle Atlantic Archaeology* 28:69–80.

Reith, Christina B., editor
2008   *Current Approaches to the Analysis and Interpretation of Small Lithic Sites in the Northeast.* New York State Museum Bulletin Series 508. New York State Education Department, Albany.

Rountree, Helen C.
2004   Look Again, More Closely: 18th Century Indian Settlements in Swamps. *Journal of Middle Atlantic Archaeology* 20:7–12.

Sanford, Douglas
2012   Towards an Archaeology of Urban Slavery: Contextual Predictions. *Journal of Middle Atlantic Archaeology* 28:143–53.

Schindler, William
2004   What Lies Beneath: Does Debitage on Plowzone Surfaces Provide Adequate Representations of Parent Subsurface Deposits? *Journal of Middle Atlantic Archaeology* 20:65–70.

Schuldenrein, Joseph
2000   Pennsylvania Geoarchaeology and Cultural Resource Management: As Assessment of Achievements and Shortcomings. *Journal of Middle Atlantic Archaeology* 16.

Smith, Steven D.
2010   "Obstinate and Strong": The History and Archaeology of the Siege of Fort Motte, South Carolina. *Journal of Middle Atlantic Archaeology* 26:31–42.

Starbuck, David R.
1996   Four Years of Archaeological Research on Rogers Island, An Encampment of the French and Indian War. *Journal of Middle Atlantic Archaeology* 12.

Troup, Charles G., Chris Espenshade, Chris Hays, and Marcey Bergman
  1977 *An Evaluation of Tracts I, II, and III, Madison and Green Counties, Shenandoah National Park, Virginia.* Laboratory of Archaeology, University of Virginia, Charlottesville. Submitted to National Park Service, Luray, Virginia.

Wilkins, Andrew
  2010 Elements of a Landscape: Soil Chemistry at Stratford Hall Plantation. *Journal of Middle Atlantic Archaeology* 26:155–64.

Wood, Alyson
  2010 Understanding Variables Affecting Data Collected During Metal Detector Survey. *Journal of Middle Atlantic Archaeology* 26:75–80.

Woodard, Buck, and Danielle Moretti-Langholtz
  2009 "They Will Not Admitt of Any Werowance From Him to Governe Over Them" The Chickahominy In Context: A Reassessment of Political Configurations. *Journal of Middle Atlantic Archaeology* 85–96.

Yamin, Rebecca
  2008 *Digging in the City of Brotherly Love: Stories from Philadelphia Archaeology.* Yale University Press, New Haven, CT.

4

+

Public Archaeology
and Outreach in the
Middle Atlantic Region

Elizabeth A. Crowell

In her PhD dissertation, Carol McDavid defined public archaeology as: "engaging the public in order to share archaeological findings and/ or promote stewardship of cultural resources or to otherwise make archaeology relevant to society by providing the public with the means for constructing their own past" (McDavid 2002:2)

Public archaeology can be defined to include cultural resource management, avocational archaeology, education programs (public and formal), heritage tourism, monument restoration, interaction with descendent communities, public activism, public comment on archaeological reports, and archaeology in popular media. There is hesitancy in the professional community to develop a concrete definition of public archaeology, because it is many things to many people. It is more than having professional archaeologists teach the public from the top down (McDavid 2005). Rather it is a collaborative process and a process that can take a wide variety of forms.

Public archaeology as we know it today includes both public outreach (educating the public about archaeology) and public participation (getting the public involved in the archaeological process). The concept of "public archaeology" was largely defined in the 1960s and the 1970s, with the passage of the National Historic Preservation Act, and other historic preservation legislation. Section 106 of the National Historic Preservation Act mandated that archaeology be done on projects that received federal funding, were on federal land, or required federal permits. As well, Section 106 provided members of the public with the opportunity to have a voice in the review process. It also mandated that archaeologists provide public outreach documentation, so that the results of archaeological studies would be readily available to the public.

Whereas this legislation defined public archaeology and provided the means for public involvement, we would be remiss to see this as the birth of public awareness of archaeology. Antiquities and archaeology captured the public imagination in a widespread manner in the nineteenth century as a result of Napoleon's expedition to Egypt. When Napoleon embarked upon his military expedition, he included more than 160 scientists, artists, and scholars as part of his team. These scholars formed the *Commission des Sciences et Arts d'Egypte,* whose mandate was to document conditions in Egypt. They produced a multi-volume treatise, *Description de L'Egypte,* which included volumes on geology, geography, zoology, natural history, the modern state, and antiquities. The information and illustrations of Egyptian antiquities combined with the return of the team with artifacts such as the Rosetta stone piqued an interest in antiquities (de Laus de Boisy 2008). In Europe and in the United States, among the upper classes and the educated, an interest in antiquities of all sorts took off like wildfire. In Europe, there were expeditions that took place to Egyptian and other ancient sites.

In the United States in the nineteenth and early twentieth centuries, there was a growing interest in archaeology. As early as 1799, the American Philosophical Society sent a circular letter to its membership asking for descriptions of antiquities in their areas (National Park Service 2013c). The Smithsonian Institution was founded in 1846 and the Department of the Interior was established in 1849. In 1879, the Bureau of Ethnology (later Bureau of American Ethnology) was established to document the culture of the quickly disappearing American Indians (National Park Service 2013c). The University of Pennsylvania Museum of Archaeology and Anthropology was established in 1889 (Grossman-Bailey 2001:23). The Antiquities Act, enacted in 1906, established penalties for the desecration of antiquities (16 U.S.C. 433) and required that permits be obtained for their investigation (16 U.S.C. 432). Each of these firsts laid the groundwork for the development of later public archaeology initiatives.

The discovery of American Indian and historical artifacts in gardens and agricultural fields sparked the interest of local intellectuals. Many individuals identified with nineteenth and early twentieth century archaeology could be categorized as "Renaissance men." They were learned, but their initial training was not in anthropology or archaeology (Crowell 2000:98). In the late nineteenth and early twentieth century, the likes of Henry Chapman Mercer, Charles Conrad Abbott, and William Henry Holmes were pursuing archaeological ventures. Henry Mercer was a Harvard- and Penn-educated law scholar who never practiced. He was an avid collector who preserved everyday objects threatened by obsolescence. He served as curator of American and Prehistoric Archaeology at the University of Pennsylvania Museum in the 1890s (Leach 2008) and later founded a museum in Bucks County, Pennsylvania, to house and exhibit his collections. Charles Abbott was a University of Pennsylvania–educated MD who was knowledgable in both cultural and natural history. He served as assistant curator at the Peabody Museum. His property, Abbott Farm, was subject to numerous archaeological investigations throughout the latter nineteenth and wentieth centuries. It has been designated a National Historic Landmark (Princeton University). William Henry Holmes graduated from McNeely Normal College and then studied art before joining the U.S. Geological Survey, where served as archaeologist. He then became chief of the Bureau of American Ethnology; curator of anthropology at the University of Chicago's Field Columbian Museum; head curator of the U.S. National Museum, and the first director of the National Gallery of Art (Smithsonian Institution, Department of Anthropology 1 and 2; Swanton 1936). Dorothy Cross was the only anthropologically trained archaeologist of those mentioned here. She earned her PhD in Oriental studies and anthropology from the University of Pennsylvania in 1936, where she specialized in Near Eastern archaeology and New Jersey prehistory. She taught at Hunter College and served as an archaeologist at the New Jersey State Museum (Levine 1994: 14–15).

These archaeologists engaged interested members of the public to assist in the excavation of archaeological sites in the Middle Atlantic region. Many of the early avocational archaeologists were members of the professional classes or the elite who had the time to spend pursuing such endeavors (Crowell 2000: 98). In Washington, D.C., this avocational interest led to the establishment of the Anthropological Society of Washington (ASW) in 1879, the first local anthropological association. Its membership was composed of anthropologists from the Smithsonian Institution, other scientists, and other male members of the interested public (Lamb 1906). Women in Washington, D.C., formed their own society, the Women's Anthropological Society of America, which was established in 1885 and was primarily composed of non-anthropologists (McGee 1889). The ASW began publication of the *American Anthropologist*, in 1888. In its earliest years, it was largely devoted to local archaeological activities. The Anthropological Society of Washington was the parent organization of the American Anthropological Association (Lamb 1906).

In the twentieth century, opportunities for those interested in archaeology expanded. Avocational interest in archaeology, in combination with the growth of archaeological projects, led to the establishment of statewide archaeological societies with local chapters. These archaeological societies were not only for professional archaeologists but also included members from the general public who had an interest in archaeology.

These societies held annual meetings and published journals (sometimes several times a year) and regular newsletters. They also sponsored archaeological investigations where members of the public could participate. The local chapters held more frequent meetings where members could hear or make presentations, share information, and make contacts. Notably, these local societies and chapters provided and continue to provide their membership with opportunities to volunteer on projects sponsored by archaeological societies, museums, and other organizations.

As well as those opportunities offered by the state archaeological societies, the Great Depression resulted in some citizens becoming involved in archaeology as a matter of economic necessity. Where these workers did not come to participate in these archaeological studies out of choice, other workers and landowners who lived where the work was being conducted developed an awareness of and an interest in archaeology. The Great Depression put a huge percentage of the population out of work. Beginning in the mid-1930s, Franklin Delano Roosevelt's New Deal initiatives provided employment for groups of unskilled and semiskilled workers

Table 4.1. Middle Atlantic State Archaeological Societies

Organization	Founding Date	Publications
New York State Archaeological Association	1916	*The Bulletin: Journal of the New York State Archaeological Association* and *The NYSAA Newsletter* (http://nysaa-web.org/)
Society for Pennsylvania Archaeology	1929	*Pennsylvania Archaeologist* (since 1931) and *SPA Newsletter* (http://pennsylvania archaeology.com)
Archaeological Society of New Jersey	1931	*Archaeological Society of New Jersey Bulletin* (since 1948), the newsletter, and a LISTSERV (http://www.asnj.org/)
Archaeological Society of Delaware	1933	*Bulletin of the Archaeological Society of Delaware* and blog (http://delawarearchaeology.org/)
Archeological Society of Virginia	1940	*Quarterly Bulletin of the Archeological Society of Virginia* (beginning 1942) and the *ASV Newsletter* (http://www.asv-archeology.org/)
West Virginia Archeological Society	1948	*The West Virginia Archeologist* (since 1949) and newsletter (http://www.wvarch.org/)
Archeological Society of Maryland	1965	*Maryland Archeology* (since 1965) and *ASM Ink* (http://www.maryland archeology.org/)

on archaeological sites. "Archaeological investigations across the nation took advantage of virtual armies of relief workers to move tons of soil and uncover thousands of American Indian sites" (Means 2013a: 1). As well, historical archaeological investigations, including those in Pennsylvania and at Jamestown in Virginia, benefited from the labor of these relief workers (Means 2013a; Johnson 2013). New Deal archaeology occurred at several locations in New Jersey, under the direction of Dr. Dorothy Cross (Lattanzi 2013) and in Pennsylvania (Means 2013b; Johnson 2013).

BEYOND THE NATIONAL HISTORIC PRESERVATION ACT

The most profound impact on engaging the public in archaeology came with the enactment of the National Historic Preservation Act. With the advent of the National Historic Preservation Act and other historic preservation legislation, more archaeology was being done. More professional archaeologists were being hired to meet the growing demand. Universities, environmental engineering companies, and enterprising individuals established archaeological departments to address the available work. The National Historic Preservation Act not only provided opportunities for professional archaeologists, it provided another means by which the public could become involved in archaeology. Section 106 mandates public participation in the process in the form of public meetings and review. It also calls for public interpretation of archaeological findings. Public involvement did not happen overnight, but it did come. Prior to this time, many academic projects were done by professional archaeologists with the assistance of students. The only information that might be disseminated to the public would have been through museum exhibits and displays. For publicly funded projects, there were more opportunities for actual participation. The enactment of this legislation has led to far more effort to engage the public at many levels in the past forty-seven years.

The National Historic Preservation Act calls for governors to appoint State Historic Preservation Officers and to ensure they had associated staff (National Historic Preservation Act, Section 101 (b) (1) (A)). Public archaeology programs are one of the many mandates of the State Historic Preservation Offices (SHPOs). Programs such as Archaeology Week (the first of which was established in Arizona in 1983) became immensely popular (Appler 2012: 45). Archaeology Week evolved into Archaeology Month. In the Middle Atlantic region, programs were being initiated out of the SHPO offices and supported by other agencies and municipalities. Archaeology Month in Maryland is held in April; in Delaware and New Jersey, it is in May; and in Pennsylvania, Virginia, and West Virginia,

Archaeology Month is celebrated in October (Society for American Archaeology 2013). Beginning in 2005, New York State designated May through September as Archaeology Season (Society for American Archaeology; New York Archaeological Council).

A number of federal agencies have been committed to public outreach and involvement in archaeology. This has included the preparation of planning and guidance documents produced by the National Park Service and Advisory Council on Historic Preservation. As part of the Section 106 process, federal agencies have made efforts to reach out to the public, including descendent communities, both to allow them a voice in the process and to allow them input into interpretation.

The other state agencies that have made meaningful contributions to archaeology are the Departments of Transportation and Highway Departments. Each state in the region has archaeologists in these agencies who are highly committed to public participation and outreach. There have been efforts to produce public documents and to make write-ups accessible to the public on websites. Pennsylvania Department of Transportation (PennDOT), Maryland State Highway Association (MDSHA), and Virginia Department of Transportation (VDOT) have easily accessible websites where archaeological materials are available for the public. Delaware Department of Transportation's (DelDOT's) archaeology website is truly impressive with pages presenting straightforward explanations about archaeology and why they are involved. They have historic maps and photographs, a detailed children's page, and an impressive public outreach page. The public outreach page provides pdfs of booklets, brochures, handouts, magazine articles, papers, postcards, posters, and presentations that have been prepared as part of transportation projects (Delaware Department of Transportation). Between 1980 and 1991, archaeologists representing DelDOT made presentations, conducted tours, or spoke to citizens' or school groups on more than 350 occasions. In the eighteen years since the initial list was compiled, the DelDOT archaeology staff has made at least one public presentation per week, which would equate to at least 936 additional presentations (Cunningham, 2013, personal communication).

THE ADVENT OF LOCAL ARCHAEOLOGY PROGRAMS

Several county and city programs have developed and included a public outreach component. Programs in New York, Philadelphia, and Baltimore had strong outreach components in the 1980s. At the county level, the Maryland National Capital Park and Planning Commission supported and continues to support archaeology programs in Montgomery and Prince Georges Counties. These programs accept volunteers and have developed outreach materials. For the purposes of this chapter, three programs are being described, which are unique and long-standing.

Archaeology has occurred at the municipal level in the Middle Atlantic with some of the earliest public programs. In the city of Alexandria archaeology was conducted at Fort Ward by concerned citizens beginning in 1961. When "urban renewal" unearthed a treasure trove of artifacts in the Old Town, the city called upon the Smithsonian for assistance. They later hired the Smithsonian staffer to assist on a project-to-project basis and finally hired the first permanent Alexandria city archaeologist in 1977. Alexandria benefits from having an Archaeology Commission, established in 1975. From the outset, the city has actively engaged the public. There is a well-established volunteer program with opportunities to volunteer to participate in field work, laboratory processing, or research activities. The city of Alexandria enacted an archaeology ordinance in 1989 that allowed the city to require archaeology prior to development. As well, the Friends of Alexandria Archaeology (FOAA) has been active since it was established in 1986. The group provides assistance and financial support to the staff (Alexandria Archaeology Timeline). Alexandria continues to provide volunteer opportunities in the field and laboratory and offers archaeology camps and field schools that allow students with an interest in archaeology to explore it.

In 1978, the Fairfax County History Commission petitioned the Fairfax County Board of Supervisors to establish an archaeology program in response to the increase in development in the county. Archaeologists, with the assistance of volunteers, documented archaeological sites prior to development. Staff developed a Heritage Resource Management Plan to guide archaeology (Renaud and Chittenden 1987). This document, through the County Comprehensive Plan, allows Fairfax County to require archaeology when rezoning occurs. A strong volunteer program was established where members of the public had the opportunity to volunteer in both the field and laboratory. In 1987, in response to the increased use of parkland, the Fairfax County Park Authority hired an archaeologist to work with cultural resources on parklands. In 1996, County Archaeology and Park Authority Cultural Resources were merged. A Cultural Resource Management Plan was prepared in 2006 to guide the operation of the Cultural Resource Management and Protection Branch. County archaeologists continue to work with volunteers, school groups, scouts, and other organizations. There is both a website and a blog. Many of the volunteers are members of the Northern Virginia Chapter of the Archeological Society of Virginia and/or the Friends of Fairfax Archaeology and Cultural Resources (FOFA), which was established in 2010 to support the organization (Fairfax County Park Authority 2012).

In 1981, the Archaeology in Annapolis program started as a collaboration between the University of Maryland and Historic Annapolis. The program has offered annual summer field schools. The program is committed to public archaeology and, as such, has offered public tours and exhibits to interpret the history of Annapolis. The program has worked on a variety of sites over the years, many of which have focused on slaves, workers, or other ordinary people. As part of the longstanding program, the archaeologists have invited the public to be part of the process, by encouraging them to provide input, including critiques of the program's motives. "This process serves as a cornerstone for the premise that through active and critical discourse social change can be wrought" (Archaeology in Annapolis).

As well, archaeology has been supported at a number of museums, and public outreach activities have occurred. This includes the long-term archaeology programs at Colonial Williamsburg, St. Mary's City, Jamestown (by both the Association for the Preservation of Virginia Antiquities and the National Park Service), Montpelier, Mount Vernon, Monticello, and Bartram's Garden, among others. These programs have volunteer opportunities in the field and or laboratory, provide opportunities for students, conduct tours, and share information on their findings through websites and brochures. In some cases, for example, at St. Mary's City, buildings have been reconstructed on the basis of archaeological research. In the summer, archaeologists contribute to heritage tourism, by conducting their work in the midst of the areas being visited and providing up-to-the-minute reporting of what is being found as it comes out of the ground. This puts the visitor in the center of the activity. Archaeology has also been used as a basis for reenactment, with everything from the building, to its furnishings, to the clothing being based on archaeological evidence. A number of these programs draw upon the expertise of local scholars, undergraduate and graduate students, and specialists to interpret the findings to the public.

One example that allowed the public to become deeply involved in archaeology and interpretation involves the archaeological investigations that occurred in the 1970s and 1980s at Thunderbird, a Paleoindian archaeological site in the Shenandoah Valley of Virginia. Professional archaeologists, geomorphologists, undergraduate and graduate students, and members of the public were involved in excavations at the site. In addition to site tours, lectures, exhibits, brochures, and volunteer opportunities, there were opportunities to learn how Virginia Indians lived by doing. As a result of experimental archaeology, the visitor could participate in flint knapping to manufacture stone tools; collect clay from the river and fire pottery over open fires; twist cordage from milkweed stems; and gather wild plant foods. When presentations were made, replica artifacts could be given to the public to hold in their hands. This type of interactive learning experience gave the visitor an intimate view and unforgettable link to people in the past. It provided a truly exciting and innovative approach to learning (Walker 2013, personal communication).

ARCHAEOLOGICAL CERTIFICATION PROGRAMS

In an effort to encourage skilled volunteers to participate in archaeological investigations, many states have developed archaeological certification programs. In 1962, the Texas Archeological Society offered the first annual field school, an eight-day training program in archaeological field methods (Texas Archeological Society 2013). This was identified by Hester Davis as the oldest formal program to train avocational archaeologists (Davis 1990). The Arkansas Training Program for Avocational Archeologists was established in 1964. The goal of the program was "(1) providing interested citizens with the opportunity to gain information on how to do archeology 'right,' and (2) multiplying many fold the eyes and ears of the few professional archeologists in efforts to preserve the state's past" (Davis 1990). A formal certification program was begun in 1972. The field and laboratory training program provides an introduction to field and laboratory. Arkansas has a tiered certification with the applicant being able to work from being a (I) Provisional Crew Member, Lab Technician, or Site Surveyor; to a (II) Certified Crew Member, Lab Technician, or Site Surveyor; to a (III) Certified Field Technician; to a (IV) Certified Field Archeologist (Davis 1990). The program requires that the students spend a significant amount of time in the field and laboratory, participate in a series of seminars, keep a log book, and participate with reporting.

Nationally, there are twelve certification programs, two of which are in the Middle Atlantic Region (National Park Service 2013a). In Virginia, the Archeological Technician Certification Program provides the opportunity for avocational certification candidates to get technical training in field and laboratory methodology. The program includes a series of lectures and workshops presented by professional archaeologists. As well, there is a list of required reading; required supervised laboratory and field time, and the requirement to discover and register an archaeological site on Virginia Cultural Resource Information System (VCRIS, formerly DSS). The program is rigorous, with the readings, workshops, and a commitment of time that is equivalent to or greater than a college-level course. Students must adhere to a code of ethics. The Virginia Department of Historic Resources (VDHR), Council of Virginia Archaeologists (COVA), and the Archeological Society of Virginia (ASV) sponsor the program (ASV website). The Facebook page states: "The aims of the program are to provide useful knowledge of the archaeological process to the public and facilitate active participation in the understanding and management of Virginia's constantly decreasing cultural resources" (Virginia Archaeological Technician Certification Program 2013). A total of seventy certification students have successfully completed the Archeological Technician Certification Program and are working with professional archaeologists to make meaningful contributions to archaeology across the Commonwealth.

Maryland also offers a certification and training program for archaeological technicians, known as the CAT program. This program is jointly sponsored by the Council for Maryland Archeology, the Maryland Historical Trust, and the Archeological Society of Maryland, Inc. The program was modeled after the certification programs in Virginia and Oklahoma and provides training for the interested public who wish to gain training in field and laboratory methods. As with Virginia, certification candidates are required to participate in field and laboratory projects, attend a series of classes taught by professional archaeologists, maintain a log book and personal journal, and complete an extensive reading list. The Maryland program certifies students in laboratory, field survey, and excavation. Candidates may be certified in one or all of these specializations.

CONCLUSION

Archaeologists fulfill their obligations to the public by keeping the public informed and involved in the process. We provide the public with opportunities for involvement in volunteer programs, field schools, and amateur certification programs. The public can also become engaged by exhibits and traveling displays. Numerous booklets, brochures, posters, postcards, and popular accounts have been displayed and distributed. Sites are often interpreted with wayside signage. Videos and media have been produced and are available on websites.

With the advent of twenty-first-century media technology, opportunities to reach the public have expanded exponentially. Printed material and interpretive signage can include QR codes that direct the reader who is looking for additional information to websites, podcasts, articles, or books. The interested public can be reached via social media, including Facebook and Twitter. There are LISTSERVs where information is exchanged. Archaeology programs are using social media, websites, blogs, and other electronic media to keep the public informed about discoveries. The benefits of working with the public are many. It provides an opportunity to exchange information. Often community members are interested in what is being discovered and sometimes can provide important information that can assist in the interpretation of the site. Projects that use volunteers allow a variety of community members to become involved in research, lab work, mapping, and other aspects of work. Local involvement imbues volunteers with "ownership" of the past (not in owning what is discovered, but in making the history their own).

In our current atmosphere of fiscal constraint, we are facing funding freezes and are challenged to do more with less. An educated constituency can advocate for archaeology. Participation in the process helps to demonstrate the contribution that archaeology can make to our collective sense of humanity. Rather than thinking that archaeology is Lara Croft, Indiana Jones, or the treasure hunters on reality television, an educated public can see the value of archaeology in our interpretation of past lifeways. The experience can enhance their understanding, broaden their worldview, and help the future learn from the past.

> There is a need in every generation to study the past, to absorb its spirit, to preserve its messages. . . . It's a collaboration of ourselves and our ancestors, the result is a deeper understanding for individuals and in consequence, a broader culture for the nation.
>
> —Christopher Tunnard (National Park Service Awards)

REFERENCES CITED

Appler, Douglas R.
  2012 Municipal Archaeology Programs and the Creation of Community Amenities. *The Public Historian* 34(3):40–67.

Crowell, Elizabeth A.
  2000 Walking in the Shadows of Archaeologist Past: Researching Museum Collections and Associated Records to Elucidate Past Lifeways. *North American Archaeologist* 21(2):97–106.

Davis, Hester
  1990 Training and Using Volunteers in Archaeology: A Case Study from Arkansas. *Archeology Program: Brief 9*. Washington, DC: National Park Service.

de Laus de Boisy, Louis
  2008 The Institute of Egypt. In *Napoleon: Symbol for an Age, A Brief History with Documents*, edited by Rafe Blaufarb, pp. 45–48. New York: Bedford/St. Martin's.

Fairfax County Park Authority
  2012 *Cultural Resource Management Plan*. Fairfax County, VA.

Grossman-Bailey, Ilene
  2001 Toward a History of Archaeological Research in the Outer Coastal Plain of New Jersey. *Bulletin of the Archaeological Society of New Jersey* 56.

Johnson, Janet R.
  2013   Historical Archaeology's "New Deal" in Pennsylvania. In *Shovel Ready: Archaeology and Roosevelt's New Deal for America*, edited by Bernard K. Means, pp. 33–47. Tuscaloosa: University of Alabama Press.

Lamb, Daniel S.
  1906   The Story of the Anthropological Society of Washington. 1–8. http://aaanet.org/sections/gad/history/062lamb.pdf. Originally published in *American Anthropologist*, 8:564–79.

Lattanzi, Gregory D.
  2013   The First Stimulus Package: The WPA and the New Jersey Indian Site Survey. In *Shovel Ready: Archaeology and Roosevelt's New Deal for America*, edited by Bernard K. Means, pp. 21–32. Tuscaloosa: University of Alabama Press.

Leach, Mallory
  2008   Henry Chapman Mercer. Accessed October 5, 2013. http://pabook.libraries.psu.edu/palitmap/bios/Mercer_Henry_Chapman.html

Levine, Mary Ann
  1994   Creating Their Own Niches: Career Styles Among Women in Americanist Archaeology between the Wars. In *Women in Archaeology*, edited by Cheryl Claassen, p. 9–40. Philadelphia: University of Pennsylvania Press.

McDavid, Carol
  2002   From Real Space to Cyberspace: The Internet and Public Archaeological Practice. Doctoral dissertation, University of Cambridge.
  2005   Comments made by Carol McDavid about a "Careers in Archaeology" handout, Society for American Archaeology (March 23, 2005). http://www.saa.org/publicftp/PUBLIC/primaryDocuments/Comments_Carol_McDavid.pdf

McGee, Anita Newcomb
  1889   The Women's Anthropological Society of America. *Science: A Weekly Newspaper of All the Arts and Sciences* 13(321):240–42.

Means, Bernard K.
  2013a Alphabet Soup and American Archaeology. In *Shovel Ready: Archaeology and Roosevelt's New Deal for America*, edited by Bernard K. Means, pp. 1–18. Tuscaloosa: University of Alabama Press.
  2013b Archaeologist #.ooooooooooooooooo: Edgar E. Augustine and New Deal Excavations in Somerset County, Pennsylvania. In *Shovel Ready: Archaeology and Roosevelt's New Deal for America*, edited by Bernard K. Means, pp. 48–65. Tuscaloosa: University of Alabama Press.

National Park Service
  2013a Amateur Certification. http://www.nps.gov/archeology/public/certify.htm
  2013b Appleman-Judd-Lewis Awards. http://www.nps.gov/aboutus/appleman-judd-lewis-awards.htm

2013c   Public Archaeology in the United States: A Timeline. http://www.nps.gov/ archeology/timeline/Timeline.htm

Renaud, Susan L. Henry, and Betsy Chittendon
1987   *Heritage Resource Management Plan: Fairfax County.* Office of Comprehensive Planning, Heritage Resources Branch.

Swanton, John Reid
1936   Biographical Memoir of William Henry Holmes, 1846-1933. *National Academy of Sciences (US) Biographical Memoirs, XVII.* Washington: The National Academy of Sciences, 223–52. http://www.nasonline.org/ publications/biographical-memoirs/memoir-pdfs/holmes-william.pdf

Texas Archeological Society
2013   Texas Archeological Society Field School. www.txarch.orgVirginia Archaeological Technician Certification Program
2013   DHR, COVA, ASV Archaeological Technician Certification Program. Facebook Page. https://www.facebook.com/pages/DHR-COVA-ASV -Archaeological-Technician-Certification-Program/124764550913632

OTHER SOURCES

Alexandria Archaeology Museum. "History of Alexandria Archaeology." Page updated August 30, 2013 11:59 AM. https://www.alexandriava.gov/historic/ archaeology/default.aspx?id=39146
American Anthropological Association. "A Brief History of Anthropology." Updated 9/15/2000. http://www.aaanet.org/about/Governance/history/
Antiquities Act of 1906. http://www.cr.nps.gov/local-law/fhpl_antiact.pdf
Archaeological Institute of America. "History" *About the AIA, 2013.* http://www .archaeological.org/about/history
"Archaeology in Annapolis." http://www.aia.umd.edu/
Comer, Elizabeth Anderson. "Public Archaeology as a Tool for Community Preservation and Empowerment." http://www.eacarchaeology.com/public.html
Delaware Department of Transportation. "DelDOT's Cultural Resources Archaeology/Historic Preservation Public Outreach." http://www.deldot.gov/ archaeology/brochures.shtml
National Historic Preservation Act. http://www.nps.gov/history/local-law/ nhpa1966.htm
Princeton University, "Collection Creator Biography," *Princeton University Finding Aid.* http://findingaids.princeton.edu/collections/C0290#description
Smithsonian Institution, Department of Anthropology 1. "An Artist's View: William Henry Holmes." *Expeditions People.* http://anthropology.si.edu/laexped/ ch4ns.htm
Smithsonian Institution. Department of Anthropology 2. "William Henry Holmes Biography." http://anthropology.si.edu/laexped/holmes2ns.htm

Society for American Archaeology. "State Archaeology Month Information." http://
www.saa.org/ForthePublic/NewsEvents/ArchaeologyWeeksMonths/
ArchaeologyWeekMonthbyState/tabid/143/Default.aspx

STATE ARCHAEOLOGICAL SOCIETIES

- The Archaeological Society of Delaware. http://delawarearchaeology.org/
- The Archeological Society of Maryland. http://www.marylandarcheology
  .org/
- The Archaeological Society of New Jersey. http://www.asnj.org/
- The Archeological Society of Virginia. http://www.asv-archeology.org/
- New York State Archaeological Association. http://nysaa-web.org/
- The Society for Pennsylvania Archaeology. http://pennsylvania
  archaeology.com
- The West Virginia Archeological Society. http://www.wvarch.org/

5

The Research Potential
of Museum Collections
and Their Influence
on Archaeology
in the Middle Atlantic

Gregory D. Lattanzi and Jessie C. Cohen

This chapter adds another pillar to the foundation of Middle Atlantic archaeology through its focus on the role played by museums in the region. While the authors understand the region consists of many local historical societies that do contain archaeological collections, we are limiting this discussion to museums, which contain the bulk of private, and compliance archaeological donations. Museums are vast repositories of archaeological collections, not only from individual donations, but also from mandated cultural resource management projects. While only a tiny percentage of these artifacts go on display, the rest remain in compact storage units untapped of their true potential. The care and use of these artifacts and collections are important to our understanding and knowledge of Middle Atlantic prehistory. This chapter discusses some of the research potential these collections have on Middle Atlantic regional prehistory, and the role and responsibility of museum professionals and cultural resource managers toward collections.

There are many aspects of Middle Atlantic archaeology that come to mind when we hear that word *foundations* (donations, compliance archaeology, etc.); however, we believe that the museum, home to compliance archaeology collections and individual donations, is foundational for a number of reasons. Museums are the most significant and sometimes the only repositories for archaeological, anthropological, as well as natural history collections. They house the material culture of past and present people; human skeletal remains; faunal, paleontological, ethnobotanical, and geological specimens; and archival and photographic documents (Rothschild and Cantwell 1981:2).

In the Middle Atlantic region there are a number of museums associated with universities or with federal and state governments, as well as many small public historical society museums, holding everything from vast amounts of archaeological collections to small personal items. State museums contain a wide breadth of collections. The New York State Museum, New Jersey State Museum, and the State Museum of Pennsylvania all center primarily upon the early histories of their particular state, and have strong emphases on prehistoric and historic archaeological collections as they are the repositories for many of the states' contract archaeology-generated materials. While a Delaware archaeological museum no longer exists, the Delaware Natural History Museum has a rich assortment of objects, including some of the country's most complete and informative mollusk and bird collections. Archaeology collections are curated at the University of Delaware Center for Archaeological Research and at the Delaware Archaeological Collections, Tudor Park Annex (part of Delaware Division of Historical and Cultural Affairs). Archaeological collections from Maryland are curated at the Maryland Archaeological Conservation Lab (MAC Lab). Besides in-person research opportunities, the MAC Lab also makes a significant amount of the collection, including important sites and diagnostic artifacts, accessible online. Virginia's official archaeological repository is the Archaeological Collections Management Program, which falls under the umbrella of the state's Department of Historic Resources. The West Virginia Archaeological Research and Collections Management Facility, located within the Grave Creek Mound Archaeological Complex, serves as the state's archaeological repository. All of these institutions provide students, professional researchers, and scholars with research opportunities, as well as provide the general public with educational exhibitions.

We argue that the nature of museum holdings permits an important and necessary two-fold focus: (1) comparative analyses of materials that have already been collected, and (2) an emphasis on curation stewardship and archaeological responsibility. In this chapter, we will discuss the problems and assets of the different types of collections, and the active role both museum professionals and CRM archaeologists need to take to help old and new collections maintain viability, educate the general public, and make data available within the discipline. Examples used to illustrate our discussions are taken from work carried out in New Jersey.

BACKGROUND

In past decades archaeological and ethnographic fieldwork have resulted in museum compact storage facilities, which are chock-full of objects representing vast assemblages of material culture. In the late nineteenth century, anthropologists and archaeologists alike "dug" through the past by salvaging data from fast disappearing cultures. Entities like the Bureau of American Ethnology (BAE) effectively founded and then promoted the field of American anthropology by conducting extensive research on North American Indian cultures through ethnology, archaeology, and linguistics. BAE researchers returned from the field with copious amounts of material objects and supplementary written documents, photographs, and audio recordings. These rapidly growing collections were deposited at the National Museum, which fell under the umbrella of the Smithsonian Institution, thus initiating the systematic collecting of anthropological assemblages to be deposited at museums. It is also important to note that the BAE established the River Basins Surveys, which sought to "supervise and conduct archaeological research in areas where dams were flooding many of the centers of prehistoric cultures within the U.S." (Smithsonian Institution 2013). This could very well be considered as one of the precursors to the cultural resources management projects and initial sources of archaeological museum collections. However, archaeologically based fieldwork and research emanating from national and state museums soon underwent a change that resulted in a dramatic shift. This shift, occurring sometime in the 1920s, saw an increase in university archaeological research programs, while at the same time museums "became more concerned with direct public service" (Sullivan and Childs 2003:9). As a result, the curation of archaeological collections became more of an exercise in training archaeologists as well as basic research (academic context), while simultaneously becoming inaccessible to the general public (Sullivan and Childs 2003:10) .

For an example, the New Jersey State Museum collections include a variety of grossly underutilized, yet systematically collected historic and prehistoric materials from sites throughout the state, including a National Historic Landmark site. The systematic feature of these collections is obviously their greatest asset. However, most of the State Museum's collections are donations from amateur archaeologists and collectors from as far back as the 1920s. Many of these older donated collections lack much of the organization that systematic collections have, as provenience information on individual objects is scanty at best or non-existent. The passage of Section 106 of the National Historic Preservation Act marked the beginning of cultural resource management and in 1976, the New Jersey State Museum started receiving these systematic collections; today they are the

fastest growing segment of repository collections, and the influx of materials now far exceeds the demand for comparative research or exhibition
potential. Systematic and non-systematic collections have advantages and
disadvantages, yet they both provide the interpretive foundation for a
Middle Atlantic region prehistory.

COMPARATIVE ANALYSIS OF COLLECTIONS—
DONATION AND SYSTEMATIC

Conducting archaeological fieldwork requires an infallible degree of
systematic methodology. Once artifacts are transferred to the museum
repository, systematic methodologies help to define the research potential
each assemblage will yield. Old collections are often undervalued due
to the lack of documentation and collection controls that are standard in
today's fieldwork (Brown 1981:65). While current collecting standards
might not have been used in decades past, many of these older collections
still include a certain amount of consistency in their documentation.

One of the most prolific collectors in New Jersey was Charles A. Philhower (1878–1962). His collection was originally donated to Rutgers
University and comprises thousands of artifacts as well as boxes of personal files and field notes. Finding his first artifact at the age of seven in
1885, he continued collecting until 1962 when he died. While the bulk of
his collection stems from New Jersey, a large portion of it comes from
states such as California, Arizona, Maine, Ohio, and Texas where he also
collected prehistoric and ethnographic objects. Philhower was not only
an artifact collector but also amassed an extensive amount of publications about his findings. Many of Philhower's publications can be found
in the *Archaeological Society of New Jersey Bulletin* and the *Proceedings of
the New Jersey Historical Society*. The Philhower artifacts are an example
demonstrating that while earlier collections may not include documentation up to today's standards, they still include supplemental information
that will enable future research. The Philhower collection includes an
extensive amount of prehistoric artifacts, which does not always include
documentation associated with each object. It appears that around 1971
all of the archaeological and ethnographic material was sent to the New
Jersey State Museum on permanent loan. This loan was permanently ac-
cessioned to our collections in 2010.

Documentation in the Philhower collection includes pieces of paper or
ink on the artifacts themselves. These notes often contain the town or other
locational information about the artifact, which can be extremely helpful.
Philhower also included whether or not he purchased the collection from
another collector, which typically occurred in his case. Those little bits of

information he provided are sometimes the only contextual information given. A large portion of his archaeological collection comes from "Ahaloking," or "the Beautiful Place," translated from the Delaware. This site was literally on Philhower's summer property along the Delaware River in Sussex County. Opposite Minisink Island, a large National Historic Landmark archaeological property, Philhower excavated on his property human burials, large pits, and post molds for over forty years. This site also saw archaeological excavations by Edmund Carpenter (1950), Dr. Edmund Darymple (1893–1894), Heye and Pepper (1916), Herbert Kraft (1977), and William Ritchie (1949). The significance of this site is attested to by the many years of excavations, which started with Philhower. Presently, staff of the Bureau of Archaeology and Ethnography are scanning all of the Philhower papers at Rutgers University in order to add additional information that may be lacking on the archaeological and ethnographic objects in our collections. Aside from all of the archaeological material currently at the New Jersey State Museum, Philhower also collected or purchased a large number of ethnographic objects, with a large portion of them being made by the Delaware. Hand-made baskets with beautifully colored block-stamped designs are not only impressive but a valuable educational resource.

The sheer volume of archaeological material from numerous significant archaeological sites makes the Philhower collection a valuable resource for staff, students, volunteers, interns, and scholars. The research potential of this collection still continues to prove itself. Presently bureau staff have begun to examine the Philhower papers currently housed at the Archives and Special Collections at Rutgers University. The presence of photographs with negatives and additional written material on some objects has enabled us to connect objects with more detailed information on excavation locations, missing objects, and locations of other sites through correspondence found within this collection.

The Pennella site (28-Oc-60), located in Ocean County, New Jersey, a Middle and Late Woodland period site, is an example of a systematic collection from the New Jersey State Museum. It was first visited by archaeologists in 1937. In the early 1970s controlled archaeological excavations were initiated. Continued over two summer seasons these excavations included the establishment of a grid system and the excavation of contiguous blocks of measured five by five units (Thomas and Stanzeski 2001:4). A third and final archaeological survey conducted by MAAR Associates in 2001 sought to comply with investigations per the guidelines of the New Jersey Historic Preservation Office in response to planned residential development.

The faunal assemblage of approximately two thousand fragments recovered during the 1970s excavations was donated to the State Museum.

These remains were inventoried, though many were not accurately identified. Unfortunately, an overall site map and field notes were not included in the donation. In the past, this lack of identified faunal materials may have proven a deterrent to researchers looking for complete collections to analyze. The Pennella site collection, with its lack of documentation and unidentified faunal remains, has actually proven to be a fruitful project for the bureau's student interns.

An intern from the Rutgers University anthropology program has worked on faunal identification, entering data into MNISQL, a program designed by Dr. Richard Kline of Rutgers University. The program uses basic information given by bone fragments, including element, side, and species to interpret minimum number of individuals (MNI). The program also has the capacity to include archaeological excavation locations such as unit and level and permit paleoecological and dietary analysis on the collection. The museum greatly benefits from these student projects as well: as the material is identified, the collection is properly stored according to museum best practices, thereby reducing the overall footprint of the collection and increasing available space within compact storage areas.

Professional researchers have also begun to utilize the richness of our collections, bringing their analysis and insight to inform the classroom. Professors from Temple University, Washington College, and Monmouth and Montclair universities have conducted large research-based analyses as well as object-based learning in an effort to educate and inform students. As an example, Dr. R. Michael Stewart spent about four months at the museum analyzing a number of collections for his research on early pottery and stone bowls of the region. The result of his efforts led to the publication of a large manuscript as well as invaluable knowledge for his prehistoric pottery classes. It is research like this that exemplifies the richness of collections and the professionals who want to see them used.

Museum professionals and CRM archaeologists alike play important roles in making sure that collections such as these continue to be viable comparative tools for not only archaeological but also anthropological research. This brings us to the point where we must ask ourselves "what kind of foundation must we as professional archaeologists set in order to continue to make meaningful discoveries, curate according to best practices, and finally promote these collections and their research potential?" (Warfel 2000:116). We have found that unless you actively promote your museum's collections no one will know what you have and the research potential it possesses. Unfortunately as is the case, the onus falls upon the staff to promote, encourage, and disseminate the type and kind of collections that the museum houses. The ability to "sell" your museum collection all depends on the potential research that those collections hold. The following are some examples of past and present work conducted using collections from private donations as well as cultural resource management projects.

USE OF MUSEUM COLLECTIONS

Numerous archaeological collections housed in museums in the Middle Atlantic region have been utilized to further promote archaeological knowledge in the form of reanalysis or reevaluation. However, the public, students, and professional researchers must be made aware of the types of collections housed at these state museums and the number of artifacts in their holdings. A quick preliminary survey of a couple of state museums indicates the extent of their total collections as well as how it breaks down (Figure 5.1). This kind of information is important, not only to the sustainability of the institution, but also to the entire public, professional and non-professional alike. These numbers, while not wholly accurate, are a first step in making old and new collections accessible to all researchers.

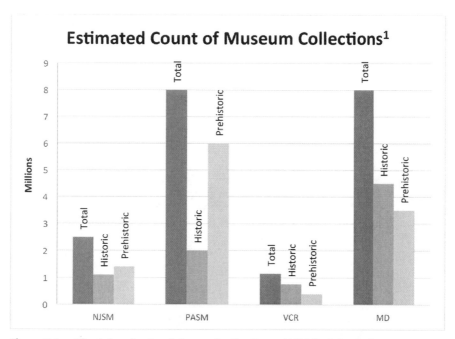

Figure 5.1.   Chart showing breakdown of collections at Middle Atlantic State Museums.

[1] The data used for this chart are estimates provided by the collection managers/curators of the New Jersey State Museum, Pennsylvania State Museum, the Virginia Department of Cultural and Historic Resources, and the Maryland Archaeology Laboratory.

A number of universities that have senior honors theses as well as graduate students have recently made it almost a requirement to seek out answers to pertinent research questions using museum collections. The following are just a few examples of the type of projects that have used these old collections across the Middle Atlantic region.

Starting in the 1970s and then again in the early 1980s cultural resource management work was carried out on the Abbott Farm National Historic Landmark as part of new highway and interstate construction (Pollak 1977). Then in the 1980s, Louis Berger and Associates carried out major data recovery excavations at the Abbott Farm (Wall et al. 1996). Archaeologists from this firm made use of the New Jersey State Museum's collections to help in reconstructing settlement and subsistence patterns for the Middle Delaware Valley. Byrne and Parris (1987) examined trace elements in the bones of prehistoric native peoples (well before the implementation of NAGPRA) to examine the prehistoric diet at the Abbott Farm site in New Jersey. For her dissertation research, Ann Guida (1989) analyzed deer teeth from the Abbott Farm to infer about prehistoric seasonality.

More recently, Timothy Messner (2008) examined a couple of ceramic sherds from Middle Woodland deposits in order to identify phytolith and starch grain information. Messner's work follows on the heels of John Hart and his colleagues (Hart et al. 2003; Hart and Lovis 2013) and his work with Owasco and Iroquois pottery from the collections at the New York State Museum. Pevarnik et al. (2007, 2008) examined Abbott Farm ceramics to examine clay sources and trade and exchange between the Middle Atlantic and coastal Virginia. His examination looked at petrographic and chemical analyses of the clays and tempers to help identify distinct patterns. Lattanzi (2013) examined prehistoric copper artifacts from not only the New Jersey State Museum but also the Pennsylvania State Museum and the Maryland Archaeological Laboratory from sites and locales, examining potential copper sources.

Finally, undergraduate students from a number of Middle Atlantic universities (Monmouth University, Rutgers University, Temple University, West Chester University, and William & Mary) are encouraged by their professors to pick a topic and examine collections in museums as part of their senior honors theses. Some of these projects involve ceramic analysis, examination of faunal collections from historic sites, and analysis of prehistoric lithics. The ability to provide access to collections for future research is paramount not only to the viability of the museum itself, but also for the collections themselves. Furthermore, those collections must be kept in a professional state so as not to lose provenience information or objects through neglect. This leads us to the problem of the condition of the collection as it is presented to the museum for eventual curation.

"CAREFUL HOW YOU CURATE"

In 1981, James B. Griffin stated that he had the "unhappy feeling that many contract archaeology programs of the recent past, and now being carried out, do not have an adequate support base for the proper preservation and curation of the materials and data being recovered" (Griffin 1981:12). Similarly in 2000, Steve Warfel also stated that the curation or "caring for" collections needs to be an obligation not only of museum professionals but also of contract archaeologists (Warfel 2000). This is an obligation we have to researchers, scholars, and the general public. Museum professionals assume responsibility for all collections, providing for their continued use for present and future researchers and the general public. Similarly, practicing archaeologists in cultural resource management must have an ethical responsibility to see that a project is completed and left in such a state whereby it can be easily used and researched (Sullivan and Childs 2004; Warfel 2000:116).

One of the downsides of collections management relates to the so-called nature of the beast and something that Griffin alluded to. CRM firms, unless they are part of larger diverse companies, appear to low bid projects, leaving out sometimes altogether any money for curation of collections let alone artifact analysis. If the company is small, over time it may ultimately fold. This is when archaeological collections are the last thing on anyone's mind, and the collections they house may be left vulnerable to theft, vandalism, neglect, or the elements. The New Jersey State Museum was recently faced with a situation whereby a New Jersey–based CRM firm went bankrupt. The employees were vacated and the doors were locked with artifacts left drying on the racks. This firm had carried out a number of projects over the entire state, some of which were data recoveries with many storage boxes of collections and associated paperwork. Both the main building for the firm and three tractor-trailer containers outside the firm building were full of collections, some from National Historic Landmark sites. The boxes, which contained original photographs, negatives, project correspondence, and field notes, were all damaged by water, mold, and rodents. These collections now need many hours of cleaning, rehousing, and retagging. Some of the collections are too far gone or have lost provenance information and thus research potential. This is an extreme case and one that should never have happened. As professional archaeologists and anthropologists we would hope that our first priority is to the collections.

WHAT CAN WE DO?

A challenge (also common to all kinds of museums) is to find more dynamic ways of integrating the public with the potential research use of all collections. Problems with those non-systematic collections need to be examined and re-inventoried. Problems with non-archival materials used to house collections also need to be addressed. The collections also need to be promoted to the outside archaeological community as well as academic archaeologists, as their potential for being utilized for research projects, theses, or dissertations are great. Steve Warfel, retired curator at the Pennsylvania Historical and Museum Commission, stated, "How well are we (museum professionals) preserving the past for the future?" (Warfel 2001:115). We believe that today's museum professionals are doing their best with the resources given to them. With state and federal funding for public museums ever shrinking, curators and registrars are left to spread the word not only about exhibits and programming but also their collections. They are trying to do more with less all the while adhering to museums' best practices.

A tactic of the New Jersey State Museum has been to expand internship and volunteer programs to local and statewide colleges and universities, particularly through the Rutgers University Douglass College Extern program. We receive students for a one- or two-week slot two times a year. Sometimes they may want to continue their internship during the semester. Additionally seniors at Rutgers within the Anthropology Department must produce a senior thesis. Using the collections at the New Jersey State Museum and our local universities with well-established anthropology and archaeology programs, we are helping a number of students to develop topics of interest that will utilize the collections.

We are also in the development stages of initiating distance-learning classes for elementary and high school students in archaeology and museum studies, helping them fulfill core curricular standards in social science. We are also offering an undergraduate class in the archaeology of New Jersey at The College of New Jersey, which will be offered at the NJSM using the collections and providing hands-on opportunities to the students. We are taking advantage of local historical events, festivals, and history fairs, widening the museum and the collections' exposure to the public. The collections are used as teaching tools, all part of an object-based learning initiative at the State Museum. The combined effort of these different approaches renews interest in both old and new collections by highlighting their viability as potential student and professional research projects. While the topic of digitally available collections is fully discussed in chapter 6, it is worth mentioning here. At the New Jersey State Museum, we have started to upload object images to our collections management software program. However, we currently do not have Wi-Fi in our public museum let alone control over our own website to be able to upload collection photos. The bureau does have a blog with entries of specific objects; however, it is not online, as we still need permission from the Department of State to publish it.

We do not believe that museum professionals are prone to the same danger as Warfel (2000) predicted twenty years ago. The problem we see and alluded to by both Griffin (1981) and Warfel (2000) is that CRM firms, while now experiencing a resurgence after the economic recession, need to be honest not only with themselves and their clients, but with the resources they are excavating. Knowing that you have a state and/or national register–eligible site that is going to a data recovery, you must make sure that CRMs hand off the entire collection to an official certified repository, in such a state as to promote its research potential. Standards have to be set and guidelines have to be met; otherwise, these culturally valuable collections are worthless for any future use.

CONCLUSION—WHERE DO WE GO FROM HERE?

Public museums in the Middle Atlantic region, especially those repositories for CRM collections as well as type collections, cannot wait for scholars, researchers, and students to come to us; we have to go to them. Museum professionals must make the resources of these collections available to everyone who wants to learn about the past even if that involves developing creative ways of doing so. While some state museums may be affiliated with the State Historic Preservation Office or a university and thus have additional monetary and academic resources, others are not and as such must obtain funding in new innovative and sometimes unattractive ways—like charging admission or curation fees. Most anthropology departments and their faculty have no idea of the vast resources available to them through the collections housed at museums. We must reach out to those departments, where undergraduate and graduate students can help promote our collections through research projects, theses, and dissertations.

Setting up the equivalent of a research center where professional museum staff can participate in either distance-learning classes or be affiliated with a local university can help promote collections and their research potential. Making collections or even portions of them available to students, both undergraduate and graduate, breathe new life into old and unused artifacts. Student projects using non-systematic collections benefit not only the collection itself but also the museum as a whole, reducing the footprint creating additional collection space. These often-comparable materials become part of education programs, community outreach projects, and research projects by professionals and students. Professionals in turn inform their students in the classroom. Access to artifacts as type collections offers a research library for comparing evidence between fields. They can also inform administrative decisions and provide information for policy statements and management reports. These projects exemplify the effects of using collections, to facilitate the ability of communities to build skills in communication and teamwork, to foster a heritage preservation ethic in students, and to create networks between ethnic groups. The results of research using all types of archaeological collections can also significantly impact the public's conception of the past by challenging traditional assumptions or interpretations. This also goes for exhibits where those artifacts are presented to the public.

Archaeological collections have great potential, but collections managers must first know what they have, curate it appropriately, promote it, and work not to let archaeological processing be the final step in the life of the collections. It is our responsibility, then, "to improve the value, image and perceived importance of archaeological assemblages to many audiences statewide" (White and Breen 2012:2). So too, cultural resource managers must be cognizant of the fact that the resources they excavate need to be given the same amount of attention and detail as the proposal that got them to excavate that significant site in the first place.

REFERENCES CITED

Brown, James A.
  1981   The Potential of Systematic Collections for Archaeological Research in *The Research Potential of Anthropological Museum Collections,* edited by Nan Rothschild and Anne-Marie Cantwell, pp. 65–76. *Annals of the New York Academy of Sciences,* Volume 376. New York Academy of Sciences, New York.

Byrne, Kevin B., and David C. Parris
  1987   Reconstruction of the Diet of the Middle Woodland Amerindian Population at Abbott Farm by Bone Trace-Element Analysis. *American Journal of Physical Anthropology* 74:373–84.

Carpenter, Edmund S.
  1950   Five Sites of the Intermediate Period. *American Antiquity* 15(4):298–314.

Dalyrmple, Edmund
  1893–1894   Catalogue of Indian Relics. Field notes from excavations at Bell-Philhower property. Rutgers University Special Collections and Archives. Box P18, Folder 8.

Griffin, James B.
  1981   The Man Who Comes after; or, Careful How You Curate. In *The Research Potential of Anthropological Museum Collections,* edited by Anne-Marie Cantwell, James B. Griffin, and Nan A. Rothschild, pp. 7–15. *Annals of the New York Academy of Sciences,* Volume 376. New York Academy of Sciences, New York.

Guida, Ann H.
  1989 Seasonality of Occupation of Upper Delaware Valley Sites Based on an Analysis of Dental Cementum Annulations of White-tail Deer. Unpublished Master's Thesis. Department of Anthropology, New York University.

Hart, John P., and William A. Lovis
  2013 Reevaluating What We Know About the Histories of Maize in Northeastern North America: A Review of Current Evidence. *Journal of Archaeological Research* 21:175–216.

Hart, John P., Robert G. Thompson, and Hetty Jo Brumbach
  2003 Phytolith Evidence for Early Maize (Zea mays) in the Northern Finger Lakes Region of New York. *American Antiquity* 68(4):619–40.

Heye, George G., and George H. Pepper
  1916 *Exploration of a Munsee Cemetery Near Montague, New Jersey.* The Museum of the American Indian, Heye Foundation.

Kraft, Herbert C.
  1977 *The Minisink Settlements. An Investigation into a Prehistoric and Early Historic Site in Sussex County, New Jersey.* Archaeological Research Center, Seton Hall University.

Lattanzi, Gregory D.
  2013 *The Value of Reciprocity: Copper, Exchange and Social Interaction in the Middle Atlantic region of the Eastern Woodlands of North America.* Temple University. UMI University microfilms.

Messner, Timothy
  2008 *Woodland Period People and Plant Interactions: New Insights from Starch Grain Analysis.* Temple University. UMI University microfilms.

Moyer, Teresa S.
  2006 *Technical Brief 19: Archaeological Collections and the Public: Using Resources for the Public Benefit.* National Park Service, Washington, DC.

Pevarnik, George L., Matthew T. Boulanger, and Michael D. Glascock
  2008 Instrumental Neutron Activation Analysis of Middle Woodland Pottery from the Delaware Valley. *North American Archaeologist* 29:239–68.

Pevarnik, George L., and R. Michael Stewart
  2007 Typology and Pottery: Problems and Prospects. Paper presented at the *37th Annual Meeting of the Middle Atlantic Archaeological Conference.* Virginia Beach, VA.

Pollak, Janet
  1977 Prehistoric Resources. In *Case Report – Route I-195 Arena Drive to I-295 Interchange, Route I-295 – US 130 to Kuser Road, Route NJ 29 – Ferry Street to I-295 Interchange, Route NJ 129 – US 1 to NJ 29; Cities of Trenton and Bordentown, Townships of Hamilton and Bordentown, Counties of Mercer and*

Burlington, State of New Jersey. Prepared for the Federal Highway Administration and the New Jersey Department of Transportation, Trenton.

Ritchie, William
 1949 *The Bell-Philhower Site: Sussex County, New Jersey. Indiana Historical Society, Prehistoric Research Series* vol. 2 no. 2. Indianapolis.

Rothschild, Nan A., and Anne-Marie Cantwell
 1981 The Research Potential of Anthropological Museum Collections. In *The Research Potential of Anthropological Museum Collections,* edited by Anne-Marie Cantwell, James B. Griffin, and Nan A. Rothschild, pp. 1–6. *Annals of the New York Academy of Sciences,* Volume 376. New York Academy of Sciences, New York.

Smithsonian Institution
 2013 http://anthropology.si.edu/outreach/depthist.html. Accessed 12/6/2013.

Sullivan, Lynn P., and S. Terry Childs
 2003 *Curating Archaeological Collections, From the Field to the Repository.* Archaeologist's Toolkit Volume 6. Alta Mira Press, Walnut Creek, CA.

Thomas, Ronald, and Andrew Stanzeski
 2001 Archaeology Investigations at a Portion of the Pennella S Site – 28-Oc-60, Willis Creek, Ocean County, New Jersey. Submitted to Mr. Eugene Lasuen, Kennelworth, NJ.

Wall, Robert D. R., Michael Stewart, John Cavallo, Douglas McLearen, Robert Foss, Philip Perazio, and John Dumont
 1996 *Prehistoric Archaeological Synthesis.* Trenton Complex Archaeology: Report 15. The Cultural Resource Group, Louis Berger & Associates, Inc., East Orange, New Jersey. Prepared for the Federal Highway Administration and the New Jersey Department of Transportation, Bureau of Environmental Analysis, Trenton.

Warfel, Steve
 2000 Comments on "Making a Future for the Past." *North American Archaeologist* 21:115–18.

White, Ester, and Eleanor Breen
 2012 *A Survey of Archaeological Repositories in Virginia.* Council of Virginia Archaeologist's Committee.

6

✝

Not Just Bells and Whistles

Changes in Technological Applications to Middle Atlantic Archaeology

Bernard K. Means

Today, most archaeologists are no strangers to applying technology to solve their work's basic challenges. We routinely use smartphones on a daily basis: checking on the weather; taking pictures; finding our way around with our GPS apps; and accessing research that is becoming increasingly and readily available across the Internet. Some archaeologists even use these small digital devices to locate and document sites. Smartphones can be readily integrated into public archaeology efforts via the immediacy of social media. The potential these everyday devices hold to aid our investigations of the past is likely to grow immensely over time. This acceptance of readily available technology should not be too surprising. Over the last half century, archaeologists in the Middle Atlantic region have increasingly turned to technological applications for the discovery, recovery, and analysis of the archaeological record. We have moved beyond punch cards and computers the size of buildings to more powerful digital devices that fit snugly in the palms of our hands. Middle Atlantic archaeologists are increasingly turning to sophisticated technological applications that are transforming the very questions we ask about the past—and how we answer them.

This reliance on technological tools to approach our studies of the prehistoric people that inhabited the Middle Atlantic region is not something new. As I started my review of how Middle Atlantic archaeologists employ technology in their studies, I had to decide how narrowly—or how broadly—I was going to define technology as it is applied to Middle Atlantic prehistory. After all, the trowel, the shovel, and even the lowly ¼-inch mesh screen are forms of technology. These manifestations of technology are ever present on most excavations—so much so that we take them for granted. But, these tools all need training and special skills to use or interpret. A poorly wielded shovel or trowel can damage the irreplaceable fabric of the past. Training and practice are needed to ensure that the physical landscape is deftly removed—layer by careful layer—and the knowledge contained in the ground is not lost, destroyed, or altered into an unrecognizable form. Users of the ¼-inch mesh screen need to understand that they are sampling the past, and take this into consideration in their statistical analyses of artifact frequencies and their maps of artifact distributions.

To keep this overview manageable, I focus on technological applications—many developed originally outside the field of archaeology—that traditionally require specialized and often expensive equipment or computer software and that may require extensive training and expertise. Some of this specialized equipment can be obtained and used by archaeologists who train themselves to master it with varying levels of competence and success. Other specialized equipment—and the expertise needed to coax appropriate results from it—is tucked away in sometimes distant laboratories managed by faceless individuals whose utterances may prove challenging to interpret. Without the necessary training or even basic understanding of this specialized equipment, the archaeologist is reduced to a mere supplicant who sacrifices his or her fragments of the past on an altar that blinds them with a cascade of fluctuating, multicolored, and bright lights occasionally and jarringly punctuated by odd whirring, grinding, and beeping sounds.

This overview concentrates on four broad topics: chronology; discovery and documentation; origins and identification; and analysis and data presentation. I do not look at the full suite of technologies currently available for use by archaeologists, or that archaeologists have drawn upon in the past, but more specifically on those technologies employed in the Middle Atlantic region. My review emphasizes published and accessible research, and I have combed through the pages of regional archaeology journals, including the *Journal of Middle Atlantic Archaeology* and *Archeology of Eastern North America*, as well as select journals from state archaeological societies that fall into the Middle Atlantic region, especially *Maryland Archeology, Pennsylvania Archaeologist, Quarterly Bulletin of the Archeological Society of Virginia*, and the *West Virginia Archaeologist*. The cultural resource management (CRM) world relies increasingly on advanced technology for discovery, analysis, and interpretation—but, too often, their approaches and findings at best make it out of the gray literature into conference presentations but not into more accessible published venues.

CHRONOLOGY

One of the earliest—and still prevalent—technologies embraced by archaeologists in the Middle Atlantic region is radiocarbon dating. Inashima (2008, 2011) has compiled lists of many of the published and unpublished radiocarbon assays from sites in Virginia, Herbstritt (1988) has done the same for Pennsylvania, and Boyce and Frye (1986) assembled Maryland's radiocarbon assays. These lists tend to become outdated quickly in print form and are somewhat onerous to update. Placing radiocarbon assays on the Internet is an obvious solution, but even these lists have to be maintained and updated regularly.

Shortly after the radiocarbon dating technique was introduced, archaeologists enthusiastically began to submit single samples from their sites to the various radiocarbon laboratories that sprung up—and which were later determined to not all have been created equal. In some cases, exuberant archaeologists overstepped their careful attention to context and submitted burned organic matter to laboratories simply because they had sufficient material for a dateable sample. Keeping track of provenience and associations for radiocarbon samples was often a secondary consideration, if considered at all—size and not context was often the most important criterion for sample selection. The potential of—and concerns over—the application of radiocarbon dating were explicitly articulated by archaeologists practicing in the Middle Atlantic region almost forty years ago (Brennan 1974; Dragoo 1974; Ralph et al. 1974). More recently, Levine (1990) examined dates ascribed to fluted points in the Middle Atlantic region and throughout eastern North America and noted uncritical use of radiocarbon dates and often poor associations between samples selected for dating and the "cultural target events" (e.g., the period of manufacture, use, and deposition of the fluted points).

The inattention to critical details bedeviled my recent assessments of all radiocarbon assays in Virginia and all radiocarbon assays associated with the Late Prehistoric Monongahela tradition in Pennsylvania (Means 2005a, 2005b, 2014; Means and McKnight 2010). Even if careful attention was paid to provenience and associations, my reviews showed that researchers were often content to obtain a single date from a single context within a site—and then would extend that date to the entire site, ignoring the complex formation processes that create the archaeological record. The resulting date would also often be misinterpreted—assumed to represent a single point in time and not a segment of a probability curve. Radiocarbon dating is a critical tool but must be applied cautiously—and we must not forget that we are still dependent on outside experts and laboratories to produce dates from our samples. Radiocarbon dating laboratories will date what is submitted to them; this does not mean what is submitted to them is always worthy of dating. Archaeologists must practice due diligence when selecting samples for radiocarbon dating, pay attention of course to provenience and context, and also carefully assess exactly what event they are hoping to date.

The misuse of radiocarbon dating, unfortunately, is a problem that is still with us today. A recent article reported on radiocarbon assay from a raccoon bone recovered from the Totuskey Creek (44RD0206) site in Richmond County, Virginia (Key et al. 2009). The exact provenience for this raccoon bone is unclear—we only know that it was found roughly 35 centimeters below the ground's surface. A Late Woodland age determination was made for this raccoon jawbone, and this date was extended to all other diagnostic ceramics and chipped stone tools found anywhere on the site within a layer 30–45 centimeters below the surface (Key et al. 2009:164–65). This connection between the date and the temporally diagnostic artifacts is tenuous at best—the so-called associations seem site-wide and not from a discrete context, such as a single layer or single feature. The radiocarbon assay seemingly only shows that raccoons were around during the Late Woodland period—something we knew already. Authors of an earlier study (McCracken and Lucy 1989) developed an entire new chronological period that overlaps the proto-Susquehannock and early Schultz Phases of the Susquehannock tradition from a single radiocarbon assay—this is quite an impressive feat. In either case, we should be long past the time where we consider a single radiocarbon assay suitable for dating an entire site and all its associated artifacts, or for generating new temporal phases in an outmoded culture-historical temporal framework.

This is not to say that archaeologists have not made good use of radiocarbon dating in the Middle Atlantic region, especially following the advent of accelerator mass spectrometry (AMS) dating (Haynes 1984). Numerous researchers have used radiocarbon dating to date sites and to build regional chronologies. In Pennsylvania, Beverly Chiarulli, Richard George, John Hart, William C. Johnson, Sarah Neusius, Robert Oshnock, and myself—among many others—have used AMS dating on sites—drawing on old collections and newly excavated materials—to ascertain the age of individual components, or to build regional chronologies (Auffart and Oshnock 2011; Hart and Scarry 1999; Johnson and Means 2016; Johnson et al. 2010; Means 2005a, 2005b; Means and Tippins 2010; Neusius and Chiarulli 2012; Oshnock 2009; Tippins and George 2010).

I employed AMS dating on old collections from Work Projects Administration (WPA)-excavated sites to build a chronology for Monongahela tradition villages in Somerset County, Pennsylvania. These WPA-excavated sites were assigned dates based on the prevailing culture-historical temporal framework, which proved grossly inaccurate (Means 2005a). Overall, AMS dating of sites demonstrates that families regularly joining together and congregating in discrete village communities did not become common until after A.D. 1100 amongst the peoples associated with the Monongahela tradition, and not as early as A.D. 900 as had been thought.

Similar conclusions have been reached about culture-historical constructs, chronology, and the occupational histories of villages in New York State, notably related to the Owasco (Hart and Brumbach 2003) and the earliest construction dates for Iroquoian longhouses (Hart 2000a). This has been primarily through the efforts of John P. Hart of the New York State Museum and his colleagues. Their research has emphasized how curated collections are integral to reexamining and challenging past preconceptions of Middle Atlantic culture-historical taxa and temporal frameworks, especially through AMS dating of residue found on cooking vessels (Hart and Brumbach 2003; Hart and Lovis 2007). The important work by Hart and his colleagues related to the histories of maize, beans, and squash will be considered below.

In Virginia, Klein (1994) used radiocarbon dating to examine the relationship between ceramic types and temper, and emphasized in particular the need to make sure that a radiocarbon assay links to a targeted event. Dennis Blanton and his colleagues drew on radiocarbon dates to explore the occupational history of the Potomac Creek site located in Stafford County, Virginia (Blanton et al. 1999). Radiocarbon assays were employed in part to argue that the people of the Potomac Creek complex who occupied the eponymous Potomac Creek site represented an intrusive group that relocated to the lower Potomac River basin (Blanton et al. 1999:92–104). Across the Potomac River in Maryland, Richard J. Dent submitted residue on a curated ceramic vessel fragment to obtain the sole absolute date that exists for the Accokeek Creek site, and used this date to also consider the origins of the Potomac Creek complex (Dent and Jirikowic 2001). His dating result is definitely intriguing, but single dates from archaeological sites are not ideal. Robert Wall has drawn on radiocarbon assays to explore the myriad overlapping occupations at the Barton site complex located in the floodplain of the Potomac River in western Maryland (Wall 2008).

We also should not forget the important role that radiocarbon dating— particularly AMS dating of archaeobotanical remains—has played in understanding the history of plant domestication in the Middle Atlantic region, especially the timing of the introduction and widespread adoption of maize and beans. This is particularly evident from research by Hart and his colleagues throughout the Northeast, and McKnight and her colleagues in Virginia (Hart 1999, 2000; Hart and Scarry 1999; Hart and Sidell 1997: McKnight and Gallivan 2007; Means and McKnight 2010). We now know that maize (*Zea mays*) has much greater antiquity in the Middle Atlantic region than had been previously thought, having been identified in ceramic residue dating to over two thousand years ago in central New York—with a similar age for squash (*Cucurbita pepo*) use (Hart et al. 2007). The common bean (*Phaseolus vulgaris*) is not archaeologically visible in the Middle Atlantic region and elsewhere in northeastern North America until after A.D. 1300 (Hart and Scarry 1999; Means 2005 and b; Means and McKnight 2010). What this essentially means is that we have to discard our simplistic associations between maize-beans-squash agriculture and the appearance of settled village life in the Middle Atlantic region during the Late Woodland period. Village life was once thought to have occurred as a response to the domestication of maize at the onset of the Late Woodland period, ca. A.D. 900, and that maize agriculture was a necessary precondition for village life and could not be maintained without the existence of village communities. Thanks to new excavations throughout the Middle Atlantic region and beyond, as well as AMS dating of cultigens in museum collections, we know that the association between maize-beans-squash agriculture and American Indian populations is much more complex than we thought a few decades ago (Hart and Lovis 2013; Hart and Means 2002).

Less common forms of dating applied in the Middle Atlantic region include oxidizable carbon ratio (OCR) carbon dating, obsidian hydration, and optically stimulated luminescence dating. OCR carbon dating was introduced to archaeology by Douglas Frink in the early 1990s as an experimental procedure and applied to sites throughout the world, including a few in the Middle Atlantic region (Frink 1992, 1994, 1995, 1999). According to Frink (1999), OCR carbon dating "has the potential to provide reasonably accurate and precise age estimates from organic carbon within an aerobic soil context at an affordable cost." The technique has not been without its critics (Killick et al. 1999), and it would appear that archaeologists in the Middle Atlantic region prefer the more established and less controversial radiocarbon dating technique. Radiocarbon dating is applicable to all carbonized material—including that curated in museum collections—while OCR carbon dating is limited to carbonized organic matter found in soils.

The obsidian hydration dating technique has had very limited application in the Middle Atlantic region, given the small amount of obsidian artifacts found here. The technique can be employed to test the authenticity of obsidian artifacts found in museum collections or recovered from questionable or poorly documented contexts (Boulanger et al. 2007). Boulanger et al. (2007) actually discuss an example from Vermont—outside our study region—but their use of obsidian hydration did show that an obsidian point supposedly recovered from the Connecticut River Valley was prehistoric in age. However, the obsidian hydration technique is destructive and collections repositories may prove reluctant to approve this type of analysis for rare objects, as Dillian et al. (2006:44) found with an obsidian projectile point curated by the University of Pennsylvania Museum (discussed further below).

One of the more controversial questions in Middle Atlantic archaeology today relates to the timing of when American Indians first occupied this region—notably whether there were people present that pre-dated the widespread and well-known Paleoindian Clovis culture. One of the most studied possible pre-Clovis sites in the Middle Atlantic region is the Cactus Hill site (44SX202), which is located in Sussex County, Virginia, in a sand deposit above an alluvial terrace of the Nottoway River. The site has two layers dating to the late Pleistocene: one with Clovis artifacts and another below it that contained quartzite blades. Using radiocarbon dating, the Clovis layer was dated to around 11,000 B.P., while the lower layer was dated to around 15,000 B.P. (Feathers et al. 2006:167). Because only 7–15 centimeters of sand separates the artifacts in these two layers, some have questioned the radiocarbon assays and the site's overall stratigraphic integrity. Feathers et al. (2006:167) "selected luminescence dating of sediments because, unlike radiocarbon, it directly addresses depositional events and has the potential to identify mixing of sand grains of different depositional ages." Optically stimulated luminescence (OSL) dating determines the last time that sediment was exposed to sunlight (Feathers et al. 2006:171). While OSL dating did support the radiocarbon assays, the authors did not assess a more important question: Are the artifacts associated with the layers within which they were found? (Feathers et al. 2006:167).

DISCOVERY AND DOCUMENTATION

Not all important technological tools used by the archaeologist depend on high-tech computerized machinery located in distant and inaccessible laboratories. Flotation of feature fill and other archaeological contexts has been practiced more or less continuously throughout the United States since at least the late 1960s (Bryant 2000), but the extent to which flotation has been used in the Middle Atlantic region during this time is not clear. Moeller (1986) discusses flotation from a theoretical and practical standpoint, based largely on his lengthy experience in the Middle Atlantic region. Barber and Madden (2004) recently stressed that archaeologists in Virginia need to incorporate more flotation of feature deposits into their research designs, especially for the recovery of archaeobotanical remains. They enacted a program of flotation of all feature contexts at their excavations of the Sawyer site (44RN39) in Roanoke County, Virginia, and the Keyser Farm site (44PG1), a multicomponent village occupation located in Page County, Virginia (Barber and Madden 2004). They argue that not only does flotation lead to enhanced recovery of archaeobotanical and micro-remains but that the procedure should also be viewed as comparatively cost effective. While the equipment costs associated with wet screening are more expensive than those associated with dry screening, the savings in time help counter these costs (Barber and Madden 2004:230). Flotation of feature contents at the Sawyer site produced very small flakes, revealing the full lithic reduction phases that took place there (Barber and Madden 2004:231). Archaeobotanical remains recovered from pit features at the Keyser Farm site enabled the history of occupation of this Late Woodland village to be explored, showing that there were likely two occupations at the site and that, contrary to an earlier interpretation, both occupations pre-dated European contact (Means and McKnight 2010).

The mapping of site locations and the locations of features within sites certainly has been eased by readily accessible and moderately priced technological developments. Aerial photography and satellite mapping have made considerable inroads into the discovery and documentation of archaeological sites. Google Earth has brought satellite mapping quite inexpensively to our desktops (Ur 2006). GPS was once a specialized and expensive tool, but now many of us regularly hold decent GPS devices in our hands via our smartphones. Anecdotal evidence and my personal experience suggest that GPS on smartphones may not always be suitable for remote—or not so remote—regions where archaeologists often work. The integration of Google Earth and GPS into our daily lives has happened so fast that it seems few in Middle Atlantic archaeology have written explicitly about this phenomenon. Unmanned aerial vehicles, usually referred to as drones, are becoming commonly available for everyone ranging from hobby enthusiasts to medical professionals. It is not surprising that some archaeologists have eagerly integrated drones into their own work (Gutiérrez et al. 2016; Gutiérrez and Searcy 2016; Smith et al. 2014; Wechsler et al. 2016), although they need to be aware of legal concerns (Searcy 2016).

Having the ability to view what lies hidden below the ground's surface before or even instead of excavating is a welcomed technological development. Archaeological prospection, or geophysical survey, allows us to explore the nature of subsurface deposits without extensive—and expensive—excavation. We are still at a stage, however, where results need to be verified through ground "truthing" (e.g., excavation) (Hargrave 2006; Johnson 2006). A whole host of techniques are used in the Middle Atlantic region, including ground penetrating radar, magnetometry, and electrical resistivity (Chadwick 2014). These techniques hold tremendous potential for allowing us to examine sites on scales rarely possible in this region since the days of large crews associated with New Deal work relief programs. We do not have the cheap labor today needed to expose entire village sites and reveal community patterning—but we can determine basic site layouts using a combination of archaeological prospection and targeted excavation. Indiana University of Pennsylvania's Beverly Chiarulli, Sarah Neusius, and their students have taken the lead on this with respect to Late Prehistoric village sites in central and western Pennsylvania, and have produced some very intriguing results (Chiarulli 2012; Espino et al. 2012; Dehaven 2011; Rubino 2010; Smith 2009).

Espino et al. (2012) used magnetometry and ground penetrating radar to search for subsurface anomalies at the Hatfield Site (36WH678), a Monongahela tradition village site. These techniques helped reveal aspects of the site's ring-shaped community pattern that would not have been possible given the limited funds available for excavation—most of which was undertaken by avocational and professional members of the Society for Pennsylvania Archaeology Allegheny Chapter. Another major study has been work on the Barton site complex by Horsley and Wall (2010), who used magnetometry to map a known Late Woodland village site and identify previously unknown palisaded components. Archaeological prospection techniques are increasing in accuracy and decreasing in cost and complexity, and so should become a more common tool employed in the archaeologist's arsenal.

ORIGINS AND IDENTIFICATION

A number of technologies rooted in the "hard sciences" of chemistry and physics have relevance to archaeology and allow us to examine microscopic or even atomic-level data that is not only invisible but also often not preserved at a macroscopic scale. In addition to radiocarbon dating the residues found burned on the interior of ceramic vessel fragments, Hart and others have also worked to identify the types of food remains represented in burned residue, using gas chromatography/mass spectrometry to look for traces of lipids (fats, oils, etc.) and extracting phytoliths to identify maize, squash, and other foods rarely preserved at macroscopic scales in the archaeological record (Hart et al. 2003, 2005). One stunning result is the identification of maize in dated cooking residue from over 2,500 years ago in New York assemblages, as noted above, well before the widespread adoption of maize as a staple crop in northeastern North America (Hart et al. 2007). Discoveries such as these highlight how something as humble as burned food on a fragment of a pottery can nonetheless radically rewrite our sometimes tenuous understanding of the past.

Another way to examine the complex history of introduced tropical cultigens and locally domesticated plants is to examine skeletal material using a variety of techniques, such as stable isotope analysis. Almost two decades ago, Sciulli (1995) used stable carbon isotope analysis to make inferences about the paleodiet of human skeletal remains associated with the Monongahela tradition. He concluded that Monongahela maize consumption levels did not differ between upland and lowland populations, and were similar to those seen among other horticultural groups in eastern North America (Sciulli 1995). Today, for the most part, cultural sensitivity and concerns over issues related to the Native Americans Grave Protection and Repatriation Act (NAGPRA) have generally discouraged this type of research on human skeletal remains, so some archaeologists have turned to proxy animals. Explicitly citing concerns over NAGPRA and destructive analyses of human remains, Allitt et al. (2008) examined stable isotope ratios from dog bone as a surrogate to human bone to look for traces of maize. They found maize traces in dog bone recovered from the outer coastal plain of New Jersey, an area where maize consumption (and production) was previously not well known.

Messner and his colleagues (Messner et al. 2008) have also conducted important research with starch grain analysis in the Middle Atlantic region. Starch grain analysis looks for plant microfossils adhering to plant processing tools, ceramics, and sediments and can be used to identify the presence of various foods and artifact function and even help with reconstructing paleoenvironments (Messner et al. 2008:111). They have used starch grain analysis to examine Late Woodland plant use in the Upper Delaware Valley and have increased the archaeological visibility of maize in this region to around A.D. 1000 (Messner et al. 2008:123). Clearly a multitude of technological tools exist that enable us to explore the complex histories embodied in plant domestication and adoption as it varied among social groups and over time throughout the Middle Atlantic region.

The concerns embodied within NAGPRA have discouraged but not halted molecular studies of human bone. DNA analysis shows great potential for examining past American Indian populations in terms of movement and geographic extent, while also linking these populations to historically known or contemporary groups. DNA analysis of human remains from the Fort Ancient tradition Man site in Logan County, West Virginia, for example, has tentatively linked the site's occupants to Siouan groups (Maslowski 2011).

Analysis of raw materials used to create archaeological objects in the past was once limited to differences in color, texture, and composition ascertained largely through visual inspection. Visual inspection is not without its utility but can be affected by observer bias, and there are issues with different researchers communicating their observations. Didier (1975:90) decades ago encapsulated this by noting:

> It is standard archeological procedure to pick up an artifact, "eye-ball" it to get an idea of texture, density, and other attributes, and then to make an "identification" of the material. This method of lithic "identification" is often all the archeologist has to rely on, for she or he cannot usually remove the artifacts from the museum or collection for further testing and comparison and, certainly cannot even take a hammer, as a geologist quickly would, and break the specimen to get a fresh surface to examine.

One solution to examining raw materials is to view them on an elemental level. Trace element studies of various metals, stones, and clays provide clues to trade and exchange networks, social interaction at varying scales, and, possibly, geographically circumscribed cultural entities akin to historically known tribes. Sourcing studies seek to identify the locations from which various materials were obtained, with a special emphasis in the Middle Atlantic region on chert, jasper or rhyolite chipped stone tools, steatite carved stone containers, clay sources for ceramics, or copper ornaments and other artifacts. Techniques used include instrumental neutron activation analysis, laser ablation-inductively coupled plasma-mass spectrometry, X-ray diffraction, and X-ray fluorescence, the latter of which is becoming more widespread thanks to portable devices (Chiarulli et al. 2000; Dillian et al. 2006; Key and Gaskin 2000; Klein 1990; Lattanzi 2007, 2008a, 2008b; Pevarnik 2007; Pevarnik et al. 2008; Rafferty et al. 2007; Rieth 2007; Steadman 2008; Stevenson et al. 1990, 2004, 2008).

Sourcing studies often seek to find the elemental signature of quarry locations and link them to artifacts recovered from various archaeological sites, with the goal of determining the distances from source to site (e.g., from the immediate vicinity of the site or from a non-local source). For example, Chiarulli et al. (2000) used instrumental neutron activation analysis as part of their effort to determine the locations of raw material sources for prehistoric artifacts recovered from archaeological sites in western Pennsylvania. They focused their initial efforts on chert artifacts and worked to link them to distinct quarry sources. The researchers noted that their use of trace element analysis was actually new to Pennsylvania, even though examination of trace element concentrations to determine raw material sources had long been common in the western United States (Chiarulli et al. 2000).

Lattanzi (2007, 2008a, 2008b) used trace element analysis to examine the origins of pre-contact copper in the Middle Atlantic region, challenging the notion that all copper artifacts in this area necessarily were traded from distant sources in the Great Lakes region. His analyses do not simply seek to determine whether copper artifacts are local or non-local in origin, but to examine social factors as well. Lattanzi (2008a:2) asked a series of interesting questions regarding the source(s) of pre-Contact copper artifacts from the Delaware Valley that have regional implications:

> If copper artifacts from the Middle Atlantic region are not from the Great Lakes, but actually from local sources, what does this say about previous explanations for their presence in this region? If there is a shift in copper procurement over time, what does this imply about the social contexts supporting procurement and use? Is this shift an adaptive response by local groups to the conditions of regional information and exchange networks? Do these patterns imply some type of social inequality among Delaware Valley peoples?

Laser ablation-inductively coupled plasma-mass spectrometry of four copper artifacts from Pennsylvania showed that they were not similar on an elemental level to samples from the Great Lakes area (Lattanzi 2008a:8). However, their specific location of origin could not be definitively tied to a known source in the Middle Atlantic region. Source locations mapped by geologists today may not have been used prehistorically, or past peoples may have used drift (surface) copper moved by glacial action some distance from their actual source. An expanded sample of pre-Contact copper artifacts and geologic specimens are necessary before the sources of these objects can be determined (Lattanzi 2008a:10) and before the questions Lattanzi raised above can be answered.

Application of trace element analysis in an unusual case includes Dillian et al.'s (2006:41) examination of an obsidian projectile point curated by the University of Pennsylvania Museum, from a larger collection of chipped stone bifaces from eastern Pennsylvania. As the closest known source of obsidian to eastern Pennsylvania is located in South Dakota, the obsidian point—or at least the material from which it was made—traveled some distance. The obsidian artifact could not be dated through obsidian hydration, as mentioned earlier, and Dillian et al. (2006:44) could not determine whether it was manufactured prehistorically or during the historic period. Through X-ray fluorescence, they were able to source the obsidian biface to a source in Oregon. Because the biface was recovered in the late 1800s, when travel was relatively rare between eastern Pennsylvania and Oregon, Dillian et al. (2006:44) suggest that the object was obtained in antiquity. They noted that a handful of obsidian artifacts were known from other sites in the eastern United States, further suggesting long-distance trade of at least unique items prior to European contact.

What can sometimes be lost in these trace element studies is the human dimension. It is not sufficient to document the origins of stone or copper artifacts—one must link them to the people that made them, used them, and then discarded them (Adovasio 1997:7). I certainly echo Adovasio's (1997:6) concern with "the disparity between the empirical results of instrumentally based research and its interdigitation with contemporary theory" and efforts to reconstruct complex human behaviors from the archaeological record (Adovasio 1997:6–7).

ANALYSIS AND PRESENTATION

There are a number of enhanced visualization techniques that produce aesthetically pleasing representations of archaeological data, but that also hold tremendous analytical potential. Two techniques, one now getting a bit hoary in age and the other still very much cutting edge, are considered here: geographic information systems (GIS) and three-dimensional (3D) artifact documentation. GIS is not a new technology, but it has become increasingly more popular and easier to use as computer interfaces have become streamlined and more user-friendly. GIS software has also become more affordable as well. And, fortunately, GIS is now familiar enough to new and old archaeologists alike that presenters do not need to spend 80 percent of their presentation time describing what a GIS is, but rather can present their findings.

At a recent formal gathering of Middle Atlantic archaeologists featured two presentations that highlight the way GIS has been integrated into research and preservation planning efforts. Strickland (2013) developed a GIS of Late Woodland settlements in the Potomac Valley based on previously identified sites, particularly in relationship to environmental characteristics. He plans to incorporate the limited ethnohistorical record into his GIS model and make comparisons to existing theoretical models for the distribution of Late Woodland groups throughout the Chesapeake region. For the Lost Towns Project, Poulos and Sperling (2013) built a GIS model using recorded site data along the Patuxent River in Anne Arundel County, Maryland. Their basic goals were to predict the locations of new sites and examine shifting settlement patterns throughout prehistory. The latter goal was intended to understand how highly significant sites fit into broader regional patterns, such as the "Delmarva Adena" ritual and mortuary complex at the Pig Point (18AN50) site (Luckenbach 2013).

Lowery (2002:34) is skeptical of overreliance on GIS and outlines his two major concerns: a GIS can only be as good as the data entered into it; and the modern landscape variables that some rely on in a GIS may not have existed the same way in the past. He concludes his discussion by noting that "GIS seems to be an excellent database management tool. But, researchers and observers should never forget to question the quality of the data in the database before they attempt to access aspects of the past" (Lowery 2002:34). Landscape reconstructions based on sound geomorphological studies (such as Cremeens and Hart 2009) can provide us with the accurate variables we need for a dynamic GIS that extends to the beginnings of human occupation of the Middle Atlantic region.

We should also not be too quick to dismiss the importance GIS as a database management tool, even if our site locational variables rely on modern landscape data. The sites that we study exist in the contemporary landscape, and many are in danger of partial or complete destruction at an accelerated rate due to a wide variety of forces—most with a proximate human cause, such as construction or climate change (Means 2011a). Knowing what sites are most in danger from these destructive forces will allow us to target our research efforts to those that are most vulnerable. The Delaware Department of Transportation has been very proactive in examining the impact that climate change will have on heritage resources in their state—not surprising given the low-lying nature of the state and its long coastline. Clarke (2011) stressed that it is not just current sites in direct coastal impact areas that are in danger, but also that sites outside the direct impact zones will be affected by major construction of new infrastructure, including the rerouting of coastal highways. Chadwick-Moore (2011) noted that 20 percent of all known sites in Maryland might potentially be impacted by sea level rise, including mapped Paleoindian sites, and that steps need to be taken to protect or document these sites before they vanish under the waves or as a result of coastal erosion. Schiszik et al. (2011) detailed efforts by the Cultural Resources Division of Anne Arundel County's Department of Planning and Zoning to try to "develop solutions, actions, and policy responses that will best protect or mitigate threatened resources." Funding through Virginia's Threatened Sites program is currently being directed toward those sites most affected by coastal erosion and rising sea levels related to climate change (Barber 2013). GIS is ideally suited to tracking the multitude of forces that actively are threatening sites, or have the potential to do so at some point in the near future.

We can also use GIS to examine the historical development of prehistoric archaeology in the Middle Atlantic region and beyond. I recently developed a GIS of archaeological projects conducted as work relief projects during the Great Depression (Means 2011b, 2013a). One might think that a geographic approach to the history of archaeology has limited utility for the contemporary researcher. However, significant archaeological investigations took place as a result of New Deal–funded projects that continue to drive archaeological research today and influence how we still view the past. Most of New Jersey and much of Pennsylvania were subject to major work relief excavations, particularly through the WPA (Lattanzi

2013; Means 2013b). Who knows what a geographic approach to the entire history of archaeology in the Middle Atlantic region would reveal about our current approaches to questions that bedevil and intrigue us?

Some GIS geographic-based analyses do not use the full potential inherent within GIS—digital maps are produced that are not much better than the pen and ink maps they replace and, with microscopically thin lines on a bright white background, may be worse! But other studies use GIS not only as a way to create colorful and aesthetically pleasing maps but also as a technique for modeling the way past peoples moved across and through landscapes—both real and metaphorical. A recent and interesting application of GIS that moves beyond approaches that could be just as easily done with paper maps is Mike Klein's and Marco Gonzalez's (2012) study of John Smith's well-known map of 1612. They combined this map with a view shed analysis that examines the movement of Contact-era populations through the York River Valley in Virginia. They showed how movement through the physical landscape was structured in such a way as to help create and maintain a hierarchically organized social order. And that "movement appears to [have] become increasingly ritualized as the setting shifted from mundane to sacred landscapes." Thus, the intangible landscapes manipulated to produce "new forms of political status and social personhood" were as real as the tangible landscapes that we can see today as archaeologists. Some GIS analyses integrate light detection and ranging (LIDAR) data, such as Martin's (2015) reexamination of nineteenth-century excavations at the Abbot Farm National Historic Landmark in New Jersey.

Another development in archaeological visualization is three-dimensional (3D) artifact documentation technology. 3D documentation technology allows unprecedented sharing of digital models created from artifacts readily and easily across cyberspace. Digital artifact models generated through 3D documentation technology can be shared, manipulated, and measured from the comfort of one's laboratory, home, or even field site. 3D digital models increase our ability to generate new interpretations and new insights into archaeological remains—and open interpretation not only to the professional archaeologist but also interested individuals located anywhere in the world. Archaeologists and non-archaeologists can display many details of an object from multiple viewpoints—without directly interacting with or even ever seeing the actual object itself. With 3D artifact models, we are no longer limited to static representations of artifacts presented in two dimensions from a limited number of vantage points. 3D artifact documentation allows us to virtually curate artifacts, generating intangible digital models from tangible objects. This technology is becoming increasingly more common as prices drop (Means et al. 2013a, 2013b).

My current research, and that of my students, in the Virtual Curation Laboratory at Virginia Commonwealth University utilizes a NextEngine Desktop 3D scanner to create digital topological models of archaeological objects (McCuistion 2013; McCuistion et al. 2013; Means 2015; Means et al. 2013a, 2013b). Another increasingly popular method of generating 3D digital models of archaeological discoveries, including artifacts, ecofacts, and features, is Structure from Motion (SfM) photogrammetry. Photogrammetry uses dozens or even thousands of photographs of the subject being recorded and combines them using specialized software to generate a 3D model (Selden et al. 2014:22). Virtual curation can be combined with social media as part of a dedicated strategy to promote and build a truly participatory culture that changes how we experience and think about heritage. 3D digital archaeological models offer tremendous potential for expanding our understanding of the past. Our engagement as archaeologists with material culture can cease to be unidirectional and become a two-way conversation—a true dialogue—with a broader and more inclusive community drawn to places of heritage. 3D documentation and virtual curation further integrate the tangible and intangible remains of the past. This integration might also benefit from efforts to create virtual worlds that people can "visit," such as the digital Monongahela village created by archaeologists at Indiana University of Pennsylvania (Chiarulli et al. 2010).

Some archaeologists are also calling for a revolution in how we document archaeological sites, arguing that we should use technological devices to go completely paperless (Walldrodt 2015). To what extent this might be happening in the Middle Atlantic region has not yet been discussed in print. A search of the Internet finds most applications of paperless archaeology being implemented primarily in Old World contexts (Paperless Archaeology 2016). Certainly, Middle Atlantic archaeologists are no strangers to some aspects of digital documentation, with digital cameras and tablets so seamlessly integrated into site documentation that most people do not feel the need to mention their use as standard archaeological equipment.

DISCUSSION

Both cost and unfamiliarity act as barriers to the integration of existing and developing technologies into archaeological practice. We should be careful to not let technological illiteracy prevent us from learning about the latest devices that will allow us to pierce through the veils that shroud the past from our gaze. However, employing sophisticated technology is no substitute for analytical rigor. A piece of technical equipment is not a magic black box that produces findings ready to be seamlessly inserted into one's interpretive frameworks. Whatever is being scrutinized or probed by our shiny machines must be carefully linked to the targeted events that hold our interest. Our technologies are designed to give us results, regardless of whether we present our devices with good or bad data. The misapplication of technology will generate bad results from bad data—or even bad results from good data. Assuming that one's data are good, and that due diligence has been paid to ensure they are linked to the targeted events of interest, uncritical acceptance of the results generated by our technologies still remains an issue. In my review of the literature, I came across a few archaeologists who lacked the expertise to properly interpret results presented to them and ceded the interpretation of the data they had paid for to non-archaeological technicians. Why? We would not let an outsider tell us how to categorize and analyze our bits of stones, bones, and clay. If we are using a particular type of technology to view the past, we must at least understand the basics of what that technology is doing to our data. We also must not let the colored lights of technology hypnotize us and forget that our questions and interpretations need to be solidly grounded in archaeological theory. Otherwise, we are simply applying technology in search of an idea.

CONCLUSIONS

A not uncommon theme in a number of the articles I reviewed for this chapter is how archaeologists in the Middle Atlantic region lag behind their colleagues elsewhere in the United States—or the rest of the world—when it comes to embracing and incorporating new technologies into archaeological practice. Most of these technologies have been almost universally developed by people working outside our field—sometimes far outside our field—and have to be modified, massaged, tweaked, or radically redesigned to facilitate our exploration of the past. We may need special training or have to rely on outside experts to adopt these technologies—but this alone cannot account for the apparent regional lag in the Middle Atlantic region regarding the adoption of new technologies. After all, archaeologists laboring anywhere across the planet also had to become familiar and comfortable with new technological developments. Perhaps Middle Atlantic archaeologists are simply more poorly funded, use these technologies but do not publish about them, or, alternatively, are just plain technophobic. I suspect this latter situation is changing with the rising generation of archaeologists—many of whom are digital natives. Younger scholars are enmeshed in an integrated digital world—and have been since they were born. Knowledge of innovative technologies—and how they can be applied to address archaeological questions—is spreading readily and rapidly, and Middle Atlantic archaeologists must be poised to embrace the future as they study the past.

ACKNOWLEDGMENTS

I would like to thank Heather Wholey and Carole Nash for inviting me to participate in this volume, and Michael Klein for his comments on an earlier version of this chapter. Any errors, omissions, or mischaracterizations of the individuals cited here are my sole responsibility.

REFERENCES CITED

Adovasio, James M.
  1997 A Comment on Lithic Raw Material Analyses: Examples from the Old and New Worlds. *Journal of Middle Atlantic Archaeology* 13:5–8.

Allitt, Sharon, R. Michael Stewart, and Timothy Messner
  2008 The Utility of Dog Bone (*Canis familiaris*) in Stable Isotope Studies for Investigating the Presence of Maize (*Zea mays ssp. mays*): A Preliminary Study. *North American Archaeologist* 29:343–67.

Auffart, Albert, and Robert Oshnock
  2011 Keyhole Features from the Consol Site (36WM100). *Pennsylvania Archaeologist* 81:44–53.

Barber, Michael B.
  2013 From the Office of the State Archaeologist. *Newsletter of the Archeological Society of Virginia* Number 210. Electronic document: http://www.asv-archeology.org/PDF/ASVNL13-09.pdf, accessed May 1, 2016.

Barber, Michael B., and Michael J. Madden
  2004 Float, Sink, or Swim: An Argument for Archaeological Flotation. *Quarterly Bulletin of the Archeological Society of Virginia* 59 (4):228–37.

Blanton, Dennis B., Stevan C. Pullins, and Veronica Deitrick
  1999 *The Potomac Creek Site (44ST2) Revisited.* Virginia Department of Historic Resources Report Series No. 10. Richmond, VA.

Boulanger, Matthew T., Thomas R. Jamison, Craig Skinner, and Michael D. Glascock
  2007 Analysis of an Obsidian Biface Reportedly Found in the Connecticut River Valley of Vermont. *Archaeology of Eastern North America* 35:81–92.

Boyce, Hettie L., and Lori A. Frye
  1986 *Radiocarbon Dating of Archeological Samples from Maryland.* Maryland Geological Survey, Baltimore.

Brennan, Louis A.
　1974　Date Reporting. *Archaeology of Eastern North America* 2:37–39.

Bryant, Jr., Vaughn M.
　2000　Flotation. In *Archaeological Method and Theory: An Encyclopedia*, edited by Linda Ellis, pp. 216–18. Garland Publishing, Inc., New York.

Chadwick, William J.
　2014　What Are the Current "Best Practices" for the Application of Geophysics to Archaeological Projects in the Middle Atlantic Region? Paper presented in the session "Alternative Mitigation Results from the Route 301 Archaeology Program in Delaware," organized by David Clarke at the Middle Atlantic Archaeological Conference, Langhorne, PA.

Chadwick-Moore, Jennifer
　2011　Going, Going, Gone: Impacts of Sea Level Rise on Archeological Resources in Maryland. Paper presented in the session "Climate Change, Cultural Variability, and Archaeology: Past, Present, and Future," chaired by Bernard K. Means and David Clarke, at the Middle Atlantic Archaeological Conference, Ocean City, MD.

Chiarulli, Beverly A.
　2012　Using Geophysical Instruments to Investigate Late Prehistoric Villages in Western Pennsylvania. Paper presented at the Middle Atlantic Archaeological Conference, Virginia Beach, VA.

Chiarulli, Beverly A., R. Scott Moore, Sarah W. Neusius, Ben Ford, and Marion Smeltzer
　2010　Public Archaeology in Virtual Worlds. *Anthropology News* 51 (6):35.

Chiarulli, Beverly A., Paul Raber, Christopher Stevenson, and Michael Glascock
　2000　The Use of Neutron Activation Analysis to Identify Raw Material Sources for Prehistoric Artifacts in Western Pennsylvania. Paper presented at the 71st annual meeting of the Society for Pennsylvania Archaeology, Williamsport, PA.

Clarke, David
　2011　Climate Change Impact on Archaeological Sites in Transportation Corridors: Delaware Department of Transportation Case Study. Paper presented in the session "Climate Change Implications for Transportation Systems and Archaeological Sites in Transportation Corridors," organized by David S. Clarke and Ileana Ivanciu, at the 90th annual meeting of the Transportation Research Board of the National Academies, Washington, DC.

Cremeens, D. L., and Hart, John P.
　2009　Holocene Alluvial Geoarchaeology of the Memorial Park Site (36Cn164), West Branch Susquehanna River, Pennsylvania. *Archaeology of Eastern North America* 37:47–64.

Dehaven, Lydia
    2011   Geophysics at the Squirrel Hill Site. Unpublished Master's thesis, Department of Anthropology, Indiana University of Pennsylvania, Indiana, PA.

Dent, Richard J. and Christine A. Jirikowic
    2001   Accokeek Creek: Chronology, the Potomac Creek Complex, and Piscataway Origins. *Journal of Middle Atlantic Archaeology* 17:37–55.

Didier, Mary Ellen
    1975   The Argillite Problem Revisited: An Archeological and Geological Approach to a Classical Archeological Problem. *Archaeology of Eastern North America* 3:90–101.

Dillian, Carolyn, Charles Bello, and M. Steven Shackley
    2006   Long Distance Exchange: The Case of an Obsidian Projectile Point from the University of Pennsylvania Museum. *Pennsylvania Archaeologist* 76 (2):41–47.

Dragoo, Don W.
    1974   Radiocarbon-14 Dates and the Archaeologist. *Archaeology of Eastern North America* 2:21–29.

Espino, Jason, Seth Van Dam, and Ashley Brown
    2012   Archaeological Prospection of the Hatfield Site, a Monongahela Tradition Village in Washington County, Pennsylvania. *North American Archaeologist* 33:107–134.

Feathers, James K., Edward J. Rhodes, Sebastian Huot, and Joseph M. McAvoy
    2006   Luminescence Dating of Sand Deposits Related to Late Pleistocene Human Occupation at the Cactus Hill Site, Virginia, USA. *Quaternary Geochronology* 1:167–87.

Frink, Douglas S.
    1992   The Chemical Variability of Carbonized Organic Matter through Time. *Archaeology of Eastern North America* 20:67–79.
    1994   The Oxidizable Carbon Ratio (OCR): A Proposed Solution to Some of the Problems Encountered with Radiocarbon Data. *North American Archaeologist* 15:17–29.
    1995   Application of the Oxidizable Carbon Ratio (OCR) Dating Procedure and its Implications for Pedogenic Research. *Pedological Perspectives in Archaeological Research.* SSSA Special Publication 44. Soil Science Society of America, Madison.
    1999   The Scientific Basis of Oxidizable Carbon Ratio (OCR) Dating. *SAA Bulletin* 17 (5). Electronic document, http://www.saa.org/Portals/0/SAA/publications/SAAbulletin/17-5/index.html, accessed May 1, 2016.

Gutiérrez, Gerardo, Grace Erny, Alyssa Friedman, Melanie Godsey, and Machal Gradoz
    2016   Archaeological Topography with Small Unmanned Aerial Vehicles. *The SAA Archaeological Record* 16(2):10–13.

Gutiérrez, Gerardo, and Michael T. Searcy
  2016 Introduction to the UAV Special Edition. *The SAA Archaeological Record* 16(2):6–9.

Hargrave, Michael
  2006 Ground Truthing the Results of Geophysical Surveys. In *Remote Sensing in Archaeology: An Explicitly North American Perspective*, edited by Jay K. Johnson, pp. 269–304. The University of Alabama Press, Tuscaloosa.

Hart, John
  1999 Dating Roundtop's Domesticates: Implications for Northeast Late Prehistory. In *Current Northeast Paleoethnobotany*, edited by John Hart, pp. 47–68. New York State Museum Bulletin 494. University of the State of New York, Albany.
  2000a New Dates from Classic New York Sites: Just How Old Are These Longhouses? *Northeast Anthropologist* 60:1–22.
  2000b New Dates from Old Collections: The Roundtop Site and Maize-Beans-Squash Agriculture in the Northeast. *North American Archaeologist* 21:7–17.
  2008 Evolving the Three Sisters: The Changing Histories of Maize, Bean, and Squash in New York and the Greater Northeast. In *Current Northeast Paleoethnobotany II*, edited by John P. Hart, pp. 87–99. New York State Museum Bulletin 512. University of the State of New York, Albany.

Hart, John P., and Hetty Jo Brumbach
  2003 The Death of Owasco. *American Antiquity* 68:737–52.
  2005 Cooking Residues, AMS Dates, and the Middle-to-Late-Woodland Transition in Central New York. *Northeast Anthropology* 69:1–34.

Hart, John P., Hetty Jo Brumbach, and Robert Lusteck
  2007 Extending the Phytolith Evidence for Early Maize (Zea mays ssp. mays) and Squash (Cucurbita sp.) in Central New York. *American Antiquity* 72:563–83.

Hart, John P., and William A. Lovis
  2007 A Multi-Regional Analysis of AMS and Radiometric Dates from Carbonized Food Residues. *Midcontinental Journal of Archaeology* 32:201–61.
  2013 Reevaluating What We Know About the Histories of Maize in Northeastern North America: A Review of Current Evidence. *Journal of Archaeological Research* 21:175–216.

Hart, John P., and Bernard K. Means
  2002 Maize and Villages: a Summary and Critical Assessment of Current Northeast Early Late Prehistoric Evidence. In *Northeast SubsistenceSettlement Change: A.D. 700–A.D. 1300,* edited by John P. Hart and Christina Rieth, pp. 345–58. *New York State Museum Bulletin* 496. University of the State of New York, Albany.

Hart, John P., and C. Margaret Scarry
  1999 The Age of Common Beans (*Phaseolous vulgaris*) in the Northeastern United States. *American Antiquity* 64(4):653–58.

Hart, John P,. and Nancy Asch Sidell
   1997   Additional Evidence for Early Cucurbit Use in the Northeastern Wood-
          land East of the Allegheny Front. *American Antiquity*: 653–58.

Hart, John P., Robert G. Thompson, and Hetty Jo Brumbach
   2003   Phytolith Evidence for Early Maize (*Zea mays*) in the Northern Finger
          Lakes Region of New York. *American Antiquity* 68:619–40.

Haynes, C. Vance, D. J. Donahue, A. J. T. Jull, and T. H. Zebel
   1984   Application of Accelerator Dating to Fluted Point Paleoindian Sites. *Ar-
          chaeology of Eastern North America* 12:184–91.

Herbstritt, James
   1988   A Reference for Pennsylvania Radiocarbon Dates. *Pennsylvania Archae-
          ologist* 58 (2):1–30.

Horsley, Timothy J, and Robert D. Wall
   2010   *Archaeological Evaluation of Alluvial Landscapes in Western Maryland* Report
          prepared for the Maryland Historical Trust, Crownsville, MD.

Inashima, Paul
   2008   Establishing A Radiocarbon Date Based Framework for Northeastern
          Virginia Archeology. *Quarterly Bulletin of the Archeological Society of Vir-
          ginia* 63 (4):187–290.
   2011   Supplement No. 1 to "Establishing a Radiocarbon Date Based Frame-
          work for Northeastern Virginia Archeology." *Quarterly Bulletin of the
          Archeological Society of Virginia* 66(3):89–140.

Johnson, Jay K. (editor)
   2006   *Remote Sensing in Archaeology: An Explicitly North American Perspective.*
          The University of Alabama Press, Tuscaloosa.

Johnson, William C., Jay Babich, and Natale Kirshner Shaw
   2010   The Kirshner Site (36Wm213): A Preliminary Reassessment of a Multiple
          Monongahela Component Site. Paper presented at the 77th Annual Meet-
          ing of the Eastern States Archeological Federation, Williamsburg, VA.

Johnson, William C., and Bernard K. Means
   2016   The Monongahela Tradition of the Late Prehistoric and Protohistoric Peri-
          ods, 12th–17th Centuries A.D., in the Lower Upper Ohio River Valley. In
          A Synthesis of Native American Archaeology in Pennsylvania, by Kurt W. Carr,
          Christopher Bergman, Christina B. Rieth, Bernard K. Means, and Roger W.
          Moeller. Manuscript under review at the University of Pennsylvania Press.

Key, Marcus M., Jr., and Emily S. Gaskin
   2000   Dating the Prehistoric Davis Site (44la46) in Lancaster County, Virginia.
          Quarterly Bulletin of the Archeological Society of Virginia 55 (3):135–60.

Key, Marcus M., Jr., Steven Vaughn, Todd Davis, and William Parr
   2009   C14 age Control on a Rappahannock Native American Site on Totuskey
          Creek (44RD0206) in Richmond County, Virginia. *Quarterly Bulletin of the
          Archeological Society of Virginia* 64(4):163–76.

Killick, D. J., A. J. T. Jull, and G. S. Burr
  1999 A Failure to Discriminate: Querying Oxidizable Carbon Ratio (OCR) Dating. *SAA Bulletin* 17 (5). Available online at http://www.saa.org/Portals/0/SAA/publications/SAAbulletin/17-5/index.html.

Klein, Michael J.
  1990 The Potential of X-Ray Diffraction Analysis of Prehistoric Ceramics in the Middle Atlantic Region: An Analysis of the Clay Mineralogy, Firing Temperature, and Clay Source of Sherds from Virginia. *Journal of Middle Atlantic Archaeology* 6:13–26.
  1994 An Absolute Seriation to Ceramic Chronology in the Roanoke, Potomac and James River Valleys, Virginia and Maryland. Unpublished Ph.D. Dissertation, Department of Anthropology, the University of Virginia, Charlottesville, VA.

Klein, Michael J., and Marco Gonzalez
  2012 View shed Analysis of Contact-Period Settlements in Coastal Virginia. Paper presented in the session "Forging Identities: The Shifting Temporal and Geographic Boundaries of the Contact Period," chaired by Bernard K. Means and Michael B. Barber, at the Society for Historical Archaeology annual meeting, Baltimore, MD.

Lattanzi, Gregory D.
  2007 The Provenance of Pre-contact Copper Artifacts: Social complexity and Trade in the Delaware Valley. *Archaeology of Eastern North America* 35:125–37.
  2008a Chemical Characterization of Four Pre-Contact Copper Artifacts from Pennsylvania. *Pennsylvania Archaeologist* 78 (1):2–15.
  2008b Elucidating the Origin of Middle Atlantic Pre-Contact Copper Artifacts Using Laser Ablation ICP-MS. *North American Archaeologist* 29:297–326.
  2013 The First Stimulus Package: The WPA and the New Jersey Indian Site Survey. In *Shovel Ready: Archaeology and Roosevelt's New Deal for America*, edited by Bernard K. Means, pp. 21–32. The University of Alabama Press, Tuscaloosa.

Levine, Mary Ann
  1990 Accommodating Age: Radiocarbon Results and Fluted Point Sites in Northeastern North America. *Archaeology of Eastern North America* 18:33–63.

Lowery, Darrin
  2002 The Distribution of Miocene Silicified Sandstone in the Archaeological Record and Interpretations Based on the Observed Patterns: A Test of GIS in Archaeology. *Journal of Middle Atlantic Archaeology* 18:17–34.

Luckenbach, Al
  2013 The Discovery of a Major "Delmarva Adena" Ritual and Mortuary Complex at Pig Point on the Patuxent River, Maryland. Paper presented in the session "Early & Middle Woodland Settlement and Subsistence, Technology, and Social Organization: New Investigations and New

Interpretation," organized by Darrin L. Lowery and Stuart Fiedel, at the Middle Atlantic Archaeological Conference, Virginia Beach, VA.

Martin, Andrew
  2015 A Reexamination of Ernest Volk's Excavations at the Abbott Farm through GIS. Paper presented in the session "The Applications of GIS in Archaeology," organized by Sean McHugh at the 2015 Middle Atlantic Archaeological Conference, Ocean City, MD.

Maslowski, Robert
  2011 Cultural Affiliation Statement: New River Gorge National River and Gauley River National Recreation Area. Prepared under cooperative agreement with Bureau of Applied Research in Anthropology, School of Anthropology, University of Arizona, Northeast Region NAGPRA Program, National Park Service, Boston, MA.

McCracken, Richard J. and Charles L. Lucy
  1989 Analysis of a Radiocarbon Date from the Blackman Site, an Early Susquehannock Village in Bradford County, Pennsylvania. *Pennsylvania Archaeologist* 59 (1):14–18.

McCuistion, Ashley
  2013 Promoting the Past: The Educational Applications of 3D Scanning Technology in Archaeology. *Journal of Middle Atlantic Archaeology* 29:35–42.

McCuistion, Ashley, Courtney Bowles, Bernard K. Means, and Clinton King
  2013 *Protocols for Three-Dimensional Digital Data Collection from Artifacts Using the NextEngine Desktop 3D Scanner*. Prepared for the Department of Defense, Legacy Resource Management Program, Legacy Project #11-334. Prepared by the Virtual Curation Laboratory, Virginia Commonwealth University, Richmond, VA.

McKnight, Justine and Martin Gallivan
  2007 The Virginia Archeobotanical Database Project: A Preliminary Synthesis of Chesapeake Ethnobotany. *Quarterly Bulletin of the Archeological Society of Virginia* 62 (4):181–89.

Means, Bernard K.
  2005a New Dates for New Deal Excavated Monongahela Villages in Somerset County. *Pennsylvania Archaeologist* 75 (1):49–61.
  2005b Late Woodland Villages in the Allegheny Mountains Region of Southwestern Pennsylvania: Temporal and Social Implications of New Accelerator Mass Spectrometry Dates. *Uplands Archaeology in the East* VII and IX, edited by Carole L. Nash and Michael B. Barber, pp. 13–23. Archeological Society of Virginia Special Publication 38-7.
  2011a Climate Change, Cultural Variability, and Archaeology: Past, Present, and Future. Paper presented in the session "Climate Change, Cultural Variability, and Archaeology: Past, Present, and Future," chaired by Bernard K. Means and David Clarke, at the Middle Atlantic Archaeological Conference, Ocean City, MD.

2011b The Future Meets the Past: Digital Mapping of New Deal Archaeology Projects across the Lower 48 States. Bernard K. Means, guest editor. *The SAA Archaeological Record* 11 (3):29–33. Electronic document, http://online digeditions.com/publication/?i=70732, accessed May 1, 2016.

2013a Shovels at the Ready: Work Relief and American ArchaeologyToday and Tomorrow. In *Shovel Ready: Archaeology and Roosevelt's New Deal for America*, edited by Bernard K. Means, pp. 235–42. University of Alabama Press, Tuscaloosa.

2013b Archaeologist #.00000000000000000: Edgar E. Augustine and New Deal Excavations in Somerset County, Pennsylvania. In *Shovel Ready: Archaeology and Roosevelt's New Deal for America*, edited by Bernard K. Means, pp. 48–64. The University of Alabama Press, Tuscaloosa.

2014 Time Marches On? Rethinking the Monongahela Chronological Framework. In *Instances of Prehistoric and Historic Archaeology in Mountainous Areas of the Eastern United States: Papers from Uplands Archaeology in the East Symposium XI*, edited by Clarence Geier, pp. 94–111. James Madison University, Harrisonburg, VA.

2015 A Promoting a More Interactive Public Archaeology: Archaeological Visualization and Reflexivity through Virtual Artifact Curation. *Advances in Archaeological Practice* 3(3):235–48.

Means, Bernard K., Courtney Bowles, Ashley McCuistion, and Clinton King
2013a *Virtual Artifact Curation: Three-Dimensional Digital Data Collection for Artifact Analysis and Interpretation*. Prepared for the Department of Defense Legacy Resource Management Program, Legacy Project #11-334. Prepared by the Virtual Curation Laboratory, Virginia Commonwealth University, Richmond, VA.

Means, Bernard K., Ashley McCuistion, and Courtney Bowles
2013b Virtual Artifact Curation of the Historic Past and the NextEngine Desktop 3D Scanner. *Technical Briefs in Historical Archaeology* 7:1–12. Electronic document, http://www.sha.org/documents/VirtualArtifacts.pdf, accessed May 1, 2016.

Means, Bernard K., and Justine McKnight
2010 Constructing Chronologies from Curated Collections for Northern Virginia's Late Woodland Period: A Threatened Sites Project. *Quarterly Bulletin of the Archeological Society of Virginia* 65(1):16–29.

Means, Bernard K., and William H. Tippins
2010 A Discussion of New Radiocarbon Dates from the Gnagey 3 (36SO55), McJunkin (36AL17), and Household (36WM61) Sites. *Pennsylvania Archaeologist* 80 (1):63–74.

Messner, Timothy J., Ruth Dickau, and Jeff Harbison
2008 Starch Grain Analysis: Methodology and Applications in the Northeast. In *Current Northeast Paleoethnobotany*, edited by John Hart, pp. 111–27. New York State Museum Bulletin 494. The University of the State of New York, Albany.

Moeller, Roger W.
   1986   Theoretical and Practical Considerations in the Application of Flota-
          tion for Establishing, Evaluating, and Interpreting Meaningful Cultural
          Frameworks. *Journal of Middle Atlantic Archaeology* 2:1–19.

Neusius, Sarah W. and Beverly A. Chiarulli
   2012   Dating the Late Pre-Contact Period in Central Western Pennsylvania.
          Paper presented at the 77th annual meeting of the Society for American
          Archaeology, Memphis, TN.

Oshnock, Robert
   2009   Consol site (36WM100), Sewickley, Township, Westmoreland County,
          Pennsylvania, Report Number 5. Paper presented at the 80th annual
          meeting of the Society for Pennsylvania Archaeology, Harrisburg.

Paperless Archaeology
   2016   Paperless Archaeology. Electronic document, https://paperlessarchaeology
          .com/, accessed May 1, 2016.

Pevarnik, George L.
   2007   A Polarizing View of Middle Woodland Pottery from the Delaware Val-
          ley. *Archaeology of Eastern North America* 35:139–51.

Pevarnik, George L., Matthew T. Boulanger, and Michael D. Glascock
   2008   Instrumental Neutron Activation Analysis of Middle Woodland Pottery
          from the Delaware Valley. *North American Archaeologist* 29:239–68.

Poulos, Anastasia, and Stephanie Sperling
   2013   A Comparative Study of Prehistoric Settlements on the Patuxent River in
          Anne Arundel County, Maryland. Paper presented in the session "Early
          & Middle Woodland Settlement and Subsistence, Technology, and Social
          Organization: New Investigations and New Interpretation," organized
          by Darrin L. Lowery and Stuart Fiedel, at the Middle Atlantic Archaeo-
          logical Conference, Virginia Beach, VA.

Ralph, E. K., H. N. Michael, and M. C. Han
   1974   Radiocarbon Dates and Reality. *Archaeology of Eastern North America*
          2:1–20.

Rafferty, Sean M., Candis Wood, and Christina B. Rieth
   2007   A Trace Element Analysis of New York Chert Sources. *North American
          Archaeologist* 28:167–86.

Rieth, Christina B., Sean Rafferty, and Derek Saputo
   2007   A Trace Element Analysis of Ceramics from the Pethick Site, Schoharie
          County, New York. *North American Archaeologist* 28:59–80.

Rubino, Sara
   2010   Geophysics at the Byrd-Leiphart Site. Unpublished Master's thesis,
          Department of Anthropology, Indiana University of Pennsylvania, In-
          diana, PA.

Schiszik, Lauren, C. Jane Cox, and Stephanie Sperling
   2011   Archaeological Site Vulnerability Assessment and Sea level Rise in Anne Arundel County, MD. Paper presented in the session "Climate Change, Cultural Variability, and Archaeology: Past, Present, and Future," chaired by Bernard K. Means and David Clarke, at the Middle Atlantic Archaeological Conference, Ocean City, MD.

Sciulli, Paul W.
   1995   Biological Indicators of Diet in Monongahela Populations. *Pennsylvania Archaeologist* 65 (2):1–18.

Searcy, Michael T.
   2016   Dealing with Legal Uncertainty in the Use of UAVs in the United States. *The SAA Archaeological Record* 16(2):43–45.

Selden, Jr., Robert Z., Bernard K. Means, Jon C. Lohse, Charles Koenig, and Stephen L. Black
   2014   Beyond Documentation: 3D Data in Archaeology. *Texas Archaeology* 58 (4):20–24. Electronic document, http://www.txarch.org/Publications/newsletters/index.html, accessed April 29, 2015.

Smith, Donna
   2009   Geophysical Investigation of Stockades. Unpublished Master's thesis, Department of Anthropology, Indiana University of Pennsylvania, Indiana, PA.

Smith, Neil G., Luca Passone, Said al-Said, Mohamed al-Farhan, & Thomas E. Levy.
   2014   Drones in Archaeology: Integrated Data Capture, Processing, and Dissemination in the al-Ula Valley, Saudi Arabia. *Near Eastern Archaeology* 77(3):176–81.

Steadman, Laura
   2008   Uncovering the Origins of Abbott Zoned Incised Pottery in Coastal Plain Virginia: An LA-ICP-MS Study. *Journal of Middle Atlantic Archaeology* 24:79–86.

Stevenson, Christopher M., Michael D. Glascock, Robert Speakman, and Michelle MacCarthy
   2008   Expanding the Geochemical Database for Virginia Jasper Sources. *Journal of Middle Atlantic Archaeology* 24:57–78.

Stevenson, Christopher M., Michael D. Glascock, and Robert J. Speakman
   2004   Instrumental Neutron Activation Analysis of Chert from the Williamson and Bolster's Store Sources, Dinwiddie County, and the Mitchell Plantation Source, Sussex County, Virginia. *Quarterly Bulletin of the Archeological Society of Virginia* 59 (4):211–27.

Stevenson, Christopher M., Maria Klimkiewicz, and Barry E. Scheetz
   1990   X-Ray Fluorescence Analysis of Jaspers from the Woodward Site (36CH374), the Kasowski Site (36CHl61), and Selected Eastern United States Jasper Quarries. *Journal of Middle Atlantic Archaeology* 6:37–47.

Strickland, Scott
   2013   A GIS Approach to Late Woodland Settlement in the Potomac Valley. Paper presented in the session "Material Approaches to Contact and Colonization in the Lower Potomac Valley," organized by D. Brad Hatch and Julia A. King, at the Middle Atlantic Archaeological Conference, Virginia Beach, VA.

Tippins, William H. and Richard L. George
   2010   Richard George's 2008 C14 Dating Project. *Pennsylvania Archaeologist* 80 (1):60–62.

Ur, Jason
   2006   Google Earth and Archaeology. *The SAA Archaeological Record* 6 (3):35–38.

Wall, Robert D.
   2008   Deep Testing and Radiocarbon Dates from the Barton Site (18AG3), Allegany County, Maryland. *Maryland Archeology* 44(2):1–4.

Walldrodt, John
   2015   Keynote Lecture: Why Paperless? Digital Technology and Archaeology. Paper presented at *Mobilizing the Past for a Digital Future: The Potential of Digital Archaeology*, February 27–28. Wentworth Institute of Technology, Boston, MA.

Wechsler, Suzanne, Carl Lipo, Chris Lee, and Terry L. Hunt
   2016   Technology in the Skies Benefits of Commercial UAS for Archaeological Applications. *The SAA Archaeological Record* 16(2):36–42.

7

+

Ethnohistoric Studies

Documentary Evidence for Variation in Late Prehistoric Cultures Across the Middle Atlantic Region

Marshall J. Becker

The evolution of the many distinct Native cultures of the Middle Atlantic realm was strongly influenced by the development of the bow and arrow, around A.D. 1000–1100. This innovation appears to have initiated the Late Woodland period that witnessed the formation of a wide variety of Native cultures. Each of the distinct tribes that inhabited the region in A.D. 1500 had perfected a specialized and locally adapted economy. The tribes first encountered by Europeans utilized not only a variety of economic strategies but also various political systems, including true chiefdoms, low-level egalitarian horticulturalists (shifting villages), and basic foragers. These systems continued to operate long after earliest contact, in some cases beyond A.D. 1830, providing us with the opportunity to study massive numbers of relevant documents that record these various traditional systems as they operated during a long "Contact period." Archaeologists have long been interested in the connections between the evidence for the peoples of the Late Woodland Period and their "descendants" of the historic period who interacted with early colonists. Written records provide insights into these many cultures as they existed during that long period of interactions. The early documents recording aspects of Native life reveal a great deal about cultural diversity during the Late Woodland period as well as providing an understanding of how European immigrant groups, with their different and competing interests and goals, came to dominate the cultural landscape. The dynamics of Native cultures, and their continuities even as they gradually were absorbed into modern states, are better understood using the vast documentary record as interpreted through the anthropological lens of ethnohistory.

DEVELOPMENT OF ETHNOHISTORY IN THE MIDDLE ATLANTIC

In 1888 the founding of the *Journal of American Folklore* emulated its British ancestor in examining traditional and regional customs that were slowly disappearing. Scholars interested in the curious languages and behaviors of Native peoples around the world used these journals to report on a wide variety of traditional societies still available for firsthand study. A decade later the *American Anthropologist* would begin to publish the workings of traditional cultures as distinct from social behaviors that were remnants of fading cultural traditions within modern societies. While early anthropologists were collecting ethnographic information from various living cultures, the rich archival collections relating to these people were almost entirely ignored. The methods of conducting ethnography with the living were quite distinct from gathering the archived records that provide us with histories of the same people. Archival explorations during the past three-score years have provided an "archaeology" of documents that contain layers of information about the past. This technique, called *ethnohistory*, is a method increasingly integrated into anthropological research.

Formal conceptualization of ethnohistory as a bridge between history and anthropology in the study of Native peoples began in the 1950s. The link solidified when the Ohio Valley Historic Indian Conference of 1953 led to the 1954 founding of the journal *Ethnohistory*. Within a few years, the focus of the papers in *Ethnohistory* expanded to include North and South America, and then the world. *Ethnohistory* offers anthropologists, historians, and other scholars an outlet for publishing their understanding of traditional peoples. These data were drawn from the documents once overlooked (e.g., Royce 1899) but now interpreted using an anthropological understanding of culture. The goals of the journal were articulated in three early papers written by an anthropologist (Voegelin 1954), a historian (Smith 1954), and an "archaeologist" (Black 1954). An emic approach, fundamental to anthropology, is basic to most of the papers in this journal. Archaeologists utilizing ethnohistoric data remained disposed to publishing in the archaeological literature. Given the early association between the journal *Ethnohistory* and the Ohio Valley, a zone into which a few northeastern groups had shifted their territories after 1650, it is not surprising that two of the earliest papers are related to the so-called Delaware. Both were authored by a linguist (Mahr 1955a, 1955b). A dozen years later, in a reprise of those three 1954 papers, Sturtevant (1966) dropped the archaeological component and focused on anthropology, history, and ethnohistory. Not until volume 16 do we find a paper in *Ethnohistory* intended to link the prehistoric record to historical patterns (Upper Great Lakes region: Fitting and Cleland 1969). A second archaeological paper also appeared in that issue, but papers using excavated information to augment the documentary record remain rare (e.g., Becker 1979c).

In regional journals the fusion of historical approaches to the native past in the form of ethnohistoric research soon became an adjunct to archaeology and ethnography, providing clearer views of that portion of time during which records were kept. Among the more important revelations derived from modern studies is the recognition that tribal "areas" were relatively small zones surrounded by extensive territorial buffers. Understanding the function and dynamics of these generally large and unoccupied (unclaimed) areas that surrounded the core residential region of each native tribe remains one of the features of native life that seems difficult for most non-anthropologists to understand. Buffer zones, also called no-man's-lands or "shared resource areas," served a number of purposes (Becker 1983a, 1998:45–46). Milner et al. (2001:9) were among the first archaeologists to take note of this common cultural phenomenon, terming the occupation pattern "discontinuous." A buffer zone could be entered by anyone wishing to extract resources, but remained an area not claimed by any nearby tribe. After European land purchases became a means by which natives could gain access to European goods, tracts in these buffer zones were often "sold," often with vendors and purchasers complicit in what they knew to be fraudulent transactions (see Becker 2013). Not only were tracts in these areas subject to "sales" by people who did not own them (Becker 1998), but they commonly became locations in which displaced groups could relocate (Becker 1993). Both of these activities became common during the latter phases of tribal disruption in the Middle Atlantic zone, ca. 1635–1740s.

Despite some broad and inclusive reviews of cultures in contact (e.g., Fausz 1985), most historians' studies of the colonial Middle Atlantic zone tended to focus on those immigrants who were writing in English rather than the Native peoples with whom they interacted (but, see Lewis and Loomie 1953). Documents for the Dutch in this region had been gathered (e.g., O'Callaghan 1848, and after, also Trelease 1962), and recently been afforded much greater attention (Waterman et al. 2009, also Jacobs 2009). The Swedish colonial venture has received sporadic attention since the efforts of Amandus Johnson (1911, 1925). Despite the gathering of data relating to early European explorers and traders, scholars continued to lump the several Native tribes in the area of New Sweden into a single "people" who came to be called "Delaware." Each portion of the Middle

Atlantic region has its own history and cast of characters that merits study. The following overview provides a very brief introduction to the growing numbers of studies of the Native peoples and how this research developed, and it offers some suggestions regarding the many questions yet to be answered.

DELINEATION OF THE CULTURAL GROUPS IN THE MIDDLE ATLANTIC

Ethnohistoric research confirms that each of the many tribes in northeastern North America had a unique and distinct social and economic system. A previous model for the Middle Atlantic peoples held that all of them were horticulturalists, living in large villages just like the historically known Five Nations Iroquois. This idea now can be documented as a nineteenth-century invention that became the popular model to describe Native peoples. The evidence reveals that this idea derives from firsthand reports published about the Five Nations Iroquois in the early 1800s. Only recently has this stereotypic view given way to more specific understanding of individual cultural differences based on direct documentary and archaeological evidence. The true chiefdoms of coastal Virginia and Maryland were easily distinguished from the egalitarian Iroquoian villagers of central New York. Exploration of the records on coastal societies living north of Bombay Hook in Delaware and up through New England and into Canada recognize these individual cultures as unique foraging societies.

The Late Woodland period in the Northeast, or that period after ca. A.D. 1000, differs greatly in its dates from the period of that same name as it is described in the Ohio Valley. Prior to 1950, archaeological reports from the Northeast commonly inferred that Late Woodland sites generally represented some variation of the villages of the historically known Five Nations Iroquois villages. These preconceptions influenced archaeological interpretations of the past and colored understanding of the excavated information. By the 1950s, utilization of anthropological models to interpret written records, and more sophisticated archaeological research, led to greater understanding of the recent past. These innovations in methods continue to bring greater clarification to the distinct histories of the many peoples of the Middle Atlantic region.

The recognition of cultural territories, boundaries, and buffer zones has been of importance since the first Europeans arrived in the Northeast and made efforts to purchase land from Native owners, or from "occupants." The limitations of Swanton's (1952) regional approach soon were recognized, with efforts to create a more ethnographic accounting begun soon after. By the 1970s the impressive, but still largely traditional, orientation offered by the many volumes of the *Handbook of North American Indians* offered "comprehensive" summaries of Native cultures, as delineated by the editors and various consultants. The cultural boundaries that were selected reveal the slow progress that had been made toward understanding specific cultural borders for the known tribal groups. By the time that these volumes were planned, the "Eastern Woodland" cultural region, comprising all the peoples east of the Mississippi River, had only recently been divided into Northeastern and Southeastern zones. The idea that adjacent cultures might have radically different sets of organizing principles had only recently been suggested by young "splitters" who were departing from the anthropological "lumpers" who envisioned adjacent cultures as fundamentally all the same (the "culture area" concept). Using a "lumper" model seemed adequate to the editors of the *Handbook* who assigned many sections of volume 15 ("Northeast" 1978) to young scholars, reflecting the dearth of scholars working in this region.

In addition to problems in the delineation of cultural ("tribal") territories many of the entries in volume 15 fail to address economics and political organization. Many of the authors deeply misunderstood the economics of egalitarian foragers. To this day, the forager-horticulturalist-agriculturist debate remains a poorly understood, yet important, matter, particularly as we recognize the extent of regional and temporal variations in cultures. These difficulties are compounded by the many different perspectives and different approaches to this body of knowledge, not limited to archaeology, history, and ethnohistory. These differences may produce conflicting narratives. The result is that major problems are often ignored, or not even understood, by many historians and scholars working with archaeological data sets.

Particularly problematical in the history of Middle Atlantic studies has been the portrayal in the *Handbook* of all the peoples in the Middle Atlantic region as longhouse dwelling, maize farming villagers (Goddard 1978:218). The important work of MacLeod (1922) on foraging economies had been entirely ignored. More recently the efforts of Bruce Smith (1989, 1992) to describe what is called the "eastern agricultural complex" in the riverine interior have been distorted to support ideas regarding Native uses of food sources in the coastal Northeast. Smith proposes that goosefoot, sunflower, sumpweed, squash, and several other plants were cultivated ("farmed") as crops and that this complex constituted a form of agriculture specific to eastern North America. These various wild plants were included in the array gathered by peoples throughout much of the Americas, including Northeastern foragers such as the Lenape, but this collecting activity does not constitute an "agricultural" system (cf. Becker 1995). More problematic is the belief that the term *eastern agricultural complex* refers to the use of maize, beans, and squash rather than those plants proposed by Smith (e.g., Mansius 2011:25).

Only recently has a collection of papers (Blanton and King 2004) addressed subjects specifically concerned with ethnohistory within the Middle Atlantic region. Scholars such as Elizabeth Little (2010, also Becker 2006b) have made efforts to clarify the record regarding plant use. The following review of the studies pertaining to this realm is an effort to indicate the progression of scholarly studies that have enabled us to trace specific tribal histories and to understand processes of change and survival among some groups as proto-industrial European agrarian societies entered their spheres of activity. We will begin in the southern part of the Middle Atlantic area, or that zone that has become the most abundantly studied and for which the individual Native groups are among the best known.

VIRGINIA AND MARYLAND, BUT NOT DELAWARE

The numerous chiefdoms and paramount chiefdoms occupying the southern portion of the Middle Atlantic region were among the more politically sophisticated tribes within this zone. Perhaps, as a consequence of their political structures, these polities have a rich and interesting history of study (see Fausz 1985). Noteworthy is that this southernmost sector of the Middle Atlantic region has garnered much more attention from ethnohistorians than has been paid to all of the Native peoples north of Delaware's Indian River combined. This attention does not appear to be related to the early Spanish and English entries into this southern portion of the Middle Atlantic region. Nor do the financial rewards available from government benefits to surviving "native communities" identified as federal recognized tribes explain the numbers of excellent scholars who have long endeavored to describe these peoples. Surviving Native "communities" in the United States are eligible for significant benefits from the federal government if they can document their historic connections and maintenance of "group integrity" to the present. Ethnohistoric research in Virginia, however, has been ongoing since long before the passage of laws regarding provisions for claimant groups for alleged injustices (e.g., Morrison 1921). In modern Virginia, some remnant or related Native populations have had strong continuity to the present, leading to considerable early research focusing on their cultural survival. The many Native peoples of Virginia (see Robinson 1983a, 1983b) and Maryland (see Robinson 1987) also are extensively documented in the colonial records (see also Vaughan and Rosen 1998). The sheer abundance of documents, however, does not explain why there are so many scholars who have focused an enormous amount of effort on the culture histories and complex dynamics of these coastal chiefdoms and their neighbors in the Piedmont.

The modern era of these cultural studies began with John Garland Pollard's (1894) examination of the Pamunkey, a pioneering effort to conduct serious research in this part of Virginia. This future governor of Virginia wrote one of the earliest "historical" works incorporating extensive cultural information about Native peoples gleaned from the documentary records. Another major early contributor to the anthropology of Virginia was James Mooney. Mooney's studies of Cherokee mythology became an early contribution to *The Journal of American Folklore* (1888). He later examined the Powhatan Confederacy (Mooney 1907), with Frank Speck's study of this tribe (1928, see also 1935) representing an attempt to expand on Mooney's research. Swanton's (1952) review provides only a rudimentary gathering of data, but Christian Feest's three chapters in the *Handbook* (1978) provide a more amplified examination. There Feest (1978) delineates the Nanticoke quite well (see below), but his data were placed under the assigned rubrics of "Virginia Algonquians" and "North Carolina Algonquians" as if they represented two distinct cultural systems. Much more specific and focused tribal research had just become a goal of a younger generation of scholars developing new methods as the traditional "culture area" concept was being inundated by more extensive ethnographic and ethnohistoric research.

Helen Rountree's (1975) study of the Powhatan was not included in the *Handbook,* nor was the early work of Lewis Binford (1964). Rountree's efforts had been omitted because the *Handbook* was prepared earlier and long delayed in publication. With few exceptions, the *Handbook* now can be seen as the climax of traditional ethnohistorical studies that now have advanced into research involving much more extensive and detailed data collection. For example, the examination of the relevant documents for each of the many Native polities in the Virginias has vastly improved our understanding of these many peoples (e.g., Potter 1993, McCartney 2004). Rountree's many works (1975, 1989, 1990, 1993, 2005; also 2002) reveal the extent of the evidence and what can be gleaned from these vast numbers of documents. These recent efforts have clarified and vastly expanded on the accumulated research into the lives of the Powhatan and other Native peoples (see also Townsend 2004). Rountree has also reviewed the efforts of some of Speck's students who were active in this area during the late 1930s and early 1940s. Theodore Stern's (1952) work with the Chickahominy, the less productive efforts of Royal B. Hassrick (Speck et al. 1946), and several others, characterize that interesting early period of research.

Efforts on the part of the hyperactive and often error prone Lewis Binford (1964, 1991, also 1967) to differentiate among the Nottoway, Meherrin, and Weanock Indians of southeastern Virginia provide some of the earliest modern ethnohistorical attempts to understand the peoples of that region. Binford's research focused on the pre-1750 period. Rountree (1987) has expanded the Nottoway data far beyond Binford's efforts (see also Dawdy 1995, Dent 1995:60). Rountree's numerous works (1989 etc.) on the Powhatan, a paramount chiefdom in 1607, are complemented by those of E. Randolph Turner (1985, 1993). The English title "emperor" linked with the head of the Powhatan in the early documents reveals that Wahunsenacawh was recognized as a paramount chief, distinct from the less powerful "kings" (tributary chiefs) of other tribes (cf. Turner 1976). Turner's significant study (1986) of the Powhatan as they relate to the archaeology of chiefdoms, plus Potter's (1993) contribution of ethnohistoric data, have done much to aid our understanding of Powhatan society as a paramount chiefdom. Working together, Rountree and Turner (1994, 2004) have extended our knowledge of Virginia's Native peoples after 1600 (see also Potter 1993; Gallivan 2011). Rountree and Davidson (1997) also produced a significant volume on the Native peoples of the Chesapeake Bay Eastern Shore in Virginia and Maryland.

These many ethnohistoric studies have complemented if not stimulated archaeological research directed toward the identification and excavation of the villages of these largely sedentary peoples. After years of field research Randolph Turner (1986) noted how difficult it was to provide archaeological identification for any of the many villages of the many chiefdoms for which extensive documentary evidence is available. Many suspect locations had been tested, but only in recent years have we seen archaeological verification. In 2003, Martin Gallivan began excavations at the site of what is believed to be Werowocomoco (44GL32), an early principal habitation of the Powhatan named Wahunsenacawh. Recent research often identifies him by the name of his people (see Gallivan 2011; also Turner 1976).

The modern and more rigorously based approaches to the study of these many tribal peoples have led anthropologists to consider models based on specific cultures and their relationships with other Native and colonial peoples. Turner (2004) expanded on his earlier work with the archaeology of the Powhatan with a broad overview of the archaeology of Contact (see also Hantman, below). The use of excavation data to interpret the documentary record and to expand on written documents through the examination of the material evidence further contributes to the anthropological methods used to understand our past (see elsewhere, this volume).

While the coastal peoples of Virginia and Maryland have attracted significant attention for more than a century, less effort has been expended in decoding the histories of peoples living to their west and southwest. The ethnogenesis of the well-known and increasingly well documented

Cherokee, at the extreme southwest of the Middle Atlantic realm, has been reviewed by Rodning (2011), with their proto-Iroquoian origins reviewed by Whyte (2007). The lasting power and importance of these peoples have attracted a great deal of study. The reasons for their dominance and survival, in contradistinction to the interior peoples to their north in Virginia, have yet to be decoded.

A good introduction to the people of the interior parts of Virginia (the Piedmont, etc.) can be found in Bushnell's (1935) pioneering assemblage of data relating to the Monacan. The Saponi (Miller 1957), believed to be related to the Monacan, are another of several Eastern Siouan–speaking tribes in this region (see also Brown 1995). These data were first put into a larger cultural perspective, relevant to the Powhatan, by Mouer (1981) and later by Hantman (1993; see Williamson 2003 for a largely theoretical examination of the Powhatan polity). Gleach (1997) provides excellent data for the interior tribes of Virginia and how they related to the Powhatan. Hantman (1990, 2001, 2010) has integrated the archaeological record with the documentary evidence for the Powhatan and Monacan peoples, and also offers important views of the peoples of western Virginia and West Virginia (see also Gallivan 2003; Blanton and King 2004; Rountree and Turner 1994, 1998, 2002). Hantman now is writing a history of the Monacan. Exploration of the complementary archaeological record for these people has been expanded greatly by Nash (n.d.).

The interior tribes of Virginia, as those in western Maryland and Pennsylvania, have attracted increasing attention in recent years. A comprehensive bibliography of ethnohistoric research conducted with the Virginia piedmont tribes has been assembled by Turner (2013). Lapham's (2004) study of deer exploitation in the "hinterlands" offers information crucial to understanding Native continuities in colonial trade along the coast as well as far into the interior (cf. Becker 2011b). These peoples, as well as groups such as the Tutelo in the Ohio Valley (Hale 1883, Speck 1935, Griffin 1942, see also Smith 1954), are increasingly the subject of recent ethnohistoric research. All these tribes commonly appear in the early documents by the names used by their neighbors to identify them. Our increased understanding of the multiple epithets assigned by other peoples to each tribe helps us to decode the records of their individual histories.

One of the questions regarding tribal identification and nomenclature relates to the people known in the seventeenth-century records as the Massawomeck. Pendergast (1991) described them as "raiders and traders into the Chesapeake Bay." The concern for their identification has been sustained by Helen Rountree, who gathered ethnohistorians and archaeologists concerned with these matters for a series of focused roundtable discussions. These meetings, as a model for cooperative scholarship, identified one of the candidates for the Massawomeck as the culture known archaeologically as "Monongahela." Thanks to the extraordinary archaeological work of William C. Johnson (2001), Bernard Means (2001, 2007; also Hart et al. 2005), and Heather Lapham (Lapham and Johnson 2002), these village-dwelling peoples of southwestern Pennsylvania and adjacent regions have been extraordinarily well documented from about A.D. 1050 (or earlier) to about 1635. Occupation at several contemporary Monongahela villages ended in the 1630s, the decade during which the Five Nations Iroquois had begun to systematically dislodge or exterminate all their neighbors. Johnson and Means (2009) make a connection between the Massawomeck-Monongahela and peoples called Antouhonoron in the documents. Since Monongahela villages had been located along the major trade routes for peltry that crossed Pennsylvania, I suspect that by 1640 the people whom archaeologists identify as "Monongahela" had relocated to the east and allied themselves with the Susquehannock, becoming the "Black Minquas" in the documentary record.

Portions of Maryland had been part of the homeland of the Nanticoke (Busby 2010) and the Piscataway, and perhaps others (Rountree and Davidson 1997). James Merrell (1979) provided an important delineation of the Algonquian speaking Piscataway people, and was one of the first to understand the cultural continuity of these people. Paul Cissna's (1986) dissertation on the Piscataway attempts to delineate the history of this tribe. His study, however, uses the seasonal rounds documented for the Powhatan, for whom the year included five seasons. A recent effort to document the seasonal movements of the Piscataway (Mansius 2011:23) is deeply flawed by assumptions regarding "agriculture" and biases derived from Cissna's inferences from the Powhatan rather than evidence from the Piscataway records. A new volume by Seib and Rountree (2015) delineates all the tribes of southern Maryland and summarizes their individual histories. This work significantly updates Christian Feest's (1978) contribution to the *Handbook*, "Nanticoke and Neighboring Tribes." Nanticoke territory extended across the present Maryland-Delaware border, perhaps up to the riverine buffer zone formed by the Indian River in southern Delaware. This rich area provided an excellent shared resource area separating the Nanticoke from their Sekonese neighbors to the north. Today, claimant groups of "Nanticoke" are widely dispersed throughout the Middle Atlantic region and beyond (see Speck 1915b, 1927), but Maryland today has no federally recognized Native group.

North of Nanticoke territory, occupying the center of the state of Delaware, were the Sekonese (Ciconicin), the northernmost true chiefdom in eastern North America. The Sekonese were the only tribe located entirely within the borders of the modern state (Becker 2004, 2012c). The documentary record provides important evidence allowing us to recognize the Sekonese as a hereditary chiefdom with an all-powerful chief, but as yet there is no archaeological evidence providing the slightest clue to the settlement pattern or the people of this important polity (cf. Turner 1986). While the records reveal the Sekonese as a true chiefdom, the absence of archaeological confirmation leads us to wonder how different their lives may have been from those of the Iroquoian peoples to their west or from the Algonquian speakers to the north. Aside from two very early documents (Kent 1979:5–7, also Graymont 1985:20–21) references to the Sekonese remain few and widely scattered. They were known as Mattwas (variously spelled) by their neighbors in Maryland and Virginia, where Sekonese activities are sporadically recorded in the colonial records. The Sekonese may have been a foraging society, but their political organization was similar to the chiefdoms to their south and distinct from the Lenape bands to their immediate north (Becker 2012c:165–82). This suggests a horticultural economy, which in turn might explain why the members of the fragile Sekonese chiefdom could merge effectively into the multiethnic European population that settled Pennsylvania's lower counties, now the state of Delaware.

FORAGERS: THE PEOPLES
NORTH OF BOMBAY HOOK

The Lenape bands, living to the north of the Sekonese and separated from them by the swamps of the Bombay Hook buffer zone, were a distinct culture but remain archaeologically nearly invisible (but, see Becker 1992c). The best description of the workings of a foraging society in the Middle Atlantic region before 1900 is that of William Penn (1683). How the Lenape lifestyle became confused with that of the Five Nations is described below. Some individuals and entire bands of these fish-oriented foragers (Becker 2006a) were relocating to the west by 1660 to take advantage of opportunities in the pelt trade (Becker 2011c). Other Lenape bands left their homeland over the next seventy-five years, with the last of the traditionalists abandoning the Delaware Valley in 1737. Lenape foraging in the Delaware Valley ended during the 1730s when the last bands still operating along the River shifted their operations to western Pennsylvania or beyond. Scholarly return to Penn's 1683 description took many years.

The development of anthropology programs at a few universities during the end of the 1800s renewed interest in the lives of foragers, who had become prominent in the world's imagination with reports of Plains Indians. This interest was especially robust at the University of Pennsylvania. Frank G. Speck's (1915) brief study of family hunting territories took place among Algonquian bands then living in the Ottawa Valley. This research provided an early example of a modern examination of how foragers, not living on the Plains, distributed themselves over their collective holdings in the post-Contact period. European trade provided them with a connection to a cash-like economy for European goods as well as supplemental foodstuffs. Speck's rudimentary efforts to conduct ethnographic research among the several peoples that he visited were seriously distorted by poor record keeping. The records reveal that, from publication to publication, he paid even less attention to his own data (see Becker 2007a). Even more problematical was Speck's efforts to "revive" Native traditions, using stereotypic views of "Indians" created in the late 1800s during the Plains Wars. His introduction of war bonnets and other garb worn by various Plains cultures to various Native claimant groups in the Northeast presaged the contemporary "social work cum applied anthropology" that has come to prominence in some departments of anthropology. The rise of modern ethnohistoric approaches in the Middle Atlantic may have been impeded by the fictions created during this early era of "applied anthropology."

Following the publication Speck's study of hunting territories there appeared a series of related papers on family territories, among which MacLeod's (1922) study of the foraging Lenape was perhaps the most significant. MacLeod's conclusion was that the territorial land use pattern was a result of contact economics and the pelt trade (contra Becker 2006a). MacLeod applied the term *family*, the winter hunting unit, to the extended family, or band. His subjects were the groups that, as band units, had sold their territories to William Penn (Kent 1979). Despite MacLeod's efforts to understand Lenape culture as it operated during the 1600s, the popular view of these people had become completely distorted through that chain of events extending back to the 1730s, described below.

THE LENAPE FORAGERS, FORMALLY CALLED "DELAWARE"

The best eyewitness account of the Lenape was written by William Penn (1683). His brief but perceptive narrative summarizes their foraging lifestyle long before anthropologists began to understand the concept. In addition to some Swedish documents, there are many texts of interest in the development of an awareness of how the Lenape organized their socioeconomic system. Documents dating from July 10, 1680, and May 5, 1681, on which Alom [sic] made his mark (Dunlap and Weslager 1961; Kent 1979:48–49) offer clues to the lifestyle that Penn's narrative describes so accurately. Penn had purposefully written an ethnography of the aboriginal people whose land rights he tried to protect, expecting them to become the neighbors of anyone, of any religion or language or culture who was literally buying into his experiment in land development. How these foragers became viewed by the public, and a great many scholars after 1800, is summarized here.

Early colonists understood the differences between village dwelling horticulturalists and those Native tribes who had no permanent abodes. Their efforts to describe a foraging lifestyle was embodied in the reference to "Unsettled Ubiquitarians" used in Maryland in October 1725. In a long statement to the General Assembly concerning securing title to Native land rights on the Nanticoke River, mention was made of the commonly known "Indians manner of Planting and habitation in their Towns . . . [being] . . . far different" from the ways of those "Unsettled Ubiquitarians" (Hall 1915, 35:365)—that is, those tribes of Indians who have no permanent villages but seem to be everywhere over the countryside. Foraging tribes are mobile, and in the case of the Lenape bands, had been shifting to the west since the 1660s. Securing title to land whose owners had abandoned them was at issue in Maryland in 1725 and was diligently pursued by the members of Pennsylvania's Provincial Council in 1737 who sought to determine the intentions of Native landholders who had abandoned tracts allotted to them (Becker 1976, 1986a).

The archival records reveal that in their aboriginal state at least twelve, and sometimes more, Lenape bands foraged within the drainages of the rivers that enter the Delaware River from the west. Their entire territorial range lay in the area between old Duck Creek, in northern Delaware, up the Delaware to Tohiccon Creek, which flows parallel and just to the south of the Lehigh River (Kent 1979, Becker 2006a). The southernmost Lenape bands operated in the region that today is northern Delaware, separated from the Sekonese tribe to their south by a swampy buffer zone region now called Bombay Hook.

There are three reasons to focus on the Lenape, and to consider the use of the term "Delaware" in the past and in modern usage. First, all the peoples primarily identified as "Delaware" are located in the center of the Middle Atlantic region. Second, the confusion engendered by the term "Delaware" continues to obstruct historical research, and to baffle the public, including the descendants of this group. Third, this was a problem in the process of tribal self-identification confronted more than forty years ago, when I recognized significant confusion in terminology. This problem led me to begin a program of "deep ethnohistory" to determine what was going on. The specific territorial range and details of culture history specific to the Lenape, and by contradistinction the territories of the Lenopi, Sekonese, and Susquehannock, have been the subject of my studies for forty-five years.

Not long ago the entire region from Long Island down to Maryland once was identified as land inhabited by the "Delaware" (Goddard 1978). The English name "Delaware" (from Thomas West, Third Baron De La Warr) became applied, at a late date, to the several distinct Native tribes occupying the regions adjacent to the Delaware River and bay. In the 1600s the common term applied to the foraging peoples of the lower South (Delaware) River was "River Indians" and these same people later became identified as "Delaware." The foraging tribes along the North (Hudson) River also were collectively called River Indians but these several tribes (except for the Mahican) later became identified in the popular literature as "Delaware Indians" rather than "Hudson Indians" as they all spoke Delawarean languages. The foragers along the South (Delaware) River, Lenape on the west side and Lenopi on the east, were clearly distinct from the people of the Sekonese (Ciconicin) chiefdom. The Sekonese are identified as a separate people in the colonial documents where they are referred to as the Bay Indians. The Lenape were also distinguished from the peoples of the Susquehannock confederacy in the early documents. The main palisaded villages of the Susquehannock are similar in form to those of the Five Nations Iroquois (but, see also Howard 2003). Archaeologically these people are very well known. Even after their dispersal and complete loss of power in 1675, members of Susquehannock remnant communities were commonly identified by the Lenape term *Minquas*. A small group of them even took refuge among those Lenape still foraging in the Delaware Valley. Other Susquehannock taken as slaves by the Five Nations are often mentioned in the documents as resident among the Iroquois. No ethnohistoric account of the Susquehannock has yet been written.

Evidence from the western side of the lower Delaware Valley demonstrates that traditional land use patterns among the fish-oriented Lenape foragers continued into the 1730s (Becker 2006a, 2010a; cf. Bishop 1970 for the Northern Ojibwa). Their Lenopi neighbors, across the river to the east (Becker 2008, 2010a, 2012c:747–64), maintained their traditional foraging systems *within* their ancestral borders and for at least a century longer (Becker 2011d). The search for the "palisaded villages" created by popular historians characterized much of the archaeology of this region.

As early as the 1740s the Moravians identified the Lenopi by the term *Delawar*, distinguishing them from the Lenape. By the early 1800s the popular term "Delaware" had become used interchangeably for all the speakers of Algonquian languages, even those Algonquian speakers as far north as Mi'kmaq territory (Becker 1992b). By the late 1800s, the European term "Delaware" had become attached to the several cultures occupying the territory between southern Delaware and southeastern New York State, out to eastern Long Island.

THE DELAWARE AS VILLAGE HORTICULTURALISTS:
AN ALTERNATE VIEW

Why did so many laymen and scholars alike come to believe that the Lenape, and their neighbors to the east and north, lived in palisaded villages just like the Iroquois when all of the documentary evidence indicates that the Lenape were foragers at the time of contact? By the 1850s, the Lenape were uniformly depicted as having lived in a large village that became buried beneath Philadelphia. In fact, by the 1630s, Lenape bands were using sales of small tracts of land to Europeans as one of multiple means to get access to trade goods, primarily cloth (Becker 2005, 2014b). By the 1640s, the warm-weather fishing stations of the Lenape, generally located at the mouths of feeder streams in their territory along the Delaware River, had become interspaced between small parcels of land bought by Swedish and other European immigrants. In addition to providing the source by which Lenape could secure desired European trade goods, the availability of woolens and supplemental foodstuffs may have enabled an increase in the Lenape population. The complementary resources afforded to a foraging population by a nearby agrarian society had been suggested for some time (Becker 1985, 1995). A post-Contact increase in population density for Native peoples also has been suggested for the horticultural peoples in the Chesapeake Bay region based on biological evidence (Graver 2005).

The land sales that provided one of many means by which Lenape gained access to European goods accelerated around 1655 as a result of the rise in the numbers of English colonists from the New England colonies moving into the Delaware Valley, then still under Dutch control. By 1660 the number of English purchasing tracts along the lower Delaware River was growing at a rapid rate. Many of the Lenape bands selling small tracts along the Delaware River shifted their warm-weather fishing stations to locations a kilometer or two farther up their respective feeder streams. The documents also reveal that by 1660 many Lenape families, and some entire Lenape bands, had moved west to engage in the extremely lucrative pelt trade (Becker 2011c). The pelt trade through Pennsylvania and out to the Ohio Valley and beyond was controlled by the Susquehannock confederacy. By 1660, the Susquehannock, increasingly subjected to Five Nations Iroquois depredations, had sent invitations to Swedish and other colonists to relocate into freely offered tracts of land within their orbit and thus to become allies. These invitations also extended to the Lenape. Iroquois raiding ultimately led to the dispersal of the Susquehannock confederacy in 1675 (Egle 1890), leaving the lucrative pelt trade across Pennsylvania almost entirely in the hands of the Lenape.

By the time of William Penn's 1682 arrival in New Castle, now in Delaware, many Lenape bands had left their traditional foraging areas, posing a challenge to the proprietor who wanted to purchase all Native land in the area of his grant. During the twenty long years between 1682 and 1701 Penn gradually arranged for the purchase of all Lenape lands (see Kent 1979) while protecting the residual or de facto land rights of those bands choosing to remain in the Delaware Valley (e.g., Becker 1986). Penn often had difficulty in getting Lenape to return to negotiate the sale of their abandoned lands. By the 1730s increasing contacts with Europeans and changing cultural patterns among the Lenape led the elders of those remaining bands still foraging in the Delaware Valley to relocate to the more profitable pelt trade in the frontier areas. There they joined their kin in areas away from the culture-distorting influences of colonial interactions.

At least one small family of Lenape and a few isolated individuals remained in the Delaware Valley after 1740, all tightly integrated into colonial society (Becker 1990). By the early 1800s, the last of these individuals, as well as any elder colonists who had witnessed the pre-1740 lifeways of the Lenape, had reached the ends of their long lives. After 1800 the deaths of these remaining Natives were often eulogized as being "the last" of their tribe in Bucks (or other) County in southeastern Pennsylvania (Becker 1990; cf. Nash n.d.). The last of the Lenape who once had lived a traditional lifestyle in their homeland, and the last colonial farmers to have been eyewitnesses to how they lived, were dead by the end of the first decade of the nineteenth century. Their passing left no individuals with actual firsthand knowledge of how the Lenape had lived when they were foraging in the Delaware Valley (Becker 2014a).

The deaths of these last eyewitnesses to traditional Lenape lifestyle occurred during the same years that young Quakers were being sent from the Philadelphia area to live among the Seneca. By the 1790s, some progressive members of the Seneca tribe desired to learn the skills needed to shift from their low-level horticulture to the modern agrarian economy of the settlers. In 1792, after years of discussion that followed the Condolence Conference at Tioga in 1790, Colonel Timothy Pickering invited representatives of the Six Nations to come to Philadelphia "to complete the arrangements for introducing farming to the Indians" (Campisi and Starna 1995:474). The Quakers realized that "survival" (continuance) of the Iroquoians on their traditional lands, or on recently allotted reserves, would be dependent on their shifting from foraging supplemented by horticulture, with its requirements for huge territories, to intensive agriculture that could be practiced on the lands then available to them (Belknap and Morse 1796; Munoz et al. 2014).

The years between 1798 and 1815 marked the maximum period during which a number of young Quakers from Philadelphia lived among the Seneca on the northwestern frontier to teach "farming" as well as barn raising and farm related technologies such as sawmills that were basic to the complex agrarian system that had developed by the end of the eighteenth century. They also taught the English language. Other young Quakers lived among the Oneida and their dependent groups, the immigrants at New Stockbridge and Brothertown (see Swatzler 2000, Densmore 2013). The young men, and an occasional woman, sent on these training missions all had been born at least two generations after the last Lenape foragers had left the Delaware Valley. They had no idea how those "Indians" lived. Subsequently, the many publications of these Quakers who returned had the greatest impact on how the "Indians" of Pennsylvania became perceived (Aborigines 1844:107). Their reports also indicate that most of the traditional Five Nations groups, such as the Oneida, remained resistant to the alteration of male roles that were essential to developing an agricultural economy. Conversely, many of the people in the multi-ethnic groups at New Stockbridge and Brothertown, coming from diverse Native backgrounds in New England, had mastered some of the skills needed to conduct plow agriculture. These individuals were able to sell foodstuffs to their government-subsidized Five Nations neighbors who had not developed these skills (Aborigines 1844:118–123; Gilkison 1885, in Loyer 2013:44; but, see Ricciardelli 1963).

The ethnographic "reports" of those young Quakers provided intimate exposure to Iroquoian longhouses and related settlement patterns. During the 1830s, these accounts of Five Nations' life became a stereotypical "record" of generic "Indian life." This model then was applied, in retrospect, to the peoples of the Delaware Valley and then to all of New England. In the public mind the different cultures and cultural patterns of each Native tribe became fused into one model, represented by the Five Nation villages and longhouses described in these Quaker accounts (e.g., Jackson 1830a; Jackson 1830b; Friends 1840; also see Swatzler 2000). By the 1850s, historians referring to the "Delaware" Indians in Pennsylvania were describing life as it had been witnessed by these young Quakers who had lived among the Seneca, not among Penn's Lenape. To some extent this mistaken idea of a "village model" for Lenape society was later reinforced by excavations at several Susquehannock villages in central Pennsylvania (Kent 1984). The Iroquoian Susquehannock shared similar economic and social systems as their Five Nations neighbors, but that was a lifestyle completely different from that of the Lenape.

Even the modern "Delaware" people in the Bartlesville, Oklahoma area, who graciously hosted me during my visit to them twenty-five years ago, had come to believe that their ancestors were a "civilized" or "village" dwelling peoples. Mrs. Nora Thompson Dean and her kin were quite content to have me excavate a Lenape cemetery (36CH60) in search of direct evidence, and to host me graciously despite my then dark beard. Their only concern was with my ideas regarding the Lenape as a foraging people (Becker 2006a). Just like their non-Native neighbors in Oklahoma, these modern "Delaware" wanted their ancestors to have been "agriculturalists" and not foragers chasing game like Native peoples seen in documentary films. The "cultural memory" of these "Delaware," some of whom still spoke a Delawarean language when I was visiting, certainly did not extend as far back as the early nineteenth century, let alone back to the 1700s. But they did retain some recall of mortuary customs as they had been in the 1920s and, as documented by archaeology, back at least to the 1720s.

At this time, I do not know of a single academic who still believes that the Lenape ever lived in longhouses, either within large palisaded villages or anywhere else (cf. Becker 1993b). Yet in 1968, when I began to study the people then commonly called "Delaware" I found that only three anthropologists recognized that these people had been foragers and not village-based "horticulturalists": William MacLeod (1922), Mark R. Harrington (1938; also 1963), and Carol Barnes (1968). These scholars had to contend with journalistic accounts that merged all the peoples of the Delaware Valley and Bay area as "Delaware" (Weslager 1972). This fiction also applied the term "Delaware" to other cultures far from the lower Delaware Valley, all said to have lived in longhouses within large, maize dependent palisaded villages with large populations. Some archaeologists active during the mid-twentieth century later became the strongest proponents of the "horticultural" model, a model still commonly found in CRM reports filed in this region (see Milner et al. 2001:9).

Daniel G. Brinton's interest in Native languages commonly focused on the Lenâpé (1888), including efforts to revive the Native pronunciation of their name (Leh-NAH-peh). In the Lenape homeland, where those people had been gone for nearly 150 years when Brinton wrote, the word itself had become popularly pronounced as "LEN-uh-pee." The degree to which fundamental information about these people had been lost is demonstrated by this pronunciation of their Native self-identifier even in their aboriginal region, and the replacement of it with the English term "Delaware." It continued to be used as a collective term for an undifferentiated aggregate of Native Algonquian speaking peoples (Goddard 1978), including cultures resident far beyond the Delaware Valley. Since the 1970s, when the documents revealing the ethnohistoric complexity in the Middle Atlantic region began to be mined, the distinct lifestyles of these multiple cultures have become better recognized. Yet for basic information on Native cultures, anthropologists trained in the 1960s and 1970s turned to volume 15 of the *Handbook* (Trigger 1978), even though those entries were out of date at publication.

POPULATION DYNAMICS
AND CULTURE HISTORY

Coupled with the idea of the "Delaware as village dwelling horticultural-ists" is the disease decimation theory used to account for the extremely low population densities of Native American peoples in the Middle Atlantic and elsewhere. Many scholars cannot conceptualize population dynamics within a foraging society, or that a foraging culture gener-ally includes no more than five hundred individuals dispersed over an extremely large territory. Foragers generally operate in small groups, generally called bands, averaging about twenty-five persons each. This idea is incomprehensible to the ethnocentrically challenged. The Esopus, Lenopi, Lenape, and Hudson River tribes such as the Waping each num-bered fewer than five hundred members before Contact (Becker 1989, also 1988). In 1490, what is now the Commonwealth of Pennsylvania had a total Native population of six or seven thousand individuals, based on all recent archaeological evidence. Most of these peoples were village dwell-ing peoples living far from the coast. Perhaps a high estimate might be ten thousand inhabitants, although even doubling this would not alter its importance to understanding Native cultural dynamics. A theorized mass die-off of Native peoples helps naïve scholars reconcile why there were so few people in the Middle Atlantic area and how Europeans could effort-lessly invade a supposedly "depopulated and culturally disorganized" region. This model ignores the complex interactions among native and immigrant powers over more than 250 years (1500–1750), during which the tribal peoples of the Middle Atlantic realm only gradually lost power in their respective territories.

Many contemporary historians continue to use the term "Delaware" for a wide range of Native peoples of the past, or simply substitute the term "Lenape" for any peoples listed in the documents as "Delaware." The use of the term "Delaware" for the many distinct cultures known by the Eu-ropean colonists was reinforced in the popular literature by the extensive works of the amateur historian C. A. Weslager. Weslager began what he called his "journalistic" career in association with the scholar Leon De Valinger (1941), one of the first to examine Indian land sales as sources of important ethnographic evidence. Weslager also worked briefly with A. R. Dunlap (Dunlap and Weslager 1950) before returning to the more profitable writing of popular history (Weslager 1943, 1953a, 1953b, 1972). His accounts, which put into print many useful parts of the documentary record, invariably repeated nineteenth-century ideas regarding "Dela-ware" settlement pattern and social organization (Weslager 1953b). The continued use of the term "Delaware" among anthropologists (cf. Becker 1976) was largely a function of Goddard's linguistically oriented research.

Based on data from the various Algonquian languages, and perhaps the popular literature, Goddard (1990, 1994, also 1978) lumped Delawarean-speaking peoples into a single cultural unit. A history of the Algonquian languages on the order of detail provided by Julian (2010) for the Iroquoian languages would be useful.

A. F. C. WALLACE: A BIOGRAPHY OF TEEDYUSCUNG AND THE BEGINNINGS OF MODERN ETHNOHISTORY

Of considerable importance to the development of the ethnohistorical approach in the Middle Atlantic is Anthony F. C. Wallace's (1949) biographical account of a Native player named Teedyuscung, who was born about 1709 and died on April 19, 1763 (Becker 1987, 1992).

Wallace's narrative not only revealed the vast extent of the documentary record, but also demonstrated that the Native peoples were far from passive victims of "colonization" even after 1750. Following in the tradition of historical research employed by his father, Paul A. W. Wallace (1946, 1961), the young Wallace's view of Teedyuscung is curiously lacking in basic concerns of anthropology such as cultural dynamics and kinship. Documents revealing Teedyuscung's birth and kinship, and thus his cultural interactions as a Lenopi ("Jersey"), were not identified until many years later (Becker 1987, 1988a, 1992). Nevertheless, the information that Wallace extracted led him to question the popular historical view that the many bands of each of the tribes of the Delaware Valley region belonged to a single "culture," called "Delaware." The specific tribal boundaries that can be extracted from an overview of the documentary record (land sales, treaty groups) have revealed a great deal about these people that was not considered in 1949.

Wallace's biography of Teedyuscung predated Philip Barbour's biography of Pocahontas (1970) by more than twenty years but follows in the path of John Papunhank (1823). Unlike the deculturated historical studies within which the Pocahontas biography industry has blossomed (see Gallivan 2003), other significant anthropological studies of individual natives in the Middle Atlantic region began to emerge some forty years after Wallace set the stage (McCartney 1989, Becker 1987, 1998, 2011d). Wallace's biography also predated the 1954 origin of the journal *Ethnohistory*. This journal began at a gathering focused on the Ohio Valley, the area into which several groups of Natives from various parts of the Middle Atlantic zone had begun to move after the 1650s. The huge collections of documents from the Ohio Valley provide a remarkable database that had attracted little interest from anthropologists concerned with the aboriginal tribal groups that were resident there, or with those groups migrating into that region from New York, New Jersey, and Pennsylvania. Studies of this region during this period still remain the purview of historians (e.g., Grimes 2013).

One of the first anthropologists to research Indians who entered the Ohio Valley after 1600 was William W. Newcomb. His 1956 study of the culture and acculturation of "the Delaware Indians," like studies by his imitators (e.g., Weslager 1972, Thurman 1973) failed to review the earliest documents or to establish a basic chronology. Original Native boundaries, territories, or the processes of culture change influencing the several groups who later became identified as "Delaware" were not addressed. When Newcomb published his "Delaware Indians" (1956), Wallace's review of his work (1957) pointed out Newcomb's failure to recognize the braggadocio in Teedyuscung's claims to be a leader of all the "Delaware." More specifically Wallace was the first to question when "the numerous autonomous 'Delawaran' communities [now recognized as Lenape, Lenopi, etc.] ever consolidated into a politically definable Delaware tribe." Newcomb (1956:84) had placed a process of "tribal formation" in the early eighteenth century, while Wallace points out (1957) that even when these several peoples were in residential proximity along the White River (now Indiana, ca. 1770–1800+), various groups only "claimed to be representatives of the political unification of the Delawares." Wallace points out that in the late 1700s various tribal groups supported impermanent alliances and were far from being a single polity. Wallace recognized that the several tribes identified by outsiders as "Delaware" rarely interacted, let alone operated in a united manner.

The dynamics of kinship within Teedyuscung's band, and within the other Lenopi bands originally resident south of the Raritan River in New Jersey, now can be traced in an extensive genealogy. The Lenopi people commonly had been referred to by another European term—"Jerseys"—to distinguish them from the closely homonymous Lenape. This is best revealed in the treaties of 1756 and 1758 in which the Lenopi are distinguished as a distinct culture (Becker 2008). Research on the many bands of Lenopi (e.g., Becker 1998, 2012b) has revealed a great deal about their territories, varied foraging strategies, and multiple complex adaptations to European colonization (Becker 2011a).

NATIVES AND NEWCOMER NATIVES IN PENNSYLVANIA: WILLIAM HUNTER

After becoming the "historian" for the Pennsylvania Historical and Museum Commission in 1945, William Albert Hunter (1908–1985) gathered masses of information for his impressive *Forts of the Pennsylvania*

Frontier, 1753–1758 (1960). In the course of doing deep research in the archives, and while reading through the extensive *Colonial Records of Pennsylvania* and the many series of volumes that compose the *Pennsylvania Archives* (cf. Witthoft and Hunter 1955), Hunter recognized how extensively the names of individual Indians had been recorded. Hunter recognized that biographies could be written for many if not most of these Natives, a discovery that may have influenced Wallace's research. Hunter also used his German language skills to review documents from the extremely important Moravian Archives. From their base in the Forks of Delaware, the Moravian missionaries provide documentation regarding those "Jerseys" (now recognized as "Lenopi") who began to enter this buffer zone in 1733–1734, less than a decade before the Moravians first arrived. The Moravians' impressive written documentation for every individual, including Native converts who provided life histories, is particularly important in establishing Lenopi genealogies (Hunter 1974).

Hunter also observed that the names of Lenape who appeared on documents such as land sales, to which they affixed their marks (see Kent 1979), were in order of their status ranking. This reflects an egalitarian social organization based on membership in bands where status is based on age, gender, and ephemeral personal characteristics. The position of a name in a list of vendors to a piece of land, signed by all the adult males present, and occasionally a female, reflects status within the band. Young men, perhaps fifteen to eighteen years of age or younger, were the last to sign. Through time, the position of an individual's name on these signatory lists shifted as their status increased. The more able elders in these bands might eventually reach the top of a later list, while some individuals never became the senior member of their band.

LAND SALES AND OTHER DOCUMENTS: ENTER ALDEN T. VAUGHAN

The process of extracting data from the archives of each state, and from Native land sale records, remains an approach not commonly employed. By 1970, through searching for details on documents cited by Wallace for Teedyuscung's biography, I had come across the transcripts of early Native land sales in Pennsylvania. I remained ignorant of parallel land sales documents from most of the other colonies, believing that early explorers simply claimed land that they wanted! This popular school child's view goes along with the idea that Native peoples were biologically inferior and powerless to resist Europeans. The detailed histories of each tribe that belie this fantasy were still far in the future.

During the 1970s the insight of Alden T. Vaughan led him to launch a project to publish relevant Native documents from each colony, creating an essential set of volumes entitled "Early American Indian Documents: Treaties and Laws, 1607–1789." The first of these to emerge includes documents from colonial Pennsylvania, including Delaware, which had begun as Pennsylvania's three "lower" counties (Kent 1979). This superlative volume omits a series of specious land sales that I call "the Delaware Deeds" (Becker 1998:44–45, 50–51, 65–68). These are, in effect, fraudulent land "sales" made by a few Sekonese as well as the Lenopi named Mehoxy. The tracts sold all are in the Bombay Hook buffer zone that separated Lenape from Sekonese territory. Kent recognized that something was amiss with these land "sales" and chose to omit them from his compilation. We now have the anthropological information enabling us to decode the problems associated with these transactions, and to recognize other specious sales of land in buffer zones that actually had no Native owners. Regions between areas used and held by specific tribes were literally "no-man's-lands."

Vaughan's volume editors often have difficulties in decoding the cultural meanings of their target texts, but these twenty volumes provide an essential source of information for anyone undertaking ethnohistoric studies in these areas. While many of the volumes in Vaughan's series are centered on documents from specific colonies, others cover regions such as the Middle Atlantic area (Vaughan and Rosen 2004). Although Native territories are not necessarily bounded in the same way as modern state borders, Vaughan commonly uses these geographic markers.

NEW JERSEY: THE LENOPI, ESOPUS, AND "NEWCOMERS"

Prior to 1950, at least three New Jersey scholars had recognized that the colonial records in that state clearly delineated the separate identity of distinct Native tribes foraging within the state borders (see in Becker 2008, also 2012c). The Esopus, north of the Raritan River, and immigrant Raritan and Waping still require further study (Becker 2016a). Graymont's (1985) collation of the Indian documents from New York and New Jersey, colonies once under a single governor, does not distinguish the Lenopi from their northern neighbors, or from any of the New York tribes (cf. Graymont 2001:273). The descendants of the Esopus and various immigrant groups resident in northeastern New Jersey are the peoples who became identified as "Munsee" when numbers of them moved into the upland regions in the northwestern parts of the colony (but, cf. Grumet 2009).

In New Jersey, south of the Raritan River, the Lenopi made specific adaptations to local ecologies (e.g., Becker 1998, 2011d). The northern

Lenopi groups, including Teedyuscung's band, migrated into Pennsylvania during the years 1733–1734 to take advantage of resources in a newly available buffer zone (Becker 1992a). Some members of the central Lenopi bands collected at Brotherton after 1758, but most left for New York in 1802 (Becker 2011d). The southern, or Delaware Bay area Lenopi, bands sold their lands in the late 1600s, often using Mehoxy of the Cohansey band as an intermediary (Becker 1998, 2012b). The southern bands then shifted their foraging activities into the central parts of the state. These and other Lenopi families remained in the back country pursuing traditional lifeways and retaining their language beyond the 1830s, and the essence of their culture throughout the nineteenth century. Their descendants may be found among families still making a living from fishing and hunting, retaining a remarkable cultural continuity despite the loss of language and other explicit aspects of culture.

LONG ISLAND AND NEW ENGLAND

In volume 15 of the *Handbook*, Bert Salwen (1978) was assigned the "Early Period" of the Indians of southern New England and Long Island. He recognized the specific areas of most of the tribal entities, but describes their "culture" as a single, homogeneous entity. Much of the rationale seems to derive from close linguistic relationships, parallel to those used to define "Delaware" (cf. Bragdon 2009). Bert Salwen's (1978) review of the tribes of southern New England and Long Island for the *Handbook*, as Christian Feest's review of the Nanticoke (see above), provided important early indications of the range of cultural diversity within the Middle Atlantic region at a time when most anthropologists were still lumping groups into linguistic clusters (Goddard 1978). Salwen's recognition of the cultural diversity in the areas of his study was carried forward by the work of Goddard and Bragdon (1988), and also by Wojciechowski (1992). A popular volume by Bragdon (1996, reissued 2009) aims at a wider market area.

Laura Conkey was lead author for the chapters on the Indians of southern New England and Long Island during the "Late Period" (Conkey et al. 1978). Conkey, then a research assistant to editor Sturtevant, was only peripherally concerned with this project and went on to complete a doctorate in geosciences at Arizona in 1982. The number of scholars working with southern New England tribes is now far larger, but those cultures lie beyond the purview of this Middle Atlantic study. The early elision of data on the Long Island tribes soon was superseded by extensive documentary research by Gaynell Stone (1983) and her colleagues, and later by John Strong's important and detailed investigations (1996, 2001). Their significant efforts, however, have done little to dissuade popular authors and some archaeologists from considering all of southeastern New York and Long Island as part of the "Delaware" territory, recently re-christened as "Lenape." The borrowing of a well-documented name from the tribe in southeastern Pennsylvania rather than from local records reveals the extent to which the colonial documents continue to be ignored.

FORAGERS IN NEW YORK

The many tribes native to New York State included Iroquoian horticulturalists in the interior and Algonquian-speaking foragers resident along the Hudson River (called the North River by the Dutch) and its estuary (e.g., Starna 2013). These foraging tribes collectively were identified as the River Indians, the same term collectively used during the Dutch period for the tribes along the Delaware (South) River. Both groups included only foraging tribes, being similar only in their significant dependence on riverine and/or maritime resources. The individual tribes of the lower Hudson River Valley and region surrounding the mouth of that river are only now gaining attention, and their specific local foraging strategies are becoming better known.

Not surprisingly, the power, dynamics, and central location of the more numerous Five Nations Iroquois proved to be the epicenter for colonial-native interactions throughout the Northeast. The impressive geopolitical force of this confederacy, united only by a non-aggression "treaty," can be seen in the impressive series of documents revealing interactions between them and their Native neighbors, both near and far (Graymont 1985, 1996; Vaughan and Rosen 2004).

The Iroquoian villagers of New York as well as central Pennsylvania were all low-level horticulturalists, or perhaps egalitarian foragers using supplemental horticulture. They occupied relatively poor resource zones and used economic systems adjusted to survival in areas of relative food scarcity. These inland regions may be compared with the coastal and river dwelling Algonquians at the eastern margins of Iroquoia who had available abundant riverine and/or marine resources. The Five Nations villagers have been documented in considerable detail, with some significant volumes emerging in recent years (Jordan 2008, Wallace 2012).

ETHNOHISTORY: APPROACHES
AND POSSIBILITIES

One of the principal achievements of ethnohistoric research, in the Middle Atlantic and in general, is the recognition of the varied histories of tribal cultures interacting with a series of competing European business ventures that led to the colonization process. Early economic ventures from various European polities to the Americas were extremely small in scale, and those from the same region commonly were uncoordinated, if not disjointed (Worsley 2003). Private ventures, such as the Dutch West India Company, often had the greatest success. The fragility of these trade enterprises is perhaps best seen in the short-lived early Dutch whaling station in southern Delaware and the Swedish "colony" on the Delaware, enabling foraging societies with only a few hundred members to form alliances that offered countering forces to these colonial efforts.

The many documents from the Swedish colony that have been published in *The New York Colonial Documents* (e.g., Fernow 1877, O'Callaghan 1848) provide an important entry to the study of the Natives with whom the immigrant entrepreneurs interacted (cf. Becker 1979c). Popular efforts to understand the Natives from a colonial point of view (Johnson 1911, Weslager 1987, 1988) generally ignore cultural dynamics as seen from a Native perspective (e.g., Dahlgren and Norman 1988, Craig 2006, cf. Becker 1989).

After forty-five years of conducting "deep ethnography" in the archives, reading early documents relating to the Lenape and their immediate neighbors, I recognize those studies based on very limited evidence, and resulting interpretations that are anthropologically naïve. An awareness of culture theory is what provides ethnohistorians with a singular advantage in reconstructing the Native past. This viewpoint enables us to recognize that the members of the Sekonese chiefdom in central Delaware remained within their homeland and merged into the multiple ethnic groups or immigrant traditions that came to surround them. By the middle of the nineteenth century, these people were no longer identifiable as a separate Native American culture, or as Natives at all. Popular histories, ignoring the documents, have simply merged the Sekonese into the "Delaware" and repeat the belief that they were "forced off their land." The non-Native term "Delaware," which has become used by the descendants of a number of distinct tribal entities, remains "good enough" for those for whom the basic workings of anthropology are simply beyond their interest.

Archaeologists working in the Middle Atlantic realm often attempt to generate cultural models of pre-1500 societies solely based on the archaeological record. Borrowing from faulty histories (Lenape "villages") and other popular ideas about past cultures has constrained researchers by limiting their access to valid models that can be deduced from the historical record. When efforts are made to construct Late Woodland land-use patterns using only the archaeological evidence (e.g., Walwer and Pagoulatos 1990) the results are far different from those revealed by the documents (Becker 1992a; 1998, 2012b; 2011d).

DISCUSSION AND CONCLUSIONS

The ethnohistoric record of the Middle Atlantic realm is largely dependent on the documents that record behaviors and interactions with the Native populations made by a few members of literate societies. Many early "narrations" were published not by primary observers, but by scribes to whom "tales" or adventures were related after the fact, often decades after the events took place. Determining the accuracy of all these records is part of the academic process, but the primary documents must be consulted. Terminology and definitions are always issues in any scholarly enterprise, and often are subject to the "fashion" of the times. We need to be particularly careful in our use of terms and to make clear the definitions that often are in our heads but not spelled out for our readers.

Oral tradition, or elements of cultural history that are maintained by a people through rote learning and repetition of a narrative, have impressive potential for preserving knowledge. Not every culture sustains such an "oral literature." Ethnohistorians are particularly interested in oral accounts (cf. Brown 1973, Hantman 2005), but most statements said to represent the survival of Native traditions in the Middle Atlantic realm cannot be agreed upon even by members of the same claimant group. Recall of historical rituals may be precise, but transmission of these observations has yet to be tested. Examples are completely absent from *Ethnohistory* and similar journals, reflecting an absence of testable possibilities. Folktales often provide a strong surviving "literature" from the past (e.g., Beauchamp 1888). As with oral traditions, no folktales have been verified to survive as part of any cultural entity anywhere in the Middle Atlantic region. Even the "recorded versions" of early tales reveal deterioration in most aspects of folktales after 1850 (e.g., Adams 1997; cf. Becker 2000).

The term "Contact Period," long the subject of debate, has largely been replaced by terms such as "proto-historic" or "historic." The many and widely diverse cultures encountered by Europeans are generally held to have been operating with some variation of a "Late Woodland" tradition. This includes the use of bow and arrow, but each developed as a strongly localized system of resource extraction. The extent to which the many Late Woodland cultures were altered by interaction with Europeans also is a matter of considerable debate. The documents relating to trade and land sales indicate that all the Natives successfully maintained traditional cultures, some of them for hundreds of years. They all wanted cloth above all other trade goods (Becker 2005, also 2010c), but soon came to desire an enormous range of "modern" materials. The variety of goods that Natives wanted became as impressive as the basic inventory stocked at general stores of a much later date. In exchange the Natives provided peltry and a wide range of other goods and services (Becker 2014b). While trade goods vastly altered some aspects of Native material cultures in a relatively short period of time, the essence of each cultural system—those implicit designs for living—survived much longer than can be easily detected through archaeology (cf. Rubertone 2000). Changes in material culture, so evident in the archaeological record, are a poor indication of changes in the values and mores among each of these Native peoples.

Seventeenth-century documents directly relating to each of the many tribal groups in the Middle Atlantic region reveal an impressive congruence between each Native culture as revealed in the historical records and the archaeology of the Late Woodland period. The documents confirm that each of the now-known social entities sustained a unique cultural pattern, one that also can be detected in the archaeological record (Becker 2016b). The evidence from the documents reveals that local ecologies can be exploited in ways that enable cultural differences to allow maximum resource extraction. The particularly successful combination of plow agriculture and animal husbandry that had been perfected on other continents, however, was not operant in the Americas. These complex agrarian systems, over the course of centuries, sustained populations that inexorably came to dominate and largely absorb the cultures of the Middle Atlantic region.

Examination of the rich collections of documents archived throughout the Middle Atlantic provides a means by which individual tribal entities can be delineated and their specific histories traced. These documents enable us to make better estimates of population size, and to understand the significance of possible alliances between Native groups and immigrant colonists. An increased understanding of tribal territories, and the extent and functions of buffer zones, further aids in understanding population dynamics. As scholars recognize the great extent of the documentary evidence, and pursue records specific to the individual tribal entities only recently delineated, new vectors open for understanding the Native past. Our ability to reconstruct the cultural history of each tribe, and the complex dynamics among all of them, and after A.D. 1500 with European immigrants, becomes increasingly easy.

ACKNOWLEDGMENTS

My sincere thanks are due the editors for their kind invitation to contribute to this volume. Thanks are due to Martha McCartney for sharing data and for her many important suggestions, and to Helen Rountree and E. Randolph Turner III for data on early ethnohistorians in Virginia. Thanks are due to Jonathon Erlen, Jonathan Friedman, Ives Goddard, Jeffrey L. Hantman, Bernard K. Means, and Jennifer J. Reynolds for their help in various matters. Thanks also are due Stephen Marvin, Traci Meloy, and the entire staff of the Francis Harvey Greene Library of West Chester University for their continued support of this research. Thanks also are due to the entire staff in Academic Computing Services, West Chester University, for their efforts on my behalf. The ideas expressed here as well as any errors of interpretation or presentation, of course, are solely the responsibility of the author.

REFERENCES CITED

Aborigines' Committee, The
   1844   Some Account of the Conduct of the Religious Society of Friends To-
          wards the Indian Tribes in the Settlement of the Colonies of East and
          West Jersey and Pennsylvania; with a Brief Narrative. London: Edward
          Marsh for the London Yearly Meeting (Society of Friends).

Adams, Richard C.
   1997   *Legends of the Delaware Indians and Picture Writing.* Syracuse: Syracuse
          University Press.

Barbour, Philip L.
   1970   *Pocahontas and Her World; a Chronicle of America's First Settlement on Which
          is Related the Story of the Indians and the Englishmen, Particularly Captain
          John Smith, Captain Samuel Argall, and Master John Rolfe.* Boston: Hough-
          ton Mifflin.

Barnes, Carol
   1968   Subsistence and Society of the Delaware Indians: 1600 A. D. *Bulletin of the
          Philadelphia Anthropological Society* 20 (1):15–29.

Beauchamp, William M.
   1888   Onondaga Tales. *Journal of American Folklore* 1 (1):44–48

Becker, Marshall Joseph
   1976   The Okehocking: A Remnant Band of Delaware Indians in Chester
          County, Pennsylvania during the Colonial Period. *Pennsylvania Archae-
          ologist* 46:25–63.
   1979a Priests, Peasants and Ceremonial Centers: The Intellectual History of a
          Model. In *Maya Archaeology and Ethnohistory*, edited by Norman Ham-
          mond and Gordon R. Willey, pp. 3–20. University of Texas Press, Austin.
   1979b *Theories of Ancient Maya Social Structure: Priests, Peasants, and Ceremo-
          nial Centers in Historical Perspective. Katunob*: Occasional publications
          in Mesoamerican Anthropology, No. 12, Greeley, Colorado. (Reissued
          in 1984 as Number 53 in the Occasional Publications in Anthropology
          [Ethnology Series], Museum of Anthropology, University of Northern
          Colorado.)

1979c Ethnohistory and Archaeology in Search of the Printzhof, the 17th Cen-
       tury Residence of Swedish Colonial Governor Johan Printz. *Ethnohistory*
       26 (1):15–44.
1983a The Boundary Between the Lenape and the Munsee: The Forks of Dela-
       ware as a Buffer Zone. *Man in the Northeast* 26:1–20.
1983b An Overview of Cultural Diversity in the Lower Delaware River Valley:
       An Ethnohistorical Perspective. In *Proceedings of the 1983 Middle Atlantic
       Archaeological Conference*, pp. 67–79. Rehoboth Beach, DE.
1984a The Lenape Bands Prior to 1740: The Identification of Boundaries and
       Processes of Change Leading to the Formation of the "Delawares." In *The
       Lenape Indian: A Symposium*, edited by H. C. Kraft, pp. 19–32. Archaeo-
       logical Research Center Publication Number 7, Seton Hall University.
1984b Lenape Land Sales, Treaties, and Wampum Belts. *Pennsylvania Magazine
       of History and Biography* 108:351–356.
1986a The Okehocking Band of Lenape: Cultural Continuities and Accommoda-
       tions in Southeastern Pennsylvania. In *Strategies for Survival: American In-
       dians in the Eastern United States*, edited by Frank W. Porter III, pp. 43–83.
       Westport, CT: Greenwood Press.
1986b Cultural Diversity in the Lower Delaware River Valley, 1550–1750: An
       Ethnohistorical Perspective. In *Late Woodland Cultures of the Middle Atlan-
       tic Region*, edited by Jay F. Custer, pp. 90–101. Newark, DE: University of
       Delaware Press.
1987   *The Moravian Mission in the Forks of the Delaware: Reconstructing the Migra-
       tion and Settlement Patterns of the Jersey Lenape during the Eighteenth Cen-
       tury through Documents in the Moravian Archives.* Unitas Fratrum. Special
       Issue: "The American Indians and the Moravians," 21/22:83–172.
1988a Native Settlements in the Forks of Delaware, Pennsylvania in the
       18th Century: Archaeological Implications. *Pennsylvania Archaeologist*
       58(1):43–60.
1988b A Summary of Lenape Socio-Political Organization and Settlement Pat-
       tern at the Time of European Contact: The evidence for Collecting Bands.
       Journal of Middle Atlantic Archaeology 4:79–83.
1989a Lenape Population at the Time of European Contact: Estimating Native
       Numbers in the Lower Delaware Valley. In, "Symposium on the Demo-
       graphic History of the Philadelphia Region, 1600–1860," edited by Susan
       E. Klepp. *Proceedings of the American Philosophical Society* 133(2):112–22.
1989b Review of, The Rise and Fall of New Sweden: Governor Johan Risingh's
       Journal 1654–1655 in its Historical Context, by Stellan Dahlgren and
       Hans Norman (1988). *Pennsylvania Archaeologist* 59(2):100–101.
1990   Hannah Freeman: An Eighteenth-Century Lenape Living and Working
       Among Colonial Farmers. *Pennsylvania Magazine of History and Biography*
       114:249–69.
1992a Teedyuscung's Youth and Hereditary Land Rights in New Jersey: The
       Identification of the Unalachtigo. *Bulletin of the Archaeological Society of
       New Jersey* 47:37–60.
1992b Lenape Clothing of the Early 19th Century as Indicated by Artifacts in
       the Ethnographic Collections of the Historical Museum of the University

of Lund, Sweden. Meddelanden från Lunds universitets historiska museum. Papers of the Archaeological Institute (1991/1992): NS 9:131–54.

1992c The Lenape of the Historic Contact Period. In *The Buried Past: An Archaeological History of Philadelphia,* edited by John L. Cotter, Daniel G. Roberts, and Michael Parrington, pp. 17–29. Philadelphia: University of Pennsylvania Press.

1993a Connecticut Origins for Some Native Americans in New Jersey During the Early Historic Period: Strategies for the Use of Native American Names in Research. *Bulletin of the Archaeological Society of New Jersey* 48:62–64.

1993b Lenape Shelters: Possible Examples from the Contact Period. *Pennsylvania Archaeologist* 63(2):64–76.

1995 Lenape Maize Sales to the Swedish Colonists: Cultural Stability during the Early Colonial Period. In *New Sweden in America,* edited by Carol E. Hoffecker, Richard Waldron, Lorraine E. Williams, and Barbara E. Benson, pp. 121–36. Newark: University of Delaware Press.

1998 Mehoxy of the Cohansey Band of South Jersey Indians: His Life as a Reflection of Symbiotic Relations with Colonists in Southern New Jersey and the Lower Counties of Pennsylvania. *Bulletin of the Archaeological Society of New Jersey* 53:40–68.

2000 Review of, Legends of the Delaware Indians and Picture Writing (1997), edited by Richard C. Adams [and] The Mythology of Native North America (1998), by David Leeming and Jake Page. *Journal of American Folklore* 113:230–32.

2004 The Archaeology of Ethnicity: Can Historical Archaeology Extract the Ciconicin from the Melting Pot of Delaware? *SAA Archaeological Record* (The Archaeology of Ethnicity II) Volume 4(5):26–28.

2005 Matchcoats: Cultural Conservatism and Change. *Ethnohistory* 52(4):727–87.

2006a Anadromous Fish and the Lenape. *Pennsylvania Archaeologist* 76(2):28–40.

2006b Foragers in Southern New England: Correlating Social Systems, Maize Production and Wampum Use. *Bulletin of the Archaeological Society of Connecticut* 68:75–107.

2007a Unique Huron Ornamental Bands: Wampum Cuffs. *Material Culture Review* 66:59–67.

2007b Native Lives in New Jersey. *Bulletin of the Archaeological Society of New Jersey* 62:93–95.

2008 Lenopi, Or, What's in a Name? Interpreting the Evidence for Cultural Boundaries in the Lower Delaware Valley. *Bulletin of the Archaeological Society of New Jersey* 63:11–32.

2009 A Quaker Farmstead in the Delaware Valley: Research at the Taylor Burying Ground Site (36-CH-117) Revealing Changes in Settlement Patterns and Culture During the Agrarian-Industrial Transition. *Bulletin of the Archaeological Society of Delaware* 46 (New Series 2013):47–70.

2010a "Late Woodland" (CA. 1000–1740 CE) Foraging Patterns of the Lenape and Their Neighbors in the Delaware Valley. *Pennsylvania Archaeologist* 80(1):17–31.

2010b The Armewamus Band of New Jersey: Other Clues to Differences Between the Lenopi and the Lenape. *Pennsylvania Archaeologist* 80(2):61–72.

2010c Match Coats and the Military: Mass-Produced Clothing for Native Americans as Parallel Markets in the Seventeenth Century. *Textile History* 41, No. 1: Supplement (Textile History and the Military):153–81.

2010d Wampum Use in Southern New England: The Paradox of Bead Production without the Use of Political Belts. In *Nantucket and Other Native Places: The Legacy of Elizabeth Alden Little*, edited by Elizabeth S. Chilton and Mary Lynne Rainey, pp. 137–58. Albany, NY: SUNY Press.

2011a The Prinzhof (36DE3), A Swedish Colonial Site that was the First European Center of Government in Present Pennsylvania. *Bulletin of the Archaeological Society of Delaware* 43:1–34.

2011b Rockshelter Use during the "Late Woodland" Period in the Northeast: Increased Use as an Aspect of the Pelt Trade. *North American Archaeologist* 32(1):81–93.

2011c Lenape Culture History: The Transition of 1660 and its Implications for the Archaeology of the Final Phase of the Late Woodland Period. *Journal of Middle Atlantic Archaeology* 27:53–72.

2011d Jacob Skickett, Lenopi Elder: Preliminary Notes from Before 1750 to after 1802. *Pennsylvania Archaeologist* 81(2):65–76.

2012a Birdstones: New Inferences Based On Examples from the Area around Waverly, New York. The Bulletin. *Journal of the New York State Archaeological Association* 126:1–31.

2012b Mehoxy of the Cohansey Band of Lenopi: a 1684 Document that Offers Clues to the "Missing" Part of His Biography. *Bulletin of the Archaeological Society of Delaware* 44 (New Series, 2007):1–29.

2012c "Delaware" (I: 165–82) and "New Jersey" (II: 747–64) in, *Native America: A State-by-State Historical Encyclopedia* (3 volumes), edited by Daniel Murphree. Westport, CT: Greenwood Press/ ABC-CLIO.

2013 Review of, *On Records: Delaware Indians, Colonists, and the Media of History and Memory*, by Andrew Newman (2012). *Pennsylvania Magazine of History and Biography* 137(4):445–46.

2014a Ethnohistory of the Lower Delaware Valley: Addressing Myths in the Archaeological Interpretations of the Late Woodland and Contact Periods. *Journal of Middle Atlantic Archaeology* 30:41–54.

2014b Lenape ("Delaware") in the Early Colonial Economy: Cultural Interactions and the Slow Processes of Culture Change Before 1740. *Northeast Anthropology* 81–82:109–29.

2016a The Raritan Valley Buffer Zone: A Refuge Area for Some Wiechquaeskeck and other Native Americans During the 17th Century. *Bulletin of the Archaeological Society of Connecticut* 17:55–93.

2016b The Lenape and the Origins of Indian Trade Silver: Brooches from Southeastern Pennsylvania as Cultural Markers. In review, *Pennsylvania Archaeologist*.

Belknap, Jeremy, and Jedidiah Morse
1796 [1955] *Report on the Oneida, Stockbridge and Brotherton Indians. 1796.* Indian Notes and Monographs, No. 54. New York: Museum of the American Indian, Heye Foundation.

Binford, Lewis R.
1964   Archaeological and Ethnohistorical Investigation of Cultural Diversity and Progressive Development among Aboriginal Cultures of Coastal Virginia and North Carolina. Doctoral Dissertation in Anthropology, University of Michigan. Ann Arbor, MI.
1967   An Ethnohistory of the Nottoway, Meherrin and Weanock Indians of Southeastern Virginia. *Ethnohistory* 14(3/4):103–218.
1991   *Cultural Diversity among Aboriginal Cultures of Coastal Virginia and North Carolina.* New York: Garland Press.

Bishop, Charles A.
1970   The Emergence of Hunting Territories among the Northern Ojibwa. *Ethnology* 9(1):1–15.

Black, Glenn A.
1954   The Historic Indians of the Ohio Valley: An Archaeologist's View. *Ethnohistory* 1 (2):155–65.

Blanton, Dennis B., and Julia A. King (editors)
2004   *Indian and European Contact in Context: The Mid-Atlantic Region.* Gainesville: University Press of Florida.

Bragdon, Kathleen J.
2009   *Native People of Southern New England, 1500–1650* (reissue of 1996). Norman: University of Oklahoma Press.

Brinton, Daniel Garrison
1888   Lenâpé Conversations. *Journal of American Folklore* 1(1):37–43.

Brown, Jane Douglas Summers
1995   The Saponi Indians: Their Town and Fort of 1708–1714. *Archeological Society of Virginia Quarterly Bulletin* 28(1):41–47.

Brown, Marley III
1973   The Use of Oral and Documentary Sources in Historic Archaeology: Ethnohistory at Mott Farm. *Ethnohistory* 20(4):347–60.

Busby, Virginia Roche
2010   Transformation and Persistence: The Nanticoke Indians and Chicone Indian Town in the Context of European Contact and Colonization. Doctoral Dissertation in Anthropology, University of Virginia. Ann Arbor: UMI Dissertations Publishing.

Bushnell, David I., Jr.
1935   The Manahoac Tribes in Virginia, 1608. *Smithsonian Institution Miscellaneous Collections* 94(8). Publication 3337. Washington, DC: Government Printing Office.

Campisi, Jack, and William A. Starna
1995   On the Road to Canandaigua: The Treaty of 1794. *American Indian Quarterly* 19 (4):467–90.

Cissna, Paul B.
1986   The Piscataway Indians of Southern Maryland: An Ethnohistory from Pre-European Contact to the Present. Doctoral dissertation in Anthropology. American University: Washington, DC.

Conkey, Laura E., Ethel Boissevain, and Ives Goddard
1978   Indians of Southern New England and Long Island: Late Period. In *Handbook of North American Indians, Volume 15: Northeast*, edited by Bruce Trigger, pp. 177–89, Washington, DC: Smithsonian Institution.

Craig, Peter Stebbins (editor)
2006–2008   *Colonial Records of the Swedish Churches in Pennsylvania* (4 volumes). Philadelphia: Swedish Colonial Society.

Dahlgren, Stellan, and Hans Norman (editors)
1988   *The Rise and Fall of New Sweden: Governor Johan Risingh's Journal 1654– 1655 in its Historical Context*. Stockholm: Almqvist & Wiksell.

Dawdy, Shannon Lee
1995   The Meherrin's Secret History of the Dividing Line. *North Carolina Historical Review* 72(4):386–415.

Densmore, Christopher
2013   "Quakers Among the Haudenosaunee: A Projected Online Resources [sic] of Primary Documents [Swarthmore College]." Poster exhibited at the Conference on Iroquois Research. Cortland, NY (Hope Lake Lodge, 4–6 October).

Dent, Richard J., Jr.
1995   *Chesapeake Prehistory: Old Traditions, New Directions*. New York: Plenum Press.

De Valinger, Leon
1941   *Indian Land Sales in Delaware*. Wilmington, DE: Archaeological Society of Delaware.

Dunlap, Arthur R., and C. A. Weslager
1950   *Indian Place-Names in Delaware*. Wilmington: Archaeological Society of Delaware.
1961   Names and Places on an Unrecorded Indian Deed (1681). *Delaware History* IX(3):282–92.

Egle, William H. (editor)
1890   The Breviat in the Boundary Dispute between Pennsylvania and Maryland [1742]. *Pennsylvania Archives* Second Series, Volume XVI. Harrisburg: Edwin R. Meyers.

Fausz, J. Frederick
1985   Patterns of Anglo-Indian Aggression and Accommodation along the Mid-Atlantic Coast, 1584–1634. In *Cultures in Contact: The European Impact on Native Cultural Institutions in Eastern North America, A.D. 1000–*

1800, edited by W. W. Fitzhugh, pp. 225–68. Washington, DC: Smithsonian Institution.

Feest, Christian
   1978   Nanticoke and Neighboring Tribes, pp. 240–52. Virginia Algonquians, pp. 253–70. North Carolina Algonquians, pp. 271–81. In *Handbook of North American Indians, Volume 15: Northeast*, edited by Bruce Trigger. Washington, DC: Smithsonian Institution.

Fernow, Bertold (editor)
   1877   *Documents Relative to the Colonial History of the State of New-York. Volume XII: Documents relating to the History of the Dutch and Swedish Settlements on the Delaware River*. Albany: Argus Company.

Fitting, James E. and Charles E. Cleland
   1969   Late Prehistoric Settlement Patterns in the Upper Great Lakes. *Ethnohistory* 16(4): 289–302.

Friends, Society of
   1840   *The Case of the Seneca Indians in the State of New York, Illustrated by Facts*. Philadelphia: Merrihew and Thompson.

Gallivan, Martin D.
   2003   *James River Chiefdoms: the Rise of Social Inequality in the Chesapeake*. Lincoln: University of Nebraska Press.
   2011   Powhatan's Werowocomoco: Constructing Place, Polity, and Personhood in the Chesapeake, C.E. 1200–C.E. 1609. *American Anthropologist* 109(1) 85–100.

Gilkison, J. P.
   1885   Report of the Visiting Superintendent. Page 2 in, *Annual Report* of the Department of Indian Affairs [Dominion of Canada] for the Year Ended 31st December, 1884. Ottawa: Maclean, Roger & Company.

Gleach, Frederic W.
   1997   *Powhatan's World and Colonial Virginia: A Conflict of Cultures*. Lincoln: University of Nebraska Press.

Goddard, Ives
   1978   Delaware. In, *Handbook of North American Indians, Volume 15: Northeast*, edited by Bruce Trigger, pp. 213–39. Washington, DC: Smithsonian Institution.
   1990   Algonquian Linguistic Change and Reconstruction. In *Linguistic Change and Reconstruction Methodology*, edited by Philip Baldi, pp. 99–114. Berlin: Walter de Gruyter.
   1994   The West-to-East Cline in Algonquian Dialectology. In, *Actes du Vinct-Cinquième Congrès des Algonquinistes*, edited by William Cowan, pp. 187–211. Ottawa: Carleton University.

Goddard, Ives, and Kathleen J. Bragdon
   1988   *Native Writings in Massachusett* (2 volumes). Philadelphia: American Philosophical Society.

Graver, Sally M.
2005　Dental Health Decline in the Chesapeake Bay, Virginia: The Role of European Contact and Multiple Stressors. *Dental Anthropology* 18(1):12–21.

Graymont, Barbara (editor)
1985　*Early American Indian Documents: Treaties and Laws, 1607–1789*. General editor, Alden T. Vaughan. Volume VII: *New York and New Jersey Treaties, 1609–1682*. Frederick, MD: University Publications of America.
1996　*Early American Indian Documents: Treaties and Laws, 1607–1789*. General editor, Alden T. Vaughan. Volume IX: *New York and New Jersey Treaties, 1714–1753*. Bethesda, MD: University Publications of America.
2001　*Early American Indian Documents: Treaties and Laws, 1607–1789*. General editor, Alden T. Vaughan. Volume X: *New York and New Jersey Treaties, 1754–1775*. Bethesda, MD: University Publications of America.

Griffin, James B.
1942　On the Historic Location of the Tutelo and the Mohetan in the Ohio Valley. *American Anthropologist* 44:275–81.

Grimes, Richard S.
2013　We "Now Have Taken up the Hatchet against Them": Braddock's Defeat and the Martial Liberation of the Western Delawares. *Pennsylvania Magazine of History and Biography* 137(3):227–59.

Grumet, Robert S.
2009　*Munsee Indians: A History*. Norman: University of Oklahoma Press.

Hale, Horatio
1883　The Tutelo Tribe and Language. *Proceedings of the American Philosophical Society* 24(114):1–47 [Philadelphia].

Hall, Clayton Colman (editor)
1915　Archives of Maryland, Volume 35: *Proceedings and Acts of the General Assembly* (14)1724–26. Baltimore, MD: Maryland Historical Society.

Hantman, Jeffrey L.
1990　Between Powhatan and Quirank: Reconstructing Monacan Culture and History in the Context of Jamestown. *American Anthropologist* 92:676–90.
1993　Powhatan's Relations with the Piedmont Monacans. In *Powhatan Foreign Relations, 1500–1722*, edited by H. Rountree, pp. 94–111. Charlottesville: University Press of Virginia.
2001　Monacan archaeology in the Virginia Interior, A. D. 1400–1700. In *Societies in Eclipse: Archaeology of the Eastern Woodland Indians, A. D. 1400–1700*, edited by David S. Brose, C. W. Cowan, and R. C. Mainfort Jr., pp. 107–24. Washington, DC: Smithsonian Institution Press.
2005　Monacan Meditation: Individual and Regional Archaeologies in the Contemporary Politics of Indian Heritage. In *Places in Mind: Public Archaeology as Applied Anthropology*, edited by Paul A. Shackel and Hervé J. Chambers, pp. 19–34. New York: Routledge Press.

2010   Long Term History, Positionality, Contingency, Hybridity: Does Rethinking Indigenous History Reframe the Jamestown Colony? In *Across a Great Divide: Continuity and Change in Native North American Societies*, edited by Laura L. Scheiber and Mark D. Mitchell, pp. 42–60. Tucson: University of Arizona Press.

Harrington, Mark Raymond (1882–1971)
1938   *Dickon among the Lenape Indians.* Philadelphia: John C. Winston.
1963   *The Indians of New Jersey: Dickon among the Lenapes.* New Brunswick, NJ: Rutgers University Press.

Hart, John P., John P. Nass, and Bernard K. Means
2005   Monongahela Subsistence-settlement Change? *Midcontinental Journal of Archaeology* 30(2):327–65.

Howard, J. Smoker
2003   The Chronologiocal Placement of the Hershey Site on a Dynamic Socio-Cultural Landscape. *Pennsylvania Archaeologist* 73(2):16–30.

Hunter, William A.
1960   *Forts of the Pennsylvania Frontier, 1753–1758.* Harrisburg: Pennsylvania Historical and Museum Commission.
1974   Moses (Tunda) Tatamy, Delaware Indian Diplomatic. In *A Delaware Indian Symposium*, edited by Herbert C. Kraft, pp. 71–88. Harrisburg: Pennsylvania Historical and Museum Commission.

Jackson, Halliday
1830a   *Sketch of the Manners, Customs, Religion, and government of the Seneca Indians in 1800.* Philadelphia: Marcus T. C. Gould.
1830b   *Civilization of the Indian Natives.* Philadelphia: Marcus T. C. Gould.

Jacobs, Jaap
2009   *Colony of New Netherland—A Dutch Settlement in Seventeenth-Century America.* Ithaca: Cornell University Press.

Johnson, Amandus
1911   *The Swedish Settlements on the Delaware: Their History and Relation to the Indians, Dutch and English, 1638–1664: With an Account of the South, the New Sweden, and the American Companies, and the Efforts of Sweden to Regain the Colony* (2 volumes). Philadelphia: University of Pennsylvania.
1925   *Geographia Americae* with an Account of the Delaware Indians. Philadelphia: Swedish Colonial Society.

Johnson, William C.
2001   The Protohistoric Monongahela and the Case for an Iroquois Connection. In *Societies in Eclipse: Archaeology of the Eastern Woodlands Indians, A.D. 1400–1700*, edited by David S. Brose, Robert C. Mainfort Jr., and C. Wesley Cowan, pp, 67–82. Washington, DC: Smithsonian Institution Press.

Johnson, William C., and Bernard K. Means
  2009 "In Defense of James Pendergast: The Massawomeck-Monongahela-Antouhonoron Connection." Paper presented at the Iroquois Research Conference, Rensselaersville, New York (2–4 October).

Jordan, Kurt A.
  2008 The Seneca Restoration, 1715–1754: An Iroquois Local Political Economy. Gainesville: University Press of Florida.

Julian, Charles
  2010 A History of Iroquoian Languages. Doctoral Dissertation in Linguistics and Native American Studies, University of Manitoba. Ann Arbor, MI: UMI Dissertations Publishing.

Kent, Barry A.
  1984 *Susquehanna's Indians*. Harrisburg: Pennsylvania Historical and Museum Commission.

Kent, Donald H. (editor)
  1979 Early American Indian Documents: Treaties and Laws, 1607–1789. General editor, Alden T. Vaughan. Volume 1. *Pennsylvania and Delaware Treaties, 1629–1737*. University Publications of America, Washington, DC.

Lapham, Heather A.
  2004 "Their Complement of Deer-Skins and Furs": Changing Patterns of White-Tailed Deer Exploitation in the Seventeenth-Century Southern Chesapeake and Virginia Hinterlands. In *Indian and European Contact in Context: The Mid-Atlantic Region*, edited by Dennis B. Blanton and Julia A. King, pp. 172–92. Gainesville: University Press of Florida.

Lapham, Heather A., and William C. Johnson
  2002 Protohistoric Monongahela Trade Relations: Evidence from the Foley Farm Phase Glass Beads. *Archaeology of Eastern North America* 30:97–120.

Lewis, Clifford M., and Albert Loomie (editors)
  1953 *The Spanish Jesuit Mission in Virginia, 1570–1572*. Chapel Hill: University of North Carolina Press.

Little, Elizabeth
  2010 Limestone, Shell, and the Archaeological Visibility of Maize and Beans in New England: A Fertilizer Hypothesis. In, *Nantucket and Other Native Places: The Legacy of Elizabeth Alden Little*, edited by Elizabeth S. Chilton and Mary Lynne Rainey, pp. 181–200. Albany, NY: SUNY Press.

Loyer, Stacey Anna-Marie
  2013 Belonging and Belongings: Ethnographic Collecting and Indigenous Agency at the Six Nations of the Grand River. Doctoral Dissertation in Cultural Mediations, Carleton University: Ottawa, ON.

MacLeod, William Christie
  1922 The Family Hunting Territory and Lenape Political Organization. *American Anthropologist* 24:448–63.

Mahr, August C.
  1955a Semantic Analysis of Eighteenth-Century Delaware Indian Names for Medicinal Plants. *Ethnohistory* 2(1):11–28.
  1955b Eighteenth-Century Terminology of Delaware Indian Cultivation and Use of Maize: A Semantic Analysis. *Ethnohistory* 2(3):209–40.

Mansius, Mary Kale
  2011 Incidents of Violence and the Annual Movements of the Piscataway Indians. *Maryland Archeologist* 47(2):22–34.

McCartney, Martha W.
  1989 Cockacoeske, Queen of Pamunkey: Diplomat and Suzeraine. In, *Powhatan's Mantle: Indians in the Colonial Southeast*, edited by Peter H. Wood, Gregory A. Waselkov, and M. Thomas Hatley, pp. 243–66. Lincoln: University of Nebraska Press.
  2004 Last Refuge: Tribal Preserves in Eastern Virginia. In, *Indian and European Contact in Context: The Mid-Atlantic Region*, edited by Dennis B. Blanton and Julia A. King, pp. 222–43. Gainesville: University Press of Florida.

Means, Bernard K.
  2001 Circular Reasoning: Ring-Shaped Village Settlements in the Late Prehistoric Southwestern Pennsylvania and Beyond. *Journal of Middle Atlantic Archaeology* 17:109–31.
  2007 *Circular Villages of the Monongahela Tradition*. Tuscaloosa: The University of Alabama Press.

Merrell, James H.
  1979 Cultural Contacts among the Piscataway. *William and Mary Quarterly* 36(4):548–70.

Miller, Carl F.
  1957 Reevaluation of the Eastern Siouan Problem with Particular Emphasis on the Virginia Branches—The Occaneechi, the Saponi, and the Tutelo. Smithsonian Institution, *Bureau of American Ethnology, Bulletin 164*. Anthropological papers 52:115–211.

Milner, George R., David G. Anderson, and Marvin T. Smith
  2001 The Distribution of Eastern Woodland Peoples at the Prehistoric and Historic Interface. In *Societies in Eclipse: Archaeology of the Eastern Woodlands Indians, A.D. 1400–1700*, edited by David S. Brose, Robert C. Mainfort, and C. Wesley Cowan, pp. 9–18. Washington, DC: Smithsonian Institution Press.

Mooney, James
  1888 Myths of the Cherokee. *Journal of American Folklore* 2:97–108.
  1907 The Powhatan Confederacy, Past and Present. *American Anthropologist* 9(1):129–52.

Morrison, A. J.
  1921 The Virginia Indian Trade to 1673. *William and Mary Quarterly Historical Magazine* (Second Series) 1(4):217–36.

Mouer, L. D.
   1981   Powhatan and Monacan Regional Settlement Hierarchies: A Model of
          Relationship Between Social and Environmental Structure. *Quarterly Bul-*
          letin of the Archeological Society of Virginia 36(2):1–21.

Munoz, Samuel E., David J. Mladenoff, Sissel Schroeder, and John W. Williams
   2014   Defining the Spatial Patterns of Historical Land Use Associated with the
          Indigenous Societies of Eastern North America. *Journal of Biogeography*
          41(12). doi: 10.1111/jbi.12386.

Nash, Carole L.
   2009   Modeling Uplands: Landscape and Prehistoric Native American Settle-
          ment Archaeology in the Virginia Blue Ridge Foothills. Doctoral Disser-
          tation in Anthropology, Catholic University of America.
   n.d   Blind Tom, Foolish Jack, and the Never-Ending Contact Period of West-
          ern Virginia: Searching for the Historic Manahoac of the Piedmont and
          Blue Ridge. In *Upland Archaeology in the East Symposium* XI Archeological
          Society of Virginia.

Newcomb, William W.
   1956   *The Culture and Acculturation of the Delaware Indians.* Museum of An-
          thropology, University of Michigan. Anthropology Papers, No. 10. Ann
          Arbor, MI.

O'Callaghan, E. B.
   1848   *History of New Netherlands; or, New York Under the Dutch. Volume II.* New
          York: Bartlett and Welford.

Papunhank, John
   [1823] *John Papunhank, a Christian Indian of North America: A Narrative of Facts.*
          Dublin: Christopher Bentham, Eustace Street.

Pendergast, James F.
   1991   The Massawomeck: Raiders and Traders into the Chesapeake Bay in the
          Seventeenth Century. *Transactions of the American Philosophical Society,*
          Volume 81 Part 2. Independence Square, Philadelphia: The American
          Philosophical Society.

Penn, William
   1683 [1982] "A Letter from William Penn . . . [to] the Free Society of Traders."
          16 August 1683. Document 139, pages 442–60 in, *The Papers of William
          Penn. Volume II: 1680–1684,* edited by Richard S. Dunn and Mary Maples
          Dunn. Philadelphia: University of Pennsylvania Press.

Pollard, John Garland
   1894   *The Pamunkey Indians of Virginia.* Bureau of American Ethnology, Smith-
          sonian Institution. Washington, DC: Government Printing Office.

Potter, Stephen R.
   1993   *Commoners, Tribute, and Chiefs: The Development of Algonquian Culture in
          the Potomac Valley.* Charlottesville: University Press of Virginia.

Ricciardelli, Alex F.
    1963   The Adoption of White Agriculture by the Oneida Indians. *Ethnohistory* 10(4):309–28.

Robinson, W. Stitt (editor)
    1983a   *Early American Indian Documents: Treaties and Laws, 1607–1789.* General editor, Alden T. Vaughan. Volume IV: Virginia Treaties, 1607–1722. Frederick, MD: University Publications of America.
    1983b   *Early American Indian Documents: Treaties and Laws, 1607–1789.* General editor, Alden T. Vaughan. Volume V: Virginia Treaties, 1723–1775. Frederick, MD: University Publications of America.
    1987   *Early American Indian Documents: Treaties and Laws, 1607–1789.* General editor, Alden T. Vaughan. Volume VI: Maryland Treaties, 1632–1775. Frederick, MD: University Publications of America.

Rodning, Christopher B.
    2011   Cherokee Ethnogenesis in Southwestern North Carolina. In *The Archaeology of North Carolina: Three Archaeological Symposia*, edited by Charles R. Ewen, Thomas R. Whyte, and R. P. Stephen Davis Jr., pp. 16–1 to 16–18. North Carolina Archaeological Council Publication No. 30.

Rountree, Helen
    1975   Change Came Slowly: The Case of the Powhatan Indians of Virginia. *Journal of Ethnic Studies* 3(3):1–20.
    1987   The Termination and Dispersal of the Nottoway Indians of Virginia. *Virginia Magazine of History and Biography* 95:193–214.
    1989   *The Powhatan Indians of Virginia: Their Traditional Culture.* Norman: University of Oklahoma Press.
    1990   *Pocahontas's People: The Powhatan Indians of Virginia Through Four Centuries.* Norman: University of Oklahoma Press.
    1993   (editor) *Powhatan Foreign Relations, 1500–1722.* Charlottesville: University Press of Virginia.
    2002   Trouble Coming Southward: Emanations Through and From Virginia, 1607–1675. In *The Transformation of the Southeastern Indians, 1540–1760*, edited by Robbie Ethridge and Charles Hudson, pp. 65–78. Jackson: University Press of Mississippi.
    2005   *Pocahontas, Powhatan, Opechancanough: Three Indian Lives Changed by Jamestown.* Charlottesville: University of Virginia Press.

Rountree, Helen C., and Thomas E. Davidson
    1997   *Eastern Shore Indians of Virginia and Maryland.* Charlottesville: University Press of Virginia.

Rountree, Helen C., and E. Randolph Turner III
    1994   On the Fringe of the Southeast: The Powhatan Paramount Chiefdom in Virginia. In *The Forgotten Centuries: Indians and Europeans in the American South, 1521–1704*, edited by C. Hudson and C. Tesser, pp. 355–72. Athens: University of Georgia Press.

1998 The Evolution of the Powhatan Paramount Chiefdom in Virginia. In *Chiefdoms and Chieftaincy: an Integration of Archaeological, Ethnohistorical, and Ethnographic Approaches*, edited by Elsa M. Redmond, pp. 265–96. Gainesville: University Press of Florida.

2002 *Before and after Jamestown: Virginia's Powhatans and their Predecessors*. Gainesville: University Press of Florida.

Royce, Charles C. (Compiler)
1899 Indian Land Cessions in the United States. *Bureau of American Ethnology Eighteenth Annual Report*, for 1896–'97. Part II: 521–997. Washington, DC: Smithsonian Institution.

Rubertone, Patricia E.
2000 The Historical Archaeology of Native Americans. *Annual Review of Anthropology* 29:425–46.

Salwen, Bert
1978 Indians of Southern New England and Long Island: Early Period. In *Handbook of North American Indians, Volume 15: Northeast*, edited by Bruce Trigger, pp. 160–76. Washington, DC: Smithsonian Institution.

Seib, Rebecca, and Helen C. Rountree
2015 *Indians of Southern Maryland*. Baltimore, MD: Maryland Historical Society.

Smith, Bruce D.
1989 Origins of Agriculture in Eastern North America. *Science* 246:1566.

1992 *Rivers of Change: Essays on Early Agriculture in Eastern North America*. Washington, DC: Smithsonian Institution Press. Reissued in 2006 by University of Alabama Press.

Smith, Dwight L.
1954 The Problem of the Historic Indian in the Ohio Valley: The Historian's View. *Ethnohistory* 1(2):172–80.

Speck, Frank G.
1915a *Family Hunting Territories and Social Life of Various Algonkian Bands of the Ottawa Valley*. Anthropological Series, No. 8. Ottawa: Government Printing Office.

1915b *The Nanticoke Community of Delaware*. New York: Museum of the American Indian, Heye Foundation.

1927 *The Nanticoke and Conoy Indians with a review of Linguistic Material*. Wilmington, DE: Historical Society of Delaware.

1928 *Chapters on Ethnology of the Powhatan Tribes of Virginia*. New York: Museum of the American Indian, Heye Foundation, pp. 225–455.

1935 Siouan Tribes of the Carolinas as Known from Catawba, Tutelo, and Documentary Sources. *American Anthropologist* 34(2–1):201–25.

Speck, Frank G., R. B. Hassrick, and Edmund B. Carpenter
1946 *Rappahannock Taking Devices; Traps, Hunting and Fishing*. Philadelphia: University Museum of the University of Pennsylvania.

Starna, William A.
　2013　*From Home Land to New Land: A History of the Mahican Indians, 1600–1830.* Lincoln: University of Nebraska Press.

Stern, Theodore
　1952　Chickahominy: The Changing Culture of a Virginia Indian Community. *Proceedings of the American Philosophical Society* 96(2):157–225.

Stone, Gaynell (editor)
　1983　*The Shinnecock Indians: A Culture History.* Stony Brook, NY: Ginn Custom Publishing for the Suffolk County Archaeological Association.

Strong, John A.
　1996　*"We are still here!": The Algonquian Peoples of Long Island Today.* Interlaken, NY: Empire State Books.
　2001　*Montaukett Indians of Eastern Long Island.* Syracuse, NY: Syracuse University Press.

Sturtevant, William C.
　1966　Anthropology, History, and Ethnohistory. *Ethnohistory* 13(1/2):1–51.

Swanton, John R.
　1952　The Indian Tribes of North America. *Bureau of American Ethnology, Bulletin* 145. Washington, DC: Smithsonian Institution.

Swatzler, David
　2000　*A Friend Among the Senecas: The Quaker Mission to Cornplanter's People.* Mechanicsburg, PA: Stackpole Books.

Trelease, Allen W.
　1962　Indian-White Contacts in Eastern North America: The Dutch in New Netherlands. *Ethnohistory* 9(2):137–46.

Thurman, Melburn D.
　1973　The Delaware Indians: A Study in Ethnohistory. Doctoral Dissertation in Anthropology, University of California, Santa Barbara.

Townsend, Camilla
　2004　*Pocahontas and the Powhatan Dilemma: An American Portrait.* New York: Hill and Wang.

Turner, E. Randolph, III
　1976　An Archaeological and Ethnohistorical Study of the Evolution of Rank Societies in the Virginia Coastal Plain. Doctoral Dissertation in Anthropology, Pennsylvania State University. Published by University Microfilms, Ann Arbor, MI, 1979.
　1985　Socio-Political Organization within the Powhatan Chiefdom and the Effects of European Contact, A.D. 1607–1646. In *Cultures in Contact: The European Impact on Native Cultural Institutions in Eastern North America, A.D. 1000–1800,* edited by W. W. Fitzhugh, pp. 193–224. Washington, DC: Smithsonian Institution Press.

1986   Difficulties in the Archaeological Identification of Chiefdoms as Seen in the Virginia Coastal Plain During the Late Woodland and Early Historic Periods. In *Late Woodland Cultures of the Middle Atlantic Region*, edited by Jay F. Custer, pp. 19–35. Newark, DE: University of Delaware Press.

1993   Native American Protohistoric Interactions in the Powhatan Core Area. In *Powhatan Foreign Relations: 1500–1722*, edited by H. C. Rountree, pp. 76–93. Charlottesville: University Press of Virginia.

2004   Virginia Native Americans During the Contact Period: A Summary of Archaeological Research Over the Past Decade. *Archeological Society of Virginia Quarterly Bulletin* 59:14–24.

2013   Virginia Piedmont Ethnohistory: A Working Bibliography (10 Oct.). Manuscript on file, Becker Archives at West Chester University of Pennsylvania.

Trigger, Bruce G. (editor)
1978   *Handbook of North American Indians. Volume 15*: Northeast. Washington, DC: Smithsonian Institution.

Vaughan, Alden T., and Deborah A. Rosen
1998   Early American Indian Documents: *Treaties and Laws, 1607–1789*. General editor, Alden T. Vaughan. Volume XV: Virginia and Maryland Laws. Bethesda, MD: University Publications of America.

2004   Early American Indian Documents: *Treaties and Laws, 1607–1789*. General editor, Alden T. Vaughan. Volume XVII: New England and Middle Atlantic Laws. Bethesda, MD: University Publications of America.

Voegelin, Erminie W.
1954   An Ethnohistorian's Viewpoint. *Ethnohistory* 1(2):166–71.

Wallace, Anthony F. C.
1949   *King of the Delawares: Teedyuscung, 1700–1763*. Philadelphia: University of Pennsylvania Press.

1957   Review of, *The Culture and Acculturation of the Delaware Indians*, by William W. Newcomb (1956). *Ethnohistory* 4(3):322–24.

2012   *Tuscarora: A History*. Albany: State University of New York Press.

Wallace, Paul A. W.
1946   *White Roots of Peace*. Philadelphia: University of Pennsylvania Press.

1961   *Indians of Pennsylvania*. Harrisburg: Pennsylvania Historical and Museum Commission, Commonwealth of Pennsylvania.

Walwer, Gregory, and Peter Pagoulatos
1990   Native American Land-Use Patterns of the Outer Coastal Plain of New Jersey. *Bulletin of the Archaeological Society of New Jersey* 45:77–95.

Waterman, Kees-Jan, Jaap Jacobs, and Charles T. Gehring (editors)
2009   *Indianen Verhalen: de Groegste Beschrijvingen van Indianen Lands de Hudsonrivier (1609–1680)*. Zutphen: Walberg Pers.

Weslager, Clinton A.

1943 *Delaware's Forgotten Folk: The Story of the Moors & Nanticokes.* Philadelphia: University of Pennsylvania Press.

1953a *Brief Account of the Indians of Delaware.* Newark, DE: University of Delaware Press.

1953b *Red Men on the Delaware.* Wilmington, DE: Hambleton Company.

1972 *Delaware Indians:* A History. New Brunswick, NJ: Rutgers University Press.

1987 *Swedes and Dutch at New Castle.* New York: Bart.

1988 *New Sweden on the Delaware: 1638–1655.* Lanham, MD: Middle Atlantic Press.

Whyte, Thomas R.

2007 Proto-Iroqoian Development in the Late Archaic–Early Woodland Transition of the Appalachian Highlands. *Southeastern Archaeology* 26:134–44.

Williamson, Margaret Holmes

2003 *Powhatan Lords of Life and Death: Command and Consent in Seventeenth-Century Virginia.* Lincoln: University of Nebraska Press.

Witthoft, John, and William A. Hunter

1955 The Seventeenth-Century Origins of the Shawnee. *Ethnohistory* 2(1):42–57.

Wojciechowski, Franz Laurens

1992 *Ethnohistory of the Paugussett Tribes: An Exercise in Research Methodology.* Amsterdam: De Kiva.

Worsley, Peter

2003 The Nation State, Colonial Expansion and the Contemporary World Order. In *Companion Encyclopedia of Anthropology: Humanity, Culture and Social Life,* edited by Tim Ingold, pp. 1040–66 (from the 1994 edition). London and New York: Routledge.

8

+

Experimental Research in Middle Atlantic Archaeology

Bill Schindler

Experimental archaeology has been an important component of archaeological research in the Middle Atlantic region for decades. In fact, experimental archaeologists from the region have made significant contributions to the discipline on a global scale. Considering its continued regional importance and global presence, the placement of experimental archaeology in the Middle Atlantic in temporal and geographic context, the focus of this chapter, is long overdue. This chapter will also attempt to acknowledge the significant contributions to experimental archaeology researchers from the Middle Atlantic region have made on a global scale.

DEFINITIONS

To some, the notion of experimental archaeology conjures romantic images of crafting tools in a manner consistent with prehistoric techniques and using them to test archaeological theories and improve our interpretation of the past. To others, it means countless hours spent flintknapping in the backyard as a means of reconnecting with some long forgotten ancient roots. Some believe it to be an extremely effective pedagogical tool in the classroom and use it to engage students and enhance learning. And, to others, experimental archaeology is considered "playing Indian" and something better left to those engaging with fantasy play, having no place in serious archaeological research.

These various perspectives on experimental archaeology are confusing and beg the question, "What *is* experimental archaeology?" For decades, researchers have attempted to provide a clear-cut definition (Ascher 1961; Callahan 1995; Coles 1973; Wescott 1995) yet, defining and re-defining of experimental archaeology has ultimately served to provide a multitude of different definitions—each specific to a particular researcher's strengths or agenda. This practice also divides and fractions "would-be" experimental archaeologists into smaller groups of experimenters, archaeologists, primitive technologists, hobbyists and craftspeople, and re-enactors (Schindler 2009). Some of these divides have become so great that organizations including REARC (Reconstructive and Experimental Archaeology Conference) and EXARC (International Organization of Archaeological Open-Air Museums and Experimental Archaeology) have emerged, in part, to bring these different groups back together.

There are many different ideas about, and approaches to, experimental archaeological research. Elsewhere (Schindler 2009, 2010a), I have proposed that the most comprehensive and useful characterization of experimental archaeology merges definitions proposed by Schick and Toth (1993:20) and Errett Callahan (1995:3, 1999). Experimental archaeology is here defined as that branch of archaeology which seeks to interpret material culture, technology, or life-ways by using the same materials, techniques, and strategies believed to have been employed in the past through structured, scientific experimentation. Experiential archaeology, on the other hand, lacks the scientific rigor required of experimental archaeology and can often be a useful educational tool or as a "step" in a larger experimental research project requiring familiarity with a particular technology or medium (see, for example, Messner and Schindler 2010).

Finally, living archaeology can be experimental, as with Peter Reynolds's work at Butser Hill in England (see Reynolds 1976, 1979), and Callahan's Old Rag and Pamunkey projects (see Callahan 1973, 1976b, 1981); experiential, as with Lynx Vilden's current work near the Kootenai River in Montana (see Vilden 2005); or a combination of the two. The difference with living archaeology is that the researcher is deeply concerned with creating the proper context and immersing his- or herself in this context for an extended period during which time experimental and/or experiential archaeological research is conducted. The advantage to this style of research is that "immersion" has the ability to affect the decision-making processes of the researchers, the way they carry out experiments, and hopefully "constrain," as much as possible, results to produce only outcomes probable in the past. The drawback to this approach is a perceived lack of control, which can be offset through extensive documentation (Schindler 2010a). Documentation provides the context within which the experiment took place. It is this narrative that allows others to understand what variables were present in the experiment and let them decide how they may have impacted the results.

Callahan (1985:18–19), in order to further distance experimental research from other manifestations of a primitive technological approach, identified three levels, defined by adherence to authenticity and the scientific method. Level 1, defined as Play, is considered non-authentic and non-scientific; Level 2, defined as Primitive Technology, is considered authentic and non-scientific; and Level 3, defined as Experimental Archaeology, is considered authentic and scientific (Callahan 1995). While this system is useful in understanding how the results of these activities impact interpretation of the archaeological record, it also reinforces the divide between practitioners of primitive technology and suggests that some activities are more important than others.

Most researchers today take a holistic and encompassing approach to experimental archaeology. For example, Peter Kelterborn (personal communication, March 27, 2008) feels that someone conducting experimental research does not need to pigeonhole him- or herself into a distinct subcategory of the discipline, nor adhere to every principle of the scientific method for their work to have meaning. All that is required is accurate, detailed, and truthful documentation. In 1991, as co-founder and president of the Swiss Society of Experimental Archaeology, Kelterborn helped to create a solution to the battle over various definitions of experimental archaeology by integrating six different activities he considers "equally valuable, important, and necessary components" into the philosophy of the society. According to this philosophy, all six of these activities are considered *experimental archaeology* and include:

1. Emotionally experiencing situations in a prehistorical context. (This is for children as natural as for students or researchers.)
2. Teaching and learning archaeological skills and techniques. (This is a precondition for all other activities.)
3. Offering or applying demonstrations in schools, in museums or at other occasions. (As correct as possible, but often this allows a much lower-level authenticity than activity 4 or 5.).
4. Offering or using replications or reconstructions in research, in schools, during exhibitions and in other events. (Authenticity only where required by the goal.)
5. Executing true scientific experiments. (This is sometimes the formal procedure in industry and the really hard natural sciences, but where time and climate and human nature is involved, the experimental criteria may or must be very different.)
6. Reporting the results (and if possible make them public).

The all-important pre-condition to become a member in our Society was only to honestly tell the public in which of above categories one is working, to truthfully report and document what has happened (always clearly separating facts from opinions), so that the event could be repeated by others (Peter Kelterborn, personal communication, December 12, 2008).

It is easy to get lost in semantics and the practice of dividing the field of experimental archaeology into various levels, imbuing different values on each. Regardless of the definition, experimental archaeology, in all of its manifestations, is an exciting, visceral way to teach, learn, and interpret the past. Taken holistically and including people engaged in experimental archaeological research, experiential archaeology, primitive technology, historical reenactment, and pedagogy utilizing any of the above, the practice of experimental archaeology is a vibrant component of archaeology and interpretation of the past in the Middle Atlantic region.

EXPERIMENTAL ARCHAEOLOGY: WORLDWIDE CONTEXT

Jodi Flores, a recent PhD graduate in experimental archaeology from Exeter University, has constructed the most recent detailed synopsis of the history of the discipline of experimental archaeology to date (Flores 2010). In it, she credits a shift to a romantic view of the past in eighteenth-century Europe coupled with an increased interest in material remains as the driving forces behind the earliest roots of experimental archaeology. Some early research during this time includes experiments with bronze musical instruments unearthed in both Britain and Denmark. These early forms of experimentation were often as simple as playing the instruments to determine the type and quality of the sounds that were produced. Other experiments at the time worked to create a better understanding of taphonomic processes. Over time, experimental research shifted its focus to the technologies used to create tools and artifacts, or *chaîne opératoire*. For instance, in the nineteenth century experiments were focused on creating a better understanding of the production of artifacts, especially stone tools. More recently, experimental archaeology has been influenced by processual archaeology in the 1960s as well as an influx of ethnographic research that has become increasingly more available to researchers. The rich European tradition of experimental archaeology research has carried over into academia. Currently, there are two universities, Exeter University in England and University College Dublin in Ireland, that boast remarkable graduate programs in experimental archaeology.

Undoubtedly, the strongest driving force behind bringing like-minded people interested in and practicing experimental archaeology from around the world into a shared conversation is EXARC, an ICOM affiliated organization representing archaeological open-air museums, experimental archaeology, ancient technology, and interpretation (www .exarc.net). The Netherlands-based organization has board representation from around the world including the United States. Through its publication, website, thorough online bibliography, social media presence, collaborative projects, and support for conferences held all over the world it raises the standard of experimental archaeology scientific research and public presentation.

EXPERIMENTAL ARCHAEOLOGY: LOCAL HISTORICAL CONTEXT

In the United States, experimental archaeology has a long history in and near the Middle Atlantic region. For example, as early as the late nineteenth century, Frank Hamilton Cushing (1894) conducted a number of experiments designed to investigate the manner in which Native Americans could have produced the figures fashioned from sheet copper found in Hopewell mounds. Here, he was reacting against the proposition that "primitive people like the so-called moundbuilders, being unpossessed of a knowledge of smelting or of tools of iron or steel, could not have fashioned plates of such size and uniformity as many of those from which these objects had been made, merely with implements of stone." In fact, his experiments did indicate that such production was entirely possible using stone-age technology.

During the late twentieth century experimental archaeology really began to build momentum in the Middle Atlantic region. Driving experimental archaeology were *three spheres of influence*, the effects of which can still be seen today. At the center of the first sphere is Dr. Errett Callahan. Callahan has been flintknapping since 1956 and recording his work since the early 1960s. As of 2010, he has produced 9,884 meticulously recorded knapped tools, including well over a thousand hafted cutlery knives. As a self-described reconstructive archaeologist, Callahan has developed and ran numerous living and experimental archaeology projects including Old Rag (Callahan 2008), five phases of the Pamunkey Project (Callahan 1972, 1973, 1974, 1976a, 1981), St. Mary's Longhouse (Callahan 1985), the Thunderbird House Reconstruction, the Cahokia House Project (Callahan 2005, 1993), and dozens of smaller projects. No doubt his research over the past forty-plus years has influenced the field and provided a more accurate appreciation for the past. However, many, including Callahan himself, would consider teaching his most important contribution. He is currently retired after having taught various primitive technologies to over a thousand students since 1971.

The second sphere of influence began in 1971 at the Gulf Branch Nature Center in Arlington, Virginia, where Scott Silsby started organizing an annual primitive technology event. This event persisted successfully for years until it was turned over in 1988 to Kirk Drier, who then moved it to the Oregon Ridge Nature Center in Cockeysville, Maryland, where it remained until 2016. In 2016, still under the direction of Kirk Drier, it was moved to Cromwell Valley Park in Towson, Maryland. This event includes two days of theme-driven primitive technology demonstrations, opportunities for the public to in engage in hands-on learning, an evening lecture, and an archery-roving course. The event continues to serve as a gathering place for experimental archaeologists, primitive technologists, professional and avocational archaeologists, hobbyists, scouts, home-schoolers, and craftspeople.

The third sphere of influence is centered in Moorestown, New Jersey. Here professional archaeologist and skilled primitive technologist Jack Cresson provides flintknapping classes and conducts experimental research. Jack first tried his hand at knapping while in Scouts in 1955 using a nail and pieces of glass. In the early 1960s, while an undergrad at Pennsylvania State University, he resumed his knapping experiments with both argillite and Cretaceous European flint. Later, Callahan encouraged him to embrace all varieties of stone working applications, which became the inspiration for his concentration on using wooden percussors. He launched his Primitive Industries workshops in 1986 and his classes have been running in the spring and summer ever since. Jack Cresson represents the ultimate in an experimental archaeologist. He is simultaneously a field archaeologist and a primitive technologist highly skilled in a number of ancient technologies. He continues to teach, conduct archaeological and experimental archaeological research, and present at professional archaeology meetings. A founding member of the Society of Primitive Technology, he is still active in the Reconstructive and Experimental Archaeology Conference.

SPARKS THAT IGNITED THE FIELD

These three spheres have ignited the spark that continues to fuel the majority of experimental archaeology research taking place today in the Middle Atlantic region. Errett Callahan's experimental work has received worldwide recognition (see, for example, Callahan 1987) and decades ago he began a process of bridging the gap between experimental research in the United States and that taking place in Europe, a process that continues today. Regular trips to the open air museum and experimental archaeology center Lejre, in Denmark, to conduct experimental research on

Danish Daggers laid the groundwork for a European-U.S. cooperation/ communication that is still ongoing. Several experimental archaeologists from the region have visited Lejre as a result of Callahan's initial contacts, including Jack Cresson and the author, who has visited three times to conduct experimental research and now regularly takes students from Washington College there as a study abroad experience.

While much of the flintknapping community was concerned with making works of art out of the finest lithic materials in the world, Jack Cresson instead focused on learning how to use the rocks that prehistoric tools he found on local sites were actually fashioned from. Through years of practice he skillfully learned to transform quartzite, rhyolites, and argillites into fully functional tools mimicking what he unearthed in his excavations. Both his research and the flintknapping classes he offers are focused on learning how to master these materials for the purpose of obtaining a better understanding of the local archaeological record. In a manner similar to the way Bordes and Crabtree did decades earlier, both Callahan and Cresson have continue to teach and inspire a whole new generation of flintknappers, many of whom have utilized their skills to conduct archaeological experiments, and some continue the tradition of passing on knowledge through teaching.

The model offered by what is known as the Oregon Ridge Primitive Skills Gathering has been repeated throughout the world. For example, here in the Middle Atlantic region the Center for Experimental Archaeology Knap-In just finished its twelfth consecutive year. Over the decade, it has been common to see a number of skilled primitive technologists teaching courses, demonstrating, and interacting with the public at the event. Additionally, a number of experiments have been conducted at the event to take advantage of the infrastructure and resources provided by the setting as well as the opportunity to engage the public. Other local knap-ins and primitive technology gatherings have popped up throughout the region, including the Schiele Museum Knap-In, the Bald Eagle Knap-In, Letchworth, and Robert Godall's annual event in Virginia.

Middle Atlantic archaeologists, primitive technologists, and experimental archaeologists Errett Callahan, Jack Cresson, and Maria Sidoroff were key founders of the Society of Primitive Technology (SPT). Officially formed in 1989, the SPT's primary function was the publication of the *Bulletin of Primitive Technology*, which has served to disseminate valuable and exciting information related to experimental archaeology, primitive technology, and open-air museums on a worldwide scale for over twenty years (Schindler 2012; Wescott 1995). During this long run, the journal published contributions from a variety of authors, ranging from highly skilled primitive technologists with no academic training to academic archaeologists lacking hands-on primitive technology skills—and everything in between.

It has been an invaluable resource and has served to let primitive technologists know that "yes, there are others out there like them!" In 2013 the Society of Primitive Technology's board decided to disband after a very successful run. However, the editor, Dave Wescott, agreed to continue to publish the journal on his own and is continuing to do so under his company, Backtracks.

Four years ago the Reconstructive and Experimental Archaeology Conference was founded. For the majority of its existence, the yearly conference has been held slightly outside of the geographic range of the Middle Atlantic region, yet the majority of the board is composed of a number of researchers from the Middle Atlantic and the conference itself is primarily attended by archaeologists, primitive technologists, experimental archaeologists, and students from our region. This organization has been based out of the Schiele Museum in Gastonia, North Carolina (the same location where the Society of Primitive Technology was officially created), because of its close ties with primitive technologist Steve Watts. In 2015, the conference took a hiatus as a result of this author's participation in a National Geographic television project (see below). In 2016, REARC held its annual conference at Colonial Williamsburg in Virginia.

CURRENT STATUS

Currently, a great deal of experimental research originating from our region has found its way into state, regional, national, and international conferences and site reports, which over the years has helped to shape our regional interpretation of the past. It is interesting to note that as experimental archaeology gained prominence in the Middle Atlantic region, the influence provided by the three original spheres grew primarily as a result of the students and participants they produced. This "new" generation's focus has primarily been in academia. The following list is not suggestive of an exhaustive list of experimental studies from the Middle Atlantic in any form. Rather, the following is designed to reflect the contribution that this new generation of academics from the Middle Atlantic region have recently made to experimental archaeology studies. This includes experimental research such as Michael Stewart's experiments with ceramics (Stewart 1998a, 2005, 2010; Stewart and Pevarnik 2007, 2008, 2010; Sidoroff et al. 2008; Lattanzi and Stewart 2010), lithics (Stewart 1981, 1984, 1989, 1998b, 1998c), fire altered rock (Stewart 2003, 2005b, 2008a, 2008b, 2013), and site formation processes (Stewart et al. 2002) at Temple University, Jay Custer's work with fire altered rock at the University of Delaware (Custer and DePetris 2013), Heather Wholey's work with soapstone (Wholey 2010, 2011, 2012) at West Chester University, John Shea's extensive experimentation with lithics (see, for example, Shea et al. 2001), Coastal Carolina's Carolyn Dillian's work with pigments (Dillian et al. 2007), and the author's work at Monmouth University and now at Washington College with lithics (Schindler 2003; Schindler and Koch 2012; Stewart and Schindler 2008), ceramics (Sidoroff, et al. 2008), fishing (Schindler 2005, 2011, 2013), taphonomic processes (Schindler 2004), penetration tests (2010b), and food technologies along with Tim Messer (Messner and Schindler 2010; Schindler et al. 2011) from SUNY Potsdam. By taking an experimental approach to their research, and including experimental archaeology and primitive technology in their teaching, the researchers in these positions have also planted the seed of experimental research in the up-and-coming generation of archaeologists in our region.

Experimental archaeology is a powerful teaching tool and its pedagogical potential has been realized in many institutions of higher education throughout the United States, albeit not at the graduate level like the two aforementioned European examples. According to a list compiled by EXARC of colleges and universities located in the Middle Atlantic region that either offer full-blown experimental archaeology courses or at least incorporate experimental archaeology into other archaeology courses include Buffalo State College, Monmouth University, Oswego State University of New York, Potsdam University of New York, Stony Brook University of New York, University of Delaware, Washington College, and West Chester University. Undoubtedly, this list is not exhaustive but indicative of the presence of the academic experimental archaeology in the Middle Atlantic and the impact this type of teaching and learning has on archaeologists graduating here.

In 2016, experimental archaeology in the Middle Atlantic region also crossed over into another arena—television. This author was fortunate enough to co-star with Cat Bigney, a survival instructor from the Boulder Outdoor Survival School in Utah, on a groundbreaking National Geographic television series, *The Great Human Race* (http://channel.national geographic.com/the-great-human-race/). A blend of experimental archaeology, primitive technology, and prehistory, this series capitalized on the popular survival television genre to tell the story of our shared human experience in a very unique way. Beginning in Tanzania, the co-stars of this program followed an idealized migratory route over ten episodes and two and a half million years through Africa, the Middle East, Asia, and across the Bering Sea, eventually ending in Oregon. The location and time period represented in each episode was selected because at each particular time and place a technological development allowed our ancestors to interact with their environment in a different way. In each episode the co-stars were restricted to only the technologies available at the time they were representing to subsist for typically a period of eight days. This program eventually aired in 171 countries.

FUTURE DIRECTIONS

What is perhaps most exciting about looking at experimental archaeology in the Middle Atlantic region is identifying trends and providing suggestions for future development. The following sections describe a few examples.

Materials. Experimental archaeology in our region has notoriously focused on materials that do not degrade over time and are easily recognizable in the archaeological record, such as lithics and ceramics. This makes sense since they are the most ubiquitous artifacts categories on prehistoric sites. However, there are entire classes of material culture that in many ways are still only partially understood. In fact, those few sites with rare examples of organic preservation suggest that organic material culture grossly outweighs that fashioned from stone or ceramic on prehistoric sites. Thanks to ever-advancing field recovery and analytical techniques we are finally gaining a better picture of this world. Further, we now have more immediate access to ethnographic data, which include a foci on organic technologies (such as eHraf), and, increasingly, more primitive technologists are working toward becoming experts in organically based technologies. As a result, we are now witnessing an increasing number of archaeological experiments focused on obtaining a better understanding of organic residues on archaeological sites.

Time Periods. In the United States much experimental work has traditionally been focused on prehistoric technologies and obtaining a better understanding of prehistoric life. More recently, however, this is changing. For example, in Williamsburg and Jamestown several researchers have been experimenting with creating bloomery furnaces to better understand early iron production in the New World. More experiments focused on obtaining a better understanding of the historic archaeological record are necessary.

Worldwide Scale. The seed that Callahan planted decades ago has recently grown into a full-fledged movement. There are currently two major organizations in the world focused on experimental archaeology—in the United States the Reconstructive and Experimental Archaeology Conference, and in Europe, EXARC, the international organization of Archaeological Open-Air Museums (AOAM) and Experimental Archaeology (and, in the United States the Society of Primitive Technology just finished a successful run of more than twenty years). Both organizations have an international reach; however, over the past few years there has been a push for a more formal cooperation between the organizations to ensure that a true worldwide audience is reached. Bridging this gap and making our world smaller will result in a number of opportunities, including increased dialogue, transmission of knowledge, and cooperative efforts in research.

The future of experimental research in the Middle Atlantic region is bright. Many of the next generation of archaeologists in the region are now armed with hands-on understanding and practical knowledge about life in the past and, more importantly, know how to create practical experiments to test archaeological hypotheses and interpret the past. The next generation is prepared to shed a new light on the archaeology of the Middle Atlantic region.

REFERENCES CITED

Ascher, Robert
  1961   Experimental Archaeology. *American Anthropologist* 63(4):793–816.

Callahan, Errett
  1972   *Experimental Archaeology Papers (APE), vol. 1.* Virginia Commonwealth University, Richmond, VA.
  1973   *Experimental Archaeology Papers (APE), vol. 2.* Virginia Commonwealth University, Richmond, VA.
  1974   *Experimental Archaeology Papers (APE), vol. 3.* Virginia Commonwealth University, Richmond, VA.
  1976a   *Experimental Archaeology Papers (APE), vol. 4.* Virginia Commonwealth University, Richmond, VA.
  1976b   The Pamunkey Project: An Overview. In *Experimental Archaeology Papers* 4 (Vol. 4, pp. 1–15). Richmond, VA: Virginia Commonwealth University.
  1981   Pamunkey Housebuilding: An Experimental Study of Late Woodland Construction Technology in the Powhatan Confederacy. Unpublished Dissertation, the Catholic University of America, Washington DC.
  1985   The St. Mary's Longhouse Experiment: the first season. *Archaeological Society of Virginia Quarterly Bulletin* 40:12–40.
  1987   An Evaluation of the Lithic Technology in Middle Sweden during the Mesolithic and Neolithic. *Societas Archaeologica Updaliensis*, Uppsala, Sweden.
  1993   Celts at Pamunkey and Cahokia. *Bulletin of Primitive Technology* 5:36–40.
  1995   What Is Experimental Archaeology? *Primitive Technology Newsletter* 1:3–5.
  1999   *What Is Experimental Archaeology? Primitive Technology: A Book of Earth Skills.* Gibbs-Smith Publishing: Salt Lake City, UT.
  2005   The Cahokia Project: A Case Study in Reconstructive Archaeology. Society of Primitive Technology Publications, Schiele Museum of Natural History.
  2008   Old Rag Archaeology: Experimentation and Excavation. Society of Primitive Technology Publications, Schiele Museum of Natural History.

Coles, John
    1973 *Archaeology by Experiment.* Charles Scribner's Sons, New York.

Cushing, Frank Hamilton
    1894 Primitive Copper Working. *Anthropologist* 7(1):93–117.

Custer, Jay, and Darcy DePetris
    2013 Preliminary Results of Experimental Studies of Fire-Cracked Rock. Manuscript submitted to the *Journal of Middle Atlantic Archaeology.*

Dillian, Carolyn, Charles Bello, and Nequandra Bowen
    2007 True Blue: Vivianite as a Mineral Pigment. *Journal of Middle Atlantic Archaeology* 23:73–84.

Flores, Jodi R.
    2010 Creating a History of Experimental Archaeology. In *Experimentation and Interpretation: The Use of Experimental Archaeology in the Study of the Past,* edited by Dana Millson. Oxbow Books, Oxford.

Lattanzi, Gregory, and R. Michael Stewart
    2010 Technological Style in Pottery Analysis. Exhibit/Presentation at the Annual Meeting of the Middle Atlantic Archaeological Conference, Ocean City, MD.

Messner, Timothy, and Bill Schindler
    2010 Plant Processing Strategies and their Effect upon Starch Grain Survival in Rendering Arrow Arum (*Peltandra virginica* L.) Edible. *Journal of Archaeological Science* 37(2):328–36.

Reynolds, Peter J.
    1976 *Farming in the Iron Age.* Cambridge University Press: Cambridge.
    1979 *Iron-Age Farm: The Butser Experiment.* British Museum Publications Ltd: London.

Schick, Kathy, and Nick Toth
    1993 *Making Silent Stones Speak: Human Evolution and the Dawn of Technology.* New York: Simon & Schuster.

Schindler, Bill
    2003 An Evaluation of Three Argillite Tools Used in a Deer Butchering Experiment. *Bulletin of Primitive Technology* 25:84–87.
    2004 What Lies Beneath: Does Debitage on Plowzone Surfaces Provide Adequate Representations of Parent Subsurface Deposits? *Journal of Middle Atlantic Archaeology* 20:73–78
    2005 Poisoned Water? Latent Piscicide Use in the Prehistoric Delaware Valley. *Bulletin of the Archaeological Society of New Jersey* 59:4–7.
    2009 The Old Rag Symposium: a discussion. *Bulletin of Primitive Technology,* 37.
    2010a Documentation Strategies for Experimental Research. *The Bulletin of Primitive Technology* 40:64–68.
    2010b *What's the point? Systematic testing of projectile performance when confronted with various body coverings.* Report submitted to the Research Department at Lejre: Land of Legends, Lejre, Denmark.

2011   Experimental Perspectives on Prehistoric Fishing. In *Experiments and Interpretation of Traditional Technologies: Essays in Honor of Errett Callahan.* Editor Hugo Nami, Smithsonian Institution. Special edition of Arquelogia Contemporanea.

2012   The Society of Primitive Technology. *EuroREA,* 3.

2013   Location, Location, Location: The Archaeology of Prime Fishing Site Selection. Chapter to appear in "The Inescapable Significance of Cultural Ecology and Environmental Sciences in Archaeology: Papers in Honor of William M. Gardner." Editors Carole Nash and Heather A. Wholey, *Journal of Middle Atlantic Archaeology,* 29.

Schindler, Bill, Aaron Krochmal, Katie Eckenrode

2011   *What's for Dinner? Rethinking Relative Utility Factors to Better Model Resource Potential in Prehistoric Diets.* Paper presented at the annual Middle Atlantic Archaeology Conference: Ocean City, MD.

Schindler, Bill, and Jeremy Koch

2012   Flakes Giving You Lip? Let Them Speak: An Examination of the Relationship Between Percussor Type and Lipped Platforms. *Archaeology of Eastern North America* 40:99–106.

Shea, John, Zachary Davis, and Kyle Brown

2001   Experimental Tests of Middle Paleolithic Spear Points Using a Calibrated Crossbow. *Journal of Archaeological Science* 28(8):807–16.

Sidoroff, Maria, George Pevarnik, William Schindler and R. Michael Stewart

2008   An Experimental Approach to Understanding Clay Selection by Ancient Potters in the Delaware Valley. Paper presented at the Annual Meeting of the Society for American Archaeology, Vancouver, BC.

Stewart, R. Michael

1981   Archaeologically Significant Characteristics of Maryland and Pennsylvania Metarhyolites. Paper presented at the Annual Meeting of the Middle Atlantic Archaeological Conference, Ocean City, MD.

1984   Archaeologically Significant Characteristics of Maryland and Pennsylvania Metarhyolites, In *Prehistoric Lithic Exchange Systems in the Middle Atlantic Region,* edited by Jay Custer, pp. 1–13, Center for Archaeological Research, University of Delaware, Monograph No. 3, Newark.

1989   Micro-cores and Blade-like Flakes from Cobbles in Middle and Late Woodland Assemblages. *Bulletin of the Archaeological Society of New Jersey* 44:47–50.

1998a   Ceramics and Delaware Valley Prehistory: Insights from the Abbott Farm. Trenton Complex Archaeology, Report 14. Special Publication of the Archaeological Society of New Jersey and the New Jersey Department of Transportation, Trenton.

1998b   Inferences Based Upon the Weathering of Rhyolite. Paper presented at the Annual Meeting of the Archaeological Society of Maryland, Frederick.

1998c   Native American Argillite Quarries of the Delaware Valley. Paper presented at the Annual Meeting of the Eastern States Archaeological Federation, Wilkes Barre, PA.

2003 Context, Interpretation, and Fire Altered Rock. Paper presented at Annual Meeting of the Middle Atlantic Archaeological Conference, Virginia Beach, Virginia. (Earlier version presented at the Annual Meeting of the Eastern States Archaeological Federation, Mt. Laurel, NJ, 2002.)

2005a Clay Sources and Variability in Native American Pottery. Paper presented at the Annual Meeting of the Middle Atlantic Archaeological Conference, Rehoboth, DE.

2005b Some Thoughts on Fire Altered Rock. *Bulletin of the Archaeological Society of New Jersey* 60:37–42.

2008a Formation of Hearth Basin Features: Implications for the Interpretation of Archaeological Sites in the Middle Atlantic Region. Paper presented at the Symposium in Honor of the Archaeological Research of William M. Gardner, Shepherdstown, WV.

2008b Formation of Hearth Basin Features: Implications for the Interpretation of Paleoindian and Later Archaeological Sites in the Middle Atlantic Region, Eastern United States. Paper presented at the Annual Meeting of the Society for American Archaeology, Vancouver, BC.

2010 Stone Bowls and Pottery. Paper presented at the Annual Meeting of the Middle Atlantic Archaeological Conference, Ocean City, MD. Updated version of paper presented in 2011 to a meeting of the Archaeological Society of New Jersey, Trenton.

2013 Formation of Hearth Basin Features: Implications for the Interpretation of Prehistoric Archaeological Sites in the Middle Atlantic Region. *Journal of Middle Atlantic Archaeology* 29:1–26 (in press).

Stewart, R. Michael, Darrin Lowery, and Jesse Walker
2002 Site Formation Processes in Tidal Environments: Another Cautionary Tale. Paper presented at the annual meeting of the Middle Atlantic Archaeological Conference, Virginia Beach, VA.

Stewart, R. Michael, and George Pevanik
2007 Artisan Choices and Technology in Native American Pottery Production. Paper presented at the Annual Meeting of the Eastern States Archaeological Federation, Burlington, VT. Also presented at the Annual Meeting of the Middle Atlantic Archaeological Conference, Ocean City, MD (2008).

2008 Artisan Choices and Technology in Native American Pottery Production. *North American Archaeologist* 29 (3–4):391–409.

2010 Typology and Pottery: Problems and Prospects in Delaware Valley Archaeology. *Journal of Middle Atlantic Archaeology,* in press.

Stewart, R. Michael, and William Schindler
2008 Analysis of Artifacts from the Kings Quarry Site (36Lh2). Report prepared for the Pennsylvania Heritage Society and the Pennsylvania Historical and Museum Commission, Harrisburg.

Wescott, David
1995 The Society of Primitive Technology and Experimental Archaeology: Who Are We? *Primitive Technology Newsletter* 1:8–11.

Wholey, Heather
   2010 Ethnoarchaeological and Scientific Approaches to Soapstone Vessel Usage. Presented at the Middle Atlantic Archaeological Conference, Ocean City, MD.
   2011 "Steatite Vessel Use Alteration: Experiment and Observation." *Journal of Middle Atlantic Archaeology* 27:125–32.
   2012 Experiments with Soapstone. Presented at the Annual Meeting of the Reconstructive and Experimental Archaeology Conference, Shiele Museum of Natural History, Gastonia, NC.

Vilden, Lynx
   2005 Kootenai River Project II: Part 1 and 2. *Bulletin of Primitive Technology,* 25.

Part 2

TOPICS IN MIDDLE ATLANTIC PREHISTORY

9

The Use, Misuse, and Abuse of Typology

Roger Moeller

Insanity is doing the same thing over and over again but expecting different results.

—Rita Mae Brown 1983:68

Middle Atlantic archaeologists studying prehistory have struggled with techniques for organizing cultures in time and space. Artifact typology is one tool in classificatory schemes to better understand prehistoric occupations of the Middle Atlantic region. These schema begin with type descriptions of artifacts (especially projectile points and pottery) infused with raw material(s), manufacturing process(es), function(s), date(s), and frequently associated artifacts and features. Elaborate explanations of cultural processes are discussed to account for their origin, means of travel from their home territory to where they are found, and changes across time and space. My argument is that typologies should only be used to describe the physical features of large numbers of objects to facilitate their analysis. Using types for any other purposes (including relative dating and seriation) spans the continuum of misuse to abuse of the type concept.

CLASSIFICATORY SCHEME

McKern (1939) is often credited with creating the first major classificatory scheme for prehistoric archaeology. He saw a need for "introducing order into the previously existing chaotic status of general culture concepts throughout the greater Mississippi Valley" (McKern 1939:313). His taxonomic scheme of "focus, aspect, phase, pattern, and base, progressing from localized details to large general classes" (McKern 1939:310) followed the hierarchical Linnaean system of the natural world. This system (with regional variations in nomenclature) gained widespread acceptance in the Middle Atlantic region thanks to several prolific and influential archaeologists [e.g., James B. Griffin (1952), William A. Ritchie (1965), W. Fred Kinsey III (1972), and Herbert C. Kraft (1972)]. Griffin's major synthesis (1952) using the McKern system with scores of excavations conducted before the introduction of absolute dating techniques (especially radiocarbon dating) clearly demonstrated its utility. Ritchie's (1965) excellent overview of prehistoric New York State excavations and collections showcased artifacts also commonly seen in Pennsylvania, New Jersey, Delaware, Virginia, and Maryland. In the Upper Delaware Valley Kinsey (1972, Pennsylvania) and Kraft (1972, New Jersey) expanded the Ritchie model with more dates and details on individual excavations. Component, phase, horizon, tradition, and period became the accepted taxonomic terms in Middle Atlantic archaeology because of the very high profile presence at Middle Atlantic Archaeological Conference (MAAC) meetings of Louis Brennan (from New York), Kinsey, Kraft, and their students/associates.

While the taxonomic system established by McKern was modified as it moved to the East, the concept of regularizing nomenclature, providing scientific rationales for categorizing, and revisiting syntheses became part of the culture of MAAC. Middle Atlantic archaeology would not exist as a serious, cohesive, scientific pursuit without MAAC. This regional organization has brought people together into a common culture with its own language. Individuals may say "Susquehanna culture," "Broadspear tradition," "Terminal Archaic period," "Transitional," and "Late Archaic regional adaptation" without confusion. The specific terminological applications depends upon one's context, but each needs to begin with typology to identify the objects under discussion.

The ultimate application of any classificatory system depends upon the user regardless of the intentions of the designer. The Linnaean system for organizing plants (i.e., class, order, family, genus, and species) was based upon phenotypic traits controlled (originally) by natural selection. Once the typology was established, newly discovered specimens could be placed accurately; if this is not possible, then a new genus or species is named. A binomial naming system (e.g., *Phytolacca americana*) instead of just a common name (e.g., pokeweed) ensured that everyone was talking about the same plant. But once classified, is one supposed to use the traits of existing members of a family/genus/species to fill in the blanks on the recently placed one? Are we assuming that phenotypic similarities will beget physiological and ecological identity? If that is the case, one example will illustrate the dangers. The Solonaceae family includes three genera (i.e., *Solanum*, *Nicotiana*, and *Atropa*) with their species (i.e., *S. lyco-persicum*, *S. tuberosum*, *Atropa belladonna*, *N. tabacum*, and *N. rustica*). While Linnaeus had his reasons for putting tomato, potato, deadly nightshade, common tobacco, and a tobacco with ten times the nicotine of common tobacco (Plot55.com 2002) into the same family, potential users of each should be warned. Just because two of the family are in a meal does not mean you should add the other three.

In the absence of anthropogenic intervention, random mutation, or natural selection, all plants carry all physiological traits of their class, family, genus, and species. The same cannot be said for a given component at an archaeological site. Paleoindian sites are not assigned that designation in the absence of a fluted point. However, there is no need for a fluted point while one is processing plants, accessing tool stone sources, or fishing. The variety of Paleoindian implements is not apparent until they are found in valid association with a fluted point. While one might be "certain" that a site has a Paleoindian component based on radiometric dates, lithic reduction technology, or stratigraphy, the "proof" is in the flute.

The flaw in any archaeological taxonomic schema based on a hierarchical system that categorizes cultures in time and/or space is that too few components have enough data to be defined accurately. A single object (one trait) cannot be used to define an archaeological occupation as part of a particular phase, time period, or adaptation. Archaeologists seldom have the data to separate a long-term occupation into all the activities practiced or which implements were used in one activity or multiple activities. Regardless of the research question, the analysis begins with the types.

CREATING TYPES

All cultures or subcultures have a large variety of terms to describe the nuances of objects they consider more significant than others. A car enthusiast has to include manufacturer, make, year, stock equipment, modifications, and race classification to give an accurate description (e.g., little deuce coupe, flat head mill, ported and relieved, stroked and bored, competition clutch, four on the floor, lake pipes, rubber in all four gears [Beach Boys, *Little Deuce Coupe*]). The English language has 654 words referring to sexual experiences (Online Slang Dictionary 2012).

QUIZ

Now for a quick test on how good you are at determining types. These are not esoteric items made thousands of years ago by pre-literate individuals. These are common items found in our own culture today.

Which of these four animals does not belong with the others and why?

A. Cow
B. Horse
C. Chicken
D. Rabbit

Which number does not belong in the following list and why?

A. 1
B. 3
C. 5
D. 8

Which item does not belong in the following list and why?

A. Cucumber
B. Turnip
C. The Planet Earth
D. Pineapple

The answers are found at the end of the chapter.

GENERAL BACKGROUND OF ARCHAEOLOGICAL TYPOLOGY

Types were intended to be organizational tools

1. to standardize comparison of specimens over wide areas,
2. to save time in sorting, tabulating, and describing masses of materials, (and)
3. to provide convenient reference forms and terms to expedite field recording, surveys, and cataloging (Krieger 1944:275).

A goal, intention, parameter, or expectation of a type is "to group specimens into bodies which have demonstrable historical meaning in terms of behavior patterns" (Krieger 1944:272).

If analytical methods fail to interpret archaeological materials in terms of "concrete human behaviors," the historical reconstructions based upon them must be in greater or lesser degree fictitious. Traditionally, masses of specimens are grouped in one way or another to facilitate their description or to demonstrate "culture complexes" and "cultural change" through space and time (Krieger 1944:271).

Ford and Steward (1954:54) were cultural anthropologists concerned with the reality of types in living societies. They distinguished morphological types (i.e., ones based upon form) from historical-index ones (i.e., ones with temporal significance). They argue that types can be created (based upon observed behavior and the rationales provided by the practitioners), but express doubt that types can be discovered. They trust the practitioners of a given culture to provide an emic accounting for their behavior; if someone merely observes the behavior or the results of a behavior (i.e., artifact), they might not focus upon the correct criteria to form a typology. Of course, the underlying assumption is that people know why they do what they do. Taxonomy is then used to put the types into a meaningful sequence.

Dunnell (1971:118) critiqued the creation, logic, usefulness, application, and underlying theoretical assumptions of classifications very succinctly:

> Classifications are logical constructs whose justification lies in their utility. They are not inherent, nor do they explain. They are imposed constructs that function to order data so that explanation is possible.

USING TYPOLOGY

Typology is a very useful tool, but one must remember that it is only a construct, a mnemonic device, a heuristic creation. Lamoka, Perkiomen, Susquehanna, and Orient bifaces are classificatory schemes created as shorthand for pages of metric and stylistic descriptions associated with a temporal span ranging from hundreds to a thousand years more or less. Archaeologists do not know what was in the minds of the makers (e.g., function, style, personal or group identification, limitations of their technology or their available materials) when they produced a tool with particular characteristics, nor why they changed.

Despite all the caveats and demurrers, archaeologists have a bad habit of getting too loose with the terminology: evolution of projectile point styles and migrations of types. These are inanimate objects incapable of breeding. They are sessile, not ambulatory. These animistic attempts stop short of personification. Progressing to that point carries the inference of reason and rational thought where the stone artifacts can tell us what was in the minds of their makers.

MAAC has a very long history of hosting discussions (sometimes in very heated terms) about typology. Standards for establishing types were a concern at early meetings around 1974. To illustrate the degree of (dis) agreement among archaeologists on projectile point types, numbered flash cards with outlines of various bifaces were distributed to the assembled multitude. Individuals put their name for the type next to the number on a sheet of paper. This exercise led to the formation of the MAAC Board of Typological Nomenclature in 1985 (Evans and Custer 1990:31–41). Despite the scientific thoughtfulness and discussion going into this process, I am unaware of any agreement or a draft nomenclature. We will never know the "correct" answers.

SPECIFIC EXAMPLES OF TYPES WITH PROBLEMS

The publications of *New York Projectile Points: A Typology and Nomenclature* (Ritchie 1961) and *The Archaeology of New York State* (Ritchie 1965) were a boon to avocational archaeologists and professional researchers throughout the Northeast and Middle Atlantic regions: at last, an authoritative typological, cultural, historical guide to the prehistory of New York. The logical assumption was that objects from the Northeast and Middle Atlantic that look identical to the ones in these books would have the same associations, dates, and functions and be part of the same cultural package. While there were some seemingly minor exceptions to this assumption noted over the years, the fatal flaws were not documented for forty years (Hart and Brumbach 2005).

The original classificatory schemes lose their value as we move farther from the locale where the type was defined originally, which may or may not coincide with where the style actually originated. The descriptive traits of the type itself might remain through time and space, but the accompanying baggage of associated artifacts needs to be re-defined. The real question to be answered is how/why did identically appearing projectile points/pottery motifs appear in archaeological contexts hundreds of miles apart? People had to be vectors, transporting them or copying designs seen elsewhere.

Gregory Lattanzi (2009:8) reported a deep pit feature from Harry's Farm in New Jersey with Levanna Cord-on-Cord, Clemson Island Punctate, Otstungo Notched, Chance Incised, Owasco Corded, Garoga Incised, and a Munsee design over cording pottery types. These pottery styles represent a possible seven-hundred-year (plus or minus) time span (using the published New York State typologies) within the same strata in one feature.

Rieth and Hart (2011:5) note that the issues with typology extend beyond corded Owasco motifs. Kastl and Miroff (2008) document the recovery of rocker-stamped and incised pottery from very Late Woodland features, although rocker-stamped sherds were first seen much earlier. These types or stylistic techniques do not fit neatly into discrete time periods as proposed by Ritchie and MacNeish (1949), but rather have a longer use life or recur through time.

After receiving fifty AMS dates on charred cooking residues inside pottery vessels, Hart and Brumbach (2005:1–33) realized that Owasco in New York began as early as 400 A.D. rather than previously accepted 1000 A.D. date. Using AMS dating at the Thomas/Luckey site in Ashland, New York, Miroff (2009:Table 4.3) has extended the known range of dates for Sackett Corded from no later than 1350 A.D. to Contact. Other dates from the same site show a continuity/recurrence of the very early Levanna Cord-on-Cord throughout the entire sequence and its co-occurrence with the late Shenks Ferry Incised (Miroff 2009:82). Given a far earlier date for Owasco within its homeland (as defined by the number of sites and quantities of sherds recovered at each) and a greater than previously suspected time span for these and other types, the use of Iroquoian pottery types for even relative dating is called into question.

Current research at Pig Point (18AN50) in Maryland has an association of Mockley, Accokeek, Popes Creek, and Marcy Creek sherds from Pit 4 dated to 2100±30 RCY documenting that typological issues are not limited to New York Iroquois (Luckenbach 2013:8, 13). The Marcy Creek type could (should) be eight hundred years earlier (Stewart 1982:74).

A sixteen-thousand-square-foot block excavation at the Faucett site on the floodplain of the Upper Delaware Valley uncovered one hundred Late Woodland pits (Figure 9.1). Based upon feature contents (i.e., artifacts and ecofacts), I interpreted the site as having small, repetitive, short-term camps for procuring and processing seasonally available resources (Moeller 1992). Owasco, Oak Hill, Chance, and Munsee pottery types were found in different pits, which did not cluster by type.

Nine features are considered contemporaneous based upon refitting sherd and pipe fragments as well as unique pit morphology (Figure 9.2). In *toto*, the pottery types included Sackett Corded, Wickham Corded Punctate, Oak Hill Corded, and Munsee Incised and were associated with a Contact period coiled brass earring. These types should span about five hundred years based upon dates of identical types from New York State published prior to 1975.

The features seemed to cluster by the presence of sherds regardless of type. There is an extremely high statistical association of charred maize kernels and mussel shells found in features across the site. Most of the

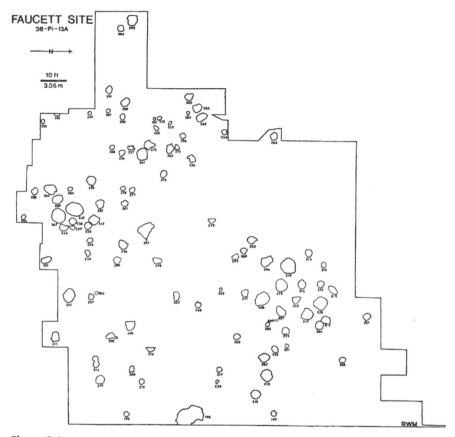

FAUCETT SITE
36-Pi-13A

Figure 9.1.

pits lacked diagnostic artifacts and were more or less in a block separated from those with implements and food remains. How could this be possible? How could any group know where another had camped and what they had done hundreds of years earlier? I can imagine that the floodplain attributes for convenient procurement and processing might endure, but why wouldn't the implements, food choices, manner of disposal, etc. change? I am now ready to accept the absolutely unthinkable. This was a single early Contact occupation for procuring and processing seasonally available resources. This means the diversity of pottery types, motifs, and design attributes (Figure 9.3) are contemporaneous. The only thing I cannot explain is why.

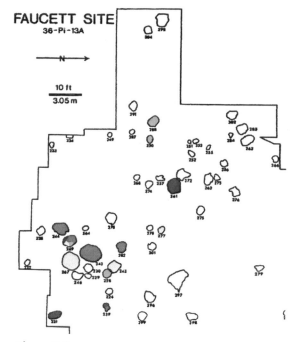

Figure 9.2.

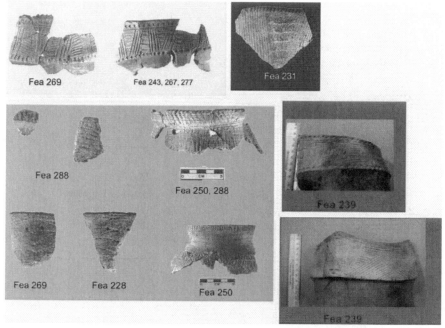

Figure 9.3.

MISUSING AND ABUSING TYPOLOGY

I am arguing that typology is not necessarily a secure means of relative dating even when considering samples close to where the type was defined originally. But dating artifacts is not the only problem. If one excavates a site in central Pennsylvania and finds a single biface, which very closely resembles an Orient Fishtail point associated with a mortuary complex on Long Island, then should we expect to find a similar complex at this site? Using the terms *phase* and *tradition* suggests that artifacts are occurring in packages in time and space and not as individual units. Using the same type name for spatially disparate objects suggests the remainder of the type description (including the date and associated artifacts) also applies.

Archaeologists have created evolutionary trajectories with diagnostic artifacts as the temporal markers. We assumed that hide, bark, or woven plant fiber containers preceded steatite bowls leading to steatite tempered pottery leading to a great variety of tempering agents. These cord- or fiber-impressed bodies begat rims decorated with corded and then incised designs of increasing complexity. Not satisfied with merely impressing and cutting wet clay, punctations, castellations, and faces were added to the design repertoire. The long-held assumption is that with each step in technological evolution and design nuance the previous was discarded in favor of the new and improved. If only. Madison Avenue would have been so proud.

Now we are seeing evidence from sites that the old prehistoric pottery types and design motifs did not slip silently into the sweet good night to make way for the new. The introduction of a new design or technological advancement does not mean that the old has been completely replaced or abandoned. The question becomes, "What accounts for the valid association of small numbers of diagnostic sherds or motifs of allegedly disparate dates?"

Ritchie's interpretation of many individual Owasco and Iroquoian sites was that they were long-term, single component villages. This was supported by the consistency of sherds, but was contradicted by the plethora of post molds which he interpreted as house patterns and palisades with many re-building episodes. Hart and Brumbach's research and AMS dates (2005) shows these sites were re-occupied repeatedly and had a wide dispersal of dates for the same type even at a single site. Obviously there was consistency through centuries. The Faucett site and others show just the opposite: amazing diversity at a point in time.

To carry the dangers of abusing typology to the extreme, consider seriation. The basic goal of seriation is to use stylistic attributes of artifacts to place a series of sites into chronological sequence. One might imagine this occurring with the techniques of applying decorations to pottery. The presumption is that when an attribute (e.g., motif) is first introduced into a group, it has a very low frequency of occurrence. There might be four other attributes already in use. Through time, the new attribute gains in popularity at the expense of the other four. People move their occupations maintaining the same frequency of occurrence of that attribute and the process continues.

The problem begins with defining a point in time. Seriation must begin with discrete occupations having contemporaneous artifact traits. A multi-component site has many discrete, non-contemporaneous occupations. Styles advent, decline, but can recur. Seriation does not take this into account. Seriation analysis assumes large numbers of objects to make the statistics reliable, but not many sites have the necessary quantities under tight controls.

SUMMARY

Archaeologists want to determine the true nature of the co-occurrence of apparently/allegedly/previously-thought-to-be temporally discrete types in the same context. What cultural processes are responsible for not only the dispersal of the types but also the longevity of cording alongside the development of incising (e.g., parallel development, cultural lag in accepting new motifs and new decorative techniques, retention of or return to old motifs, lineage identification, beginner's craft, or personal preference). Even if we assume types have no forensic value and no relative dating value, we are still left with cording, incising, high collars, low collars, no collars, fingernail impressions, punctations, castellations, effigy faces, smooth bodies, and more being contemporaneous at one site (e.g., Faucett) and possibly many or all others. I would not expect a single, small family band to exhibit such diversity at a point in time, but what about several small bands coalescing for short-term procurement and processing with each bringing their own implements?

The most conservative approach for using typology is to provide recognizable names for the objects during an analysis. Contexts and valid associations must be determined at the current site and not be based upon look-a-likes in the literature. The entire analysis must be based upon the current site's data and not be filled in with associations of similar objects found elsewhere. Without actual dates from the objects themselves (e.g., burned residue on a pottery sherd), natural or cultural admixture cannot be differentiated from valid associations. Only at the final interpretation can one include comparisons to existing descriptions and research from specific sites. The motto should be: first to thine own site be true.

CONCLUSION

The Midwestern Taxonomic Method is alive and well in the Middle Atlantic, but must be used very cautiously. McKern was not able to factor calendrical dates into the taxonomy because radiocarbon dating was unknown in 1939. He was not able to provide an areal extent to archaeological cultures, because the components at individual sites could not be separated with certainty. He did provide a stricture (McKern 1939:310):

> Archaeological data at best offer a very incomplete cultural picture of the people under investigation, and great care should be taken to base classification upon as representative a mass of data as possible.

Small camp sites or small block excavations do not necessarily provide enough information to accurately define the component. We need to rationalize the issues with typology before assigning their associated artifacts a position in the taxonomy.

ANSWERS TO THE QUIZ

1. (D). Rabbit is not kosher; the others are.
2. (A). 1, because you cannot have a one-sided polygon.
3. (B). Vietnamese use classifiers with nouns. Fruit and three-dimensional round objects use the same classifier, Trái; therefore cucumber, the planet Earth, and pineapple are a group. Although turnip is a fruit, it is an underground fruit and requires a different classifier, Củ.

or

1. (C). Chicken is not a mammal
2. (D). 8 is not a prime number
3. (C). The others are sold in supermarkets.

or

The correct answers depend upon who makes the types or who uses them.

REFERENCES CITED

Brown, Rita Mae
    1983   *Sudden Death.* Bantam, New York.

Dunnell, Robert C.
    1971   Sabloff and Smith's "The Importance of Both Analytic and Taxonomic Classification in the Type-Variety System." *American Antiquity* 36(1):115–18.

Evans, June, and Jay F. Custer
    1990   Guidelines for Standardizing Projectile Point Typology in the Middle Atlantic Region. *Journal of Middle Atlantic Archaeology* 6:31–41.

Ford, James A., and Julian H. Steward
    1954   On the Concept of Types. *American Anthropologist* New Series, 56(1):42–57.

Griffin, James B.
    1952   *The Archaeology of Eastern United States.* University of Chicago Press, Chicago.

Hart, John P., and Hetty Jo Brumbach
    2005   Cooking Residues, AMS Dates, and the Middle-to-Late Woodland Transition in Central New York. *Northeast Anthropology* 69:1–33.

Kastl, R. A., and L. A. Miroff
    2008   *Data Recovery Plan of Area L Site (NYSM # 11765), DEC-8-Moreau, Moreau Boat Launch Project, West River Road, Town of Moreau, Saratoga County, New York.* Report prepared for the New York State Museum, Albany.

Kinsey, W. Fred, III
    1972   *Archeology in the Upper Delaware Valley.* Pennsylvania Historical and Museum Commission, Harrisburg.

Kraft, Herbert C.
    1972   The Miller Field site, Warren County, New Jersey. In *Archeology in the Upper Delaware Valley,* edited by W. Fred Kinsey III, pp. 1–54. Pennsylvania Historical and Museum Commission, Harrisburg.

Krieger, Alex D.
    1944   The Typological Concept. *American Antiquity* 9(4):271–88.

Lattanzi, Gregory D.
    2009   Whatchoo Talkin' Bout Potsherd? Insights into Upper Delaware Valley Late Woodland Ceramics. *Journal of Middle Atlantic Archaeology* 25:1–14.

Luckenbach, Al
    2013   "Delmarva Adena" Mortuary Complex at Pig Point on the Patuxent River, Maryland. *Journal of Middle Atlantic Archaeology* 25:1–22.

McKern, W. C.
    1939   The Midwestern Taxonomic Method as an Aid to Archaeological Culture Study. *American Antiquity* 4(4):301–13.

Miroff, Laurie E.
2009   A Local-level Analysis of Social Reproduction and Transformation in the Chemung Valley: The Thomas/Luckey Site. In *Iroquoian Archaeology & Analytic Scale,* edited by Laurie E. Miroff and Timothy D. Knapp, pp. 69–100. University of Tennessee Press, Knoxville.

Moeller, Roger W.
1992   *Analyzing and Interpreting Late Woodland Features.* Occasional Publications in Northeastern Anthropology 12, Archaeological Services, Bethlehem, CT.

Plot55.com
2002   http://www.plot55.com/growing/nicotiana.html. Retrieved July 2013.

Rieth, Christina B., and John P. Hart
2011   Introduction to Current Research in New York Archaeology: A.D. 700–1300. In *Current Research in New York Archaeology: A.D. 700–1300,* edited by Christina B. Reith and John P. Hart, pp. 1–6. New York State Education Department, Albany.

Ritchie, William A.
1961   *A Typology and Nomenclature for New York Projectile Points.* New York State Museum and Science Service, Bulletin 384. Albany.
1965   *The Archaeology of New York State.* Natural History Press, Garden City.

Ritchie, William A., and Richard S. MacNeish
1949   The Pre-Iroquoian Pottery of New York State. *American Antiquity* 15: 97–124.

Stewart, R. Michael
1982   Prehistoric Ceramics of the Great Valley of Maryland. *Archaeology of Eastern North America* 10:69–94.

The Online Slang Dictionary
2012   http://onlineslangdictionary.com/thesaurus/words+meaning+sexuality + %28related+to%29.html. Accessed July 5, 2012.

10

+

The Contributions and Practice of Culture History in the Middle Atlantic Region

Daniel R. Griffith

Traditional culture history in archaeology is the descriptive, normative presentation of material culture within a temporal and spatial framework. The objective of culture history was to define historical societies at a given time and place by their distinct cultural or "ethnic" characteristics based on their material culture. From the late nineteenth century through the mid-twentieth century, the concept was developed and practiced by defining cultures as geographically distinct entities with their own characteristics that developed from their own unique histories.

DEVELOPMENT OF CULTURE HISTORY IN THE MIDDLE ATLANTIC REGION

For archaeologists, the "distinct cultural entities" were defined by lists of material culture traits, leading to a classification of separate cultures such as the Old Copper Culture of the Great Lakes and the Delmarva Adena Culture of the Middle Atlantic. The intent was to classify cultures based on grouping classifications of artifacts and sites from specific times and places. The ultimate goal was to create grand syntheses of the history of cultures in specific geographic areas. Works such as Griffin's "Cultural Periods in Eastern United States" (Griffin 1952) and Caldwell's "Trend and Tradition in the Prehistory of the Eastern United States" (Caldwell 1958) are of particular relevance to Middle Atlantic archaeology. These studies offered a framework of culture history over a broad area. While not ignoring what was then known through archaeology of the American Indian people in the Middle Atlantic, the scale of the syntheses was so broad and the definitions of the cultures based on such a restricted set of characteristics that one cannot see the people for the eastern woodlands.

Archaeologists in the East were quick to reduce the scale of the wide ranging syntheses by focusing on smaller geographic areas. In 1941 and 1956, Dorothy Cross published two volumes on the "Archaeology of New Jersey" (Cross 1941, 1956), while other nearby regions followed, such as Ritchie's 1965 "The Archaeology of New York State" (Ritchie 1965) and Fitting's 1970 "The Archaeology of Michigan: A Guide to the Prehistory of the Great Lakes Region" (Fitting 1970). In the 1960s, Middle Atlantic archaeology was still in its infancy in terms of understanding the range of material culture found in the region and its implications for the interpretation of American Indian history. With few exceptions, much of the work produced sub-regional summaries of current research, not syntheses of regional culture history (Kent, Smith, and McCann 1971 and Stephenson and Ferguson 1963).

What was lacking in the Middle Atlantic was a fine-scale presentation of chronological sequences of material culture working hand-in-hand with disciplined context control and theoretical frameworks that brought forth a conception of a people living in a real time in a real place. A fundamental prerequisite of fine-scale culture history, as the bases for developing areal and regional syntheses, are meaningful chronological sequences and precise context control. It is important to note here that I am speaking of chronological sequences of artifacts, features, soils, biological data, sites, and so forth, not of the traditional archaeological cultures, however they may be defined. While elsewhere in North America, the building of detailed chronological sequences began in the 1920s with Kidder's work in the Southwest (Kidder 1924) and Ford's work in the Southeast in the 1930s and 1950s (Ford 1938; Ford and Willey 1955), this type of research was not systematically undertaken in the Middle Atlantic until the 1960s. As late as 1971 it was observed that Eastern archaeology, in general, was behind other areas like the Southwest in producing fine-scale space-time ordering (Willey and Sabloff 1974:169).

In my view, there are two reasons for this lag. The chronological sequences developed in the Southwest and Southeast were based initially on detailed analysis of stratigraphic sequences and artifact seriation of overlapping sequences. The coastal plain of the Middle Atlantic lacked deeply stratified sites, while stratified sites elsewhere in the region had yet to be systematically examined. The development and refinement of radiocarbon dating beginning in the 1950s made it possible to define artifact sequences in areas without deeply stratified sites. Academic and institutional interest in the Middle Atlantic followed and expanded significantly. As an example, the first radiocarbon date from an American Indian site in Delaware was in 1963, yet the second suite of dates was twelve years later in 1975. By the 1984 publication of Jay Custer's "Delaware Prehistoric Archaeology: An Ecological Approach" (Custer 1984), sixty radiocarbon dates were reported from Delaware and the Eastern Shore of Maryland. Similar trends in refining chronological sequences elsewhere in the Middle Atlantic paved the way for a significant round of regional and areal syntheses, such as:

1. William Gardner's 1982 "Early and Middle Woodland Cultures in the Middle Atlantic: An Overview" (Gardner 1982)
2. Jay Custer's 1984 "Delaware Prehistoric Archaeology" (Custer 1984), his 1986 "Late Woodland Cultures of the Middle Atlantic Region" (Custer 1986), and the 1989 "Prehistoric Cultures of the Delmarva Peninsula" (Custer 1989)
3. Theodore Reinhart and Mary Ellen Hodges's early 1990s series on cultural period studies in Virginia (Reinhart and Hodges 1989–1992)
4. Steve Potter's 1993 "Commoners, Tributes and Chiefs: The Development of Algonquian Culture in the Potomac Valley" (Potter 1993)
5. Richard Dent's 1995 "Chesapeake Prehistory: Old Traditions, New Directions" (Dent 1995)
6. Mike Stewart's 1995 "The Status of Woodland Prehistory in the Middle Atlantic Region" (Stewart 1995)
7. Custer's 1996 "Prehistoric Cultures of Eastern Pennsylvania" (Custer 1996)

Each of these sub-regional syntheses is a culture history building on artifact and site typologies with varying degrees of temporal control in specific regions leading to the definition and description of archaeological cultures on a broad scale. Each was based on a growing body of site specific research and specialized studies of specific artifacts classes (e.g., American Indian ceramic sequences—cf. Gardner 1975) or specific behavioral practices (e.g., ossuary burials—cf. Curry 1999). While these syntheses have different emphases in terms of theoretical framework, they have in common a focus on classifications of objects, features, and sites that when placed in temporal and geographic frameworks produced a body of work that enhances our understanding of the American Indian people and their history in the region. The contributions of culture history were, and are, in:

1. Examining and organizing material culture into explicit frameworks,
2. Establishing and refining methods of fieldwork and analysis,

3. Excavating sites and archiving artifacts and field and laboratory records from sites now long gone due to modern development, erosion,
   and so on, and
4. Exhibiting a sincere interest in understanding the history of the American Indian people and in sharing that knowledge with the profession
   and the general public.

BEYOND REGIONAL SYNTHESES

The last published regional synthesis in the Middle Atlantic was seventeen years ago. Are we done with culture history? I don't think so. Are we
done with regional syntheses? Maybe. The need to establish new regional
syntheses is directly related to the scale of the research question. Nevertheless, early twenty-first-century research and publication has continued
on an accelerated pace in the region. I see four major trends in both the
nature of the subject and in the theoretical frameworks of the research:

1. Illuminating studies of American Indian people at finer and finer
   temporal and geographic scales that touch patterns at the level of
   individual communities and even individual people, such as Gallivan's "Powhatan's Werowocomoco: Constructing Place, Polity
   and Personhood in the Chesapeake, C.E. 1200–C.E. 1609" (Gallivan
   2007:85-199) and Espenshade's "Two Native Potters 'Speak' about
   Punctates: Harding Flats Data and the Clemson Island Concept"
   (Espenshade 2001:59–84).
2. Challenging the profession to examine basic data, focusing on how
   we know what we think we know and applying new analytical
   techniques, often from other disciplines like material sciences. In
   other words, "the essence of archaeological interpretation is getting
   the facts straight" (Emerson et al. 2013:62). Griffith's "Delaware
   American Indian Ceramics: Radiocarbon Dates" (Griffith 2010);
   Moeller's "The Use, Misuse, and Abuse of Typology" (this volume);
   Schindler's "Experimental Research in Middle Atlantic Archaeology" (this volume).
3. Framing research questions and research designs that humanize
   history, like Trocolli's "Women Leaders in Native North American
   Societies: Invisible Women of Power" (Trocolli 1999).
4. Embracing descendant communities as more than consumers of
   historical knowledge, but as participants in its creation, such as Gallivan and Moretti-Langholtz's "Civic Engagement at Werowocomoco:
   Reasserting Native Narratives from a Powhatan Place of Power"

(Gallivan and Moretti-Langholtz 2007); and Hantman, Wood, and Shields's "Writing Collaborative History: How the Monacan Nation and Archaeologists Worked Together to Enrich Our Understanding of Virginia's Native People" (Hantman, Wood, and Shields 2000:56–59).

These are not mutually exclusive categories. I do not know whether this is the right or best research direction for Middle Atlantic archaeology and my opinion does not really matter, but when reviewing the literature, this is what archaeologists in the region are doing.

PRACTICING CULTURE HISTORY

I subscribe to a broader definition of culture history than that practiced earlier in the twentieth century—culture history as a method of research more than a product—a method with no pre-conceived end result. By this definition, we are doing culture history whenever our research questions and interpretations are informed by a detailed examination of material culture, and associated data from multiple disciplines, in a fine-grained space and time framework. Such research cycles between data, interpretation, synthesis, and back to data, and then it starts over again as we drill down to the level of living communities and people. The objective is to know the people and to share that knowledge. And to do so, it is still a priority in any area to investigate more points or "windows" on the historical continuum to shed light on finer-scale cultural dynamics (Panich 2013:109).

I conducted recent research in Delaware that speaks to the issue of data quality and precision—how archaeologists know what we know or think we know and what we can learn from that exercise. I completed a project that cataloged, evaluated, and analyzed all radiocarbon dates from Delaware associated with American Indian ceramics. As of 2012 there are eighty radiocarbon dates from Delaware for various ceramic types. There are also types (e.g., Minguannan ceramics) for which there are no radiocarbon dates in Delaware. The types defined in Delaware, and elsewhere, are primarily "temporal" types in that the defining attributes (i.e., surface treatment and temper) have been shown repeatedly to be most sensitive to changes through time. The types combine attributes that are technological and symbolic (cf. Klein 2003). After analysis, I concluded that seventy-two of the eighty radiocarbon dates were precise, meaning their association with the target ceramics was clear and the resultant radiocarbon dates had standard deviations equal to or less than one hundred years.

The geographic distribution of precise radiocarbon dates is of historical and anthropological significance. The nature and direction of regional or sub-regional influences on American Indian ceramic technology and style can be interpreted by examining temporal and geographic distributions of the ceramic series, types, and varieties. It is possible, even likely, that ceramic types are not evenly distributed within Delaware and it is equally likely that some types are not present at all in some areas. It is precisely this kind of temporal and geographic pattern that leads to a finer-grained knowledge of social dynamics. A close look at this pattern shows that the data points for individual ceramic types are discontinuous. Of the seventy-two precise radiocarbon dates from Delaware, there are none from the Piedmont, eleven from the Delaware River drainage, forty-six from the Delaware Bay drainage, thirteen from the Atlantic Coast drainage, and two from the Chesapeake Bay drainage. This distribution skews our knowledge of geographic patterns, and I suspect that similar data patterns are found elsewhere in the region. The level of detail in a synthesis is directly associated with the fineness of the data. It is very difficult to approach research on cultural boundaries, social influences, or community and individual potter based studies without more evenly distributed data points of quality and high precision.

The temporal distribution of ceramics is of equal historical and anthropological significance. My recalibration of the seventy-two radiocarbon dates associated with American Indian ceramics produced a revised date range summary for the types (see Figure10.1). The result shows some interesting temporal patterns. For example, focusing on the temporal distribution of Mockley and Hell Island ceramics, we see a considerable temporal overlap in Delaware. Mockley, a shell tempered ceramic with cord marked or net impressed exterior surfaces, and Hell Island, a quartz and mica tempered ceramic with cord marked or fabric impressed exterior surfaces, come from two different technological traditions. The two ceramics types have not been found in the same contexts. While at one scale they share vessel form, they differ significantly in choice of surface treatment and temper, suggesting different learning networks of potters coming from slightly different technological traditions. If there is a link between technological traditions, learning networks, and broader cultural communities, this temporal pattern leads to the conclusion that two different ceramic traditions were in Delaware at the same time, creating a cultural mosaic of ceramic traditions. It is equally possible that there were short-term fluctuations in geographic boundaries between potters producing these ceramics at a time scale that falls below the threshold of detection given the 2 sigma range of the calibrated radiocarbon dates. New comparative research and new accurate and precise radiocarbon dates, from a wider range of sites, will provide information to test or refine this interpretation.

A final example from the study emphasizes the point that time and space matter. Townsend ceramics, which are shell-tempered with fabric-impressed exterior surfaces, first appeared in Delaware around *cal* A.D.

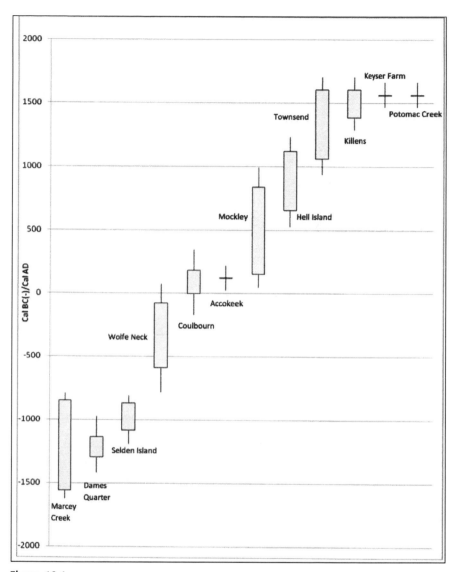

Figure 10.1.

1000. The Townsend series is distributed from the central Delmarva Peninsula south along the coastal plain through Albemarle and Pamlico Sounds
in North Carolina and west to the Fall Line in its northern distribution
and to the limit of tidewater in the south. There are two interesting patterns to note about the geographic distribution. First, the distribution of
Townsend ceramics mirrors the southern two-thirds of the shell-tempered

Mockley ceramic distribution (see Figure 10.2). Second, there is a sharp northern boundary to the Townsend distribution in central Delaware and the Delaware Bay. To the north, Late Woodland Minguannan, Riggins, and other ceramics occupy part of the area formerly covered by the regional distribution of Mockley ceramics. If there is a link between technological traditions, learning networks and broader cultural communities, this geographic pattern leads to the conclusion that different histories occurred north and south of the boundaries of Townsend distribution.

Townsend ceramics also exhibit an interesting temporal trend in design techniques and motifs (refer to Figure 10.3). Complex incised motifs are early in the series, more simplified, incised, and corded motifs are later, and a plain type is the most recent. Townsend Plain and related types (e.g., Yeocomico in Virginia) continue to be in use into the period of early European exploration and settlement (Griffith 2012; Egloff and Potter

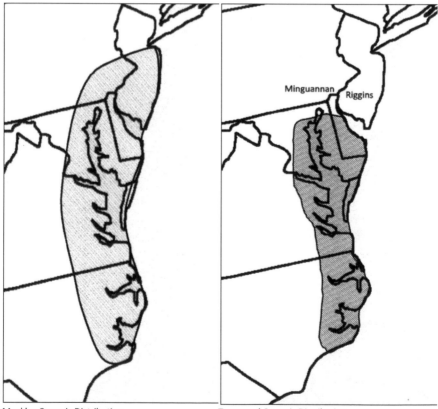

Mockley Ceramic Distribution   Townsend Ceramic Distribution

Figure 10.2.

1982:112). The range of complex motifs early in the Townsend series varies from site to site (Griffith 1977). If ceramic decorative motif is an expression of symbolic style, then the trend suggests changes from a desire by the potter to express difference to a desire to express sameness or unity. This pattern may reflect social trends in Delaware. One could propose the pattern reflects a shift in identity from smaller, lineage-based communities to identity with larger, sub-regional social networks. This hypothesis can be tested with further analysis of additional, independent data.

In the examples above illustrating the usefulness of ceramic typology, my intent was not to define archaeological cultures in the traditional sense, but to examine the history of pottery makers who learned their craft in similar social environments. Similar ceramic attributes in the same place and time are not a coincidence. Research structured on the questions of time and place of ceramic production and use yields additional hypotheses about the nature of the cultures that produced the ceramics. The definitions of those types, however, can and should vary with the nature of the research question investigated. The most critical factor in developing useful, problem-solving typologies is a clearly stated research objective supported by disciplined context control and reliable artifact associations at a local level.

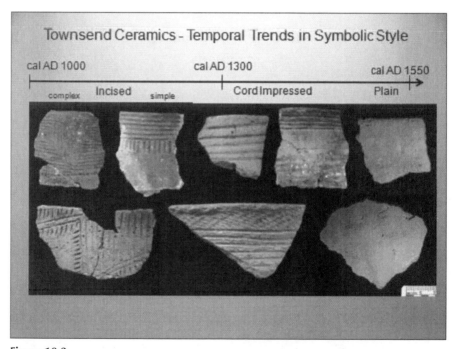

Figure 10.3.

Anticipating an anti-essentialist critique of culture history, I offer that the debate should be about research questions, research strategies, and the definition of classifications (i.e., typologies), not whether things have essences. At the level of cultures defined through archaeology, essences are not fixed through time and space. However, physical things like ceramics, which point to the culture that created them, are fixed in time and space.

REFERENCES CITED

Caldwell, Joseph R.
  1958   *Trend and Tradition in the Prehistory of the Eastern United States.* American Anthropological Association, Memoir 88, Menasha.

Cross, Dorothy
  1941   *Archaeology of New Jersey, Vol.I.* Archaeological Society of New Jersey, Trenton.
  1956   *Archaeology of New Jersey, Vol.II: The Abbott Farm Site.* Archaeological Society of New Jersey, Trenton.

Curry, Dennis
  1999   *Feast of the Dead: Aboriginal Ossuaries in Maryland.* Maryland Historical Trust, Crownsville.

Custer, Jay F.
  1984   *Delaware Prehistoric Archaeology: An Ecological Approach.* University of Delaware Press, Newark.
  1986   *Late Woodland Cultures of the Middle Atlantic Region.* University of Delaware Press, Newark.
  1989   *Prehistoric Cultures of the Delmarva Peninsula: An Archaeological Study.* University of Delaware Press, Newark.
  1996   *Prehistoric Cultures of Eastern Pennsylvania.* Pennsylvania Historical and Museum Commission, Harrisburg.

Dent, Richard J.
  1995   *Chesapeake Prehistory: Old Traditions, New Directions.* Plenum Press, New York.

Egloff, Keith, and Stephen Potter
  1982   Indian Ceramics from Coastal Plain Virginia. *Archaeology of Eastern North America* 10:95–117.

Emerson, Thomas E., K. Farnsworth, S. Wisseman, and R. Hughes
  2013   The Allure of the Exotic: Reexamining the Use of Local and Distant Pipestone Quarries in Ohio Hopewell Pipe Caches. *American Antiquity* 78:1.

Espenshade, Christopher T.
  2001   Two Native Potters "Speak" About Punctates: Harding Flats Data and the Clemson Island Concept. *Journal of Middle Atlantic Archaeology* 17:59–84.

Fitting, James E.
   1970   *The Archaeology of Michigan: A Guide to the Prehistory of the Great Lakes.*
          Garden City, NY.

Ford, James A.
   1938   A Chronological Method Applicable to the Southeast. *American Antiquity*
          3(3): 260–64, Menasha.

Ford, James A., and G. Willey
   1955   An Interpretation of the Prehistory of the Eastern United States. *American*
          Anthropologist, 43(3): 325–63, Menasha.

Gallivan, Martin D.
   2007   Powhatan's Werowocomoco: Constructing Place, Polity and Person-
          hood in the Chesapeake, C.E. 1200–C.E. 1609. *American Anthropologist*
          109:85–100.

Gallivan, Martin, and Danielle Moretti-Langholtz
   2007   Civic Engagement at Werowocomoco: Reasserting Native Narratives from
          a Powhatan Place of Power. In *Archaeology as a Tool of Civic Engagement,*
          edited by B. J. Little and P. A. Shackel, AltaMira Press, Lanham, MD.

Gardner, William M.
   1975   Early Pottery in Eastern North America: A Viewpoint. *Proceedings of the*
          1975 Middle Atlantic Archaeology Conference, Lancaster, PA.
   1982   Early and Middle Woodland in the Middle Atlantic: An Overview. In
          Practicing Environmental Archaeology: Methods and Interpretations, edited
          by Roger Moeller, Washington, CT.

Griffin, James B. (editor)
   1952   Culture Periods in Eastern United States Archaeology. In *Archaeology of*
          the Eastern United States, pp. 352–64, University of Chicago Press.

Griffith, Daniel R.
   1977   Townsend Ceramics and the Late Woodland of Southern Delaware, Mas-
          ter's thesis, American University, Washington, DC.
   2010   Delaware American Indian Ceramics: Radiocarbon Dates. *Bulletin of the*
          Archaeological Society of Delaware, Vol. 47, New Series, Wilmington.
   2012   The Gray Farm Site (7K-F-11 and 7K-F-169): Analysis of American Indian
          Ceramics. In *The Gray Farm Site: Phase II and Phase III Excavations on the*
          Murderkill River (Sites 7K-F-11 and 7K-F-169), SR 1 Frederica North Grade
          Separated Intersection, Kent County, Delaware. Delaware Department of
          Transportation Archaeology Series, Dover.

Hantman, J. L., K. Wood, and D. Shields
   2000   Writing Collaborative History: How the Monacan Nation and Archae-
          ologists Worked Together to Enrich Our Understanding of Virginia's
          Native Peoples. *Archaeology* 53(5):56–59.

Kent, Barry C., Ira F. Smith III, and Catherine McCann
   1971   *Foundations of Pennsylvania Prehistory, Vol. 1,* Pennsylvania Museum and
          Historical Commission, Harrisburg.

Kidder, Alfred V.
 1924   An Introduction to the Study of Southwestern Archaeology, with a Pre-
        liminary Account of the Excavations at Pecos. *Papers of the Southwestern
        Expedition*, Phillips Academy, No. 1, New Haven.

Klein, Michael
 2003   Ceramics, Style and Society in the Potomac Valley of Virginia. *Journal of
        Middle Atlantic Archaeology*, Vol. 19.

Moeller, Roger
 2013   The Use, Misuse, and Abuse of Typology. Paper presented at the Middle
        Atlantic Archaeology Conference, Virginia Beach.

Panich, Lee M.
 2013   Archaeologies of Persistence: Reconsidering the Legacies of Colonialism
        in Native North America. *American Antiquity*, 78 (1):105–122, Washing-
        ton, DC.

Potter, Stephen R.
 1993   *Commoners, Tribute, and Chiefs: The Development of Algonquian Culture in
        the Potomac Valley*, University of Virginia Press, Charlottesville.

Reinhart, Theodore R., and M. E. Hodges, eds.
 1989–1992   *Council of Virginia Archaeologists Special Publications*, Nos. 19, 22, 23
        and 29, Archaeological Society of Virginia, Richmond.

Ritchie, William A.
 1965   *The Archaeology of New York State*, Garden City.

Schindler, William
 2013   Experimental Research in Middle Atlantic Archaeology. Paper presented
        at the Middle Atlantic Archaeology Conference, Virginia Beach.

Stephenson, Robert L., and Alice L. L. Ferguson
 1963   The Accokeek Creek Site: A Middle Atlantic Seaboard Culture Sequence.
        Museum of Anthropology, Anthropological Papers No. 20, University of Michi-
        gan, Ann Arbor.

Stewart, Michael
 1995   The Status of Woodland Prehistory in the Middle Atlantic Region. *Ar-
        chaeology of Eastern North America* 23:177–206.

Trocolli, Ruth
 1999   Women Leaders in Native North American Societies: Invisible Women
        of Power. *In Manifesting Power: Gender and the Interpretation of Power in
        Archaeology*, edited by Tracy L. Sweely, pp. 49–61. Routledge, London.

Willey, Gordon R., and J. Sabloff
 1974   *A History of American Archaeology*. Thames and Hudson, London.

11

+

Peopling of the Middle Atlantic

A Review of Paleoindian Research

Kurt W. Carr

Research conducted in the Middle Atlantic region has been critical in the development of several models on when and how people first entered the New World and also their cultural adaptations once they arrived. Based on the Meadowcroft Rockshelter excavations in western Pennsylvania, James Adovasio (1993) has proposed a Pre-Clovis technology that was transitioning from a blade tool technology to a bifacial technology. More recently, evidence has been presented from the Middle Atlantic to support Stanford and Bradley's (2012) proposed Atlantic crossing and a Solutrean origin for fluted point technology. In 1952, John Witthoft was one of the first to propose a Paleoindian adaptation involving very high mobility. Twenty years later, William Gardner (1974, 1989) proposed a very different adaptation, emphasizing reduced mobility and a foraging subsistence pattern. In this presentation, the status of these models and Paleoindian research in general in the region will be reviewed.

The following presentation is a brief overview of the initial settlement and early cultural adaptations of the Middle Atlantic region. The term *Paleoindian* is applied to the earliest period of human occupation in the New World and begins with the entrance of humans into North America. The exact dates for this period have long been the topic of study and debate. Temporal change within this period in the environment, technology, subsistence, and settlement patterns has been demonstrated throughout North America, and the Middle Atlantic region has been especially important in some of these discussions (Dixon 1999; Meltzer 2009; Stanford and Bradley 2012). Willey (1966) divided this period into Clovis, Folsom, and Plano phases. At the early end of this continuum Krieger (1964) added the Pre-Projectile Point complex, now known as the Pre-Clovis phase or more recently "Older-than-Clovis" (Collins 2012). A large number of sites have been proposed for this phase. However, exceedingly few have stood the test of time (Adovasio and Page 2002). Gardner (1974) has added the Early Archaic phases of Charleston, Palmer, and Kirk at the end of the Paleoindian period. In the Ridge and Valley of Virginia, he argued for cultural continuity throughout this time; however, Stewart and Cavallo (1991) in the Delaware Valley and Cowan (1991) on the Appalachian Plateau do not share the same interpretation.

In this chapter, the Paleoindian period will be defined as the time from the first human populations settling in the New World dating to at least 16,000 ^{14}C yr BP (Adovasio and Page 2002) until the appearance of notched projectile points such as Thebes, Charleston, Palmer, and Kirk corner and side-notched types dating to 9,900 ^{14}C yr BP. The period is divided into the Pre-Clovis phase and the Fluted Point tradition. Although the former remains controversial, and the internal chronology of this phase is not well known, there are a reasonable number of sites in North and South America to support the existence of humans in the New World prior to the appearance of fluted projectile points. In addition, the southeastern United States has produced a great variety of fluted point types and some early dates (i.e., Page-Ladson [Webb 2006] and Little Salt Spring in Florida [Clausen et al. 1979]), demonstrating this region was occupied prior to the invention of fluting. In contrast, there is significantly more known concerning chronology, internal evolution, material culture, and settlement patterns for the Fluted Point tradition.

PALEO-ENVIRONMENTAL RECONSTRUCTION

Victor Carbone (1976) established the paleo-environmental framework for the Middle Atlantic, and several others, notably Delcourt and Delcourt (1986), Dent (1995), Foss (1977), McWeeney (2007), and Vento et al. (1994), have continued to refine this reconstruction. The dates and the terminology have since been revised with additional data (Table 11.1). Especially the identification of the Younger Dryas has improved our understanding of the environmental setting (Isarin and Bohncke 1999; Mayewski et al. 1993).

The Late Glacial Maximum is characterized as cold and wet. Glaciers covered all of New England, the Great Lakes, and into northern Pennsylvania. South of the glaciers can be characterized as a spruce parkland mosaic with no modern analogues. Deciduous species including oak may have contributed up to 10 percent of the forest (McWeeney 2007). Generally, the Middle Atlantic region became more boreal to the south in Vir-

Table 11.1. Climatic Episodes in the Middle Atlantic Region

Episodes	*¹⁴C yr B.P.*	Calendar Dates B.P.	Climatic Condition
Last Glacial Maximum	21,000	25,150	Lowest Temperatures / Highest Precipitation
Last Glacial	16,500	19,800	
Bølling / Allerød	12,600	14,950	Warming with Brief Cold Spells
	11,400	13,300	Warming
Younger Dryas	10,950	12,900	Sudden Cold and Dry
Pre-Boreal	10,150	11,800	Sudden Warming
Boreal	9,200	10,350	Warm and Dry
Atlantic	8,490	9,500	Warm and Moist
Sub-Boreal	5,060	5,850	Principally Warm and Dry
Sub-Atlantic	2,760	2,850	Warm and Moist
Medieval Warming		A.D. 900	Warm and Moist
Little Ice Age		A.D. 1300–1800	Cold and Wet

ginia including increases in pine and deciduous elements and more open, with non-arboreal species to the north in the glaciated regions of Pennsylvania and New York. Pleistocene megafauna, such as were recorded from Saltville, Virginia (or numerous sites in Pennsylvania and New York such as Barnosky et al. 1988; Kirkpatrick and Fisher 1993; Laub 2002; and Sullivan and Randall 1996), inhabited the region as late as 11,000 ¹⁴C yr BP when they became extinct. The glaciers began to melt by 14,000 ¹⁴C yr BP and had retreated across the Saint Lawrence River by 12,600 ¹⁴C yr BP. In the glaciated region and outwash area to the south, this was a time of general ecological change. New drainage patterns were being established and flora and fauna were migrating into the northern Middle Atlantic region.

The Allerød warming episode began around 11,500 ¹⁴C yr BP and probably accelerated the migration of deciduous elements into the Middle Atlantic region. It also probably facilitated the movement of the first Clovis technology into the region. The Younger Dryas episode begins at 10,950 ¹⁴C yr BP. This represents a return to significantly cooler temperatures (a drop of 5 to 15 degrees Celsius within a few generations or less) and dry conditions (Isarin and Bohncke 1999; Lothrop et al. 2011; Mayewski et al. 1993; Meltzer and Holliday 2010). These conditions would have slowed or reversed the movement of deciduous species and temperate climate animals north. It also corresponds to the end of Clovis and the beginning of a variety of Middle Paleoindian complexes (Waters and Stafford 2007). According to Delcourt and Delcourt (1986), this episode was characterized by increased erosion especially in alluvial environments. This represents a period of instability and reduced predictability of food resources. Alluvial deposits covering Middle Paleoindian occupations will be rare. In contrast, eolian deposition would have been common in the coastal zone and therefore that is where to look for buried occupations from the Middle Paleoindian period. Throughout this period, there were significant differences in flora and fauna between the northern and southern regions of the Middle Atlantic and these can roughly be defined as the glaciated and unglaciated regions. At approximately 10,100 ^{14}C yr BP, the Younger Dryas ended and there is some agreement that it ended abruptly (Meltzer and Holiday 2010:8). Temperatures and precipitation rose quickly to slightly above present conditions. The vegetation changed dramatically to a closed boreal forest with increasing deciduous species to the south and coniferous elements to the north. This corresponds to the beginning of the Holocene and the Archaic cultural period.

PRE-CLOVIS PHASE

The peopling of the Middle Atlantic region is a significant research issue in that it sets the baseline for cultural patterns in terms of population density and site distributions for future cultural adaptations. In addition, the presence of Pre-Clovis human populations would mean that the region had already been partially explored and resources located when the Clovis technological package diffused into the Middle Atlantic region.

It is interesting that the Middle Atlantic region can boast three sites dating to the Pre-Clovis phase: Meadowcroft Rockshelter in Pennsylvania (Adovasio et al. 1988; Carlisle and Adovasio 1984), Cactus Hill in Virginia (McAvoy and McAvoy 1997), and Miles Point in Maryland (Lowery et al. 2010) (see Figure 11.1 for all site locations in this chapter). All have produced multiple radiometric dates and artifacts of unquestionable human origin. For Miles Point and Cactus Hill, the problems have been in determining the depositional context and the stratigraphic separation of the Pre-Clovis and Clovis occupations. However, the geomorphological analysis by Lowery et al. (2010) at Miles Point has been able to document two wind-blown soils; the Paw Paw Cove loess dates to Clovis times and the Miles Point loess dates to at least 17,000 ^{14}C yr BP. These soils have been dated over a large area of the Delmarva Peninsula (Lowery et al. 2010:6–7). Although the artifact assemblage is small, the lower soil clearly dates to Pre-Clovis times and documents a Pre-Clovis occupation. The intensive geomorphological analysis at the Cactus Hill site by Wagner and McAvoy (2004) has clarified the stratigraphy at this site also. They conclude that some bioturbation has occurred but the particle size analysis and the pedogenic lamellae support the development of two separate stable land surfaces—one Clovis and one Pre-Clovis in age, both covered by eolian deposition.

Finally, the Meadowcroft Rockshelter has been extensively studied (Adovasio 1993; Adovasio et al. 1988; Carlisle and Adovasio 1984; Haynes 1980, 1991). The only outstanding problem for some people is the radiocarbon dates from the Pre-Clovis levels. Adovasio (1993) and Adovasio and Pedler (2013) have responded to accusations of contamination; some critics are satisfied and some will never be. In addition, the convincing data is that the Pre-Clovis sites such as Meadowcroft are beginning to exhibit a pattern—small bifaces, blade-like flakes, and mainly non-alluvial settings (Bouldurian 1985; Collins 2012; Dillehay 1989, 1997; McAvoy and McAvoy 1997; Waters et al. 2011a).

All three of these sites suggest an entrance date of 17,000 ^{14}C yr BP or earlier. Sites outside of the Middle Atlantic region such as Monte Verde in Chile (Dillehay 1997), Debra L. Friedken in Texas (Waters et al. 2011a), and Paisley Cave in Oregon (Jenkins et al. 2013), to name a few, also support this date. The technology of Pre-Clovis sites in the Middle Atlantic region consists of flake tools and small bifacial projectile points. There is a frequent reference to "blades," "blade flakes," or "elongated flakes." However, my interpretation of these artifacts is that this is not a blade tool technology similar to the Upper Paleolithic of Europe, but there seems to be a tendency to produce elongated flakes. Interestingly, they are not regularly using the formal flake tools, common on later fluted point sites but rather a more expedient tool kit of retouched and utilized flakes. In addition, the lithic material types are frequently local and do not suggest a high degree of mobility. The population density was extremely low and, unfortunately, the Pre-Clovis phase cannot be identified by diagnostic artifacts like the Fluted Point traditions—it is invisible unless radiometrically dated. Currently it seems that eolian deposits and rockshelters are the best places to find occupations from this period.

One final note, other than similarities in a few biface forms, is that there is little data to support an Atlantic crossing during Solutrean times as proposed by Stanford and Bradley (2012). Although Upper Paleolithic peoples probably possessed the maritime technology to make the crossing, as reviewed by Lawrence Straus (2000), Solutrean bifaces are part of a technology dominated by blade tools. The eastern Pre-Clovis sites may contain a small blade component but it is mainly a flake tool technology. The same is true for Clovis technology on the East Coast. A few blades may be present in these assemblages, but there are no Clovis sites along the East Coast, with the proportion of blades found at Upper Paleolithic sites (Carr et al. 2010). In addition (Carr 2000; Straus 2000), similarities in language, teeth, and DNA argue for a Siberian rather than an Iberian origin for Clovis.

FLUTED POINT TRADITION CHRONOLOGY

Although there is some debate concerning the chronological placement of the earliest fluted projectile points (Miller et al. 2013:208–09), in this chapter, the origin of fluting in North America will be dated to approximately 11,200 ^{14}C yr BP (Waters and Stafford 2007). In the Middle Atlantic region, fluted projectile points are either added to an existing Paleoindian adaptation through diffusion or they are an artifact carried by an influx of new people into the region. Although Gramly (2009:9) argues that the Cumberland type is the earliest, the Clovis type is here considered the earliest fluted point form. There are a number of later types or styles, and regional sequences have been established in the Southeast by Anderson et al. (1996), in the Eastern Great Lakes by Deller and Ellis (1988), and recently in the New England Maritimes region by Bradley et al. (2008). Unfortunately, individual types have only been dated at a few sites and rarely have several different types been recovered from the same site in a stratified context. Therefore, the so-called projectile point sequence for later types is somewhat conjectural. The chronological sequence of projectile points in these regions is primarily based on geomorphology and assumptions concerning changing fluted point morphology rather than radiometric dates for these types. The juxtaposition of the Middle Atlantic region to these regions suggests that these types have some relevance to Middle Atlantic archaeology, but the specific relationships are unclear.

The earliest radiometric dates for Clovis points in the Middle Atlantic region are from the Shawnee-Minisink site at 10,937±17 ^{14}C yr BP (Gingerich 2011:130) and the Cactus Hill site at 10,920±250 ^{14}C yr BP (McAvoy and McAvoy 1997; Wagner and McAvoy 2004). Recent dates from the Topper site in South Carolina also place Clovis at 10,958±250 ^{14}C yr BP (Smallwood et al. 2013). Nearly contemporary dates from the Hiscock site at 10,937±17 ^{14}C yr BP in New York (Laub 2002) and the Paleo Crossing site at 10,980±75 ^{14}C yr BP in Ohio (Brose 1994:65) are associated with the Gainey type (Figure 11.1). The Gainey type is considered by some (Miller et al. 2013:207) to be the same as the Clovis type and is certainly very early in the Fluted Point tradition. As documented by Anderson et al. (2010:65), the Appalachian Mountains were generally not occupied by the Fluted Point tradition and this created two avenues of entrance into the Middle Atlantic region. It would seem that the Clovis technological package entered from the southeast along the Piedmont and Coastal Plain and a second group or technology entered from the Ohio valley at the same time (Figure 11.2). See Table 11.2 for a list of radiometric dates for the Fluted Point tradition from the Middle Atlantic and Northeast regions.

In the Middle Atlantic region, the only published sequence of diagnostic artifacts from an undisturbed open-air Paleoindian site in an alluvial

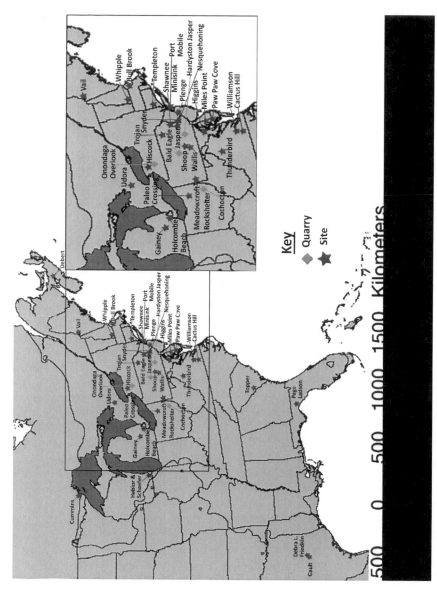

Figure 11.1.

Table 11.2. A Summary of Radiometric Dates Associated with Fluted Projectild Points in the Northeast

Site Name	Site Number	B.P. Date	1st Sigma	2nd Sigma	Median Probability	Laboratory Number	Citation
Wallis	36Pe16	9890±40	BP 11239 - 11314	BP 11220 - 11368	11,281	Beta-128231	Miller et al., .2007
Nesquehoning	36Cr142	10,340±40	BP 12064 - 12190	BP 12008 - 12253	12,189	Beta-379729	Stewart et al., 2012
Templeton	6Lf21	10,190±300	BP 11393 - 12241	BP 10888 - 10922	11,860	W-3931	Moeller, 1980
Michaud	Maine	10,200±620	BP 11093 - 12705	BP 10197 - 13262	11,783	Beta-15660	Spiess & Wilson. 1987
Whipple	New Hampshire	10,300±500	BP 11329 - 12640	BP 10574 - 13093	12,008	AA-150a	Haynes et al., 1984
Vail	Maine	10,500± (an average)	BP 12422 - 12442	BP 12416 - 12537	12,477	Average	Gramly, 1982
Debert	Nova Scotia	10,574±180	BP 12184 - 12201	BP 11831 - 11886	12,580	P-741	MacDonald, 1968: Table 4
Sheriden Cave	33Wy252	10,915±30	BP 12733 - 12790	BP 12708 - 12821	12,764	UCIAMS-38249	Waters et al., 2009
Cactus Hill	44Sx202	10,920±250	BP 12624 - 13080	BP 12158 - 12210	12,824	Beta-81589	McAvoy & McAvoy, 1997
Shawnee Minisink	36Mr43	10,937±15	BP 12746 - 12796	BP 12719 - 12821	12,772	Average	Gingerich, 2011
Topper	38AL23	10,958±65	BP 12731 - 12886	BP 12713 - 12991	12,822	AA-100294	Goodyear, 2013
Paleo Crossing	33Me274	10,980±110	BP 12744 - 12958	BP 12708 - 13059	12,854	AA-8250-E	Brose, 1994
Hiscock	New York	10,990±100	BP 12752 - 12960	BP 12715 - 13053	12,873	TO-3194	Laub, 2002

context is the Thunderbird site in Virginia. Here, Gardner (1974, 1989) documented a series of changes in projectile point types which generally parallel those of the Great Plains. The sequence begins with Clovis projectile points, which are parallel-sided with relatively short flutes that do not extend beyond the mid-point, an indented base, and grinding on the base and lower lateral edges. The Clovis type is followed by a type that Gardner (1974:15) simply defined as Middle Paleoindian. These are shorter, narrower, and more finely flaked with flutes that are longer than the Clovis type. At the time of his definition in the 1970s, fluted point chronology was based on the Great Plains Clovis-Folsom-Plano sequence. Subsequent research in the Great Lakes and in New England has shown that Folsom is rare east of the Mississippi River and that post Clovis types such as Barnes, Bull Brook/West Athens Hill types are the post-Clovis trend. These are characterized by longer flutes and are not parallel sided. I am suggesting that the specimens used by Gardner to define this type are more likely later in the fluted point sequence. Two of the Middle Paleoindian specimens were relatively thin broken bases most similar to the Crowfield type. A date of 10,340±40 BP was recovered in association with a Crowfield point from the Nesquehoning site located along the Lehigh River in Pennsylvania. Although Thunderbird has not produced any finished Bull Brook or Michaud-Neponset points, there is at least one late stage biface that could represent these types and is more likely the result of a Middle Paleoindian occupation at Thunderbird. In addition, the nearby Fifty site produced both a Clovis point and what I would consider a Michaud-Neponset type with a more wasted outline, suggesting this type existed in the region. With this refinement in the fluted point sequence, I feel that the revised sequence at Thunderbird is more like the fluted point sequence that is beginning to emerge in the Middle Atlantic region.

Although not from a stratified context, these are followed by Hardaway-Dalton types of a triangular form, with fluting generally replaced by basal thinning. Two of these were found at Thunderbird, one in the plowzone and one at the plowzone/subsoil interface. In addition, unfluted, lanceolate, parallel-flaked points (comparable to the Agate Basin type) were found in the plowzone at Thunderbird and are probably part of this sequence. There are no dates from the site's Paleoindian component, but an Early Archaic Palmer point was radiometrically dated to 9,900±340 ^{14}C yr BP (Verrey 1986:36) and marks the end of the period.

It is argued by Anderson et al. (1996:14), and others that the Clovis phase is followed by a settling in period when fluted point types evolve through a series of local types or styles. In the Southeast, the Clovis fluted point type is followed by the Cumberland type with a long flute and flaring ears; Simpson and Suwannee types which are widest in the distal half;

Table 11.3. General Chronology of Projectile Point Types by Region for the Northeast

Chronology	Cal Years	Meadian Probability	Middle Atlantic Region	New England	Eastern Great Lakes
Early Paleoindian					
11,000 ^{14}C yr BP	12,900–12,700 cal BP	12,835	Clovis	Kings Road Whipple Vail-Debert	Gainey
10,300 ^{14}C yr BP	12,700–12,200 cal BP	12,069		Bull Brook-West Athens Hill	Butler
Middle Paleoindian					
10,300 ^{14}C yr BP	12,200–11,800 cal BP	12,069	Gardner's-Mid-Paleo Crowfield	Michaud - Neponset Crowfield-related	Barnes Crowfield
10,100 ^{14}C yr BP	11,800–11,600 cal BP	11,714		Cormier-Nicholas	Holcombe
Late Paleoindian					
10,100 ^{14}C yr BP	11,600–10,800 cal BP	11,714	Plano	Agate Basin- Related	Agate Basin/Plano
9,000 ^{14}C yr BP	10,200 cal BP	10,199	Hardaway-Dalton	Ste. Anne-Varney	Eden/Plano
Early Archaic					
9,900 ^{14}C yr BP	11,250 cal BP	11,268	Charleston/Palmer	????	Kirk Notched
9,000 ^{14}C yr BP	10,200 cal BP	10,199	Kirk Notched		
Middle Archaic					
9,000 ^{14}C yr BP	10,200 cal BP	10,199	Bifurcate	Bifurcate	Bifurcate
8,300 ^{14}C yr BP	9,300 cal BP	9,349			

Radiocarbon Calibration Program, CALIB REV7.1.0, http://calib.gub.ac.uk/calib/calib.html—Copyright 1986–2016 M. Stuiver and P. J. Reimer

Beaver Lake and Quad types with a reduced emphasis on fluting; and, finally, the Dalton type (Anderson et al. 1996:10). For the Eastern Great Lakes (Deller and Ellis 1988:255–58) and the New England-Maritime region (Bradley et al. 2008), the Clovis derived forms such as Gainey and Kings-Road/Whipple are followed by Barnes and Michaud/Neponset types that exhibit a narrowing of the hafting area (face angle) and longer fluting. Toward the end of the Middle Paleoindian phase, there is a reduced emphasis on fluting. The Late Paleoindian phase in these regions is characterized by unfluted forms such as Agate Basin and Plano types. The Dalton type is rare in these regions. See Table 11.3 for a chronological summary of projectile point types from the Northeast.

Based on the projectile point sequences in the regions adjacent to the Middle Atlantic, other Middle Paleoindian point types are probably missing from the Thunderbird sequence. These probably follow the pattern found in the adjacent regions which involves the lengthening of the flutes, elongating or more pronounced ears followed by a de-emphasis on fluting and finally followed by Plano/Agate Basin-like types along with the Dalton type. It is interesting that both Plano/Agate Basin-like and Dalton types are found at Thunderbird. The Dalton type is very rare in Pennsylvania, and Thunderbird is probably near the northern boundary of this type. The Plano/Agate Basin type is found throughout the Great Lakes and into New England.

Finally, there does not seem to be a consensus on the meaning of the Clovis type or any of the other fluted point types. In this presentation, fluted projectile points are simply considered an element of the Paleoindian adaptation. Some types (e.g., Clovis or Crowfield) can be used as reasonably reliable chronological markers, but especially during Middle Paleoindian times (10,700–10,100), the temporal position of these forms is not well documented.

Fluted Point Tradition Lithic Artifacts

Paleoindian lithic technology is distinctive from later Archaic lithic technologies and this has inspired numerous analyses, including extensive experimental studies. Callahan's (1979) experimental work stands as the baseline study, but see later work by Collins (1999) and Whittaker (1994:234–42) for examples that have continued this tradition.

The distinguishing characteristic of the Paleoindian tool kit is the dependence on flake tools and the frequent use of standardized or formal tool types. These are usually produced from bifacial or polyhedral cores, most commonly using micro-cryptocrystalline cherts or jaspers. The Paleoindian durable tool assemblage in the Northeast is characterized by utilized flakes, bifaces, and a variety of prepared flake tools. Utilized flakes usually comprise at least 20 percent of the period's tool assemblages, and frequently exhibit relatively low edge angles.

Bifaces and bifacial tools are also common. Gardner (1974) stated that Paleoindian bifaces were used as tools or as preforms for projectile points. Ovate bifaces, unifacially beveled bifaces, or backed bifaces have been identified at many sites (Ellis and Deller 1997:15 and Table 2). Along with bifacial cores, they represent a very effective multi-functional technological element. Their mass allows them to be re-tooled depending on the needs of the environment so they represent a flexible technology in what was an ever-changing ecological setting. As characterized by Dent (1995:139), the Paleoindian tool assemblage can be quickly and reliably "recast or modified for unexpected contingencies."

Compared to later (i.e., post–9000 ^{14}C yr BP) technologies, flake tools following standardized shapes are very common. The most common formal flake tools are relatively small triangular endscrapers, which frequently represent 20–40 percent of the tool kit. However, at Shoop (Carr et al. 2013a) and Shawnee-Minisink (Gingerich 2013b), this tool type represents over 60 percent of the formal tool assemblage (not including utilized flakes). Sidescrapers, wedges (pieces esquilles), burins, gravers, flake shavers (limace), and awls are also common although not found at all sites. Less common tool types are fluted "drills." Double endscrapers with a scraper bit on both ends of the flake have also been found. At some sites, such as Shawnee Minisink, a high percentage of endscrapers (37 percent) are notched, presumably for hafting (McNett 1985:89). At the Shoop site, endscrapers are generally small, and evidence for notching was not common. Rule and Evans (1985:218) suggest that the non-notched scrapers from Shawnee Minisink were small and did not require this type of hafting. However, considering the small size of these artifacts, it is difficult to imagine how they could be effectively used between the fingers and un-hafted. Flake tools with multiple working edges are common, and graver-spurs are frequently found on endscrapers (Thomas Loebel analysis reported by Graham 2011:11; Loebel 2013a and Witthoft 1952).

Considering the common occurrence of endscrapers, their function has been the focus of several earlier investigations (Cox 1986; Marshall 1985; Rule and Evans 1985; Wilmsen 1970). These early analyses were based on edge angles, and woodworking was suggested as the most likely function. Cox (1986) and Wilmsen (1970) reached the same conclusion in their analysis of endscrapers from the Shoop site. Microwear analysis would seem to be the most effective avenue of investigation, although there seems to be some disagreement on the interpretation of the results. Pope (2010) analyzed fifteen specimens from the Shoop site and determined that fourteen of these were used as woodworking tools possibly in the production of handles. Loebel's (reported by Graham 2011:12–13 and Loebel 2013a) general analysis of endscrapers maintains that they were primarily used in working hides. He argues that the distinctive rounding microwear pattern resulting from this activity is frequently masked by re-sharpening near the end of the tool's use life. Loebel's (2013b) recent microwear analysis of thirty endscrapers from the Shoop site presents a strong argument for these being used on fresh hides. The large numbers of endscrapers at Shoop, along with large numbers of projectile points, certainly favor this interpretation over woodworking.

Non-utilitarian artifacts in stone are very rare from any Paleoindian sites. The Hiscock site in New York (Laub 2002:113) produced a drilled bead in stone, and Holliday and Killick list (2012:86–87) twenty other sites, mostly in the western United States, that also produced stone, bone, antler, tooth, or shell beads. The Thunderbird site in Virginia produced a single scratched piece of limestone (Carr et al. 2013b). These are lineal markings and their meaning is unknown.

As noted by Ellis and Deller (1997:21), there are certainly regional and temporal differences in tool type frequencies; however, tool and debitage forms are surprisingly similar across the East. The frequency of individual tool types varies, but the scrapers, bifaces, wedges, and awls look the same. In addition, both bifaces and flake tools are frequently re-sharpened and illustrate all the characteristics of a highly curated technology. Ground and pecked wood-working or plant-processing tools are very rare from sites in the Northeast. Two patinated, chipped adzes have been recovered from the Shoop site, although any type of hafted axe or large woodworking tool is very rare.

Lithic Material Preferences

The preference for "high-quality" lithic material has long been considered a significant characteristic of the Paleoindian period (Goodyear 1979; Wilmsen 1970). In the Middle Atlantic region, Gardner (1974, 1983, 1989) emphasized high-quality lithic sources as significant locations in the Paleoindian settlement pattern. Using only fluted points as indicators of lithic preferences, 90 percent of the fluted points from Pennsylvania are made from jaspers and cherts (Carr and Adovasio 2012:301). These lithic types have a micro-cryptocrystalline structure. Non-micro-cryptocrystalline rocks such as metarhyolite and argillite—so common in Archaic and Woodland assemblages—are rare to non-existent in Paleoindian assemblages in the Middle Atlantic region. Quartzite and quartz are rare but more common than argillite or metarhyolite in Pennsylvania.

In the Appalachian Plateau, Ridge and Valley, and Piedmont physiographic zones of the Middle Atlantic, there is no question that chert (including chalcedony) and jasper from bedrock sources were the preferred lithic types, and this preference also applies to lower-quality cherts and jaspers. At both the Shawnee-Minisink site and the Wallis site, fluted points and some tools were made from high-quality cherts, but the majority of the tools were made from a local chert of moderate flaking ability. It is important to note that Paleoindians rarely used non-micro-cryptocrystalline materials even when they may have been of comparable flaking quality compared to low-quality chert. This is clearly evident in the Archaic period use of argillite in the Delaware Valley and metarhyolite in the Susquehanna Valley. These materials are found in very large quantities in extensive bedrock formations and were extensively used during the Transitional period. They flake well, as exhibited by numerous broadspears, but as toolstone, they were practically ignored by Paleoindians.

This suggests that controlled flaking was not the primary reason that micro-cryptocrystalline lithics were preferred. As an alternative explanation, the silica content of cherts and jaspers is higher than that of argillite or metarhyolite and, possibly, the increased silica content of these materials results in a more durable edge on tools and therefore a longer use life. This would be an obvious asset to highly mobile foragers. In addition, as reported in the *Mammoth Trumpet* (January 2013) by Bradley Lepper, John Speth has noted the frequent use of colorful micro-cryptocrystalline lithics. He feels these also functioned in social, religious, or political systems and they reflect more than technological efficiency. Paleoindian lithic preferences and technological systems were obviously complex, but I would agree that both fluting and colorful lithics almost certainly had non-utilitarian meanings.

In the Coastal Plain of the Middle Atlantic region, a different pattern is evident: a variety of non-micro-cryptocrystalline lithic materials were used. Chert, jasper, and chalcedony were the dominant types, but secondary lithics include quartz, quartzite, silicified slate, and petrified wood. Dent (1995:107–17) describes sixteen sites and site complexes in the Coastal Plain and seven of these produced fluted points in these materials, mainly in quartz and quartzite. The points were usually associated with large numbers of tools in the same materials. Interestingly, ten of these sites are within 100 km of the Williamson chalcedony quarries, but this material was not always chosen. Although cherts and jaspers are the dominant lithic preference, Johnson (1996:205) reports that quartz and quartzite represent 22.5 percent of the lithic assemblage. This relatively high frequency signals a different pattern compared to the regions west of the Coastal Plain (Dent 1995).

Lithic Reduction Strategy

The lithic technology of the Fluted Point tradition has long been considered different from later Native American lithic technologies (Callahan 1979). Gardner (1989) described the lithic reduction system for the Flint Run Complex as being based on bifacial cores. Using replicative, quantitative, and refitting studies, several authors (Callahan 1979; Carr 1992; Gross 1974; Verrey 1986) have analyzed the lithic reduction sequence for the Flint Run Complex sites in northern Virginia and concluded that the Flint Run Paleoindian (along with the Early Archaic) technological organization was based on the reduction of large quarry flakes into bifacial cores. It is doubtful that the intention of the Paleoindian flintknappers was to reduce the large quarry flakes directly into bifaces at the outset. Rather, the primary flakes were treated as cores and, in the process of setting up suitable platforms and strengthening platform edges, they ultimately achieved the appearance of large bifaces. Thus, the manufacturing trajectory evidenced by the Flint Run Paleoindian Complex began at the quarry with the production of large flakes. The flakes were transformed into bifacial cores to produce flake blanks for unifacial and bifacial tools. As the bifacial flake cores were gradually reduced, some of them entered a trajectory ending in bifacial tool manufacture, including fluted points. As part of the lithic reduction and biface thinning process, overshot flaking was employed—that is, there was an effort to remove flakes from bifaces that crossed more than half of the biface's width. Callahan (1979:147) noted this technique at the Thunderbird site, although it rarely resulted in the flake removing the opposite edge. Overshot failures that removed part of the opposite edge of the biface increased the difficulty in further reducing the piece.

The Coastal Plain of the Middle Atlantic region witnesses a different reduction strategy, probably determined by the package size and shape of locally available micro-cryptocrystalline lithic resources. At the Higgins (Ebright 1992) and Paw Paw Cove (Lowery 1989) sites, cobble cherts and jaspers were the preferred material. Both sites contain Clovis components and both utilized secondary cobble sources for tool manufacture. Bifacial reduction was employed, but there is also evidence for bipolar reduction. The size of the fluted points from the Paw Paw Cove Complex is generally small (less than 31 mm), and Lowery (1989:161) believes they were made by directly reducing small cobbles. However, as discussed above, a second significant difference in this region is the use of non-micro-cryptocrystalline materials such as quartz and quartzite.

The Shoop site, located in central Pennsylvania, represents another type of Paleoindian lithic reduction system used in the Middle Atlantic region (Carr et al. 2013a). There are approximately twenty core fragments from this site and these appear to be angular or polyhedral cores rather than bifacial cores. Ninety-eight percent of the Shoop artifacts are from the Onondaga chert formation located in western or central New York, 400 km to the north of the site. The nature of the lithic source (package size and shape) is probably an important factor in determining the shape of the core. The chert lenses within the Onondaga formation of western New York are relatively thin, reaching a maximum of 130 mm in thickness (Wray 1948:41). Therefore, the tabular nature of the chert within the Onondaga formation probably explains the use of angular, polyhedral cores at Shoop. The Thunderbird cores, in contrast, were struck from massive bedrock formations, and their size and shape were not restricted by the character of the bedrock. The desired shape of the flakes and tools produced from a core also affects the choice of the core's shape. The most striking aspect of the Shoop tool assemblage is the large number of endscrapers. Cox (1986) characterizes these as being produced on thick flakes. Polyhedral or angular cores would be a better source for this type of flake than bifacial cores. Generally, the debitage at the Thunderbird site represents biface reduction while at Shoop, it is the result of producing tools, especially endscrapers, on thick flakes, and the resharpening of tools. The use of this core type at Shoop was probably a function of the distance from the quarry, the shape of the bedrock formation, and the activities conducted at Shoop.

Thus, the Paleoindian lithic reduction system in the Middle Atlantic region represents a flexible process related to the nature of the lithic sources and tool requirements. However, the production of bifaces and tools in standardized shapes such as endscrapers and side-scrapers is the result of using standardized reduction strategies that produced similar forms of debitage depending on the nature of the lithic source. The controlled flaking capabilities of micro-cryptocrystalline lithic materials facilitated the reproduction of bifaces and flake tools with the least number of errors. In addition, the high silica content of these materials extended the life of these tools and allowed them to be easily modified in response to changing environmental conditions. The emphasis on a curated technology has obvious advantages for a mobile society in an unstable environment.

In contrast to the recently reported Clovis camp site at Gault in central Texas (Collins 2007; Waters et al. 2009), the regular and systematic production of blades (specifically prepared elongated flakes) is not a characteristic of Paleoindian fluted point technology in the Middle Atlantic region or the Northeast in general (Carr et al. 2010). Working with the Shoop site assemblage from Pennsylvania, John Witthoft (1952) was one of the first to report a blade technology in association with a Paleoindian assemblage. However, re-examinations of this material by Carr (1989), Cox (1986), Krieger (1954), and Wilmsen (1970) have demonstrated that the Shoop artifacts were the result of polyhedral cores and not blade cores. The production of generally small blade-like flakes may well be a characteristic of Pre-Clovis sites such as Meadowcroft and perhaps Cactus Hill, but not of any of the fluted point assemblages in the Northeast (Carr et al. 2010).

Subsistence

Direct subsistence data for the Paleoindian period in the East is rare, and for the Pre-Clovis phase, it is practically non-existent. At the Meadowcroft Rockshelter there are meager floral remains that suggest the possible utilization of hickory (*Carya* spp.), walnut (*Juglans* spp.), and hackberry (*Celtis* spp.) (Carlisle and Adovasio 1988). It is conceivable and likely that these populations may have exploited large and now extinct Pleistocene megafauna, notably mastodon, but there is little evidence of such predation. Extinct elephant remains have been found in Paleoindian contexts at Page-Ladson in Florida (Goebel et al. 2008), Schaefer and Hebior in Wisconsin (Goebel et al. 2008), and at the Manis site in Washington (Waters et al. 2011b).

Initially, Willey (1966) characterized Paleoindians as "big game hunters" and Martin (1973) enhanced this model using it to explain the extinction of the megafauna. Haynes (2002) has continued to portray the Clovis phase adaptation as specialized big game hunters. However, in the east, north of Florida, after numerous excavations, extinct megafaunal remains have not been confidently associated with the Fluted Point tradition. Especially, the Shawnee Minisink site (Dent 1985; Gingerich 2011) has highlighted a more diverse subsistence pattern involving fish, seeds, and nuts.

There are several fluted point sites in the Northeast which have produced very small amounts of charred bone. Caribou has been identified at Bull Brook (Grimes et al. 1984) and Whipple (Curran 1984:5) in Massachusetts; Holcombe Beach in Michigan (Fitting et al. 1966:14); and Cummins (Julig 1984:194) and Udora (Storck and Spiess 1994) in Ontario. Beaver remains have been identified at Bull Brook and Udora, and artic fox has also been identified at Udora. The Shoop site produced cervid (i.e., deer, elk, moose, or caribou) blood residue on one stone tool (Hyland et al. 1992). At the Vail site, the argument for hunting—specifically of caribou—is persuasive (Gramly 1982). Robinson et al. (2009:442) also make an interesting argument for communal hunting at Bull Brook on a now drowned stretch of land (Jeffreys Ledge) that would have provided "summer grazing and a highly predictable fall migration to the mainland." Finally, Ebright (1992:242) reports hickory phytoliths and turkey feather fibers from the Higgins site in Maryland. Hickory and turkey suggest a warmer climate and also a more diverse diet. The database documenting subsistence is small, but it suggests a mixed foraging pattern with some more than casual use of caribou as part of the Northeastern Paleoindian subsistence system.

The Late Pleistocene environmental re-construction suggests a deciduous element in the forests located south of the zone affected by the glaciers. Although located in the Glaciated Plateau, hickory (Gingerich 2011) was recovered from the Shawnee-Minisink site. The date of 10,937±15 ^{14}C yr BP suggests the occupation may have occurred during the warm Allerød episode when conditions would have been more favorable for this species. Therefore, these conditions may also characterize some gallery forests in the glaciated region. These settings would contain a variety of plants and animals useful for humans. However, further north in the glaciated region, coniferous elements were more common and the forests were more open. These areas were characterized by fewer plant foods and more migratory game, at least during the Younger Dryas episode. Based on this general environmental condition, Paleoindians in the unglaciated areas of the Middle Atlantic had access to a variety of food resources and practiced a broad spectrum foraging subsistence pattern. For the glaciated region, the database is small, but suggests a mixed foraging pattern with some regular use of caribou.

Settlement Pattern Studies

Based on work in the southern Great Plains, Early Paleoindians were portrayed as highly mobile populations, exploiting large territories over 200 km in diameter (Judge 1973; Wormington 1957). Early studies in the Northeast, such as at the Shoop (Witthoft 1952), Vail (Gramly 1982), and Bull Brook (Grimes et al. 1984) sites, supported this model. A significant change in this model came with Gardner's (1974) work at the Flint Run Complex in Virginia where he proposed a settlement system that covered much smaller territories of less than 150 km (Gardner 1989).

Since that time, Paleoindian settlement pattern studies have become highly influenced by lithic sourcing studies. A word of caution is in order concerning two issues with this type of research. First, the vast majority of lithic sourcing studies depend on macroscopic analysis rather than elemental analyses such as neutron activation or X-ray fluorescence. There are notable exceptions, but these detailed studies need to be the norm, not the exception. Second, it is assumed that the lithic material is acquired through direct procurement and not trade and exchange. Some level of trade almost certainly was taking place and cannot be ignored as a source for non-local material. We would agree that trade is a mechanism to be considered, however, it is argued here that sites with a high percentage of a single lithic type (> 60 percent) are more likely the result of direct procurement rather than trade and exchange (also see Strothers 1996:204).

That said, non-local lithic material seems to be more common in Paleoindian assemblages than they are during other time periods, and there is no other time period in the East in which there are so many proposed examples of lithics consistently moving over distances of more than 200 km. Many Paleoindian sites are characterized by a variety of lithic types originating both locally and from distances of over 200 km or even over 500 km (Brose 1994 or McCracken 1989). Especially during Early Paleoindian times, there are examples where 80 percent of the assemblage apparently originated from a distance of over 200 km (Burke et al. 2008; Carr et al. 2013a; Ellis 2011; Ellis and Deller 1997; Strothers 1996). With over 98 percent of the lithic material originating from 400 km north of the site, the Shoop site is one of the most extreme examples of this type of movement in the Middle Atlantic region. In a recent sourcing analysis of tools form the Higgins site in Maryland, Singer (2017) has noted that the majority of form tools are in Normanskill chert, traveling a distance of 390 km. However, the overall frequency of this material is low, suggesting trade rather than direct procurement.

Gardner (1974, 1989) performed the pioneering work in Paleoindian settlement pattern research in the East. Based on his work at the Flint Run jasper quarries in the Shenandoah Valley of northern Virginia, he posited a settlement system that focused on the lithic quarry. The quarry served as the meeting place for related bands that could easily join together when resources were plentiful and separate when resources were more dispersed. He (1989:18–26) identified five site types as part of this settlement system: lithic quarry, lithic reduction station, quarry related base camp, base camp maintenance station, and non-quarry related base camp.

Subsequently, Custer (1984) and Meltzer (1988) refined Gardner's model to explain a greater variety of phenomena. Briefly, Custer (1984:54–55) proposed a cyclical pattern in which movements were focused on a single large quarry, and a serial pattern in which a number of small quarries were used. In the serial pattern, the collection of lithic material was incidental to the exploitation of food resources. Base camps for the cyclical pattern are located at the quarry, while the serial pattern produces base camps in other settings, especially favorable hunting areas. Sites that represent the serial system show a greater variety of lithic types. In the Piedmont and the southern Ridge and Valley sections, territories of 40–150 km have been predicated for the cyclical pattern (Gardner 1983:53). The Flint Run Complex is an example of the cyclical pattern.

However, the cyclical model has not been exactly replicated at other large micro-cryptocrystalline quarries in the Middle Atlantic region.

Paleoindian base camps have been predicted, but they have not been clearly documented at the Hardyston or Bald Eagle jasper quarries in Pennsylvania, or the Williamson chalcedony quarries in southeastern Virginia. This may be a function of archaeological context in that the Flint Run jasper quarries are located adjacent to the South Fork of the Shenandoah River and alluvial deposits have created stratified settings enabling the identification of specific living floors. A number of Paleoindian sites have been identified at the Hardyston quarries and the Williamson chalcedony quarries, for example, but these are all plowzone manifestations, mixed with later occupations and a specific function could not be ascribed to these sites. Admittedly, the large number of tools and fluted points at Williamson certainly suggest that this served as a base camp, but the context is equivocal. It seems logical that in the unglaciated region, the source of micro-cryptocrystalline toolstone will be more important in the seasonal round than favorable hunting areas and that these would serve as social aggregation sites (Anderson 1996:44). Unfortunately, this pattern is not well demonstrated beyond the Flint Run Complex.

The Shoop site is a second example of where the cyclical model applies but the lithic material (Onondaga chert) is traveling very long distances, 400 km from the north. However, this is very rare for the Middle Atlantic region where more commonly there are sites with small percentages (less than 20 percent) of the tools moving over 200 km. There are no other examples in the Middle Atlantic where 80 percent of the assemblage or more are moving these distances. The Shawnee Minisink site (McNett 1985 and Gingerich 2013b) artifact assemblage is dominated by a local chert, but produced minority pieces of Onondaga chert that traveled over 440 km from the northwest and smaller frequencies of Normanskill chert that traveled just over 100 km from the northeast. The Wallis site (Miller et al. 2007), located in the central Susquehanna River Valley, is also dominated by local cherts, but contains some jasper artifacts which traveled ca. 130 km from their source to the east. The Plenge site (Gingerich 2013a and Kraft 1973) in New Jersey has yielded at least 189 fluted points dating from the Early Middle and Late Paleoindian phases and most of these are from local toolstone. However, the minority lithic types include Onondaga chert and Normanskill chert that traveled over 200 km and Munsungun Lake chert, the latter traveling 800 km. Contrary to Gardner's (1989) model for Virginia, which proposes the direct procurement of lithics and a cyclical use of the quarries, in the northern Middle Atlantic the exploitation of lithics seems to be embedded in a serial pattern of movements usually less than 200 km in distance. Considering the low frequency of some of these exotic materials, trade may be a more economical explanation.

In a third type of pattern, as synthesized by Dent (1995:107–17) and McAvoy (1992:152–57) for the Coastal Plain of the Chesapeake Bay area, local lithic resources were commonly used along with cherts and jaspers from the adjacent Piedmont and Ridge and Valley zones. As part of these patterns, Williamson chalcedony was frequently used, but quartz and quartzite were also being chosen even though the chalcedony was readily available. This seems to represent the serial use of lithics involving short distances and the frequent use of non-micro-cryptocrystalline materials (Johnson 1996:209). Considering that the major drainages in this area commonly flow west to east, Paleoindians may be following a seasonal pattern of transhumance between the interior and the coastal regions.

In contrast to the Middle Atlantic region, the movement of lithics is different in the Eastern Great Lakes and the New England-Maritimes regions. Here, there are several examples of sites where 80 percent or more of the lithic assemblage originated more than 200 km from the source and many examples of where the lithic assemblage originated over 100 km from the source (Ellis 2011:388–89; Strothers 1996). According to Ellis and Deller (1997:12), the cyclical use of lithics of over a range of 200 km is only witnessed with Gainey phase sites. In the same region, there are more sites which represent the serial use of lithic resources. With later Paleoindian phases, the dominant lithic source is found less than 200 km from its source. However, with the Parkhill Complex, there continues to be a cyclical use of quarries and this sometimes continues into Late Paleoindian times (Ellis 2004:61). Clearly lithic quarries were an important component in the settlement system of the Great Lakes region.

In Ohio, there is evidence of very long-distance movement during the Gainey phase at the Paleo Crossing site. A variety of lithic material types have been identified at the site, but Brose (1994:66) maintains that 65 percent of the lithic assemblage is "Wyandotte Chert and Dongola or Hopkinsville Flint from quarries and outcrops in the region of the lower Ohio River Valley . . . nearly 500 km south of Paleo Crossing." The remaining lithic raw material types originate from within a 100 km radius of the site, suggesting a serial use of lithics. The projectile points are heavily re-worked and have been compared to the points at the Shoop site (Brose 1994:65).

In the New England-Maritimes region, according to Spiess et al. (1998:243) and Bradley et al. (2008), there is a different pattern in the use of quarries within the seasonal round; namely, there are far fewer examples of a single dominant lithic material type per site and fewer examples of a large percentage of any one lithic type moving distances of over 200 km. The Bull Brook locus is the best example of a site dominated by one lithic type, St. Albans chert, and the lithics are moving 300 km from this source (Spiess et al. 1998:204). The Late Paleoindian Varney Farm site is a second example where over 90 percent of the artifact assemblage is derived from Munsungun Lake, over 250 km away in northern

Maine (Peterson et al. 2002:129). A somewhat more common pattern of lithic utilization for the region is that reported by Boisvert (1998:103) for the Middle Paleoindian Israel River complex, where he found a mixture of local and exotic materials. Spiess et al. (1998:251) characterize lithic procurement in New England as "logistic, accomplished by small task groups journeying to the quarries, and not embedded in the subsistence cycle." Both Ellis (2011:389) and Strothers (1996:204) argue against this explanation. However, it is probable that trade and exchange is the more frequent explanation for the movement of lithics in this region compared to the Great Lakes.

There seem to be two patterns of lithic utilization that include both direct procurement and trade and exchange. In the unglaciated regions of the Middle Atlantic, there are only a few examples where it is possible to document what appears to be large territories used by individual bands of Paleoindians. Whether non-local lithics were obtained by direct procurement or through trade, the interaction of bands does not seem to cover large areas. However, in the northern glaciated regions of the Middle Atlantic, there are more lithic types that have traveled long distances. In these areas, individual bands may not be covering large territories, but they are interacting with other bands that seem further afield than the bands in the unglaciated regions of the Middle Atlantic.

As an additional note, sites in the glaciated region of the East frequently have high ratios of tools to debitage such as 10 percent or more at Vail, Debert, and Bull Brook. This is a pattern reminiscent of the kill sites of the western United States. In addition, they frequently have relatively large numbers of finished projectile points, for instance Debert (n=141), Gainey (n=115), Holcombe Beach (n=100+), Bull Brook (n=96), Shoop (n=92), Vail (n=79), and Paleo Crossing (n=34). Endscrapers are also frequently found in extremely large numbers and polyhedral versus bifacial cores seem to be more common. Many of these sites are also large and seem to have "multiple, apparently contemporary and interacting use areas" (Gardner 1989:30).

Exceptions to this generalization are numerous, most notably the Templeton site, (6LF21) (Moeller 1980, 1984), with a low tool frequency, and a serial lithic utilization pattern. This is to be expected, as not all sites were hunting/kill sites such as Vail, and the others simply served other functions in the seasonal cycle, such as general foraging sites or stop over camps between foraging/hunting areas.

Gardner's (1974, 1989) settlement system model has been characterized as a "lithic determinism model" (Anderson and Sassaman 1996:22). I would credit Gardner for contributing an organizational paradigm for the analysis of Paleoindian settlement systems. I think what we have learned over the past decade is that there are a variety of factors that affected the Paleoindian settlement system. The serial pattern and the cyclical pattern are not mutually exclusive and were most frequently combined in the annual cycle. There are examples of the cyclical pattern such as Shoop and Thunderbird, but the majority of sites in the Ridge and Valley, Piedmont and Coastal Plain of the Middle Atlantic region produce multiple lithic types and practiced a serial pattern of lithic utilization. However, lithic sources were important locations within the Paleoindian settlement pattern. It is probable that when food resources were plentiful and evenly distributed, quarry sites could serve as aggregation camps. In areas where food resources were not evenly distributed and varied by season, high biomass areas would be the location of aggregation camps. Generally, in the unglaciated region, high-quality lithic sources will be the location of aggregation camps and in the glaciated region aggregation camps will be located in high biomass ecotones.

Based on the above, Gardner's settlement site types can be expanded to include non-quarry related aggregation sites. The following is the proposed revised list with possible examples of each. Space does not allow descriptions of each.

- Quarry site—Flint Run, Hardyston, or Williamson quarries
- Secondary reduction station—Fifty site
- Quarry related camp/base camp/aggregation camp—Thunderbird site
- Foraging camp—Wallis site
- Foraging/processing camp—Shawnee Minisink site
- Hunting/processing/social aggregation camp—Shoop site

Gardner (1989) and Meltzer (1984) identified differences between sites in the glaciated and unglaciated regions. Subsequent work has generally supported their observations although the definition of the glaciated region needs to be extended slightly south. These two types of settlement systems represent two different adaptive strategies. In general, the Paleoindian adaptive strategy involved small bands exploiting relatively large territories in a foraging pattern using a flexible stone tool technology that could be easily modified for an unpredictable environment. The most important variable affecting seasonal movements in the southern portion of this region would have been the distribution of high-quality lithic material. Secondary to this would have been the location of high biomass ecotones. The most important variable in the northern portion of this region was the distribution of high biomass ecotones, with lithic resources a secondary variable. However, in both regions, micro-cryptocrystalline lithic resources were of prime importance and were mainly exploited through direct procurement as part of the foraging seasonal pattern. Table 11.4 summarizes the differences between the adaptation in the glaciated

Table 11.4.   Characteristics of Paleoindian Settlement Patterns in Glaciated and Un-Glaciated Regions of the Northeast partially based on Gardner 1989 and Meltzer 1984.

Glaciated Region	Un-Glaciated Region
Some sites with large numbers of finished points	*Single point sites except for quarry related base camps where projectile points are found broken in production rather than in use*
Some relatively large sites, several hectares in area	Small sites except quarry related base camps
Sites associated with riverine settings and glacial features	Sites associated with riverine settings
Bedrock lithic sources	Bedrock lithic sources except for on the Coastal Plain
Sites with lithic materials commonly moving over 150 km	Few sites with lithic materials suggesting long distance movements
Large territories decrease in size over time	Generally small territories
Polyhedral & bifacial cores	*Bifacial and bipolar cores*
Foraging & some exploitation of migratory animals	Primarily a foraging subsistence pattern
Sites with non-overlapping artifact concentrations	Few sites with multiple, non-overlapping artifact concentrations
Lithic caches in the form of flake tool blanks, fluted points and performs	Few lithic caches

region and the adaptation in the unglaciated region in the Northeast (partially following Gardner 1989, Meltzer 1984).

In the glaciated region, there are sites that produced multiple Clovis points, frequently in Onondaga or Normanskill chert that traveled over 200 km from its source to the north. These sites are part of a long-distance pattern of north-south movements typical of the Early Paleoindian phase in the Eastern Great Lakes and New England-Maritimes regions. As emphasized by Ellis (2011), these involve the direct and focused movements to specific resources. They represent hunting related base camps defined here as foraging/processing sites occupied by multiple family groups (microband). The focus of their subsistence pattern would be migratory game and probably caribou. This is almost certainly the case with the Shoop site. Pennsylvania lies on the southern edge of this pattern and the sites probably denote early winter hunting camps. There are probably other sites in the glaciated region of Pennsylvania and New Jersey that are part of this settlement system, but they represent small (micro-band) foraging or hunting camps. When migratory game was not available, Paleoindian bands would have broken into family groups to exploit other food resources such as deer and elk. The single fluted point sites may represent the exploitation of these more solitary game resources. These bands probably spent time foraging for a variety of plant foods in the spring and fall. Some of the summer camps may have been situated at the Onondaga or Normanskill quarries representing quarry related base camps.

The second Paleoindian settlement system is the more common of the two and is mostly found in the unglaciated region of the Middle Atlantic region. This pattern consists of generally micro-bands (in many cases individual nuclear families) moving over smaller territories of less than 150 km in diameter. They utilized cherts and jaspers and in the Coastal Plain, quartz and quartzite in a serial pattern. They foraged in the summer and hunted in the winter. Large bedrock sources of chert and jasper may have been the location of base camps, but this has been infrequently documented. These may have been the location of social aggregation camps or these may have been located at high biomass areas.

As discussed by Gardner (1989:24–29), quarry sites or high biomass ecotones were the location of meeting areas for several micro-bands. At such sites, a variety of social events would take place including naming ceremonies, marriage ceremonies and cultural rejuvenation ceremonies. One would expect that the ceremonies would be different if they were conducted at a quarry site versus a food resource site. Finally, as emphasized by Anderson (1996:44) "social interaction leading to marriages between groups . . . was far more important to the survival of these people in the long run than where lithic raw material sources were on the landscape or where food resources were particularly abundant." We suggest here that these social "aggregation sites" were located in the same places that contained lithic sources or abundant food resources.

Social Organization

Based on the small size of the majority of sites, the lack of any artifacts suggesting social differences, but mainly on our assumptions concerning foraging societies, it is assumed that Paleoindians participated in a band level of social organization. Their bands consisted of egalitarian family groups of fifteen to twenty-five individuals. These may have been organized around a group of related males or females although a bilateral kinship system is just as likely. It is assumed that the only social distinctions were the position of a headman and a shaman and these could have been held by males or females. Band membership was fluid although population density was probably so low that other groups were rarely encountered, at least during Early Paleoindian times. However, low population density was a real problem. In order to maintain a viable breeding population, there must have been mechanisms to bring groups and potential mating partners together.

Micro-cryptocrystalline lithic sources or high biomass settings probably served this function.

In the East, Gardner (1989) was one of the first to elaborate on Paleoindian social organization and he applied the concept of micro- and macrobands. Taking an ecological approach and emphasizing the fluidity of Paleoindian bands, he argued they would have changed size depending on local resources. The Thunderbird site was situated adjacent to a large, high-quality lithic resource and therefore functioned as a meeting place for micro-bands and frequently served as a macro-band base camp (Gardner 1989). Special task groups moved from the macro-band base camp to exploit the jasper quarries, but also to exploit food resources at nearby base camp maintenance stations. When leaving the quarries, the group broke into micro-bands and continued on their seasonal round. Micro-band base camps were situated in ecological settings where food resources or raw materials (exp. reeds for baskets) were located in large quantities. At these locations, micro-bands would divide into work parties to exploit the resource.

The hallmark of the Paleoindian period is the fluted projectile point and this clearly represents a unique artifact that carried an important symbolic meaning. The functional benefits of fluting in contrast to the rate of failures have been a point of speculation, but no definitive advantages have been identified and widely accepted (exp. Wilmsen and Roberts 1978). This technology was almost certainly wrapped in the social and supernatural realms (see Bradley and Collins 2013 and Speth et al. 2010 for a recent discussion). It is interesting to speculate on the relationship between fluted points and social organization. Kelly (2007:271) states that patrilocal post-marital residence occurs in 50–65 percent of ethnographically documented foraging societies. Bilateral kinship is practiced in about 40 percent of these groups. Several authors have acknowledged the existence of regional fluted point sequences (Anderson et al. 1996; Bradley et al. 2008; Ellis 2004; and Spiess et al. 1998). Assuming that males were the primary producers of fluted points, these regional sequences could be the result of a group of related males sharing a common "mental template" for fluted point manufacture representing a bilateral-patrilocal social organization. Through a process similar to random drift, the Clovis type would evolve through shared templates that were slightly different from adjacent macro-bands producing the current array of Middle and Late Paleoindian point types. The fluted point types in the Eastern Great Lakes and the New England Maritimes regions are particularly distinctive, but those in the Middle Atlantic region are not. The scenario described in the previous sentences may best describe these regions rather than the Middle Atlantic, but this is all very speculative.

Evolution of the Adaptive Strategy

Paleoindian people were here by 17,000 ^{14}C yr BP. Pre-Clovis groups practiced a broad spectrum foraging strategy and territories were relatively large although less than 150 km in diameter. However, the population density was extremely low and their adaptation remained generalized because it did not require any special technology or intensive measures to collect sufficient food resources to support the population. The standard social group may have consisted of extended families numbering less than fifteen individuals. At this population level, they were all but archaeologically invisible.

Populations increased through natural reproduction and possibly additional migrations from Siberia. Based on Monte Verde (Dillehay 1997), people had thinly occupied North and South America, probably moving along the coast lines and major river valleys (Anderson et al. 2013). Due to the more productive environment, populations in the southeastern United States (Georgia and Alabama) increased at a greater rate than those in the Middle Atlantic region. Anderson (2004:124) interprets the high density of Early Paleoindian sites in the Southeast as evidence for the invention of fluting and the initial spread of the Clovis technological package. It was invented in North America at approximately 11,200 ^{14}C yr BP. It had a symbolic function. At the simplest level, it allowed families to recognize other families as potential mating partners. In addition, it served to organize populations into cooperating groups, specifically allowing for a fission-fusion process so family bands could join together when resources were concentrated and divide into small family groups when resources were dispersed.

The concept of fluting entered the Middle Atlantic region with the Clovis type through both the diffusion of the idea and the immigration of people from the south. This occurred during the Allerød warming period. The people were broad spectrum foragers exploiting relatively large territories. Assuming the Appalachian Mountains formed a barrier between the Ohio Valley and the coastal regions, fluted point technology entered the Middle Atlantic region from the west and the south at about the same time; 11,000 years ago (Figure 11.2). The groups from the west had a tradition of hunting migratory game and exploiting territories over 200 km in size. Although hunting provided the most calories annually, the Clovis people from the south were more dependent on gathering. Population density remained low and they were able to move over sparsely occupied territories exploiting the most easily gathered foods. Part of the fluting tradition involved focusing on the use of micro-cryptocrystalline jaspers and cherts and these sources were the location of quarry related base camps. However, in the Coastal Plain, the preference for micro-cryptocrystalline materials was not as strong as it was on the interior. In the Great Lakes, Clovis-derived groups used Gainey style projectile points and began the exploitation of very large territories with some emphasis on caribou. The Shoop site may have been occupied by groups moving south from the Lake Ontario region.

With the onset of the Younger Dryas episode, hunting became even more important in the Middle Atlantic region. In the glaciated zone of the Middle Atlantic region, caribou became an important component of the subsistence pattern. Large territories were exploited with some focus on caribou, although other animals were taken including water fowl and fish. The Middle Paleoindian phase is a time of "settling in" and the formation of new bands through a process of "budding off." Populations were increasing and territories were established (Figure 11.3). Territories became smaller, less than 150 km in diameter. However, in most of the Middle Atlantic region, family groups did not focus on caribou, but rather exploited water fowl, fish, deer, and elk.

By the end of the Younger Dryas, smaller territories were established, as exhibited by the lithic utilization of Late Paleoindian times and most of the Middle Atlantic region continued to practice a broad spectrum foraging pattern. The Plano tradition moves into the region (Figure 11.4). This is a distinctive tradition and may well represent the movement of people from the west. However, the focus on big game hunting as observed in the Great Lakes is probably not part of the adaptation in the Middle Atlantic region (Carr and Adovasio 2012:295–96, and Peterson et al. 2002:139).

Hardaway-Dalton and Plano projectile types are reasonably distinctive and should be recognizable when they are present in the archaeological record. The former is relatively common in the Piedmont of the southeastern United States, extending into Virginia according to Gardner (1989) but decreasing in number in the Susquehanna and Delaware valleys of Pennsylvania, Delaware, and New Jersey. Their absence is a real expression of population density implying a decrease in Late Paleoindian and Early Archaic populations.

With the onset of the Pre-Boral episode at approximately 10,100 BP, a closed coniferous forest dominated by white pine and spruce developed across the Middle Atlantic. Although this situation varied by physiographic zone, the quantity and variety of food resources was reduced. I agree with Turnbaugh (1977) that based on Late Paleoindian diagnostic projectile points, such as Plano, Agate Basin, and Hardaway-Dalton, human populations decreased sharply. This is in contrast to the Southeast where Gardner (1989), Goodyear (1982), and Morse et al. (1996) argue for the reverse situation. During the Pre-Boreal, the number of Early Archaic sites in Pennsylvania, represents an increase over Paleoindian sites but, considering that a thousand years or more has elapsed since Paleoindian populations first inhabited this region, one would expect some population growth and more Early Archaic sites (Table 11.5). Although there are various problems with equating numbers of sites with relative population densities, we believe this lower number of sites supports the hypothesis that the Early Archaic period in Pennsylvania is characterized by very low population growth. Gardner (1989) argued for cultural continuity between Paleoindian and Early Archaic times. This implies that the same group of people lived in the region and we would agree. The major change during this time is in projectile point types and we assume that these ideas diffused from the south, but this process did not involve new people moving from the south as proposed by Ellis (2011) for the Eastern Great Lakes.

With the beginning of the Boreal climatic episode, there is an increase in temperature and a final transition to a closed deciduous forest. After 9000 BP, there seems to be a major change in the cultural adaptation with the introduction of bifurcate projectile point using peoples. The settlement pattern includes many more upland settings, the use of more local and non-micro-cryptocrystalline lithic materials, frequently of lesser quality and the use of fewer formal flake tools (Carr 1998). There is a significant increase in the number of sites and this can be interpreted as an increase in human population. It is assumed that these people are adapting to a more plentiful oak-hickory forest.

The fascinating aspect of Paleoindian/Early Archaic evolution is that arguably the most dramatic environmental change in the past 10,000 years (Jacobson et al. 1987:283) occurred in the middle of this time span and there is only minor archaeological (cultural) evidence for its occurrence in the Middle Atlantic region. The Late Paleoindian population increase suggested for Southeastern United States would be expected for populations exploiting a relatively more plentiful environment. In the Middle Atlantic region, Gardner (1989) also argues for a population increase for the Kirk phase of the Early Archaic. However, these changes are not evident to the north in Pennsylvania. Considering the proposed environmental change, the overall cultural adaptation for the northern Middle Atlantic does not seem to change as significantly as regions to the south. We believe this is the result of the decrease in food resources in the Pre-Boreal forest. As stated above, the significant changes do not occur until the Middle Archaic bifurcate phase beginning with the Boreal climatic episode.

In conclusion, Paleoindian research has made momentous advances since McCary's (1951) Williamson report or Witthoft's (1952) Shoop report; however, there continue to be significant problems with the database. Our understanding of the Pre-Clovis phase is based on a limited number of sites, and, obviously, more need to be uncovered. Chronology,

Table 11.5. Numbers of Sites Per Hundred Years for the Paleoindian, Early Archaic and Bifurcate Periods

Time Period	^{14}C yr BP Begin	^{14}C yr BP End	Calendar Years Begin	Calendar Years End	Duration	# of Sites	Sites/ Hundred Years
Paleoindian	11,050	10,150	12,944	11,820	1,124	304	27.05
Early Archaic	9,900	9,000	11,272	10,204	1,068	333	31.18
Bifurcate	9,000	8,100	10,204	9,109	1,068 / 1,185	809	66.37

in general, is a problem considering both internal changes and the possible dating of the various fluted point styles. The environmental reconstruction is particularly important as it relates to seasonal movements and subsistence. Finally, there has been little discussion of Paleoindian band size or social organization. Considering the anthropological implications of low population densities and "explorers" in a new land, this may be the most significant research this period has to offer.

The archaeological context of the Paleoindian period is significantly different from all succeeding time periods. It is assumed that human population densities were far below the carrying capacity, the environment was significantly different from the modern setting, and it was also constantly changing. In general, sites will be small, and they will not be frequently re-visited because of the changing ecology. This will produce many sites which cannot be easily characterized in terms of function. Lithic sourcing is a procedure which can add significantly to our understanding of this time period. It has long been a tradition in Paleoindian studies, but we have exhausted the "macro-scopic," "looks like" identification of lithic sources, and it is time to increase the effectiveness of lithic sourcing through detailed chemical and microscopic analysis.

One of the most challenging aspects of recognizing the Pre-Clovis phase is how to insert an existing population into our models of the appearance of fluting technology/Clovis in any region beyond its origin/homeland. As stated above, the general assumption is that fluting was invented in the Southeastern United States and the concept moved north and possibly west from that region. This technology became instantly highly visible in the archaeological record. What was the relationship between people using a fluting technology and people using a Pre-Clovis technology?

The Paleoindian period is a fascinating time for the anthropological study of very low population densities adapting to what appear to be relatively abundant environments. Only Australia offers a similar anthropological laboratory although the interior of that region had a significantly lower biomass. In this light, the definition of Pre-Clovis sites, such as Meadowcroft Rockshelter (Adovasio et al. 1988), Cactus Hill (McAvoy and McAvoy 1997), and Miles Point (Lowery et al. 2010) are all the more important in that they affect our explanation of the very first adaptation in the region. Paleoindians had the technology and a long cultural tradition of exploiting these types of environments, but in the Old World they were probably surrounded by significantly higher human populations. Based on the above discussion, it appears that early in Paleoindian culture history at least two different contemporary adaptations quickly emerged in eastern North America. In the glaciated region they may have focused their attention on caribou, but in the south, a much wider variety of food resources was probably being utilized.

REFERENCES CITED

Adovasio, James M.
　1993　The Ones that Will Not Go Away: A Biased View of Pre-Clovis Populations in the New World. In *From Kostenki to Clovis: Upper Paleolithic–Paleo-Indian Adaptations*, edited by O. Soffer and N. D. Praslov, pp. 199–218. Plenum Press, New York.

Adovasio, James M., Anthony Bouldurian, and Ronald Carlisle
　1988　Who Are Those Guys?: Early Human Populations in Eastern North America, prepared for Mammoths, Mastodons and Human Interaction: A National Symposium on Late Pleistocene Archaeological Interpretation, Sponsored by Baylor University and the Cooper Foundation of Waco Texas, 10/30–11/1/87.

Adovasio, James M., and Jake Page
　2002　*The First Americans: In Pursuit of Archaeology's Greatest Mystery*. Random House, New York.

Adovasio, James M., and David R. Pedler
　2013　The Ones That Still Won't Go Away: More Biased Thoughts on the Pre-Clovis Peopling of the New World. In *Paleoamerican Odyssey*, Kelly E. Graf, Caroline V. Ketron, and Michael R. Waters, editors. Center for the Study of the First Americans, College Station, TX, pp. 511–20.

Anderson, David G.
　1996　Models of Paleoindian and Early Archaic Settlement in the Lower Southeast. In *The Paleoindian and Early Archaic Southeast*, edited by D. G. Anderson and K. E. Sassaman, pp. 29–57. University of Alabama Press, Tuscaloosa.
　2004　Paleoindian Occupations in the Southeastern United states. In *New Perspectives on the First Americans*, edited by B. T. Lepper and R. Bonnichsen, pp. 119–28. Center for the Study of the First Americans, Texas A&M University, College Station.

Anderson, David G., Lisa D. Osteen, and Kenneth E. Sassaman
  1996   Environmental and Chronological Considerations. In *The Paleoindian and Early Archaic Southeast,* edited by David G. Anderson and Kenneth E. Sassaman, pp. 3–15. University of Alabama Press, Tuscaloosa.

Anderson, David G., and Kenneth E. Sassaman
  1996   Modeling Paleoindian and Early Archaic Settlement in the Southeast: A Historical Perspective. In *The Paleoindian and Early Archaic Southeast,* edited by D. G. Anderson and K. E. Sassaman, pp. 16–28. University of Alabama Press, Tuscaloosa.

Anderson, David G., Shane Miller, Stephen J. Yerka, J. Christopher Gillam, Erik N. Johanson, Derek T. Anderson, Albert C. Goodyear, and Ashley M. Smallwood
  2010   PIDBA (Paleoindian Database of the Americas) 2010: Current Status and Findings. *Archaeology of Eastern North America* 38:63–90.

Anderson, David G., Thaddeus G. Bissett, and Stephen J. Yerka
  2013   The Late-Pleistocene Human Settlement of Interior North America: The Role of Physiography and Sea-Level Change. In *Paleoamerican Odyssey,* Kelly E. Graf, Caroline V. Ketron, and Michael R. Waters, editors. Center for the Study of the First Americans, College Station, TX, pp. 183–203.

Barnosky, Anthony D., Cathy W. Barnosky, Rudy J. Nickmann, Allan C. Ashworth, Donald P. Schwert, and Stanley W. Lantz
  1988   Late Quaternary Paleoecology at the Newton Site, Bradford Co., Northwestern Pennsylvania: *Mammuthus columbi,* Palynology and Fossil Insects. In *Late Pleistocene and Early Holocene Paleoecology and Archaeology of the Eastern Great Lakes Region,* edited by Richard S. Laub, Norton G. Miller, and David W. Steadman, pp.173–85. Volume 33, Buffalo Society of Natural Sciences, Buffalo.

Boisvert, Richard
  1998   The Israel River Complex: A Paleoindian Manifestation in Jefferson, New Hampshire. *Archaeology of Eastern North America* 26:97–106.

Bouldurian, Anthony
  1985   *Variability in Flint Working Technology at the Krajacic Site: Possible Relationships to the Pre-Clovis Paleoindian Occupation of the Cross Creek Drainage in Southwestern Pennsylvania.* Unpublished PhD dissertation, Department of Anthropology, University of Pittsburgh.

Bradley, Bruce A., and Michael B. Collins
  2013   Imagining Clovis as a Cultural Revitalization Movement. In *Paleoamerican Odyssey,* Kelly E. Graf, Caroline V. Ketron, and Michael R. Waters, editors. Center for the Study of the First Americans, College Station, TX, pp. 247–56.

Bradley, James W., Arthur E. Spiess, Richard A. Boisvert, and Jeff Boudreau
  2008   What's the Point?: Modal Forms and Attributes of Paleoindian Bifaces in the New England-Maritimes Region. *Archaeology of Eastern North America,* 30:119–72.

Brose, David S.
  1994 Archaeological Investigations at the Paleo Crossing Site, a Paleoindian Occupation in Medina County, Ohio. *In The First Discovery of America: Archaeological Evidence of the Early Inhabitants of the Ohio Area,* edited by W. S. Dancy, pp. 61–76. Ohio Archaeological Council, Inc. Columbus.

Burke, Adrian., B. S. Robinson, Brian S. Robinson, and G. Gauthier
  2008 Identifying the Sources of the Cherts used at the Bull Brook Paleoindian Site. Presented at the 75th Annual Meeting of the Eastern States Archaeological Federation, Lockport, NY.

Callahan, Errett
  1979 The Basics of Biface Knapping in the Eastern Fluted Point Tradition: A Manual for Flintknappers and Lithic Analysts. *Archaeology of Eastern North America* 7:1–180.

Carbone, Victor
  1976 *Environment and Prehistory in the Shenandoah Valley.* PhD dissertation, Department of Anthropology, Catholic University of America, Washington, DC.

Carlisle, Ronald C., and James M. Adovasio
  1984 *The Archaeology of the Meadowcroft Rockshelter and the Cross Creek Drainage.* University of Pittsburgh Press.

Carr, Kurt W.
  1989 The Shoop Site: Thirty-five Years After. *New Approaches to Other Pasts,* edited by W. Fred Kinsey and Roger Moeller, pp. 5–28. Archaeological Services, Bethlehem, CT.
  1992 *A Distributional Analysis of Artifacts from the Fifty Site: A Flint Run Paleoindian Processing Station.* Unpublished PhD dissertation, The Catholic University of America, Washington DC. University Microfilms, Ann Arbor.
  1998 Archaeological Site Distributions and Patterns of Lithic Utilization During the Middle Archaic in Pennsylvania. *In The Archaic Period in Pennsylvania: Hunter-Gatherers of the Early and Middle Holocene Period,* edited by Paul A. Raber, Patricia E. Miller, and Sarah M. Neusius, pp. 77–90, Pennsylvania Historical and Museum Commission, Harrisburg.
  2000 A Discussion of Recent Pre-Clovis Investigations. *Journal of Middle Atlantic Archaeology* 16:133–42. Archaeological Services, Bethlehem, CT.

Carr, Kurt W., Christopher A. Bergman, and Crista M. Haag
  2010 Some Comments on Blade Technology and Eastern Clovis Lithic Reduction Strategies. *Lithic Technology* 35(2):91–125.

Carr, Kurt W., and James M. Adovasio
  2012 Shades of Gray Redux: The Paleoindian/Early Archaic "Transition" in the Northeast. *In From the Pleistocene to the Holocene: Human Organization and Cultural Transformations in Prehistoric North America.* Edited by C. Britt Bousman and Bradley J. Vierra, pp. 273–318, Texas A&M University Press, College Station.

Carr, Kurt W., James M. Adovasio, and Frank J. Vento
2013a A Report on the 2008 Field Investigations at the Shoop Site (36DA20). In *The Eastern Fluted Point Tradition*, edited by Joseph A. M. Gingerich. University of Utah Press, Salt Lake City.

Carr, Kurt W., R. Michael Stewart, Dennis Stanford, and Michael Frank
2013b The Flint Run Complex: A Quarry Related Paleoindian Complex in the Great Valley of Northern Virginia. In *The Eastern Fluted Point Tradition*, edited by Joseph A. M. Gingerich. University of Utah Press, Salt Lake City.

Clausen, C. J., A. D. Cohen, Cesare Emiliani, J. A. Holman, and J. J. Stipp
1979 Little Salt Spring, Florida: A Unique Underwater Site. *Science* 203:609–14.

Collins, Michael B.
1999 *Clovis Blade Technology*. University of Texas Press, Austin.
2007 Clovis at Gault and in the Western Hemisphere. Presented at the 72nd Annual Meeting of the Society for American Archaeology, Austin, TX.
2012 Preliminary Geographic Patterns in Older-Than-Clovis Assemblages of North America. Presented at the 77th Annual Meeting of the Society for American Archaeology, April 18–22, Memphis, TN.

Cowan, Verna. L.
1991 The Middle Archaic in the Upper Ohio Valley. *Journal of Middle Atlantic Archaeology* 7:43–52.

Cox, Stephen L.
1986 A Re-Analysis of the Shoop Site. *Archaeology of Eastern North America* 14:101–70.

Curran, Mary Lou
1984 The Whipple Site and Paleoindian Tool Assemblage Variation: A Comparison of Intra-site Structuring. *Archaeology of Eastern North America* 12: 5–40.

Custer, Jay. F.
1984 *Delaware Prehistoric Archaeology: An Ecological Approach*. University of Delaware Press, Newark.

Delcourt, H. R., and P. A. Delcourt
1986 Late Quaternary Vegetational Change in the Central Atlantic States *The Quaternary of Virginia—A Symposium Volume,* edited by J. N. McDonald and S. O. Bird, pp. 23–35. Division of Mineral Resources, Charlottesville.

Deller, D. Brian, and Christopher J. Ellis
1988 Early Paleo-Indian Complexes in Southwestern Ontario. *Late Pleistocene and Early Holocene Paleoecology and Archaeology of the Eastern Great Lakes Region,* edited by R. S. Laub, N. G. Miller, and D. W. Steadman, pp. 251–63. Vol. 33, Buffalo Society of Natural Sciences, Buffalo, NY.

Dent, Richard J.
1985 Amerinds and the Environment: Myth, Reality, and the Upper Delaware Valley. In *Shawnee-Minisink: A Stratified Paleoindian-Archaic Site in the Upper Delaware Valley of Pennsylvania,* edited by C. W. McNett, pp. 123–63. Academic Press, Orlando.

1995   *Chesapeake Prehistory: Old Traditions, New Directions.* Plenum Press, NY.

Dillehay, Tom D.
   1989   *Monte Verde: a late Pleistocene settlement in Chile,* vol. 1. Smithsonian Institution Press, Washington, DC.
   1997   *Monte Verde: a Late Pleistocene Settlement in Chile,* vol. 2. Smithsonian Institution Press, Washington, DC.

Dixon, E. James
   1999   *Bones, Boats and Bison: Archeology and the First Colonization of Western North America.* Albuquerque: University of New Mexico Press.

Ebright, Carol A.
   1992   *Early Native American Prehistory on the Maryland Western Shore: Archaeological Investigations at the Higgins Site.* Report prepared for the Maryland State Railroad Administration, Department of Natural Resources, Maryland Geological Survey, Division of Archaeology File Report 250.

Ellis, Christopher
   2004   Hi-Lo: An Early Lithic Complex in the Great Lakes Region. In *The Late Palaeo-Indian Great Lakes: Geological and Archaeological Investigations of Late Pleistocene and Early Holocene Environments,* edited by L. J. Jackson and A. Hinshelwood, pp. 57–83. Mercury Series, Archaeology Paper No. 165. Canadian Museum of Civilization, Gatineau, Quebec.
   2011   Measuring Paleoindian range mobility and land-use in the Great Lakes/Northeast. *Journal of Anthropological Archaeology* 30:385–401.

Ellis, Christopher J., and D. Brian Deller
   1997   Variability in the Archaeological Record of Northeastern Early Paleoindians: A View from Southern Ontario. *Archaeology of Eastern North America* 25:1–30.

Fitting, James E., J. DeVisscher, and E. J. Wahla
   1966   *The Paleo-Indian Occupation of the Holcombe Beach.* Anthropological Papers. Museum of Anthropology, University of Michigan, No. 27, Ann Arbor.

Foss, John
   1977   The Pedological Record at Several Paleoindian Sites in the Northeast. *Amerinds and their Paleoenvironments in Northeastern North America,* W. S. Newman and B. Salwen, editors. New York Academy of Sciences, New York, pp. 257–63.

Gardner, William M.
   1974   The Flint Run Complex: Pattern and Process During the Paleo-Indian to Early Archaic. In *The Flint Run Paleo-Indian Complex: A Preliminary Report 1971–1973 Seasons,* edited by W. M. Gardner, pp.5–47. Occasional Publication No. 1, Archaeology Laboratory, Department of Anthropology, Catholic University of America, Washington, DC.
   1983   Get Me to the Quarry on Time: The Flint Run Paleoindian Complex in the Middle Atlantic. Paper presented at the annual meeting of the Society for American Archaeology, Pittsburgh.

1989	An Examination of Cultural Change in the Late Pleistocene and Early Holocene (ca 9200 to 6800 B.C.). In *Paleoindian Research in Virginia: A Synthesis*, edited by J. M. Wittkofski and T. R. Reinhart, pp. 5–51. Special Publication #19 of the Archaeological Society of Virginia.

Gingerich, Joseph A. M.
2011	Down to Seeds and Stones: A New Look at the Subsistence Remains from Shawnee-Minisink. *American Antiquity* 76:127–44.
2013a	Fifty Years of Discovery at Plenge: Rethinking the Importance of New Jersey's Largest Paleoindian Site. In *The Eastern Fluted Point Tradition*, edited by Joseph A. M. Gingerich, 121–47. University of Utah Press, Salt Lake City.
2013b	Revisiting Shawnee-Minisink. In *The Eastern Fluted Point Tradition*, edited by Joseph A. M. Gingerich, 218–56. University of Utah Press, Salt Lake City.

Goebel, Ted, Michael R. Waters, and Dennis H. O'Rourke
2008	The Late Pleistocene dispersal of Modern Humans in the Americas. *Science* 319:1497–1502.

Goodyear, Albert C.
1979	*A Hypothesis for the Use of Cryptocrystalline Raw Materials among Paleoindian Groups of North America*. University of South Carolina Institute of Archaeology and Anthropology, Research Manuscript Series No. 156.
1982	The Chronological Position of the Dalton Horizon in the Southeastern United States. *American Antiquity* 47:382–95.

Graham, Dale
2011	Endscrapers: Paleoindian Workaday Tools. *Mammoth Trumpet* 26(2):14.

Gramly, R. Michael
1982	*The Vail Site: A Paleo-Indian Encampment in Maine*. Bulletin of the Buffalo Society of Natural Sciences, Vol. 30, Buffalo.
2009	*Origin and Evolution of the Cumberland Palaeo-American Tradition*. Special Publication of the American Society for Amateur Archaeology, Partners Press, New York.

Grimes, J. R., W. Eldredge, B. G. Gremir, and A. Vaccaro
1984	Bull Brook II. *Archaeology of Eastern North America* 12:159–83.

Gross, J. Ivor
1974	Some Patterns of Chipping Activity of the Thunderbird Clovis Component. In *The Flint Run Paleo-Indian Complex: A Preliminary Report 1971–1973 Seasons*. Edited by William M. Gardner, Occasional Publications, Catholic University of America, Washington, DC, pp. 100–105.

Haynes, C. Vance
1980	Paleoindian Charcoal from Meadowcroft Rockshelter: Is Contamination a Problem. *American Antiquity* 45:582–87.
1991	More on Meadowcroft Rockshelter Radiocarbon Chronology. *Review of Archaeology* 12(1):8–14.

Haynes, Gary
2002	*The Early Settlement of North America: The Clovis Era*. Cambridge University Press.

Holliday, Vance T., and David Killick
    2012   An Early Paleoindian Bead from the Mockingbird Gap Site, New Mexico. *Current Anthropology,* 54(1):85–95.

Hyland, David C., J. M. Tersak, James M. Adovasio, and Mark I. Siegel
    1992   Identification of the Species of Origin of Residual Blood on Lithic Material. *American Antiquity* 55(1):104–12.

Isarin R. B., and S. J. P. Bohncke
    1999   Mean July Temperatures during the Younger Dryas in Northwestern and Central Europe as Inferred from Climate Indicator Plant Species. *Quaternary Research* 51(2):158–73.

Jacobson, G. L., T. Webb, and E. C. Grimm
    1987   Patterns and Rates of Vegetation Change during the Deglaciation of Eastern North America. In *The Geology of North America, Vol. K-3, North America and the Adjacent Oceans During the last Deglaciation,* edited by W. F. Ruddiman and H. E. Wright, Geological Society of America, Boulder, pp. 277–88.

Jenkins, Dennis L., Loren G. Davis, Thomas W. Stafford Jr., Paula F. Compos, Thomas J. Connolly, Linda Scott Cummings, Michael Hofreiter, Bryan Hockett, Katelyn McDonough, Ian Luthe, Patrick W. O'Grady, Karl J. Reinhard, Mark E. Swisher, Frances White, Bonnie Yates, Robert M. Yohe II, Chad Yost, and Eske Willerslev
    2013   Geochronology, Archaeological Context, and DNA at the Paisley Caves. In *Paleoamerican Odyssey,* Kelly E. Graf, Caroline V. Ketron, and Michael R. Waters, editors. Center for the Study of the First Americans, College Station, TX, pp. 485–510.

Johnson, Michael F.
    1996   Paleoindians Near the Fringe: A Virginia Perspective. In *The Paleoindian and Early Archaic Southeast,* edited by D. G. Anderson and K. E. Sassaman, pp. 187–212. University of Alabama Press, Tuscaloosa.

Judge, James W.
    1973   *The Paleo-Indian Occupation of the Central Rio Grande Valley, New Mexico.* Albuquerque, University of New Mexico Press.

Julig, P. J.
    1984   The Cummins Paleoindian Site and Its Paleoenvironment, Thunder Bay, ON. *Archaeology of Eastern North America* 12:192–209.

Kelly, Robert L.
    2007   *The Foraging Spectrum; Diversity in Hunter-Gatherer Lifeways.* Percheron Press, Clinton Corners, NY.

Kirkpatrick, M. Jude, and Daniel C. Fisher
    1993   Preliminary Research on the Moon Mammoth Site. *Current Research in the Pleistocene* 10:70

Kraft, Herbert C.
    1973   The Plenge Site: A Paleo-Indian Occupation Site in New Jersey. *Archaeology of Eastern North America* 1:56–117.

Krieger, Alex D.
   1954   A Comment on "Fluted Point Relationships" by John Witthoft. *American Antiquity* 17(3):273–75.
   1964   Early Man in the New World. In *Prehistoric Man in the New World*, edited by Jesse D. Jennings and Edward Norbeck, pp. 23–84. Published for William Marsh Rice University by the University of Chicago Press.

Laub, Robert S.
   2002   The Paleoindian Presence in the Northeast: A View from the Hiscock Site. In *Ice Age Peoples of Pennsylvania.* Recent Research in Pennsylvania Archaeology Number 2, edited by Kurt W. Carr and James M. Adovasio, 105–22. Pennsylvania Historical and Museum Commission, Harrisburg.

Loebel, Thomas J.
   2013a Endscrapers, Use-wear, and Early Paleoindians in Eastern North America. In *The Eastern Fluted Point Tradition*, edited by Joseph A. M. Gingerich. University of Utah Press, Salt Lake.
   2013b *Shoop (36Da20) Endscrapers: Results of a High Powered Use-wear analysis.* Report submitted to the State Museum of Pennsylvania, Harrisburg.

Lothrop, Jonathan C., Paige E. Newby, Arthur E. Spiess, and James Bradley
   2011   Paleoindians and the Younger Dryas in the New England Maritimes region. *Quaternary International* 242:546–69.

Lowery, Darren
   1989   The Paw Paw Cove Paleoindian Site Complex, Talbot County, Maryland. *Archaeology of Eastern North America* 17:143–64.

Lowery. Darrin L., Michael A. O'Neal, John Wah, Daniel P. Wagner, and Dennis J. Stanford
   2010   Late Pleistocene Upland Stratigraphy of the Western Delmarva Peninsula, USA. *Quaternary Science Review.* doi:10.1016/j.quascirev.2010.03.007

MacDonald, George F.
   1968   *Debert: A Paleo-Indian Site in Central Nova Scotia.* National Museum of Canada, Anthropological Papers, 16, Ottawa.

Marshall, Sidney B.
   1985   Paleoindian Artifact Form and Function at Shawnee-Minisink. In *Shawnee-Minisink: A Stratified Paleoindian-Archaic Site in the Upper Delaware Valley of Pennsylvania*, edited by Charles W. McNett, pp. 165–209. Academic Press, Orlando.

Martin, Paul S.
   1973   The Discovery of America. *Science* 179(4077):969–74.

Mayewski, P. A., L. D. Meeker, S. Whitlow, M. S. Twickler, M. C. Morrison, R. B. Alley, P. Bloomfield, and K. Taylor
   1993   The Atmosphere During the Younger Dryas. *Science* 261:195–97.

McAvoy, Joseph
   1992   *Nottoway River Survey: Part 1: Clovis Settlement Patterns: The 30 Year Study of a Late Ice Age Hunting Culture on the Southern Interior Coastal Plain of*

Virginia. Archaeological Society of Virginia Special Publication Number 28. Dietz Press, Richmond.

McAvoy, Joseph, and Lynn D. McAvoy
1997 *Archaeological Investigations of Site 44SX202, Cactus Hill, Sussex County, Virginia.* Research Report Series No. 8, Commonwealth of Virginia Department of Historic Resources, Richmond.

McCary, Ben C.
1951 A Workshop Site of Early Man in Dinwiddie County, Virginia. *American Antiquity* 17(1):9–17

McCracken, Richard
1989 The Trojan Site (36BR149). *Pennsylvania Archaeologist* 59(2):1–21.

McNett, Charles W., Jr.
1985 The Shawnee-Minisink Site: An Overview. In *Shawnee-Minisink: A Stratified Paleoindian Archaic Site in the Upper Delaware Valley of Pennsylvania,* edited by Charles W. McNett, pp. 321–26. Academic Press, Orlando.

McWeeney, Lucinda
2007 Revising the Paleoindian Environmental Picture in Northeastern North America. In *Foragers of the Terminal Pleistocene in North America,* edited by Renee B. Walker and Boyce N. Driskell, 148–66. University of Nebraska Press, Lincoln.

Meltzer, David J.
1984 On Stone Procurement and Settlement Mobility in Eastern Fluted Point Groups. *North American Archaeologist* 6(1):1–24.
1988 Late Pleistocene Human Adaptations in Eastern North America. *Journal of World Prehistory* 2(1):1–52.
2009 *First Peoples in a New World: Colonizing Ice Age America.* Berkeley: University of California Press.

Meltzer, David J., and Vance T. Holliday
2010 Would North American Paleoindians have Noticed Younger Dryas Age Climate Changes. *Journal of World Prehistory* 23:1–41.

Miller, Patricia E., James T. Marine, and Frank J. Vento
2007 *Archaeological Investigations, Route11/15 Improvements, (SR 0011, Section 008), Juniata and Perry Counties, Pennsylvania, ER No. 1989-0381-042, Volume II: 36Pe16.* Prepared by: KCI Technologies, Prepared for: Pennsylvania Department of Transportation, Engineering District 8-0.

Miller, D. Shane, Vance T. Holiday, and Jordan Bright
2013 Clovis Across the Continent. In *Paleoamerican Odyssey,* Kelly E. Graf, Caroline V. Ketron, and Michael R. Waters, editors. Center for the Study of the First Americans, College Station, TX, pp. 207–20.

Moeller, Roger W.
1980 *6LF21: A Paleo-Indian Site in Western Connecticut,* Occasional Paper no. 2, American Indian Archaeological Institute, Washington, CT.

1984   Regional Implications of the Templeton Site for Paleo-Indian Lithic Procurement and Utilization. *North American Archaeologist* 5(3):235–45.

Morse, D. F., David G. Anderson, and Albert C. Goodyear
1996   The Pleistocene-Holocene Transition in the Eastern United States. In *Humans at the End of the Ice,* edited by L. Straus, B. Eriksen, J. Erlandson, and D. Yesner, pp. 319–54. Plenum Press.

Peterson, James B., Robert N. Bartone, and Belinda J. Cox
2002   The Late Paleoindian Period in Northeastern North America: A View from Varney Farm. In *Ice Age Peoples of Pennsylvania.* Recent Research in Pennsylvania Archaeology Number 2, edited by Kurt W. Carr and James M. Adovasio, pp. 123–44. Pennsylvania Historical and Museum Commission, Harrisburg.

Pope, Melody
2010   *A Microwear Study on a Small Sample of End Scrapers from the Shoop Site.* Manuscript on file at the State Museum of Pennsylvania.

Robinson, B. S., J. C. Ort, W. A. Eldridge, A. L. Burke, and B. G. Pelletier
2009   Paleoindian Aggregation and Social Context at Bull Brook. *American Antiquity* 74(3):423–47.

Rule, Pamela, and June Evans
1985   The Relationship of Morphological Variation to Hafting Techniques among Paleoindian Endscrapers at the Shawnee Minisink Site. In *Shawnee-Minisink: A Stratified Paleoindian Archaic Site in the Upper Delaware Valley of Pennsylvania,* edited by Charles W. McNett, pp. 211–20. Academic Press, Orlando.

Singer, Zachery L. and Carol A. Ebright
2017   Revisiting the Higgins Site (18AN489): Reanalysis of the First Excavated Paleoindian Site in Maryland. Presented at the Middle Atlantic Archaeological Conference, March 16–19, Virginia Beach, VA.

Smallwood, Ashley, Albert C. Goodyear, Derek T. Anderson, D. Shane Miller, and Sarah Walters
2013   Dating the Hillside Clovis Occupation of the Topper Site, Allendale County, South Carolina. Poster presented at the *Paleoamerican Odyssey.* Organized by Michael Waters, Ted Goebel, and Kelly Graf, Santa Fe, NM. Session 5A, Paleoindians of the American Southeast.

Speth, John D., Khori Newlander, Andrew A. White, Ashley K. Lemke, and Lars E. Anderson
2010   Early Paleoindian Big-Game Hunting in North America: Provisioning or Politics. *Quaternary International* 30:1–29.

Spiess, Arthur E., and Deborah B. Wilson
1987   *Michaud: A Paleoindian Site in the New England Maritimes Region.* The Maine Historic Preservation Commission and the Maine Archaeological Society, Inc. Occasional Publications in Maine Archaeology No. 6, Augusta.

Spiess, Arthur, E., Deborah B. Wilson, and James W. Bradley
  1998   Paleoindian Occupation in the New England-Maritimes Region: Beyond
         Cultural Ecology. *Archaeology of Eastern North America* 26:201–64.

Stanford, Dennis, and Bruce Bradley
  2012   *Across Atlantic Ice: The Origins of American Clovis Culture.* University of
         California Press.

Stewart, R. Michael, and John Cavallo
  1991   Delaware Valley Middle Archaic. *Journal of Middle Atlantic Archaeology*
         7:19–42.

Stewart, R. Michael, Jeremy Koch, Kurt Carr, Del Beck, and Gary Stichcombe
  2012   The Paleoindian Occupation at Nesquehoning Creek (36CR0142) Carbon
         County Pennsylvania. Presented at the 77th Annual Meeting of the Soci-
         ety for American Archaeology, April 18–22, Memphis, TN.

Storck, Peter L., and Arthur E. Spiess
  1994   The Significance of New Faunal Identification Attributed to an Early
         Paleoindian (Gainey Complex) Occupation at the Udora Site, Ontario.
         American Antiquity 59:121–42.

Straus, Lawrence G.
  2000   Solutrean Settlement of North America? A Review of Reality. *American
         Antiquity* 63:7–20.

Strothers, David M.
  1996   Resource Procurement and Band Territories: A Model for Lower Great
         Lakes Paleoindian and Early Archaic Settlement Systems. *Archaeology of
         Eastern North America* 24:173–216.

Sullivan, Robert M., and K. A. Randall
  1996   *Pennsylvania's Prehistoric Pachyderms—The Mastodonts and Mammoths that
         Once Roamed Our State: Natural History Notes of The State Museum of Penn-
         sylvania.* Harrisburg Pennsylvania Historical and Museum Commission.

Turnbaugh, William
  1977   *Man, Land, and Time.* Lycoming County Historical Society, Williamsport.

Vento, Frank J., Tony Vega, Richard S. Toomey, Leslie P. Fay, Paul A. Delcourt,
Hazel R. Delcourt, Grace S. Brush, and Frances B. King
  1994   *Paleoenvironmental and Paleoclimatic Reconstruction of Pennsylvania over the
         Last 15,000 Years.* Report submitted of the Grants Office of the Bureau for
         Historic Preservation, Harrisburg, PA.

Verrey, Robert
  1986   *Paleoindian Stone Tool Manufacture at the Thunderbird Site (44WR11).* Un-
         published PhD dissertation, Catholic University of America, Washington
         DC, pp. 1–531.

Wagner, Daniel P., and Joseph M. McAvoy
  2004   Pedoarchaeology of Cactus Hill, a Sandy Paleoindian Site in Southeastern
         Virginia, U.S.A. *Geoarchaeology: An International Journal,* 19(4):297–322.

Waters, Michael R., and Thomas W. Stafford Jr.
  2007   Redefining the Age of Clovis: Implications for the Peopling of the Americas. *Science*, 315:1122–26.

Waters, Michael R., Thomas W. Stafford Jr., Brian G. Redmond, and Kenneth B. Tankersley
  2009   The Age of the Paleoindian Assemblage at Sheriden Cave Ohio. *American Antiquity* 74:107–111.

Waters, Michael R., Steven L. Foreman, Thomas A. Jennings, Lee C. Nordt, Steven G. Driese, Joshua M. Feinberg, Joshua L. Keene, Jessi Halligan, Anna Lindquist, James Pierson, Charles T. Hallmark, Michael B. Collins, and James E. Wiederhold
  2011a The Buttermilk Creek Complex and the Origins of Clovis at the Debra L. Friedkin Site, Texas. *Science* 331:1599–1603.

Waters, Michael R., Thomas W. Stafford Jr., H. Gregory McDonald, Carl Gustafson, Morten Rasmussen, Enrico Cappellini, Jesper V. Olsen, Damian Szklarczyk, Lars Juhl Jensen, M. Thomas P. Gilbert, and Eske Willerslev
  2011b Pre-Clovis Mastodon Hunting 13,800 Years Ago at the Manis Site, Washington. *Science* 334:351–53.

Webb, S. D. (editor)
  2006   *First Floridians and Last Mastodons: The Page-Ladson Site in the Aucilla River*. Springer, The Netherlands.

Whittaker, John C.
  1994   *Flintknapping: Making and Understanding Stone Tools*. University of Texas Press, Austin.

Willey, Gordon R.
  1966   *An Introduction to American Archaeology, Vol. 1*, Prentice Hall, Inc. Englewood Cliffs, NJ.

Wilmsen, Edwin N.
  1970   *Lithic Analysis and Cultural Inference: A Paleo-Indian Case*. University of Arizona Press, Tucson.

Wilmsen, Edwin N., and Frank H. Roberts
  1978   *Lindenmeier, 1934–1974: Concluding Report on Investigations*. Smithsonian Contributions to Anthropology 24.

Witthoft, John
  1952   A Paleo-Indian site in Eastern Pennsylvania: An Early Hunting Culture. *Proceedings of the American Philosophical Society* 96(4):464–95.

Wormington, H. Marie
  1957   *Ancient Man in North America*, 4th edition. The Denver Museum of Natural History Popular Series No. 4. Denver, CO.

Wray, Charles F.
  1948   Varieties and Sources of Flint Found in New York State. *Pennsylvania Archaeologist* 18(1–2):25–45.

12

Zoological Perspectives in Middle Atlantic Subsistence Studies with an Emphasis on Virginia

Michael B. Barber

The general theme followed here will be the schema proposed by Wiley and Sabloff in their seminal 1974 work *The History of American Archaeology* although updated into the present. While earlier periods are touched upon, the real baseline for the study of subsistence in the Middle Atlantic region did not begin until the Classificatory-Historical Period and, then, with only cursory attention paid to data. At the onset of the Explanatory Period or that of the New Archaeology, faunal studies began in real earnest although usually confined to explanation involving relation to the environment. It was not until the post-processual onslaught that social issues played an active role. At the same time, ethnobotany gained a foothold and made major contributions to our understanding of social issues as well as environmental variables. The interplay of theoretical developments and key individuals will be discussed. Although the Middle Atlantic is the general focus, this chapter will use primarily Virginia data for illustration.

The study of prehistoric subsistence patterns in the Middle Atlantic region, particularly zooarchaeology, has its own set of limiting parameters the most obvious of which is the survival of animal bone and plant materials in a temperate environment. By and large, these materials decay in open air sites and it is only during the recent past (i.e., Late Woodland) that samples have been available for study. Anomalies of rockshelters and caves and carbonized nut material provide some insight into earlier periods but this is severely limited. Complicating this was the common practice through the 1970s, when many archaeologists did not collect animal bone and, if collected, did not isolate the material by provenience and/or did not analyze the assemblage. Putting this all together, much of what we "know" concerning subsistence practices during prehistoric time is speculation based on paleo-environments rather than direct archaeological evidence.

Gordon R. Willey and Jeremy A. Sabloff (1974) wrote a history of American archaeology in 1974, a daunting task at best. Drawing on 482 years of documentation, they developed a chronological and theoretical framework that summarized our discipline in 252 pages. In reading the volume, we find out who we were and what we became, as well as a prologue to who we are. Although their publication obviously ended in the 1970s, I will attempt to bring it up to the present day. Dent (1995:23–68) has offered a general historic summary which documents Chesapean archaeology and which provides a backdrop to this paper. The task at hand is to organize Middle Atlantic archaeology into a Willey and Sabloff–like typology using subsistence as a framework. As I naively approached this chapter, I thought I would take a few days and pull together the archaeological history of subsistence studies in the Middle Atlantic region. Looking for a unilinear Great Wall of China thread, I found instead a diffuse nebulous blob of a subject sprawling amorphically in all directions. Taking advice that I used to give to undergraduate students, the paper could not be all things to all people. As a zooarchaeologist by training, I will speak mostly to meat and the bones to which it adhered and the people who harvested and consumed it. It should also be noted that the dates proposed by Willey and Sabloff have been altered to reflect the time lag in theoretical developments within the Commonwealth and Middle Atlantic.

As with all periodization, the Willey and Sabloff schema should be viewed as a sliding continuum with the added complication of individual personalities. As Thomas Kuhn (1970) so eloquently related, changes in academic paradigms often require the death of the practitioner. After dedicating one's career to a particular theory, it is often taken to the grave. The competition between old theory and new theory looks more like seriation's battleship curve of yesteryear than any clean, clear-cut temporal boundary. I will add to this some evolutionary concepts in viewing the changes in the Middle Atlantic's treatment of subsistence in terms of personalities such as David Bushnell, Howard MacCord, Bill Gardner, Mike Barber, Heather Lapham, Elizabeth Moore, Martin Gallivan, and Justine McKnight.

SPECULATIVE PERIOD (1492–1840)

Hallmarks of the Period: No archaeological discipline or science, explorers' writings, un-substantiated conjecture.

The real Speculative Period in Virginia and the Middle Atlantic began in earnest with the brief Jesuit Mission of Ajaca on the York River in 1570, English settlement at Roanoke Island in 1585, and the settlement at Jamestown in 1607. St. Mary's Mission was of brief duration where Spanish missionaries attempted to bring their god to the Powhatan Indians (Mallios 2006). Spreading of the word was cut short when they were cut short by a group of local Indians led by Don Luis, a captured and returned boy from the village of Kiskiack. The missionaries joined their god and the Indians rid themselves of *in situ* European nuances for another thirty-six years. Ethhnohistoric references to subsistence were limited to the time being a period of drought, with the Jesuits bringing little in the way of food and relying heavily on the Indians for sustenance.

The settlement at Roanoke Island on Pimlico Sound (now North Carolina) in 1585 provided more grist for our understanding of the subsistence mill. This was mostly in the form of John White's water colors of local natives, flora, and fauna. At the bidding of Sir Walter Raleigh, operating under political and religious motivations, and with influences from Thomas Harriot with scientific concerns, the first English foothold at Roanoke Island in 1585 was established with a healthy contingent of soldiers, a few gentlemen, merchants, some specialists, one scientist (Thomas Harriot), and one artist (John White) (Hulton 1984:45). The watercolors of John White and the accounts of Thomas Harriot and their publication by Theodor de Bry provide some baseline data of concern here (Lourant 1946). Three of White's watercolors provide insight into subsistence practices. The first is "Indians Fishing," which demonstrates various techniques of capture plus several species of fish. The second is "The Town of Secota," where a series of crops are planted although precise identification is nebulous. The third is "A Meal," where a seated man and woman are in the act of consuming a meal.

The Englishman Captain John Smith, a mercenary soldier for both Dutch and Austrian forces, returned to England in 1604, joined the voyages to the New World for establishing a second colony there, and was named one of the Jamestown councilors upon arrival (Noel-Hume 1994:127) even though he was under arrest at the time (Dabney 1971:4). Smith remained in Jamestown until October 1609 when he was accidentally burned and returned to England. During his stay, however, he provided much needed leadership, military knowledge, cartographic skills, and a proclivity for detailed observation coupled with a dedication to writing. The result was

The Diaries of Captain John Smith: 1680–1631, which were masterfully edited by Phillip Barbour (1986). Smith (Barbour 1986: I 154–56) described in fair detail the animal populations found on the coastal plain of Virginia. For example, his list of mammals included deer, raccoon, squirrel, flying squirrel, opossum, muskrat, rabbit, bear, beaver, river otter, wild cat, fox, dog, martin, skunk, weasel, and mink. Among the birds are eagle, sparrowhawk, lanaret, goshawk, falcon, osprey, partridge, turkey, red-winged blackbird, thrush, swan, crane, heron, geese, brant, duck, Wigeon, dotterel, Oxeye, parrot, pigeon, and "diverse sort of small birds." Fish in Smith's list included sturgeon, grampus, porpoise, seal, stingray, turbot, mullet, white salmon, trout, sole, plaice, herring, conyfish, rockfish, eel, lamprey, catfish, shad, shade, and perch. Obviously, porpoise and seal are not fish although they qualified in the eyes of John Smith.

The diaries of John Smith give insight into the general aboriginal use of associated fauna which have been mined extensively by recent authors (e.g., Barber 2003; Rountree 1989; Rountree and Turner 2002). The importance of white-tailed deer is underscored in the context of venison, skins as raw material, and skins as tribute. According to Smith, subsistence patterns for the Native Americans revolved around deer, turkey, and various fish, prime among them being the sturgeon.

Other ethnohistoric renditions provide data on the aboriginal subsistence patterns. William Strachey provided a similar list to that of Smith. The expedition of Batts and Fallom in 1671 along the Roanoke River in search of the South Sea pointed to "bare meadows and old fields" left by Native American farming practices (Bushnell 1907:50). Robert Beverley (1947) in 1705 supplied a listing of locally available fauna, also like that of Smith a century earlier. John Lawson (Lefler 1967) followed suit with a cacophony of available species. In Williams Byrd's (1967) diary related to the surveying the line between Virginia and North Carolina, he lists harvested animals as deer, turkey, bear, bobcat, and buffalo.

In Virginia and the Middle Atlantic in general, the Speculative Period had many historic blocks on which to build. While the bigger questions of mound builders and the origins of Indians persisted, questions of subsistence, at least in the later period of contact, had many sources in the contemporary literature.

CLASSIFICATORY-DESCRIPTIVE PERIOD (1840–1914)

Hallmarks of the Period: Description of archaeological materials, attempts at scientific approach à la *Origin of Species.*

Archaeologists during this period paid little attention to foodways. Concerns were more focused on the distribution of villages and mounds within certain regions. One example that seems to mirror the approaches toward Middle Atlantic archaeology is Bushnell's (1907) *Research in Virginia from Tidewater to the Alleghanies*. Ethnocentrism plays a role in statements such as "The valley of the Shenandoah was undoubtedly the scene of many encounters between different tribes in the days before discovery and settlement" (Ibid:532). Focusing on old Indian trails mentioned by Kercheval (1833), Bushnell uses a regional approach to the Bath County area, pointing to various mound groups and unique artifact descriptions. Subsistence was never a serious point of study with a higher level of abstraction and broad strokes of description the rule.

While the broader questions of the Speculative Period continued, the development of regional studies by archaeological practitioners began to take hold. Subsistence remained a minor concern, with more disciplined approaches and the building of local assemblages of material culture.

CLASSIFICATORY-HISTORICAL PERIOD (1914–1940): CHRONOLOGY

Hallmarks of the Period: Concern for chronology, time-ordering of events.

For David L. Bushnell Jr., the regional approach continued with his classic study of Monacan Town in 1930. He does, however, hone his description to a particular time period, that of contact. Lip service is paid to the importance of subsistence in the village setting with Mowhemcho (or Monacan Town) described as a dispersed village with gardens scattered between the dwelling and "game abundant throughout the region" (Bushnell 1930:8–9). Likewise, Rassawek was presented as being protected by the confluence of two streams where fish and game were plentiful (Ibid:12).

It was during this period that Dr. Ben McCary began his recordation of fluted points in Virginia. Soon after the discovery of Folsom in 1922, Dr. Ben sought out Clovis projectile points and purchased many. The association of Folsom and Clovis with the killing of big game animals in the southwest fostered the concept of megafauna harvesting in the east.

CLASSIFICATORY-HISTORICAL PERIOD (1940–1970): CONTEXT AND FUNCTION

Hallmarks of the Period: Beginnings of artifacts as social indicators, settlement pattern studies, relationship between culture and environment.

There is no doubt that Col. Howard A. MacCord set the tone for this period beginning in the 1940s. In general, with regard to animals, MacCord held that Indians ate every beast encountered. When asked about the

Keyser site (44PA0001) (Manson, MacCord, and Griffin 1944), with turkey buzzard and snake identified within the recovered sample, he replied, "Of course, they ate them" (MacCord 1993). The paradigm then was that if all animals were eaten, one need not collect subsistence data as it would prove redundant to common knowledge. This theoretical attitude in Virginia led to the field methodology of not collecting bone unless human or modified into tools. When dealt with in publications, "Food Remains" were discussed in a cursory manner with apparent gross identification in the field. For the Late Woodland Irwin Site in Prince George County, Virginia, MacCord (1964a) lists only Virginia deer (*Odocoileus virginianus*), raccoon (*Procyon lotor*), squirrel (*Sciurus carolinenisis*), turkey (*Meleagris gallopavo*), and sturgeon as animals present. No further quantification or analysis is presented.

Another example of the type of subsistence study implemented during this period is Benthall's (1969) *Archaeological Investigation of the Shannon Site, Montgomery County, Virginia*. The Shannon site was a ca. A.D. 1250 palisaded Late Woodland village on the banks of the North Fork of the Roanoke River near its headwaters. While the report is packed with an amazing level of raw data, an almost complete lack of deep analysis and theory is brought to bear. With regard to subsistence, the pertinent material was succinctly divided into flora and fauna. No quantitative manipulations were attempted, and carbonized vegetal remains were listed as *Zea maize* (corn), *Prosopis* sp. (beans), *Carya glabra* (hickory nuts), and *Juglans nigra* (black walnut). Regarding fauna, Benthall (1969:143) states:

> By far the most plentiful of the remains of foodstuffs were the bushels of animal bones and the great quantities of mussel and snail shells, which indicate the great dependence placed on the animal kingdom as a source of food.

He then stated that "apparently every type of animal in the area served as a food source" and followed this with a list of mammals including only fourteen species.

The zooarchaeology and ethbotanical records were not incorporated into a holistic approach but were set aside as minor concerns, dealt with as laundry lists with only cursory analysis. While other artifact groups were analyzed at a higher level, subsistence rested at a lower threshold of acuity.

EXPLANATORY PERIOD (1970–1995)

Hallmarks of the Period: Re-emergence of evolutionary theory, system theory, positivist philosophy of science.

On the national level, it can be said that the New Archaeology origi-nated with Lewis Binford; in Virginia, it began with Dr. William M. Gardner and Catholic University. Gardner was a dyed in the wool be-liever in the power of the environment, a trait he developed no doubt at the University of Illinois under the tutelage of Julian Steward. Carr (2008) described Gardner as an "explicit cultural ecologist" and he was as close to an environmental determinist as one saw in the late twentieth century. While he was a dedicated multidisciplinary researcher, he did not strictly follow the edits of the New Archaeology and did not dabble in middle range theory, historic analogs, or intensive quantification and statistics. What he did bring to the table was the study of paleoclimate, continuity and diachronic change through time, bedrock geology, and the "big pic-ture" approach. These traits were reflected in his students, who are cur-rently, in large part, in control of the prehistory of the Middle Atlantic and remain dedicated to the environmental regime. A prime example of this is Custer's (1988) summary of coastal plain adaptions in the Middle Atlan-tic. Organized in a diachronic format, the overview deals extensively with paleoclimates and culture change through time. These changes, by and large, are all environmentally related. Paleoindian remains on a seasonal round focused on lithic sources (but also favorable hunting/gathering lo-cales) and, although plants may be collected when encountered, hunting remains the overall focus. Again, based on the evolution of the environ-mental setting, other resources are exploited through time.

What this brought to our understanding of subsistence theory was a series of settlement models based on different methods of procurement. While rocks were always of more importance than food, sex, or informa-tion, during Paleoindian times, foodways were reflected in the lithic tool kit with an emphasis on hunting. While in truth they were generalized omnivores, Gardner felt strongly that, in the paleo mind-set, they thought of themselves as hunters (Gardner 1989:30).

It was during this period that a systemic approach was applied to zoo-archaeology. No longer did one see laundry lists of mostly mammals and a few identified birds based on visual examination but a comprehensive listing of taxa identified based on comparative collections including all classes (NISP), a minimum number of individuals isolated based on ele-ment of highest frequency (MNI), and meat or biomass produced.

Many of the ethnozoological analyses during this period were guided by the environmental paradigm. For example, for the Middle and Late Woodland Taft site (44FX0544) (Norton and Baird 1994) in Fairfax County, Virginia, the faunal analysis focused on environmental exploitation sys-tems and seasonality (Otter 1994:106–14). The analysis did provide added insight into regional perspectives, diachronic change through time, and scientific methodologies. Changes between Middle and Late Woodland

subsistence patterns shifted from broad-based environmental exploitation to a focus on the riverine ecosystem with the extensive exploitation
of turtles and fish. Scientific methods were also brought into play with the
innovative analysis of gar fish scales to determine annual growth patterns
with the majority harvested in late winter/early spring.

Evidence of former periods was also noted. *The Montgomery Focus: A
Late Woodland Potomac River Culture* (Slattery and Woodward 1992:3–4) is
a prime example. Although the text indicated

> game, both large and small, was plentiful in pre-Colonial times as evidenced
> by the thousands of animal bones excavated from the Indian village flank-
> ing the rivers. Examples of almost every species of animal native to the area
> are represented in our collections, the most prevalent being the native deer
> (*Odocoileus virginianus*). Other fauna represented include fish, turtles, heron,
> waterfowl, and turkey.

This is followed by a laundry list of fifteen mammals identified from the
sample of several villages. Moore (1994) corrected this shortcoming in her
dissertation with an in-depth analysis including species/class diversity,
seasonality, ecosystem utilization patterns, feature and feature comparisons, and a regional perspective. Her analysis was a classic for the time
with a discussion of taxa, diet, environment exploitation, seasonality, and
regional perspectives. New ground was broken with a consideration of
wild faunal and floral remains augmented by new cultigens into a bal-
anced study of the subsistence economy. Her analytical approach reaches
into the post-processual period.

POST-PROCESSUAL PERIOD (1995–PRESENT)

Hallmarks of the Period: Theoretical eclecticism, cognitive archaeology, abandonment and re-emergence of science.

I am not sure what are the effects of the post-processual revolution
within the Middle Atlantic region. Many students of Gardner ignored its
implications and continued within an environmental paradigm, valuing
paleoclimates, carbon dates, lithic distribution, and jasper. Although not
quite the tendency toward Julian Steward's environmental determinism
of former years, Middle Atlantic archaeologists, by and large, obeyed the
dictates of Thomas Kuhn, and continued along their original path.

By the mid-1990s, and in some places prior, a movement was afoot
not only to abandon many of the tenets of the "new" archaeology, but to
soften the effects of the post-processual movement with its anti-scientism.
Most notably, University of Virginia, Department of Anthropology,
retained its symbolic leanings while integrating culture, data, science,

and even a nod toward the environment. Regarding subsistence studies, particularly the analysis of the zooarchaeological record, faunal analysis went well beyond diet, environment, and seasonality and led to cultural explanation. Foremost among these was Lapham's dissertation (2002) and later publication (2005) on the protohistoric deerskin trade in southwestern Virginia.

As Lapham (2005:1–6) put it, her theoretical framework evaluated the concept of overproduction of trade goods, in this case, deerskins, which could be utilized to acquire wealth, which in turn was used to create status and power. She did this by comparing the recovered vertebrate fauna between prehistoric villages, Crab Orchard (44TZ0001) and Hoge (44TZ0006) and the protohistoric Trigg site (44MY0003) with a focus on white-tailed deer. She found that the deer remains from these sites mostly represented a natural population mix of bucks and does of various ages. At the protohistoric site, however, more males than females were taken with most animals taken at three and a half years, at the center of the prime age of good hides. In tracing the distribution of trade exotica (copper and shell) found in burials, the young males at Trigg received the more of those exchange goods than in a prehistoric context. Lapham demonstrated that the seventeenth-century occupants at Trigg in southwestern Virginia were involved in the overproduction of deerskins for trade with the Europeans to the east and the eventual conveyance to England. The trade was controlled by the young males of the group who now controlled the new-found wealth and distribution of that wealth and, hence, achieved status. Going beyond subsistence consideration, Lapham demonstrated that a dearth of leather in London led to change in the social and cultural dynamics of an Indian village in southwestern Virginia, about four thousand miles away.

Barber's (2003) is another example of an analysis of faunal material lending itself to more cultural explanation, both in chronology building through a view of diachronic change, regional differences, and socio-cultural nuances. In all, a total of thirty prehistoric components was studied confined to the Late Woodland to Contact time periods in the range of A.D. 1000 to A.D. 1700. Within the core study area of the Roanoke River, this corresponds to the occupation period of the Siouan-speaking Dan River peoples. The study of bone tools underscores an image of relative stability. It is suggested that the relative lack of change continued into the proto-historic period with radical changes brought about through European contact and/or European trade goods.

To analyze the modified bone, it was necessary to develop a bone tool typology with a precise schema of definitions. At the onset, a dichotomy was put in place where functional or working tools were distinguished from visual or ornamental tools/beads. Working tools, in short, were those used in "working" activities prone to friction (i.e., hole making, scraping, grooving, etc.). Visual tools were those whose function was presumed to provide ready information about the status, wealth, and/or affiliation of the individual wearer.

The distribution of modified bone types was mapped providing a picture of the inter-relationships for the region and adjacent areas. Comparisons were made on a presence or absence basis and frequencies examined according to particular questions. The Dan River culture was centered, based on the consistency of modified bone, to the Roanoke River drainage including the Dan River along with limited settlements on the New and James Rivers with radical change occurring at European contact. These changes were reflected in an increase of *Odocoileus virginianus* metatarsal awls, and the appearance of *Ursus americanus* blunt-ended weaving tools, *Odocoileus virginianus* rib weaving tools. These were all tied into the deer-skin trade, particularly at the Trigg Site (44MY0003). The interior Indians traded surplus goods for deer skins with which to engage in the trade. In addition, to further convert their labor into higher wealth, they traded for lower value, uncured skins, thus maximizing their return. The bone tools may provide a window on this as the blunt-ended weaving tools appeared at a time when an increase in the production of baskets and mats was desired to buy skins. In this scenario, the occupants at Trigg acted as minor, interior middlemen in the deer skin trade. Although Merrill (1989) makes a convincing case that the Native Americans joined the European exchange system on their own terms, it is suggested by the ethnohistoric record and the bone tool assemblage recovered that at least some Native Americans were learning the capitalistic demand for production and maximization of labor.

These new approaches at teasing out viable hypotheses concerning culture were also augmented by new scientific techniques such as DNA testing, blood residue analysis, and amino acid analyses. One example is a recent synthesis of data with regard to the Maycock's Point site, a Middle Woodland II sedentary site on the lower James River (Barber 2016). Long known as an aggregation encampment associated with anadromous fish runs (Barber 1980; Opperman 1982), seasonality and overall subsistence remained open questions. Ethnobotanical analysis identified carbonized hickory, walnuts, and charred acorns as well as maypops and grape (McKnight 1992). Phytolith analysis identified squash/pumpkin, goosefoot, and tissue fragments from the sunflower family (Cummings and Dexter 2006). Messner's (n.d.) with starch analysis form selected ceramic and stone artifacts produced evidence of the use of water lily, other aquatic tubers, and grains. In a synthesis of the various analytical techniques, a picture of year-round site occupation emerged as well as the hypothesized presence of the Eastern Agricultural Complex.

An additional, potentially more powerful, breakthrough occurred with the initiation of the Virginia Archeobotanical Database Project (McKnight and Gallivan 2007). Funded through VDHR's Threatened Sites program, the project centralized in one database all previous data while providing funds for generating a series of dates across the Commonwealth based directly on corn and, hence, eliminating the "old wood" problem (McKnight and Gallivan 2007:185; Means and McKnight 2010:17). Coupling this with more precise accelerator mass spectrometry (AMS) dating techniques, old carbon dates were found, in many cases, to be much earlier than the new calibrated median dates. Several significant trends were noted. The first was the decline of deciduous forest species beginning with the Middle Woodland Period with an increase in earlier successive species in later times as land clearing associated with garden economies increased. This was evinced by increased successional species wood charcoal recovered used in fueling habitation fires. In addition, as the recovery of maize increased during the Late Woodland Period, the presence of deciduous species nut crops decreased (Ibid:183). It was also established that maize appeared in a coastal plain context at ca. A.D. 1100 as documented at the lower James River Maycock's Point sedentary hunter-gatherer-fisher site. Beans and squash appear in the archaeological record during the thirteenth century A.D. with a concomitant increase in maize agriculture. Such ethnobotanical re-syntheses are a hallmark of the post-processual period.

CONCLUSION

The trajectory of archaeologiocal subsistence studies in the Middle Atlantic region follows, in broad terms, the outline of American archaeology as outlined by Willey and Sabloff (1974). This pattern can be summarized as shown in Table 12.1.

In summary, the attention given to animal and plant remains has gone from a total lack of concern to a list of remains recovered to a cultural study of overall foodways and how they are included in a holistic study of the past. It is difficult to predict where the study of archaeology, in general, and prehistoric subsistence studies, in particular, will evolve in the twenty-first century. The ever more elaborate use of science will hopefully provide for many breakthroughs we could only imagine in the past. But even this is changing with the digital world. The very scientific method in which we have all invested so much of our research is in question. The formulation and testing of hypotheses is now in jeopardy, with Excel tables and digital searches fostering "let's see what happens" ilk of science. What would Thomas Kuhn say?

Table 12.1. Summary of Archaeological Subsistence Studies

Speculative Period	1580–1840	ethnohistories, untested hypotheses
Classificatory-Descriptive Period	1840–1914	focus on artifacts, little attention paid to subsistence
Classificatory-Historical Period: Chronology	1914–1940	broad generalizations, big game hunting enters lexicon
Classificatory-Historical Period: Context and Function	1940–1970	first species identification, laundry lists, sometimes collection of animal bones, overly broad concept of exploitation system
Explanatory Period	1970–1995	species identification, MNI/NSP, pounds of usable meat, diet, seasonality, base level scientific analysis
Post-Processual Period	1995–present	sophisticated scientific methods, ethnobotany moves to forefront, reconstruction of past cultures

REFERENCES CITED

Barber, Michael B.
   1980   The Vertebrate Faunal Utilization Pattern of the Middle Woodland Mockley Ceramic Users: The Maycock's Point Shell Midden Site, Prince George County, Virginia. On file with Virginia Department of Historic Resources, Richmond.
   2003   The Late Woodland Dan River People: A Social Reconstruction Based on Study of Bone Tools at the Regional Scale. Unpublished PhD dissertation, Department of Anthropology, University of Virginia, Charlottesville.
   2016   Excavations at Maycock's Point (44PG0040), Prince George County, Virginia: A Middle Woodland II Sedentary Site. Paper presented at 46th Annual Middle Atlantic Archaeological Conference meeting, Ocean City, MD.

Barbour, Philip L.
   1986   *The Complete Works of Captain John Smith (1580–1631) in Three Volumes.* The Institute of Early American History and Culture, Colonial Williamsburg Foundation, Williamsburg, VA.

Bushnell, David
   1907   Virginia from Early Records. *American Anthropologist* 9(1), Washington, DC.

Byrd, William
   1967   *William Byrd's Histories of the Dividing Line Betwixt Virginia and North Carolina.* Dover Publications, Inc., New York.

Carr, Curt
   2008   Paleoindian/Early Archaic Continuity in the Northeast: An Examination of Gardner's Criteria in the Middle Atlantic Region, New England, and

Great Lakes. Paper presented at a Symposium to Honor the Work of William R. Gardner, September 27, Shepardstown, WV.

Cummings, Linda S., and Jaime Dexter
2006 Phytolith and Starch Analysis for a Shell Midden at Maycock's Point (44PG0040), Virginia. MS. on file with Virginia Department of Historic Resources, Richmond.

Custer, Jay F.
1988 Coastal Adaptions in the Middle Atlantic Region. *Archaeology of Eastern North America* 16:121–35.

Dent, Richard J.
1995 *Chesapeake Prehistory: Old Traditions, New Directions.* Plenum Press, New York.

Gardner, William R.
1989 An Examination of Cultural Change in the Late Pleistocene and Early Holocene (circa 9200 to 6200 B.C.). In *Paleoindian Research in Virginia: A Synthesis,* J. M. Wittkofski and T. R. Reinhart (eds.), Archeological Society of Virginia: Special Publication #19, pp. 55–52, Richmond.

Hulton, Paul
1984 *America 1585: The Complete Drawings of John White.* University of North Carolina Press, Chapel Hill.

Kercheval, Samuel
1833 *History of the Valley of Virginia.* Winchester.

Kuhn, Thomas S.
1970 *The Structure of Scientific Revolutions.* International Encyclopedia of Unified Sciences, Vol. I and II, Foundations of the Unity of Science, University of Chicago Press.

Lapham, Heather A.
2002 Deerskin Production and Prestige Goods Acquisition in Late Woodland and Early Historic Southwest Virginia. PhD dissertation, Department of Anthropology, University of Virginia, Charlottesville.
2005 *Hunting for Hides: Deerskins, Status, and Cultural Change in the Protohistoric Appalachians.* University of Alabama Press, Tuscaloosa.

Lefler, Hugh T. (ed.)
1967 *A New Voyage to Carolina: John Lawson.* University of North Carolina Press, Chapel Hill.

Lourant, Stefan (ed.)
1946 *The New World: The First Pictures of America.* Duell, Sloan, & Pearce, New York.

Mallios, Seth
2006 *The Deadly Politics of Giving: Exchange and Violence at Ajacan, Roanoke, and Jamestown.* University of Alabama Press, Tuscaloosa.

Manson, Carl, Howard A. MacCord Jr., and Robert A. Griffin
  1944 The Culture of the Keyser Farm Site. *Papers of the Michigan Academy of Science, Arts, and Letters*, XXIX, pp. 375–418, Ann Arbor.

McKnight, Justine, and Martin Gallivan
  2007 The Virginia Archeobotanical Database Project: A Preliminary Synthesis of Chesapeake Ethnobotany. *Quarterly Bulletin; Archeological Society of Virginia*, 64(4):181–89, Richmond.

Messner, Timothy C.
  n.d. Starch Grain Analysis at the Maycok's Point Site (44PG0040), Prince George County, Virginia. On file with VDHR, Richmond.

Means, Bernard K., and Justine McKnight
  2010 Constructing Chronologies from Curate Collections for Northern Virginia's late Woodland period: A Threatened Sites Project. *Quarterly Bulletin; Archeological Society of Virginia* 65(1):181–89.

Moore, Elizabeth A.
  1994 *Prehistoric Economies During the late Woodland Period of the Potomac Valley.* PhD dissertation, American University, Washington, DC.

Norton, Robert F., and Edith A. Baird
  1994 The Taft Site: A Middle and Late Woodland Assemblage from the Virginia Coastal Plain. *Archaeology of Eastern North America*, 22:89–133.

Opperman, Antony A.
  1992 Middle Woodland Subsistence at Maycock's Point (44PG40), Prince George County, Virginia. Unpublished MA thesis, Department of Anthropology, University of Tennessee, Knoxville.

Otter, Edward
  1994 Faunal Analysis. In The Taft Site: A Middle and Late Woodland Assemblage from Virginia Coastal Plain, Robert F. Norton and Edith A. Baird, *Archaeology of Eastern North America* 22:106–14.

Rountree, Helen C.
  1989 *The Powhatan Indians of Virginia: Their Traditional Culture.* University of Oklahoma Press, Norman.

Rountree, Helen C., and E. Randolph Turner
  2002 *Before and After Jamestown: Virginia's Powhatans and Their Predecessors.* University of Florida Press, Gainesville.

Slattery, Richard G., and Douglas R. Wooodward
  1992 *The Montgomery Focus: A Late Woodland Potomac River Culture. Bulletin Number 2,* Archaeological Society of Maryland, Inc.

Strachey, William
  1625 *A True Reportory of the Wracke and Redemption of Sir Thomas Gates Knight.* Samuel Purchas, London.

Willey, Gordon R., and Jeremy A. Sabloff
  1974 *A History of American Archaeology.* Thames and Hudson, London.

13

Middle Atlantic Region Settlement Pattern Studies

A Review

Robert D. Wall

In settlement, man inscribes upon the landscape certain modes of his existence. These settlement arrangements relate to the adjustments of man and culture to environment and to the organization of society in the broadest sense. Viewed archeologically, settlement patterns are, like any prehistoric residue, the incomplete and fragmentary oddments of something that was once vital and whole (Willey 1956:1).

One of the earliest settlement pattern studies in ethnography was undertaken by Julian Steward (1938), who analyzed ecological data in the Great Basin region and how it articulated with ethnographic settlement data. Willey (1956) later pioneered settlement pattern studies and demonstrated how settlements tend to reflect social and economic activities (Willey 1956:1). This was in the Viru Valley of Peru where settlement patterning was first used to determine the relationship of cultural process to regional site distribution patterns (Parsons 1972:128). Willey's work involved assessing site location, the amount of refuse accumulation, architecture, and site size (Parsons 1972:129). Willey's research is considered by many to be the starting point for settlement pattern studies (Ammerman 1981:65).

One can define the meaning of "settlement patterns" by going back to Willey's original definition (1956:1).

The term "settlement patterns" is defined here as the way in which man disposed himself over the landscape on which he lived. It refers to dwellings, to their arrangement, and to the nature and disposition of other buildings pertaining to community life. These settlements reflect the natural environment,

the level of technology on which the builders operated, and various institutions of social interaction and control which the culture maintained. Because
settlement patterns are, to a large extent, directly shaped by widely held cultural needs, they offer a strategic starting point for the functional interpretation
of archaeological cultures (Willey 1953:1).

Willey (1956) also stated that socio-economic data on past cultures could
be derived from settlement pattern studies (Parsons 1972:129).

During the 1950s, many settlement pattern studies were completed with
both descriptive and theoretical-methodological foci (Parsons 1972:130).
Many of these early works focused on both community plans and intra-
site patterns as well as meaningful distributions of sites over the landscape.
Vogt (1956:173) noted that settlement patterns are important to archaeologists because of the relevance of territoriality, the ecological influence on
human culture and settlements, and other research problems that involve
geographers and ethnologists as well as archaeologists. Ritchie (1956),
also noting the importance of the environment, described the evolution of
cultures in the Northeast from their nomadic roots, to seasonal camps, to
sedentary villages, with sites increasing in size along this continuum. Parsons (1972:146) describes the importance of archaeologists working with
the ethnographic and historical records and ethnologists to develop viable
settlement pattern models (see also Vogt 1956; Willey 1953).

The 1960s brought forth a great variety of settlement pattern studies.
Also, the term *settlement pattern* became *settlement system* in the 1960s,
which involved looking more closely at settlement function within a single culture as opposed to simply looking at physiographic and geographic
relationships to sites within a culture (Parsons 1972:132). Chang (1962),
for example, analyzed the spatial aspects of prehistoric settlements. He
made the distinction between settlement patterns (site-environment association along with technology and subsistence) and community patterns
(configuration of the social group). Using examples of Arctic peoples in
Siberia and North America, he developed a typology of settlement types
based on seasonal subsistence rounds and duration of occupation, factors addressed throughout the settlement pattern literature. Specifically,
his settlement types included terminology such as sedentary settlements
with transient bases, permanent settlements, seasonal settlements, and
temporary settlements. This is not unlike some of the terminology used
in current settlement pattern analyses.

Winters (1969:110–11) described two types of analytical units, settlement
patterns ("geographic and physiographic relationships of a contemporaneous group of sites within a single culture") and settlement systems
("functional relationships among the sites contained within a settlement
pattern"). This pertains, for example, to the permanence of hunter-gatherer

sites, seasonality, and a comprehensive exploration of faunal remains and how they relate to settlement types. Also of paramount importance is what is referred to as geographic distinctions (i.e., the location of sites with respect to various types of riverine and upland environments).

In the Great Lakes region, Fitting (1969:361) recognized the lack of clear differences between what were called camps and villages, or even sites, for that matter. Fitting also emphasized the importance of tool ratios, faunal and floral remains, density of ceramics, settlement location, site homogeneity and heterogeneity, and ecological relationships as related to economic activities on a site (1969:365). He also used ethnographic models (e.g., Ottawa) to provide preliminary explanations of archaeological settlement types (1969:371).

Other 1960s studies include the basin of Mexico where one focus was to develop a typology for different settlement types (Ammerman 1981:70; Sanders, Parsons, and Santley 1979). Trigger (1967) explains, in his analysis of settlement pattern studies in the first decade since Willey's pioneer study, differences between the individual structure, the site (or community pattern), and the region. Finally, Chang (1968) brought together a number of settlement pattern studies in an edited volume on settlement patterns. This was based on an idea originally derived from a Harvard University seminar class on this "relatively unexplored field of query" in 1961.

The 1970s brought forth a variety of settlement pattern studies. Flannery's (1976) edited volume, *The Early Mesoamerican Village*, contains a series of articles that demonstrate the state of settlement pattern studies at the time using catchment analyses, survey designs, regional studies, exchange systems as related to settlement patterns, and ethnographic modeling. Catchment analysis was introduced by Vita-Finzi and Higgs (1970) as a means of describing the economic potential of an archaeological site and its surroundings. This term has been loosely applied in many studies. Predictive models were also introduced to many regions (Jochim 1976). By the 1970s, there was a greater concern for understanding why sites were located where they were (Ammerman 1981:68). This developed into increasingly more sophisticated and comprehensive spatial analyses. To a large degree most of the known archaeological sites were located in valley bottoms and on nearby river terraces so the vast upland regions were sometimes jokingly referred to as "unknowable" (Gardner 1974).

Questions on landform or site setting and archaeological site associations influenced new regional site surveys with adaptation and the environment in mind. This differed significantly from earlier twentieth century site surveys that focused more exclusively on artifacts. By the 1970s, settlement pattern studies had also pervaded the Middle Atlantic region and many of these efforts used survey data that had been compiled from surveys completed decades earlier.

EARLY SURVEYS IN THE
MIDDLE ATLANTIC REGION

Archaeological surveys conducted in the Middle Atlantic region during the first half of the twentieth century involved the compilation of archaeological site inventories that described site size and location as well as information on material culture recovered from the sites. The principal reason for conducting surveys at that time was simply to find suitable sites to excavate (Ammerman 1981:63). The purpose of excavation was, for various reasons, often designed to deal with issues of chronology.

For example, Moorehead surveyed portions of the Susquehanna valley in 1916 (Moorehead 1918). In 1929, additional testing was undertaken by the University of Pennsylvania (Davidson 1929). Other surveys, both professional and amateur, were performed in various parts of the state from the 1930s on. In southwestern Pennsylvania, surveys sponsored by the Pennsylvania Historical and Museum Commission (PHMC) and Works Progress Administration (WPA) project surveys resulted in the development of an archaeological site database (Butler 1939) though no settlement models were developed until decades later. Chronological issues were addressed by Witthoft in the 1940s and 1950s with additional data recovered from more systematic surveys and stratigraphic testing in the 1960s (see Kinsey 1972; Michels and Smith 1967).

In Maryland, Stearns's (1943) Tidewater region survey and his reconnaissance of the lower Patapsco River valley (Stearns 1949) supplied descriptions of a number of artifact assemblages and site areas not previously recorded in any systematic manner. Similar surveys had been compiled in other Middle Atlantic states like New Jersey where Skinner and Schrabisch (1913), Schrabisch (1917, 1930), and later Cross (1941) compiled lists of archaeological site locations. With regard to resources near these sites, Schrabisch described the location of lithic resources such as argillite and cherts in the upper Delaware region. A number of other surveys and compilations of site inventories, both small and large scale, can be found in the early literature for the Middle Atlantic region.

SETTLEMENT PATTERN STUDIES OF THE 1970s

Settlement models developed for the Middle Atlantic region in the 1970s through the 1980s used a variety of environmental variables to address settlement and land use patterns in prehistory. The variables were usually regional or sub-regional; for example, kame terraces and other prominent glacial landforms were considered significant landscapes within the Glaciated Plateau region. Some settlement pattern studies have analyzed environmental settings at a higher resolution to isolate key geographic features related to human land use patterns. Selected settlement pattern studies are described below by sub-region and/or theme. There are many important studies that have not been included and would serve as equally significant examples of trends in settlement pattern studies. The volume of settlement pattern analyses over the past forty years is immense.

THE POTOMAC RIVER VALLEY AND SURROUNDING REGION

Gardner and McNett (1970) established the Potomac River Basin survey in the early 1970s. The initial intent of the survey was to investigate adaptive systems during the Paleoindian period in the montane region of the Potomac River drainage and the Early and Middle Woodland periods in the Coastal Plain. These were considered critical research problems at the time. The initial phase of the survey involved the identification of more than one thousand sites. Gardner (1974) later focused on settlement patterns pertinent to seven functionally distinct Paleoindian sites on the South Fork of the Shenandoah River. Subsequent research on these sites focused on developing a chronology and studying adaptive changes over time, settlement patterns, paleoecology, and "exploitative patterns." This was the foundation for Gardner's Flint Run complex model which was developed over the next few years and settlement patterns were a significant part of this study (Gardner 1974, 1977). The quarry base camp model developed by Gardner and his students focused on Paleoindian sites that were strategically positioned in the area of high quality jasper outcrops. The sites included the quarry itself, the quarry-related station, the processing station, and the base camp (Thunderbird) (Figure 14.2).

Gardner and McNett (1970) also test excavated coastal plain sites focusing on the use of shell fish and the eventual development of agriculture. Their initial study reviewed site data based on artifact collections curated at the Smithsonian Institution as well as collections accumulated by amateurs. This provided the foundation for later works by Gardner in the mid- to late 1970s. The latter investigations were also influenced by the large volume of data compiled through cultural resource management (CRM) surveys of the mid- to late 1970s. Some examples of these surveys undertaken by Gardner and his graduate students include Poor Valley and Verona Lake, Virginia (Gardner and Custer 1978), Smith Island (Gardner et al. 1978), Massanutten Mountain (Gardner and Boyer 1978), and Piscataway Creek (Gardner 1976).

The Piscataway Creek survey conducted by Gardner (1976) and his graduate students provided some of the settlement data that was subsequently

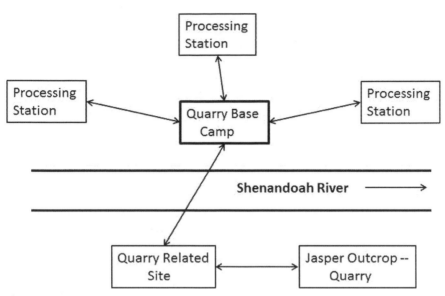

Figure 14.2.

used, along with Flint Run complex data, in his comprehensive Middle Atlantic Archaeological Conference paper (Gardner 1978) on Middle Atlantic region Archaic period settlement patterns. The paper, entitled "Comparison of Ridge and Valley, Blue Ridge, Piedmont, and Coastal Plain Archaic Period Site Distributions: An Idealized Transect (Preliminary Model)" was later published in the third volume of the *Journal of Middle Atlantic Archaeology* (Gardner 1987). This was an early effort at pulling together some of the settlement data that had been compiled over the previous decade. Continued site survey efforts of the late 1970s and into the 1980s served to augment Gardner's initial models (e.g., Gardner 1980). More recently, Nash (2009), another student of Gardner, has taken settlement pattern studies into the twenty-first century utilizing new tools such as geographic information systems (GIS) to further elicit the meaning of settlement data from carefully controlled surveys.

In the Piedmont region of the Potomac drainage, archaeological survey was conducted in the Monocacy valley as part of a multi-year study beginning in 1978 (Peck 1979; Kavanagh 1982). Kavanagh (1982:31–32) developed a predictive model using the archaeological site location data from the 205 sites identified on the survey. Environmental variables used for purposes of site association included distance from water, stream rank, height above water course, landform association, soils, and distance to interfaces between landform types. Site associations by time period were then analyzed with regard to these factors. Kavanagh (1982:100) found that predictions of site types and chronological phases associated with specific micro-environmental variables worked out well. Further upstream, in the Potomac drainage, Carr and Gardner (1979) completed a survey of Berkeley County, West Virginia, and developed a settlement model for that section of the Ridge and Valley physiographic province. Environmental variables considered to be important to prehistoric settlements included lithic resources, areas of maximum habitat overlap, distance to water, and slope with the significance of these factors varying through time.

Archaeological surveys conducted in montane regions of Virginia during the 1970s provided regional data sets that could be compared with those just described. For example, surveys of the Blue Ridge section of Shenandoah National Park (Hoffman and Foss 1980; Foss 1983) over a five-year period in the 1970s resulted in the compilation of a chronology as well as a settlement patterns analysis (Hoffman and Foss 1980:187). Though addressing permanent and temporary or transient camps as part of the settlement system, Hoffman and Foss also developed a "five-fold" settlement typology for pre–Late Woodland sites and a sixth category for Late Woodland sites (Hoffman and Foss 1980:189). The site types range from Grade 5 (large, long term and diversified) to more specialized (Grade 1) quarry sites. Others include ephemeral sites (i.e., short-term camps) and Late Woodland villages. Hoffman and Foss's work built on earlier studies of the region by C. G. Holland, who is best known for his overview of the archaeology of Southwest Virginia (Holland 1970). Holland's study was basically descriptive and focused on sites and artifacts but did provide an important foundation of survey data for further work in the region, including settlement pattern studies.

Further work in the Blue Ridge by Tolley (1983), Barber (1983), and Stewart (1983) was presented in papers during the first Uplands Archaeology in the East Conference held in Harrisonburg, Virginia, in 1981. Stewart's work focused, in large part, on the use of meta-rhyolite and how it affected prehistoric settlement patterns. Tolley and Barber's work related to archaeological sites and settlement patterning in the George Washington and Jefferson National Forests, respectively. Ecological factors such as slope, aspect, elevation, proximity to water, and other environmental variables were addressed in these settlement models. The 1980s also brought forth the first widespread use of the term "predictive model." Barber and Guercin (2012) have recently provided new data on Blue Ridge settlement patterning, specifically resource packing, risk reduction, and social interaction, based on field work at the Abbott Lake site.

Other work in the Ridge and Valley province of Virginia was directed by Clarence Geier of James Madison University in the Hidden Valley area of the Jackson River drainage (Geier 1983). As a result, a settlement sequence was developed showing that most settlements were located in alluvial settings and on mountain toe slopes. Most of the upland sites recorded were designated as temporary or short-term occupations (Geier 1983:236). The most favorable upland localities include small terraces of descending mountain streams, springs, and low saddles (Geier 1983:236). Chronologically, Geier (1983:237) noted that Early and Middle Archaic sites were primarily in alluvial settings (i.e., not in the uplands). Late Archaic sites were recorded in both alluvial settings (especially larger base camps) and in the uplands (hunting camps). Early and Middle Woodland sites were very rare and Late Woodland sites were recorded primarily in alluvial settings (Geier 1983:241).

Other areas of the Middle Atlantic region saw similar trends in settlement pattern studies at this time. For example, early Delaware coastal plain archaeology initially focused on large site excavations, such as the Slaughter Creek site (Custer 1989). With the advent of radiocarbon dating, tighter chronologies were compiled. The first systematic survey data was compiled and analyzed for settlement patterning in the 1970s (Griffith 1974; Thomas et al. 1975). These early settlement models were implicitly predictive and used ecological data to address questions of seasonality and habitat preference (Custer 1989:77; Hasenstab 1991). In nearby coastal plain New Jersey, Ranere and Hansell (1984) also analyzed ecological data with regards to settlement patterning and developed a transect survey using existing power line corridors as survey areas. This introduced a random, or at least less purposive, element to the survey design.

THE SUSQUEHANNA, DELAWARE, AND UPPER OHIO DRAINAGES

Comparable surveys and settlement patterns analyses were conducted in other regions of the Middle Atlantic such as the Delaware and Susquehanna drainages. In Pennsylvania, during the 1970s, surveys were undertaken in the Upper Delaware valley (Kinsey 1972) and the Upper Susquehanna region (Turnbaugh 1977). Smaller-scale surveys related to project-specific goals were undertaken, for example, in the Cross Creek drainage as related to the Meadowcroft Rockshelter excavations (Fryman 1982). There, an intensive survey produced information on landform association over the entire span of the Holocene.

In the Susquehanna River valley, an extensive survey was undertaken in north central Pennsylvania during the 1970s by Turnbaugh (1977) and a chronological sequence as well as a settlement pattern study was the result. Turnbaugh (1977:253) reviewed settlement patterns by physiographic province as well as by time period in order to distinguish the key ecological factors related to cultural adaptations. Key landforms used by prehistoric inhabitants included river terraces, well-drained outwash features, and tributary valleys. Site types inferred by Turnbaugh (1977:257–59) included large settlements (along the river), seasonal base camps, subsistence camps (outliers in support of seasonal base camps), fishing camps, hunting camps, gathering camps, and operation loci.

In central Pennsylvania in 1978, a site survey program was initiated in the Bald Eagle Creek drainage to collect settlement-subsistence data and show how patterns changed over time (Hatch 1980). The predictive model that was developed addressed key ecological factors for site location such as proximity to water, suitable topography, lithic resources, and ease of access to these resources (Hay and Hatch 1980). This again follows trends established in most of the other settlement pattern studies of the time. For Late Woodland sites, the nature of agricultural soils was one of the critical factors analyzed for site location preference. Hay and Hatch (1980) noted that archaeological site distributions in the Bald Eagle Creek drainage were contingent on the availability of these key resources. Related to this is the location of sites that provided routes of access to critical resources (Hay and Hatch 1980:83). This includes factors such as use of level surfaces where wild plant and animal resources were within exploitable range of hunting and gathering forays.

The Upper Delaware valley surveys were part of a long-term effort by the National Park Service and their contractual partners and volunteer organizations (e.g., Archaeological Society of New Jersey and the Society for Pennsylvania Archaeology) beginning in the late 1950s (Kinsey 1972:xx). Much of this work was part of the Tocks Island reservoir survey, which began in 1964 (Kinsey and Kent 1965; Kinsey 1969; Kraft 1975). The survey resulted in the compilation of a large inventory of sites, many of them tested for stratigraphic information to develop a regional chronology. Excavations were conducted on significant sites such as Rosenkrans (Cross 1941; Kraft et al. 1970; Ritchie 1949). Others include stratified and multi-component sites such as Brodhead (36Pi30), Zimmermann (36Pi14), and Peters-Albrecht (36Pi21 and 36Pi22) that supplied data for a local cultural sequence (Kinsey 1971; Kraft 1975). Most of these sites and the surveys that produced them were in floodplain and valley floor settings, not in the uplands.

In the Upper Ohio Valley region, settlement pattern analyses were conducted on data sets that had been compiled from earlier surveys, particularly the Upper Ohio Valley survey of the early 1950s (Mayer-Oakes 1955) and even earlier Works Progress Administration (WPA) surveys (e.g., Butler 1939). These early surveys were very descriptive and chronologically based, but they were also suitable for the settlement pattern analyses of the decades that followed. For example, George (1974) was able to use Upper Ohio Valley Archaeological Survey data to develop a settlement model for Monongahela village sites, noting their frequent movement due to poor subsistence potential and their unique location in upland saddles as well as the more typical riverine settings.

In mountainous West Virginia, similar trends in survey and settlement pattern analyses can be found in a number of project examples. Systematic survey and documentation of archaeological sites began with the creation of a state archaeologist's office in 1960. Prior to 1960, as in other regions, work involved primarily site specific investigations, Adena mounds such as Natrium and Grave Creek, in particular. Early surveys were conducted by the Bureau of American Ethnology (Thomas 1894; Fowke 1894), noting additional mound sites. Mound excavations continued into the twentieth century—for example, Beech Bottom Mound in the northern panhandle of West Virginia (Bache and Satterthwaite 1930).

Early survey work in West Virginia was undertaken by Solecki for two proposed reservoir sites (Solecki 1949a, 1949b). A few years later, the Upper Ohio Valley Archaeological Survey explored sites in the upper Ohio drainage of West Virginia (Mayer-Oakes 1955). By the 1960s, more intensive survey work was being done including a county-wide survey in Nicholas County (McMichael 1965). These early surveys provided the basis for settlement pattern studies and syntheses in the decades that followed (e.g., McMichael 1968).

New York is somewhat peripheral to the Middle Atlantic region and has its own distinct and extensive archaeological settlement pattern literature due in large part to the work of William Ritchie, Robert Funk, Ed Curtin, Nina Versaggi, Robert Hasenstab, and many others. It will not be discussed fully in this chapter but a few significant publications pertaining to survey and settlement patterns need to be mentioned. These include Ritchie and Funk's (1973) *Aboriginal Settlement Patterns in the Northeast, Recent Contributions to Hudson Valley Prehistory* (Funk 1976) and *Adaptation, Continuity and Change in Upper Susquehanna Prehistory* (Funk and Rippeteau 1977), among many others (e.g., Curtin 1981). Early CRM work, such as the I-88 Corridor survey, also contributed significantly to the archaeological site database for New York. Subsequent CRM studies of the 1980s and into the 1990s contributed additional information. Funk's two-volume set on Upper Susquehanna Valley archaeology furnished a significant update based on decades of site specific and settlement data (Funk et al. 1993).

To summarize, during the initial phase of settlement pattern studies in the Middle Atlantic region, settlement models were focused on site types as related to key environmental features such as lithic and subsistence resources and their accessibility. This was followed by tighter modeling with predictive capacity. Overall, these settlement pattern studies were very functional and ecologically oriented. Landform associations were important factors and the initiation of CRM studies furnished diverse data sets to test the models. The importance of CRM data was to more randomly supply survey data from areas that would never have been surveyed in previous decades.

SETTLEMENT PATTERN STUDIES OF THE 1980s

In a broad overview of settlement patterning for the Middle Atlantic region encompassing montane and intermontane areas, Gardner (1987) emphasized the importance of a number of environmental settings. In montane areas, most sites appear to be transitory camps marked by limited artifact scatters (Gardner 1987:61). On saddles there is a fairly continuous distribution of artifacts though these do not seem to be clustered. There is, however, a definite trend toward the use of wetlands of various types, particularly well-drained surfaces near wetlands. The primary factors influencing settlement choice were considered to be (1) zones of minimal topographic relief especially the availability of level surfaces (e.g., saddles) in what are predominantly steeply sloping lands, (2) distribution of surface water including various stream orders (including distance away from high order streams) and springs, (3) maximization of habitat overlap, (4) distribution of available daily sunlight, (5) the proximity of bogs, and (6) the presence of usable lithic raw material location (Gardner 1987). Upland flats and saddles which are relatively close to water and which had some hours of sunlight exposure were considered to be preferred locations. Gardner (1987) also noted that the valleys were most intensively utilized because of the greater variety of resources there. Upland zones were primarily for short-term, seasonally based forays. Even during the Late Archaic, when sites were scattered throughout the uplands, the greatest densities of sites are most notable along river terraces.

Gardner (1986:6) describes the diversity of Middle Atlantic region Late Archaic cultures best in stating that "there is no such thing as a standard Late Archaic response to the Middle Atlantic landscape." In other words, the settlement pattern may be characterized in various sub-regions as linear, focal, patchy, or diffuse. It may also be represented in dichotomies such as upland-lowland, headwater-tailwater, or exterior-interior. Whatever the case may be, patterns tended to apply based on spatial and physical constraints of the environment as well as sociocultural factors. The social factors include proximity to other groups, reciprocity or lack thereof, inter- and intra-group hierarchies, and the frequency of group aggregation and dispersal. Environmental factors included proximity to surface water, nature and seasonality of fish or game (e.g., anadromous fish), seasonality of exploitable plants, lithic raw materials, and the overall character of the landscape (e.g., slope, elevation, and drainage).

More intensive analysis of settlement patterns came with onset of widespread CRM archaeology in the 1980s. Before that it was associated with multi-year excavation projects in an attempt to look at a site in its broader contexts. There was an attempt to determine what other sites were found in a given area and how they related to the primary site investigation. For example, the Flint Run complex focused on the Thunderbird site and its surrounding sites in proximity to jasper quarries. These developed into more sophisticated "predictive model" surveys that delineated key environmental variables and factors relevant to settlement choice and land use. By the 1980s, in many areas, settlement pattern studies had matured into well designed research programs that based many of their assumptions on the foundations of survey work from the past two decades.

Predictive models were also developed in the 1970s to evaluate landscapes that had seen little formal archaeological survey. Much of the archaeological site data gathered in the past had been recovered from river and stream valley settings, excluding most upland terrain. Applications of predictive models (e.g., Jochim 1976) on academic data sets have since been applied to CRM studies, particularly on large-scale projects.

The decade of the 1980s brought a formalization to CRM projects and with it a set of standards for developing contexts related to both small and large project areas. In other words, project areas were seen as part of a larger landscape that contained a variety of patterned archaeological phenomena. Settlement patterns were seen as a major part of this process through which project-specific sites could be understood within surrounding contexts rather than from a site-specific perspective. The 1980s also witnessed many large projects that involved extensive site surveys including large acreages and the development of settlement patterns from survey results. Some of these projects developed regional settlement models (see Kowalewski 2008). For example, in the Potomac drainage, several of these large-scale surveys were completed in the 1980s.

In the Maryland coastal plain, Steponaitis (1983a and 1983b) surveyed a stratified sample of terrain in the Patuxent River drainage using environmental criteria (e.g., soils, geology, and physiographic setting) to distinguish the strata. The results showed primarily a dichotomy of site differences between long-term habitation sites close to the river (containing ceramics and tool diversity) and short-term procurement sites in the interior (containing projectile points). On the eastern shore of Maryland, Hughes (1980), and Davidson (1981) described some basic settlement pattern information based on known sites. Hughes (1980) described micro-environments (e.g., estuarine, fresh water, and drainage characteristics) as relevant or deterrents to prehistoric settlement. Specific geological features typically associated with archaeological sites include the well-drained Parsonsburg Sand Formation and the Sinepuxent Formation. Davidson (1981:101–02) related the importance of developing predictive models for the Lower Eastern Shore region of Maryland as a means of delineating areas of high archaeological sensitivity.

In the Piedmont region of Maryland, Kavanagh's Monocacy River Valley survey, previously described, resulted in a settlement pattern model for the Monocacy drainage. Farther west, in the Hagerstown (Great) Valley, Stewart (1980) conducted a comprehensive survey of a number of large transects to develop a settlement model for the prehistory of the Great Valley in Maryland. Stewart (1980:118) noted the presence of a range of site types including quarry and quarry reduction sites, base camps, farming villages, hunting camps, and hunting stations/stray finds. Environmental variables considered included distance to surface water, lithic raw materials, areas of maximum habitat overlap, areas of maximum sunlight exposure, and distribution of well-drained surfaces of low topographic relief. More fine-grained settings (e.g., backwater swamps, stream junctions, alluvial fans, and spring heads) were also explored. The quarrying, processing, use, and trade of meta-rhyolite also figured heavily into Stewart's analyses of unique factors affecting settlement in the Great Valley physiographic province.

Wall's (1981) survey of the Appalachian Plateau region in western Maryland resulted in the isolation of several key environmental settings relevant to prehistoric settlement. Among these are upland swamps, headwaters areas, spring heads, heights of land between drainage heads, high and low order stream settings, hollows, saddles, gaps in mountain ridges, and areas containing knapping quality lithic resources. The large sample area covered and high number of prehistoric sites recorded lends some support to the observed trends in the data. Much of the survey was done in upland terrain, areas that were largely ignored in the past. A survey in a similar Plateau region in western Pennsylvania (Stewart and Kratzer 1989) produced comparable results.

Stewart and Kratzer's (1989:28) survey in the Plateau region of Pennsylvania identified critical factors relevant to prehistoric settlements. These factors included (1) well-drained soils, (2) low relief, (3) the type and location of surface water (e.g., springs), (4) stream associations such as promontories or "peninsulas," and (5) proximity to high-quality lithic resources. High and low probabilities for the occurrence of prehistoric archaeological sites were determined from these environmental associations.

Brashler's (1984) survey in the Monongahela National Forest over several years included the development of a settlement model for the Archaic period in this very diverse and ecologically patchy mountainous terrain.

The study area cross-cuts two physiographic provinces (Ridge and Valley and the Appalachian Plateau), which further complicates the settlement patterning. The focus of the study covered how landscape use changed during the Archaic period and what distinctions were made in settlement choice between floodplain settlement and land use and the exploitation of very diverse upland terrain. A few years earlier, Wilkins (1978) had addressed the use of West Virginia mountain top terrain by Early Archaic peoples, which later became an important element in developing settlement models in eastern woodlands montane regions.

ALONG THE COAST

During the 1980s, more sophisticated settlement models were developed in Delaware based on quantitative analyses and LANDSAT satellite information (Custer 1989:77). The LANDSAT data was used to build on earlier ecological models proposed in the 1970s. Custer and Galasso (1983) looked at four major environmental zones (bay front, bay front/ mid-drainage transition, mid-drainage, and drainage divide transition). These areas were surveyed via stratified random sample and the results were incorporated into settlement models. Changes in settlement patterning over time were inferred to be related to factors of climate change, resource location, social complexity, and population densities.

Custer, Eveleigh, and Klemas (1983) built their settlement models on survey data previously acquired (Custer and Galasso 1983) by using synoptic analyses of LANDSAT data (i.e., analyzing regional sets of environmental variables associated with archaeological site locations). These data were then processed using logistal regression to create predictive site location models suitable for ground truthing (Custer, Eveleigh, and Klemas 1983:21). The purpose of this process was to develop more accurate and useful predictive models for use in, for example, CRM studies.

In the early 1980s, the multi-year Abbott Farm National Landmark project resulted in the development of a settlement model for the sequence of occupations investigated in the Trenton area of the lower Delaware Valley. Four site types were defined in the model: (1) macrosocial unit camps, (2) microsocial unit camps, (3) transient camps, and (4) stations. *Macrosocial unit camps* represented long-term semi-sedentary to sedentary occupations on floodplain and terraces that often contain structures, large storage features, burials, caches, and hearths (Wall et al. 1996:336). *Microsocial unit camps* were also long-term occupations that represented hunting, foraging, and fishing on a seasonal basis and contained varied and dense activity areas (Wall et al. 1996:337). *Transient camps* were the numerous small habitation sites of single families or task groups scattered over the landscape, particularly in stream environs. *Stations* were the smallest site type and represented the activities of individuals or small groups over a very short period of time. Such sites usually lacked features and were represented by small scatters of artifacts (Wall et al. 1996:338). Stewart (1991), for example, describes small stations dating to the Middle Archaic period within interior headwaters areas of the New Jersey Coastal Plain. All of these site types are not unlike site classes used for other regions under different names that represent (1) large, complex groups usually found in late prehistory, (2) small groups with a particular focus, and (3) small *ad hoc* groups that represent short-term groups or individual activities.

The Abbott Farm project has provided extensive data on a variety of sites in close proximity to each other; hence a more focused view of settlement patterning and the sites that comprise the pattern (Figure 14.1). Most of the sites appear to have been small camps occupied by small groups repeatedly rather than large, complex sites (macro-social unit camps) with distinctive internal patterning. This is inferred by the recovery of relatively simple tool assemblages from sites that reflect a limited range of site activities (Wall et al. 1996). The sites are also located on habitable surfaces with respect to critical resources and with regard to inter-group relationships and internal group organization.

In the Maryland coastal plain, Gardner (1982) noted that Early Woodland settlement systems centered around major base camps linked to more transient, limited-purpose interior sites. Early Woodland macroband

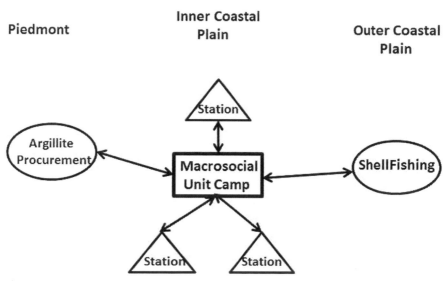

Figure 14.1.

camps on the shores of major estuaries were considered to be part of a seasonal fission-fusion cycle in which seasonal macro-band camps were established around large wetlands like Dismal Swamp. Microband camps stemmed from these locations in the vicinity of major swamps as well as in the headwaters of estuaries (Gardner 1982:57). In the Virginia coastal plain, Mouer (1991) provided settlement models that distinguished between sylvan and riverine settings. The earlier sylvan settings of the Late Archaic period were inhabited by small bands that aggregated into larger groups infrequently (Mouer 1991:10). This pattern was followed, during the subsequent Terminal Archaic, by groups who were more focused on riverine settings and the more frequent use of larger base camps in areas of high resource productivity, especially fishing grounds.

PENNSYLVANIA

Much of the survey work undertaken during the 1980s in the Susquehanna Valley of Pennsylvania was, as in most states, driven by CRM project goals. Larger projects tended to be the focus of more complex settlement and predictive models. Also stemming from these projects was the isolation of specific environmental features that were "magnets" for prehistoric settlements and/or activities. Stevenson's (1982) survey results along the Allegheny Front in the Bald Eagle drainage noted the significance of the stream hollow as a corridor for channeling prehistoric populations from the floodplain-upland interface area to headwaters zones. Stevenson (1982) also stated that most sites were located near the mouth of the hollow (i.e., in areas closer to high order stream environments). These data also showed some chronological distinctions in the patterns.

In the Piedmont of southeastern Pennsylvania, Custer and Wallace (1982) described the correlation of critical resource distributions in past environments with prehistoric settlement patterns. They distinguished some basic differences between early and late Holocene groups noting that scatters of Paleoindian through Middle Archaic procurement sites eventually developed into a large base camp pattern by the Late Archaic through Middle Woodland period. Late Woodland patterns were influenced by the location of intensive collecting areas and agricultural potential. Custer and Wallace (1982:140) also recognized the importance of regional perspectives in developing preliminary settlement models. They noted the inadequate variation of sites and settings on smaller projects. Using ethnographic models developed by Binford (1980), settlement patterns through time were analyzed within the context of forager and collector strategies.

SETTLEMENT PATTERN STUDIES
OF THE 1990S AND BEYOND

Settlement pattern studies continued into the 1990s with a continued focus on human adaptations to the environment. Surveys of both large and small areas were done with traditional settlement pattern ideas in mind (i.e., human use of the landscape). Testing of established settlement models was ongoing, including the excavation of typical examples of site types in an effort to improve the initial models. This included the study of particular aspects of settlement models through time. There were also attempts to improve settlement pattern models by more focused and comprehensive testing programs that sought to identify every possible landform attribute as related to settlement patterning (Botwick and Wall 1992). For example, an intensive survey of transects through the Delaware Water Gap National Recreation Area was designed to improve local settlement models by surveying as close to 100 percent of the selected terrain as possible. In other words, nothing testable was left out of the survey sample (Botwick and Wall 1992). The eight selected environmental settings that represent the survey area were also subdivided to include every possible landscape feature pertinent to prehistoric settlement and land use (Wall and Botwick 1992). For example, within the broad and relatively unremarkable dry upland zone category, specific environmental features included benches, outcrops, depressions (deer licks), relict drainage heads, relict stream junctions, slope side benches, and rock shelter areas.

In general, by the 1990s there were more data available due in large part to very large numbers of CRM investigations, and the compilation of more data from areas that had never seen any systematic survey (see Anderson 1991). Archaeologists were also looking at landscapes with the assistance of other scientific disciplines which had also developed vast improvements in their capabilities to analyze landscape features. Finally, the 1990s also brought the use of GIS to improve the display of settlement data and to view data in ways never before possible.

Traditionally designed settlement pattern surveys are still found in the literature for the 1990s and beyond. For example, Mounier's (1999:106) description of the New Jersey coastal plain points out the richness of resources within the Inner Coastal Plain versus the Outer Coastal Plain as it pertains to prehistoric settlement. Kraft and Mounier (1982:72) have suggested in the Maurice River area that archaeological sites in riverine settings tend to show greater tool diversity. These sites also tend to be larger, reflecting the diverse array of resources that would have been available in greater abundance. This contrasts with the smaller and less differentiated sites in headwaters areas, which show less ecological diversity and contain less variety in artifact types (Kraft and Mounier 1982:73–74). In central Delaware, Knepper and Bowen (2003) described the correlation between site distributions and proximity to streams in both tidal and non-tidal settings. They note that in some cases, stream proximity is less important than other environmental factors.

In the Virginia coastal plain, Egghart (2004) describes small sites in low order drainages noting that Middle Woodland components are as common as Late Archaic occupations. The distinct functions of these loci are addressed with descriptions of Late Archaic use of quartzite cobbles from stream beds. The Middle Woodland settlements are based on large FCR concentrations and pit features which are interpreted as disturbances to natural forest areas to promote the growth of economically (or subsistence related) useful plants (Egghart 2004:152; see also Gallivan and Blouet 2001). The Chickahominy River survey in coastal plain Virginia also provided a wealth of data to support settlement pattern studies for many years afterwards (McCary and Barka 1977; Gallivan et al. 2009; Gallivan 2009).

In the Maryland coastal plain, Lowery (1992) described a series of sites dating from the Paleoindian through the Late Woodland period. He notes several key changes in the association of environmental settings with archaeological sites of different time periods. The large surface collections derived from most of these sites permits the identification of site functions and their place within the larger settlement system. His five functional site types include macro-band camps, micro-band camps, hunting/procurement sites, cobble quarry sites, and caches (Lowery 1992:13).

In the Middle Potomac Valley, Geier and Hofstra's (1999) survey on Opequon Creek recorded 257 sites but very few base camps, no sedentary sites, and no ceramics. They note the predominance of numerous small sites, dating from the Archaic through the Late Woodland period. The general absence of large, permanent sites suggests this drainage is on the margins of a larger, more all-encompassing settlement system where the more permanent settlements were located. In other words, they are analyzing broader patterns of settlement in which permanent habitation sites are surrounded by networks of specialized and transitory sites functionally related to them.

BEYOND SURVEY DATA COLLECTION: THOUGHTS AND IMPROVEMENTS

The last two decades have seen a continuation of traditional settlement pattern studies though some improvements have been made based on a much stronger foundation of site data. There are also data sets from similar regions that have provided new ideas for approaching settlement pattern analyses. For example, Wholey (2009) examined Archaic period settlement patterns from a population ecology and settlement demography perspective, analyzing changes in population densities, group mobility, and social structure over time. Improvements in the identification of sites during surveys has also provided more complete information along with an improved ability to interpret the assemblages derived from archaeological sites.

Barber and Tolley (1999) note that in two decades of survey in mountainous terrain, the traditional typology of quarry, base camp, transient camp, and hunting/procurement site and all the variants in between do not address specific site type discrepancies. Finds of tools not specifically associated with quarrying but recovered from quarry sites suggest a more complex array of activities may have occurred on quarry sites and their quarry-related counterparts. This suggests a more complex and realistic socio-cultural pattern that goes beyond the relatively simple settlement models initially constructed (Barber and Tolley 1999:175).

Barber (2001) also notes that lithic scatters, a commonly used term for non-descript small surface sites lacking tools and ceramics, need to re-evaluated in terms of the cultural processes that create them. For example, Barber (2001:85) describes a variety of upland sites that have specific functions in mountainous regions of the Middle Atlantic. However, small and seemingly unimportant, "lithic scatters" need to be represented as real imprints of human activity rather than as unimportant debris scatters across the landscape (Barber 2001:89). In the latter sense, lithic scatters become the leftover debitage of settlement pattern studies that defy classification. Locations of rockshelters, one of the more common upland sites, have also been critically analyzed by Barber (1987) with regard to settlement patterns.

Klein (2002) also reviewed the subject of the small, low-density sites, many in inter-riverine settings. Much of these data have been accumulated from the large number of CRM surveys undertaken in the last twenty-five years. Identification and evaluation of these kinds of sites fills a significant gap in our knowledge of inter-riverine settlements and has the potential to address settlement systems in this largely unknown terrain. Perazio (2006:5) feels that so much CRM data has been accumulated, especially from upland regions, but there have been few endeavors to synthesize what has been compiled. Some states, such as Maryland, are beginning to do this.

Other relatively new contributions to settlement patterns studies include an analysis of the emergence of band territories during the Holocene in central West Virginia (McDonald et al. (2006). Carr (1998) has reviewed Early Archaic settlement patterns in Pennsylvania and compared them to

Gardner's Flint Run model, providing a broader application of the quarry-base camp phenomenon. And finally, Gallivan (2009) takes existing Middle to Late Woodland period data from a Chickahominy River survey and infers social landscapes, dispersed farmsteads, feasting locales, and other cultural phenomena.

Going beyond the survey data also means testing some of the "typical" sites that represent the principal elements of a settlement model. For example, an article by Pullens (2001) describes a Late Woodland period hunting camp excavation and focuses on settlement patterns in the Late Woodland period of southwest Virginia. Pullens (2001:50) notes, for example, the increased use of rock shelters during the Late Woodland period. Excavation of a "lithic scatter" is described as an important small site to understand given the variety of labels placed on such sites, such as lithic scatter, small camp, foraging camp and hunting station. What are the real differences among these often-described sites in settlement pattern studies? This seems to be one of the principal foci of recent settlement pattern analyses. Assumptions are often made about site types with little supporting empirical data.

A Late Woodland settlement model for the Piedmont uplands of southeastern Pennsylvania was developed by Raber (1993) based largely on excavations at site 36CH161. For the Minguannan Complex, Raber focused on the non-horticultural, seasonal, and mobile aspects of these hunting and gathering populations. He noted that much of the subsistence-settlement cycle for these groups depended on the availability and use of wild resources, not domesticated plants. In other words, Raber (1993:246) was looking beyond the patterns of the typical Late Woodland horticultural village. The Minguannan settlement types discussed include habitation sites and specialized procurement sites (Raber 1993:249). In the Piedmont uplands, habitation sites were used by both macro-bands (groups operating in productive settings) and micro-bands (groups focused on more specific zones such as ecotonal boundaries or lithic outcrop areas). The specialized procurement sites are typically found on knolls, stream headwaters and intermittent drainage and are characterized by small scatters of tools and debitage (Raber 1993). Territoriality of these mobile Late Woodland groups is another issue developed by Raber (1993:276).

Raber (2009) also looked at Monongahela settlement patterns through the excavation of a seasonal hamlet site (36FA368), which actually represent a series of small hamlets occupied over several hundred years (Raber 2009:22). The emerging pattern demonstrated a flexible settlement in both size and duration to accommodate populations facing resource scarcities. Previous models of Monongahela settlement emphasized the large, permanent village dependent on maize horticulture. The smaller, temporary settlements appear to have been a significant part of the overall

Monongahela settlement system. Monongahela studies exemplify what can be done with a wealth of data. Excavations since WPA days have provided a tremendous amount of information on Monongahela sites and excavations since then have supplied even more (Means 2007). It is not surprising that there have been a number of analyses of Monongahela settlement patterns over the years (e.g., George 1974; Johnson 1981; Hart and Nass 1995; Raber 2009) given the available information. Comparable site specific investigations related to settlement patterns have been undertaken in other regions as well. For example, Rieth (2008) reviewed Early Woodland settlement patterns in New York based on excavations at the Schoharie II site.

CONCLUSIONS

The most obvious need in settlement pattern studies is to apply the large volume of data that has been gathered over the past twenty-five years to create more empirically based settlement models. Much of these data are archived in the masses of gray literature awaiting synthesis. What actually gets published stems from a variety of sources including large CRM projects with a mandate to publish the results or simply the special interest of a particular researcher. Many of the upland survey projects have produced data that would never have been gathered if it were not for cultural resources laws and regulations requiring it.

Improvements in survey methods are likely to bring more details to settlement pattern studies in the near future. Up to this point, there have been some new studies in areas that had not been previously surveyed, or some re-formulation of settlement models based on either new data or new ideas. Improvements in survey methods and interpretations include manipulation and display of settlement data through GIS analyses. For example, Hasenstab's (1996) study of Iroquois villages demonstrated how these sites were distributed over the landscape and what influence environmental and social factors had on settlement. The findings demonstrated the paramount importance of social factors and territoriality in the distribution of village sites. Application of GIS in settlement pattern studies in the Middle Atlantic region is still in its initial phases but it should have a bright future. There are more and more examples in the last decade (e.g., Crews et al. 2009; Nash 2009; Cross 2012) though most still evaluate the same traditionally analyzed environmental factors of slope, elevation, and distance to water. Nash's (2009) GIS study of the Virginia Blue Ridge and nearby uplands of the upper Rappahannock basin utilized twenty-one variables relating to site characteristics, artifact types, and ecological contexts. The sample of 233 archaeological site

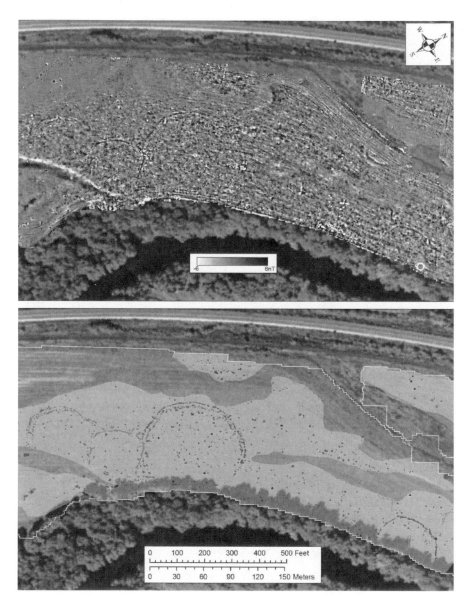

Figure 14.3.

contexts used in the study provided a comprehensive view of settlement patterns in that region of Virginia.

Finally, more consistent use of geophysical techniques will provide new forms of data to enhance settlement pattern studies. These techniques allow a clearer display of site-specific patterns as well as a view into larger landscapes that contain archaeological features. Geophysical techniques may eventually be applied to "deep site" survey where, for example, features are difficult to discern beneath thick layers of alluvium (Figure 14.3). Geophysical techniques have been used more consistently in CRM investigations, especially for cemeteries, but may prove to be a significant asset to many other landscape and site specific investigations. This includes upland surveys where contexts are often compromised and data are thin. In surveys of floodplain environments, geophysical techniques have demonstrated great effectiveness in pinpointing features and complex patterns that have subsequently been verified by test excavations (Horsley and Wall 2010). Geophysics and archaeological prospecting may eventually prove to be useful means of investigating lesser-known sites in the complex array of settlement systems throughout the Middle Atlantic region.

REFERENCES CITED

Ammerman, Albert J.
  1981 Surveys and Archaeological Research. *Annual Review of Anthropology* 10:63–88.

Anderson, David G.
  1991 Examining Prehistoric Settlement Distribution in Eastern North America. *Archaeology of Eastern North America* 19:1–22.

Bache, Charles, and Linton Satterthwaite Jr.
  1930 The Excavation of an Indian Mound at Beech Bottom, West Virginia. *University of Pennsylvania Museum Journal* 21:132–87.

Barber, Michael B.
  1983 Archaeological Perspective of the Northern Blue Ridge. In *Upland Archeology in the East: A Symposium*. USDA Forest Service, Southern Region, Cultural Resources Report Number 2, pp.116–29.
  1987 A View of Settlement Pattern Change on the Periphery of the Appalachian Plateau: Rock Shelters on the Coeburn Exchange, Wise County, Virginia. In *Upland Archaeology in the East: A Third Symposium*, edited by M. Barber, pp. 116–29. USDA Forest Service, Southern Region, Cultural Resources Report No. 87-1.
  2001 Small Sites on the Appalachian Mountain Slopes: Changes in Altitudes, Changes in Attitudes. *Journal of Middle Atlantic Archaeology* 17:85–94.

Barber, Michael B., and Richard J. Guercin
  2012   Peaks of Otter/ Abbott Lake Site (44BE0259), Bedford County, Virginia:
         New Insights into Blue Ridge Settlement Patterning. *Quarterly Bulletin of
         the Archeological Society of Virginia* 67(2):72–85.

Barber, Michael, and George A. Tolley
  1999   Lithic Utilization Patterns in the Blue Ridge of Virginia: Site Types and
         Site Boxes. *Journal of Middle Atlantic Archaeology* 15:187–200.

Binford, Lewis R.
  1980   Willow Smoke and Dogs' Tails: Hunter-Gatherer Settlement Systems
         and Archaeological Site Formation. *American Antiquity* 45:4–20.

Botwick, Bradford, and Robert D. Wall
  1992   Prehistoric Settlement in the Uplands of the Upper Delaware Valley:
         Recent Surveys and Testing in the Delaware Water Gap National Rec-
         reation Area. In *Recent Research into the Prehistory of the Delaware Valley*,
         edited by C. A. Bergman and J. F. Doershuk. *Journal of Middle Atlantic
         Archaeology* 10:73–84.

Brashler, Janet G.
  1984   Exploitation of Diffuse Resources: Archaic Settlement in Mountainous
         West Virginia. In *Upland Archaeology in the East: Symposium* 2. USDA, For-
         est Service, Southern Region. Cultural Resources Report No. 5, pp. 5–24.

Butler, Mary
  1939   Three Archaeological Sites in Somerset County, Pennsylvania. Pennsyl-
         vania Historical and Museum Commission, Harrisburg.

Carr, Kurt W.
  1998   The Early Archaic Period in Pennsylvania. *Pennsylvania Archaeologist*
         68(2):42–69.

Carr, Kurt W., and William M. Gardner
  1979   A Preliminary Prehistoric Archeological Resources Reconnaissance of
         Berkeley County, West Virginia. Report prepared by Thunderbird Re-
         search Corp. for the Berkeley County Historic Landmarks Commission.

Chang, K. C.
  1962   A Typology of Settlement and Community Patterns in Some Circum-
         polar Societies. *Arctic Anthropology* 1:28–41.

Chang, K. C. (editor)
  1968   *Settlement Archaeology*. National Press Books, Palo Alto, CA.

Crews, Rachel, Elliot Abrams, Ann Corinne Freter, and Jeffery Ueland
  2009   A GIS Analysis of the Archaic to Woodland Period Settlement Trends
         in the Margaret Creek Watershed, Athens County, Ohio. *West Virginia
         Archeologist* 55 (1&2):40–54.

Cross, Dorothy
  1941   *Archaeology of New Jersey*. Archaeological Society of New Jersey and the
         New Jersey State Museum.

Cross, Kathryn
   2012   Least Resistance? Cost-Path Analysis and Hunter-Gatherer Mobility in
          the Virginia Blue Ridge. *Journal of Middle Atlantic Archaeology* 28:1–15.

Curtin, Edward V.
   1981   Predictive Modeling of Prehistoric Site Locations in the Uplands of Cen-
          tral New York. *Man in the Northeast* 22:87–100.

Custer, Jay F.
   1989   *Prehistoric Cultures of the Delmarva Peninsula.* University of Delaware Press,
          Newark, DE.

Custer, Jay F., Timothy Eveleigh, Vytautas Klemas, and Ian Wells
   1986   Application of LANDSAT Data and Synoptic Remote Sensing to Predic-
          tive Models for Prehistoric Archaeological Sites: An Example from the
          Delaware Coastal Plain. *American Antiquity* 4:572–88.

Custer, Jay F., and George Galasso
   1983   An Archaeological Survey of the St. Jones and Murderkill Drainages.
          Bulletin of the Archaeological Society of Delaware 14:1–18.

Custer, Jay F., and E. B. Wallace
   1982   Patterns of Resource Distribution and Archaeological Settlement Pat-
          terns in the Piedmont Uplands of the Middle Atlantic Region. *North
          American Archaeologist* 3:139–72.

Davidson, D. S.
   1929   The Lock Haven Expedition. *University of Pennsylvania Museum Journal*
          20(3–4):307–17.

Davidson, Thomas E.
   1981   A Cultural Resource Management Plan for the Lower Delmarva Region
          of Maryland. Maryland Historical Trust Monograph Number 2.

Egghart, Christopher
   2004   Prehistoric Settlements of Interior Streams in the Virginia Coastal Plain.
          Quarterly Bulletin of the Archeological Society of Virginia 59(3):143–54.

Eveleigh, Timothy, Jay F. Custer, and V. Klemas
   1983   A LANDSAT-Generated Predictive Model for Prehistoric Archaeological
          Sites in Delaware's Coastal Plain. *Bulletin of the Archaeological Society of
          Delaware* 14:19–38.

Fitting, James E.
   1969   Settlement Analysis in the Great Lakes Region. *Southwestern Journal of
          Anthropology* 25:4:360–77.

Flannery, Kent W. (ed.)
   1976   *The Early Mesoamerican Village.* Academic Press, New York.

Foss, Robert W.
   1983   Blue Ridge Prehistory: A Perspective from the Shenandoah National
          Park. In *Upland Archeology in the East: A Symposium.* USDA Forest Ser-
          vice, Southern Region, Cultural Resources Report Number 2, pp. 91–103.

Fowke, Gerard
    1894   *Archeologic Investigations in the James and Potomac Valleys.* Bureau of Amer-
           ican Ethnology Bulletin No. 23. Smithsonian Institution, Washington, DC.

Fryman, R. F.
    1982   Prehistoric Settlement Patterns in the Cross Creek Drainage. In *Meadow-
           croft: Collected Paperson the Archaeology of Meadowcroft Rockshelter and the
           Cross Creek Drainage,* R. C. Carlisle and J. M. Adovasio (eds.) pp. 53–68.

Funk, Robert E.
    1976   *Recent Contributions to Hudson Valley Prehistory.* Memoir 22, New York
           State Museum, Albany.

Funk, Robert E., et al.
    1993   *Archaeological Investigations in the Upper Susquehanna Valley, New York
           State* (Vols. 1 and 2). Persimmon Press, Buffalo.

Funk, Robert E., and Bruce E. Rippeteau
    1977   *Adaptation, Continuity and Change in Upper Susquehanna Valley Prehistory.*
           Occasional Publications in Northeastern Anthropology Number 3.

Gallivan, Martin
    2009   The Chickahominy River Survey: Native Settlement in Tidewater Vir-
           ginia, AD 200–AD 1600. *Journal of Middle Atlantic Archaeology* 24:73–83.

Gallivan, Martin, and Helen Blouet
    2001   Middle Woodland Settlement in the Interior Coastal Plain: Excavations
           at 44JC1052 and 44JC1053. *Quarterly Bulletin of the Archeological Society of
           Virginia* 56(3):127–45.

Gallivan, M. D., M. F. Blakey, S. S. Mahoney, C. J. Shephard, M. A. Mahoney, J. A.
Fitzgerald, A. K. Hayden et al.
    2009   *The Chickahominy River Survey: Native Communities in Tidewater Virginia,
           AD 200–1600.* No. 2. Archaeological Research Report Series.

Gardner, William M.
    1974   The Flint Run Complex: Pattern and Process during the Paleo-Indian to
           Early Archaic. In *The Flint Run Paleo-Indian Complex: A Preliminary Report
           1971–73 Seasons,* edited by William M. Gardner, pp. 5–47. Occasional
           Publication No. 1, Archeology Laboratory, Catholic University, Wash-
           ington, DC.
    1976   Paleo-Indian to Early Archaic: Continuity and Change in Eastern North
           America during the Late Pleistocene and Early Holocene. Paper pre-
           sented at the Ninth International Congress of Prehistoric and Protohis-
           toric Sciences, Nice, France.
    1977   Flint Run Paleoindian Complex and its Implications for Eastern North
           American Prehistory. In *Amerinds and Their Paleoenvironments in North-
           eastern North America,* edited by W. S. Newman and B. Salwen, pp.
           257–63. Annals of the New York Academy of Sciences 288.
    1980   The Archaic. Paper presented at the Tenth Middle Atlantic Archeological
           Conference, Dover, DE.

1982   Early and Middle Woodland in the Middle Atlantic: An Overview. In *Practicing Environmental Archaeology: Methods and Interpretations*, edited by Roger Moeller, pp. 53–86. American Indian Archaeological Institute, Washington, CT.

1986   Summary Statement: Late Archaic to Early Woodland in the Shenandoah Valley and Potomac River. Paper presented at the Annual Meeting of the Eastern States Archaeological Federation, Wilmington, DE.

1987   Comparison of Ridge and Valley, Blue Ridge, Piedmont, and Coastal Plain Archaic Period Site Distribution: An Idealized Transect. *Journal of Middle Atlantic Archaeology* 3:49–80.

Gardner, William M., and William P. Boyer
1978   A Cultural Resources Reconnaissance of Portions of the Northern Segment of Massanutten Mountain in the George Washington National Forest, Page, Warren and Shenandoah Counties, Virginia. USDA Forest Service.

Gardner, William M., and Jay F. Custer
1978   A Preliminary Cultural Resources Reconnaissance of the Proposed Verona Lake No. 2. Report submitted to the Department of the Army, Baltimore District, Corps of Engineers by Thunderbird Research Corporation.

Gardner, W. M., and C. W. McNett
1970   Proposal to the National Science Foundation for Support of a Program of Problems in Potomac River Archeology. Submitted by the American University, Washington, DC.

Gardner, William M., R. Wall, G. Tolley, and Jay F. Custer
1978   A Partial Cultural Resources Reconnaissance of Smith Island, Maryland. Manuscript on file, Department of Anthropology, Catholic University of America, Washington, DC.

Geier, Clarence R.
1983   Preliminary Observations on Aboriginal Settlement on Headwaters Streams of the James River: The Ridge and Valley Province of Virginia. In *Upland Archeology in the East: A Symposium*. USDA Forest Service, Southern Region, Cultural Resources Report Number 2, pp. 225–49.

Geier, Clarence R., and Warren R. Hofstra
2001   Native American Settlement in the Middle and Upper Drainages of Opequon Creek, Frederick County, Virginia. *Quarterly Bulletin of the Archeological Society of Virginia* 54:3:154–65.

George, Richard L.
1974   Monongahela Settlement Patterns and the Ryan Site. *Pennsylvania Archaeologist* 44(1–2):1–22.

Griffith, Daniel R.
1974   Ecological Studies of Prehistory. *Transactions of the Delaware Academy of Sciences* 5:63–81.

Hart, John P., and John P. Nass
1995   Modeling Monongahela Subsistence-Settlement Change: Introduction. *Archaeology of Eastern North America* 23:23–26.

Hasenstab, Robert J.
  1991 Wetlands as a Critical Variable in Predictive Modeling of Prehistoric Site
        Locations: A Case Study from the Passaic River Basin. *Man in the North-
        east* 42:39–61.
  1996 Aboriginal Settlement Patterns in Late Woodland Upper New York State.
        Journal of Middle Atlantic Archaeology 12:17–26.

Hatch, James W.
  1980 An Introduction to the Central Pennsylvania Archaeological Research of
        the Pennsylvania State University: 1976–1978. In *The Fisher Farm Site: A
        Late Woodland Hamlet in Context.* The Archaeology of Central Pennsylva-
        nia Volume 1. Occasional Papers in Anthropology, Number 12. Depart-
        ment of Anthropology, Pennsylvania State University, University Park,
        PA, pp. 1–5.

Hay, Conran A., and James W. Hatch
  1980 Predictive Models of Site Distribution within the Bald Eagle Creek Wa-
        tershed. In *The Fisher Farm Site: A Late Woodland Hamlet in Context.* The
        Archaeology of Central Pennsylvania Volume 1. Occasional Papers in
        Anthropology, Number 12. Department of Anthropology, Pennsylvania
        State University, University Park, PA, pp. 83–91.

Hoffman, Michael A., and Robert W. Foss
  1980 Blue Ridge Prehistory: A General Perspective. *Quarterly Bulletin Archeo-
        logical Society of Virginia* 34:4:185–210.

Holland, C. G.
  1970 An Archeological Survey of Southwest Virginia. *Smithsonian Contribu-
        tions to Anthropology,* Number 12, Washington D.C.

Horsley, Timothy, and Robert D. Wall
  2010 Archaeological evaluation of alluvial landscapes in Western Maryland.
        Report for the Maryland Historical Trust.

Hughes, Richard B.
  1980 A Cultural and Environmental Overview of the Prehistory of Maryland's
        Lower Eastern Shore Based Upon a Study of Selected Artifact Collec-
        tions. Maryland Historical Trust Manuscript Series Number 26.

Jochim, Michael A.
  1976 *Hunter-gatherer Subsistence and Settlement: A Predictive Model.* Academic
        Press, New York.

Johnson, William C.
  1981 The Campbell Farm Site (36FA26) and Monongahela: A Preliminary Ex-
        amination and Assessment. Paper presented at the 4th Monongahela Sym-
        posium, California State College, California, Pennsylvania, October 3, 1981.

Kavanagh, Maureen
  1982 Archeological Resources of the Monocacy River Region, Frederick and
        Carroll Counties, Maryland. Maryland Geological Survey, Baltimore.

Kinsey, W. Fred, III
  1969   The Tocks Island Survey in Pennsylvania: A Review of Work in Progress. *Archaeological Society of New Jersey Bulletin* 24:5–12.
  1971   The Middle Atlantic Culture Province: A Point of View. *Pennsylvania Archaeologist* 41(1–2):1–8.

Kinsey, W. Fred, III (editor)
  1972   *Archeology in the Upper Delaware Valley.* Anthropological Series No. 2, Pennsylvania Historical and Museum Commission, Harrisburg.

Kinsey, W. Fred, III, and Barry C. Kent
  1965   The Tocks Island Survey in Pennsylvania: A Preliminary Statement. *Pennsylvania Archaeologist* 35(3–4):118–33.

Klein, Michael J.
  2002   Discovering Sites Unseen, Excavating Unforeseen Sites: Survey, Sampling, and Significance in the Inter-Riverine Uplands of Virginia. *Journal of Middle Atlantic Archaeology* 18:1–16.

Knepper, Dennis, and Chris Bowen
  2003   Regional site distribution in south-central New Castle County as seen from the Sandom Branch Site Complex. *Bulletin of the Archaeological Society of Delaware* 40:25–30.

Kowalewski, Stephen A.
  2008   Regional Settlement Pattern Studies. *Journal of Archaeological Research* 16:225–85.

Kraft, Herbert C.
  1975   The Archaeology of the Tocks Island Area. Archaeological Research Center, Seton Hall University Museum, South Orange, NJ.

Kraft, Herbert C., Elizabeth Kraus, and Louis A. Dumont
  1970   Archaeological Survey and Testing on the New Jersey Side of the Delaware River from Wallpack Bend to Port Jervis, in the Delaware Water Gap National Recreation Area. Report submitted to the National Park Service by Seton Hall University.

Kraft, H. C., and A. R. Mounier
  1982   The Late Woodland Period in New Jersey (ca. A.D. 1000–1600). In *New Jersey's Archaeological Resources from the Paleo-Indian Period to the Present: A Review of Research Problems and Survey Priorities*, edited by Olga Chesler, pp. 139–84. Office of Cultural and Environmental Services, New Jersey Department of Environmental Protection, Trenton.

Lowery, Darrin
  1992   The Distribution and Function of Prehistoric Sites Within the Lower Bay Hundred District, Talbot County, Maryland. *Journal of Middle Atlantic Archaeology* 8:11–35.

Mayer-Oakes, William J.
  1955   *Prehistory of the Upper Ohio Valley.* Carnegie Museum, Pittsburgh.

McCary, Ben C., and Norman F. Barka
  1977 The John Smith and Zuniga Maps in the Light of Recent Archaeological Investigations along the Chickahominy River. *Archaeology of Eastern North America* 5:73–86.

McDonald, Douglas H., Jonathan C. Lothrop, David L. Cremeens, and Barbara A. Mumford
  2006 Holocene Land-use, Settlement Patterns, and Lithic Raw Material Use in Central West Virginia. *Archaeology of Eastern North America* 34:121–40.

McMichael, Edward V.
  1965 *Archeological Survey of Nicholas County, West Virginia.* Archeological Series, Number 1, West Virginia Geological and Economic Survey, Morgantown.
  1968 *Introduction to West Virginia Archeology.* Educational Series, West Virginia Geological and Economic Survey, Morgantown.

Means, Bernard K.
  2007 *Circular Villages of the Monongahela Tradition.* University of Alabama Press, Tuscaloosa.

Michels, Joseph W., and Ira F. Smith, III
  1967 Archaeological Investigations of Sheep Rock Shelter, Huntingdon County, Pennsylvania. Pennsylvania State University, Department of Sociology and Anthropology, University Park.

Moorehead, Warren K.
  1918 A Brief Summary of the Archaeology of the Susquehanna. *Second Report of the Pennsylvania Historical Commission*, pp. 117–26. Harrisburg.

Mouer, L. Daniel
  1991 The Formative Transition in Virginia. In *Late Archaic and Early Woodland Research in Virginia: A Synthesis*, edited by Theodore R. Reinhart and Mary Ellen N. Hodges, Special Publication Number 23, Archeological Society of Virginia, pp. 1–88.

Mounier, R. Alan
  1982 The Archaic Period in Southern New Jersey. In *New Jersey's Archaeological Resources from the Paleo-Indian Period to the Present: A Review of Research Problems and Survey Priorities,* edited by Olga Chesler, pp. 139–84. Office of Cultural and Environmental Services, New Jersey Department of Environmental Protection, Trenton.
  1999 The Environmental Basis of Prehistoric Occupation on the New Jersey Coastal Plain. *Bulletin of the Archaeological Society of New Jersey* 54:97–108.

Nash, Carole, L.
  2009 Modeling Uplands Landscape and Prehistoric Native American Settlement Archaeology in the Virginia Blue Ridge Foothills. PhD dissertation, Catholic University of America, Washington, DC.

Parsons, Jeffrey R.
  1972 Archaeological Settlement Patterns. *Annual Review of Anthropology* 1:127–50.

Peck, Donald W.
   1979   Archeological Resources Assessment of the Monocacy River Region, Frederick and Carroll Counties, Maryland: Phase I and II.

Perazio, Philip A.
   2006   The Importance of the Settlement System Concept in Middle Atlantic Archaeological Research. *Journal of Middle Atlantic Archaeology* 22:1–7.

Pullens, Stevan C.
   2001   Late Woodland Settlement Organization in Southwest Virginia's Appalachian Plateau. *West Virginia Archeologist* 53(1–2):36–51.

Raber, Paul A.
   1993   Late Woodland Period Settlement Patterns in the Piedmont Uplands of Pennsylvania: Evidence from 36CH161. *North American Archaeologist* 14:3:245–85.
   2009   Archaeological Investigations at 36FA368: Implications for the Study of Monongahela Settlement Patterns. *Pennsylvania Archaeologist* 79(1):1–29.

Ranere, Anthony J., and Patricia Hansell
   1984   An Approach to Determining Site Distributions in the Pine Barrens: Power Line Surveying. *Proceedings of the 1983 Middle Atlantic Archaeological Conference*, pp. 90–99. Rehoboth, DE.

Rieth, Christina B.
   2008   Early Woodland Settlement and Land use in Eastern New York. *Journal of Middle Atlantic Archaeology* 24:153–66.

Ritchie, William A.
   1949   The Bell-Philhower Site, Sussex County, New Jersey. *Indiana Historical Society, Prehistory Research Series* Volume 3, No. 2. Indianapolis.
   1956   Prehistoric Settlement Patterns in Northeastern North America. In *Prehistoric Settlement Patterns in the New World*, edited by Gordon R. Willey, Wenner-Gren Foundation for Anthropological Research, Inc., New York. Viking Fund Publications in Anthropology Number 23, pp. 72–80.

Ritchie, William A., and Robert E. Funk
   1973   *Aboriginal Settlement Patterns in the Northeast*. New York State Museum and Science Service Memoir No. 20.

Sanders, W. T., J. R. Parsons, and R. S. Santley
   1979   *The Basin of Mexico*. Academic Press, New York.

Schrabisch, Max
   1917   *Archaeology of Warren and Hunterdon Counties*. Reports of the Department of Conservation and Development, Bulletin No. 18. Trenton.
   1930   *Archaeology of the Upper Delaware Valley, Volume 1*. Publications of the Pennsylvania Historical and Museum Commission, Harrisburg.

Solecki, Ralph S.
   1949a   An archaeological survey of two river basins in West Virginia, Part I. *West Virginia History* 10(3):189–214. Charleston.

1949b An archaeological survey of two river basins in West Virginia, Part I. *West Virginia History* 10:4:319–432. Charleston.

Skinner, Alanson, and Max Schrabisch
  1913 *A Preliminary Report of the Archaeological Survey of the State of New Jersey.* Geological Survey of New Jersey Bulletin No. 9.

Stearns, Richard E.
  1943 Some Indian Village Sites of Tidewater Maryland. *The Natural History Society of Maryland Proceeding* Number 9, Baltimore.
  1949 Some Indian Village Sites of the Lower Patapsco River. *Proceedings of the Natural History Society of Maryland* Number 10, Baltimore.

Steponaitis, Laurie C.
  1983a An Archeological Study of the Patuxent Drainage. 2 vols. Maryland Historical Trust Manuscript Series 24.
  1983b Some Preliminary Results of Archeological Survey in the Patuxent River Drainage. In 1983 Middle Atlantic Archaeological Conference Proceedings, pp. 100–111.

Stevenson, Christopher M.
  1982 Patterns of Hollow Exploitation along the Allegheny Front, Centre County, Pennsylvania. *Pennsylvania Archaeologist* 52(3–4):1–16.

Steward, Julian
  1938 Basin-Plateau Aboriginal Sociopolitical Groups. *Bureau of American Ethnology Bulletin* 120. Washington, DC.

Stewart, R. Michael
  1980 *Prehistoric Settlement and Subsistence Patterns and the Testing of Predictive Site Location Models in the Great Valley of Maryland.* Unpublished PhD dissertation. Department of Anthropology, Catholic University of America, Washington, DC.
  1983 Prehistoric Settlement Patterns in the Blue Ridge Province of Maryland. In *Upland Archeology in the East: A Symposium.* USDA Forest Service, Southern Region, Cultural Resources Report Number 2, pp. 43–90.
  1991 Early Prehistoric Cultures and Interior Site Settings in Southern New Jersey. *Bulletin of the Archaeological Society of New Jersey* 46:59–70.

Stewart, R. Michael, and Judson Kratzer
  1989 Prehistoric Site Location on the Unglaciated Appalachian Plateau. *Pennsylvania Archaeologist* 59:19–36.

Thomas, Cyrus
  1894 Report on the Mound Explorations of the Bureau of Ethnology. *Twelfth Annual Report of the Bureau of Ethnology,* pp. 494–503. Washington, DC.

Thomas, Ronald A., Daniel R. Griffith, Cara L. Wise, and Richard E. Artusy
  1975 Environmental Adaptation of Delaware's Coastal Plain. *Archaeology of Eastern North America* 3:35–90.

Tolley, George A.
   1983   Blue Ridge Prehistory: Perspective from the George Washington National Forest. In *Upland Archeology in the East: A Symposium*. USDA Forest Service, Southern Region, Cultural Resources Report Number 2, pp. 104–15.

Trigger, Bruce
   1967   Settlement Archaeology—Its Goals and Promise. *American Antiquity* 32:2:149–60.

Turnbaugh, William A.
   1977   *Man, Land, and Time: The Cultural Prehistory and Demographic Patterns of North Central Pennsylvania*. Unigraphic, Inc. Evansville, IN.

Vita-Finzi, C., and E. S. Higgs
   1970   Prehistoric economy in the Mount Carmel area of Palestine: Site Catchment Analysis. *Proceedings of the Prehistoric Society* 36:1–37.

Vogt, Evon Z.
   1956   An Appraisal of "Prehistoric Settlement Patterns in the New World." In *Prehistoric Settlement Patterns in the New World*, edited by Gordon R. Willey, Wenner-Gren Foundation for Anthropological Research, Inc., New York. Viking Fund Publications in Anthropology Number 23, pp. 173–82.

Wall, Robert D.
   1981   *An Archeological Study of the Western Maryland Coal Region: The Prehistoric Resources*. Maryland Geological Survey, Division of Archeology, Baltimore.

Wall, R., R. M. Stewart, J. Cavallo, D. McLearen, R. Foss, P. Perazio, and J. Dumont
   1997   *A Synthesis of the Trenton Archaeological Site Complex: The Abbott Farm Prehistoric Sites, Trenton, Mercer County, New Jersey*. Report Prepared for the Federal Highway Administration and the New Jersey Department of Transportation, Bureau of Environmental Analysis by Louis Berger & Associates, Inc., The Cultural Resource Group, East Orange, NJ.

Wall, Robert D., and Bradford Botwick
   1992   Archaeological Survey of a Portion of Delaware Water Gap National Recreation Area, Pennsylvania and New Jersey. Report prepared for the National Park Service, Mid-Atlantic Regional Office, Philadelphia, PA, by the Cultural Resource Group of Louis Berger & Associates, Inc., East Orange, NJ.

Wholey, Heather A.
   2009   A Population Approach to the Middle Atlantic Archaic. *North American Archaeologist* 30(1):1–21.

Wilkins, Gary
   1978   Prehistoric Mountaintop Occupations of Southern West Virginia. *Archaeology of Eastern North America* 6:13–40.

Willey, Gordon R.
   1953   Prehistoric Settlement Patterns in the Virú Valley, Perú. *Smithsonian Institution Bureau of American Ethnology Bulletin* 155, Washington, DC.

1956 Introduction. In *Prehistoric Settlement Patterns in the New World*, edited by Gordon R. Willey, Wenner-Gren Foundation for Anthropological Research, Inc., New York. Viking Fund Publications in Anthropology Number 23, pp. 1–2.

Winters, Howard D.
   1969 *The Riverton Culture*. Illinois State Museum Report of Investigations No. 13, Springfield.

14

+

Prehistory and Population in the Middle Atlantic

Heather A. Wholey

Anthropologists have long been concerned with historical population numbers and from as early as the 1950s archaeologists, such as Robert Braidwood (1950) and Mark Cohen (1977), have addressed the relationship between population growth, food subsistence practices, and ecological sustainability. Middle Atlantic prehistorians have arguably been less willing than archaeologists within other culture areas characterized by "small-scale" society to speculate and theorize about human population. Many Middle Atlantic archaeologists regard population studies as impossible and futile and consider an understanding of past population as enigmatic. Nonetheless, population has been considered essential to a holistic cultural ecology, and population studies (including meticulously derived demographic figures, basic impressionistic estimates, and theoretical generalizations) have been part of the discourse of Middle Atlantic archaeology. This chapter will historically situate the topic of prehistoric human population in the Middle Atlantic by reviewing various driving motives and methodological approaches. It will also include discussion of how extra-regional models and approaches have influenced population studies in the Middle Atlantic as well as how Middle Atlantic population studies may contribute to the dialogue. Lastly, this chapter considers how prehistoric population studies may be applied to contemporary population ecology.

POPULATION STUDIES: PIONEERS OF
A MULTIDISCIPLINARY TRADITION

Modern population studies are founded on a multidisciplinary approach in methodical approach and theoretical orientation. At the core, one can summarize this multidisciplinary stance as the integration of history, economy, and bio-geography; bio-geography itself uniting concepts and practice from ecology, evolutionary biology, geology, and physical geography. The exact multidisciplinary configuration will be influenced by the types of questions one is attempting to address of the problems one hopes to solve. Population studies have historically been problem-oriented, often being undertaken to understand existing social, economic, or health issues. Today population studies also frequently have an applied element, with the goals of resource management, economic welfare, and even population regulation.

The Life Table Approach: Foundations of Demography (Seventeenth Century)

The pioneering days of population studies can be traced to the seventeenth century. John Graunt, an English haberdasher, is generally considered to be the Father of Demography, being credited for initiating empirical research in population studies. Graunt analyzed the vital statistics of the citizens of London over a seventy-year period and published his findings in the 1662 pamphlet "Natural and Political Observations Made upon the Bills of Mortality," also just referred to as the "Bills of Mortality." Graunt was concerned with predicting life expectancies from mortality data by examining variables such as births, marriages, and causes of death. His work later resulted in the universal registrations of these data. The publication was used by London officials to create a system to warn of the onset and spread of bubonic plague in the city. Graunt's work is considered the first important landmark in the history of population studies, establishing the Life Table Approach that underpins modern demography.

Population and Resources: The Malthusian Equation (Eighteenth Century)

Over a century later in 1798, Thomas Malthus first published his famous treatise, *Essay on the Principle of Population*. In this piece, he argued that population growth is constant and that natural increase in population is exponential. He further argued that population growth would diminish the world's ability to feed itself as food production could grow only arithmetically and that this would ultimately lead to a rise in the death rate. Population pressure, in the form of resource shortages, could only be counteracted through what he called "positive checks," such as war, famine, and disease, or self-regulatory "preventative checks." Malthus concluded that unless family size was regulated, famine would become a global epidemic and thus suggested that the family size of the lower class ought to be regulated such that poor families do not produce more children than they can support. For him the only acceptable preventative check was delaying marriage until one was financially able to support a family. He opposed the "Poor Laws" that would provide support to the poor, on the grounds that such support would only reinforce their lack of restraint at the expense of others in society. Obviously today we see the legacy of Malthusian theory in China's one child regulation, in planning policy targeted at Third World economics, and in our own welfare reform debates.

Biology and Natural Selection: Foundations of Evolutionary Ecology (Nineteenth Century)

When Charles Darwin and Alfred Wallace read *Principle of Population*, it occurred to both of them that animals and plants should also be experiencing the same population pressure described by Malthus. The world would thus be overrun by beetles or earthworms or any other species, but it is not because they cannot reproduce to their full potential. Many die before they become adults, being vulnerable to droughts, cold winters, and other environmental assaults. Moreover, individuals must compete for food within a finite supply. Nearly half a century later, in 1859 Darwin published *On the Origin of the Species*, in which he addresses the environmental limits of population increase. He postulates that each generation of species exponentially increases its population from one generation to the next. Although nature can provide an abundance of resources, environmental checks in the form of disaster, epidemic, or shifts in climate can limit resources availability. His principle of the limits of population increase is based on the notion that if each generation continues to reproduce in greater numbers than the one before, and the rate of death remains the same, the earth will eventually run out of room and will be unable to support all of its inhabitants. Since, however, there is limit on population for every species, one individual organism's survival inherently threatens the survival of another. Aside from his arguments related to natural selection, these ideas form the underpinning of modern concepts of "carrying capacity" and biodiversity. For example, he observed that habitats with greater plant diversity were associated with greater primary productivity. In 1958, Charles Eton furthered this by hypothesizing that ecosystems with greater diversity of species were more stable and less susceptible to

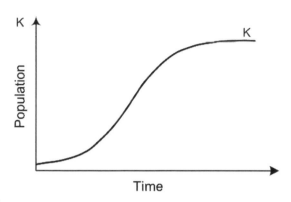

Figure 15.1.

disease and species invasion. Today, modern scholars have refocused on these tenants to promote sustainability through a concern and emphasis on the preservation of biodiversity as a key to sustainability (Tilman 2012) and reduction of resources shortages (Sanchez 2010) in the face of rapidly growing human population.

Reviving the Verhulst-Pearl Equation: The Law of Population Growth (Twentieth Century)

Frenchman Pierre-François Verhulst was also strongly influenced by reading Malthus's essay. He derived his logistic equation in 1838 to describe the self-limiting growth of a biological population (Figure 15.1). Rediscovering the Verhulst-Pearl equation rediscovery in 1920, Alfred J. Lotka reformulated the equation in 1925, calling it the *law of population growth*.

APPROACHES TO POPULATION
IN ANTHROPOLOGY

By the twentieth century anthropologists had become interested in population and were implementing multidisciplinary approaches in their studies. Approaches were grounded in demographic modeling to achieve some form of vital statistics, ecological modeling to understand adaptation, and economic modeling to understand technological advances and social complexity. Population studies in archaeology are undertaken to seek explanations for why societies become more complex, why cultural regions are abandoned, and why civilizations collapse and what is referred to as the demographic transition from the Mesolithic into the Neolithic.

Ethnohistory, the Direct Historical Approach, and "Dead-reckoning"

Some of the earliest population studies in North America were concerned with estimating so-called aboriginal population at the time of contact. In 1928, James Mooney, an ethnographer with the Smithsonian Bureau of American Ethnology, published "The Aboriginal Population of America North of Mexico through the Smithsonian." His estimate of 1.153 million is the classic population estimate for North America that he derived from a comprehensive study of historical accounts by region, which he then tallied (Haines and Steckel 2000). This approach is what Al Kroeber referred to as "dead-reckoning." In his 1934 *American Anthropologist* article "Native American Population," Kroeber revisits Mooney's work and publishes a lower estimate of 1.026 million. His revision is based on his assessment of population by culture area from his tribal maps (Figure 15.2). Kroeber's

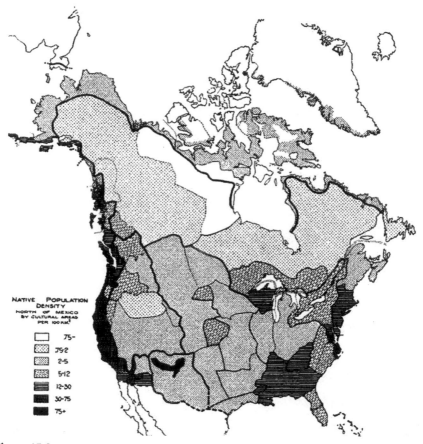

Figure 15.2.

work indicates that some of the highest population densities (according to his computations) would have been in central and coastal California, portions of the Pacific Northwest, and the central portion of the Eastern Woodlands, namely, the Middle Atlantic region. In a 1966 publication, Henry Dobyns projected a much higher estimate between 9 and 12 million and in 1983 again raised the estimate to approximately 18 million. Today Dobyns's projections are considered a high-end extreme (Haines and Steckel 2000).

John Smith and William Strachey's personal observations and information collected from Indian informants in the early seventeenth century provide primary demographic data for Virginia and Maryland Algonquians in the seventeenth century (Potter 1993). Work by Christian Feest (1973), Douglas Ubelaker (1976), and Randy Turner (1978) in the 1970s revisits Smith's observations and Mooney's work. All independently concluded that estimates for the area were too conservative and underestimated the population of the area. In 1608, John Smith provides an estimated Susquehannock population of 2,400 to 3,000 individuals. This figure was later revised by a visiting Jesuit to between 5,000 and 7,000 (Jennings 1984). Marshall Becker's work in Pennsylvania and New Jersey has been concerned with deriving estimates for the Lenape of the Delaware Valley. Utilizing primary colonial documents pre-dating 1740, Becker presents an argument in his 1989 article "Lenape Population at the Time of European Contact: Estimating Native Numbers in the Delaware Valley" that the Delaware Lenape were band-organized foragers at the time of European contact, with a rather low population density. Becker uses deeds of land sales between Lenape and Dutch and Swedish settlers, along with an estimate of about two dozen members per band, and according to his reading there would have been a maximum of fifteen bands; he thus arrives at a figure of 360 and 450 Lenape at the time of European contact. This is probably the lowest estimate for any group in the Middle Atlantic region and many people consider it to be overly conservative. The objective of works such as these is generally to assess the rates of depopulation and postcolonial demographic impacts.

Settlement Demography and the "Area-Density" Approach

In 1953, Gordon Willey published his seminal work, *Prehistoric Settlement Patterns of the Viru Valley*. In it, he defined settlement patterns as "the way in which man disposed himself over the landscape in which he lived." The work was largely descriptive, providing descriptions of the physical environment, a classification of site types, and culture periods present. It utilized this context to discuss community patterning and socio-political organization and to infer population size from settlement size. Subsequent work in the 1960s by William Saunders in the Teotihuacan Valley of Mexico incorporated early twentieth century population figures into his settlement survey to assess the intensity of subsistence agriculture over time. Large settlement pattern surveys such as these were conducted all over the Americas over the next several decades.

Shelburne Cook, a physiologist formerly of the University of California-Berkeley, is a very influential, albeit controversial, figure in what he terms the "area-density" approach in the study of pre-Columbian populations. His approach lays out many of the tenets of what now may be referred to as settlement demography. In his 1960 publication with Robert Heizer, he states that "the study of aboriginal or extinct populations rests upon a range of data quite foreign to that utilized by modern demographers" and that "absolute numerical values are usually unnecessary in work on prehistoric populations" (177). This publication includes a transcription of a discussion among Cook, Heizer, and other attendees at a conference session on the Application of Quantitative Methods in Archaeology. Various panel members stress the utility of population curves that show relative increases and decreases without numerical value, of examining the population shift. They also speculate on methods to extrapolate an estimate of population density from an average density of habitation within a given spatial unit. In my opinion, this proceeding is an important prologue to modern settlement demography. Cook and Heizer (1968) continue to formulate the area density approach by exploring statistical applications such as logarithmic conversions, goodness of fit tests, regression analysis, and so forth. In their contribution to K. C. Chang's edited volume on *Settlement Archaeology*, Cook and Heizer (1968) outlined a ranking system for two-dimensional space, with the first tier being the floor space, the second tier being the site space, and the third tier being the operating space.

The so-called operating space is brought into focus through settlement survey and the examination of settlement patterns. In the 1960s in the Middle Atlantic, as elsewhere, settlement surveys were conducted in academic settings and increasingly as cultural resources management projects. For example, the Potomac River Basin Survey was formed through a consortium between Catholic University and American University in Washington, D.C., by Bill Gardner and Charles McNett. Among the goals of the survey program were the development of culture history chronologies and the development settlement pattern models that could address adaptive strategies and resource utilization. A tremendous amount of settlement data was also generated through a rather early CRM survey, such as the Verona Lake survey in central Virginia (Gardner and Custer

1976), the Massanutten Mountain survey (Gardner and Boyer 1975), the Piscataway Creek survey (1976), and the Monacacy Valley survey (Kavanaugh 1982). Work of this nature continues to augment existing site inventories and databases and provide fodder for settlement demography studies. Some of these earlier settlement studies mention population, mostly as a remnant of site distributions. Quite often these discussions would be framed with reference to the Archaic-Woodland cultural transition and the shift from foraging to food production. For example, based on his survey of the Lower James River Valley, Reinhardt (1979) characterizes this juncture as a resource crisis wrought from overpopulation and requiring the development of a food producing economy. The strength of this approach is that it is comprehensive and can generate a wide spatial and temporal perspective necessary to address the themes of evolution and adaptation.

Habitation Space and the "Floor Area" Approach

A popular technique throughout Mesoamerica and the American Southwest has been to estimate the population of residential units based on the size of foundation remains. This has become known as the floor area approach, and in the 1960s and 1970s at least three formulations for estimating population from roofed floor areas were produced. Based on his ethnographic study of eighteen cultures, Rual Narroll (1962) proposed a constant predictor of ten square meters of roofed floor area per person. Sherburne Cook (1972) suggests twenty-five square feet for each of the first six individuals and one hundred square feet for each additional individual. Samuel Casselberry (1974) refines Narroll's formulation using the predictor of six square meters of roofed floor area per person. He goes on to use this formulation to propose a population of 1,000–1,500 individuals at the Susquehannock Schulz site. Although this approach is not as widely applied as in the American Southwest, Kinsey (1971), along with Casselberry, used the floor area approach in his work at the Susquehannock Murray site and estimated about 550 inhabitants at the site. Bernard Means (2006) has most recently applied the floor area approach in his study of Monongehela Late Woodland villages in the Allegheny Mountain section of western Pennsylvania. Means implements an approach that essentially calculates sleeping space from the perimeter measurement of a habitation structure. His analysis indicates at least two potential housing types, single and multiple family units, ranging from four to twelve individuals, although most residential units appear to have housed single families. Studies such as these contribute more broadly to considerations of kinship structures and social organization.

Population Density and the Operating Space:
Group Size, Boundaries, and Territories

In Kroeber's 1934 publication, he not only proposes North American population estimates by culture area, but he includes approximations of population densities by calculating the mean number of individuals per kilometer in each culture area. For example, he indicates that the Great Basin consisted of a territory of nearly 11,000 square kilometers, but only had a population of 26,700. Thus population density would have averaged about 2.4 individuals per 100 square kilometers, among the lowest in North America. On the other hand, the Pueblo region, with a territory of only 446 square kilometers and a population of nearly 34,000 would have had one of the highest population densities at an average of almost 76 individuals per 100 square kilometers. What he terms the Middle Atlantic Slope would have had an average density of 25.6 individuals per 100 square kilometers. This work does not derive from archaeological data, but it does implicitly employ the concept of the "operating space" in the form of bounded territories. The concept of territory and tiered territorial units, such as residential groups, local groups, and dialect groups, becomes increasingly integrated into population studies. In the 1950s, Joseph Birdsell (1957, 1958) discussed his perceived articulation between territoriality, population dynamics, and cultural cohesion, along with the role of carrying capacity as a regulatory or corrective factor in maintaining ideal population densities for a particular resource base. In a print discussion on demography and population ecology in Lee and DeVore's (1968) *Man the Hunter* publication, several contributors debate the merit and significance of the infamous "magic numbers" of twenty-five and five hundred individuals for the local group and are proposed as the ideal population for local and dialect groups. These numbers still today act as a general rule of thumb in estimating hunter-gather population densities.

Population Ecology

One of the main themes in population studies is that of growth and change—social changes, economic change, political change, and ecological change. Population ecology, the concern for how populations interact with the environment and how those interactions influence population fluctuations, is heart of this topic. Lotka's "law of population growth"—that is, the logistic curve—is an important principle of population ecology. Population ecology is multi-disciplinary developed from the intersection of biology and mathematics, a merger of practice and theory that can be traced to the 1930s and 1940s (Kingsland 1995). In anthropology, population ecology has been mostly widely applied to hunter-gatherer studies, although not always explicitly framed as population ecology *per se*.

Of primary concern in population biology is the estimation of population density with respect to environmental carrying capacity and to better understand the causes and effects of population growth. By the 1960s population ecology as a field had become preoccupied with worldwide environmental problems and incorporated mathematical modeling such as systems theory, information theory, and game theory as predictors for applied work and problem solving mainly in the way of resource management (Kingsland 1995). Human overpopulation was, and still is, of great concern. It was during this time that Esther Boserup, a Danish economist, published *The Conditions of Agricultural Growth* (1965). In this work, she essentially argues that "necessity is the mother of invention" and that during times of pressure societies innovate ways to increase food production. Thus, carrying capacity is not stationary but moveable, depending on things like organization of labor and technology. For anthropologists, the term "carrying capacity" refers to both relative environmental productivity and population density in equilibrium with that productivity (Dewar 1984). Prehistoric archaeologists, including in the Middle Atlantic region, commonly integrate the concept of carrying capacity either implicitly or explicitly in their work on population, even though the topic is only cursory to their larger research objectives.

Randy Turner's work (1976) in the Virginia Coastal Plain was concerned not only with producing population figures for at the time of contact, but also in estimating population densities and projecting a population growth trajectory throughout prehistory. Daniel Mouer (1981) suggested that population growth in the Middle James River stressed local resources and prompted group out migration. In Catlin, Stewart, and Custer's (1982) article on Late Archaic exchange, population growth, and migration, they suggest that population growth instead prompted a series of "buffering mechanisms" that included an amplified focus on riverine resources, the broadening of exchange networks, technological innovation, and decreased overall mobility. Carrying capacity is an underlying factor in accounting for diverse land use, mobility and settlement strategies, and shifting group size in Middle Atlantic prehistory (see Wholey 2009, 2013, 2016).

FUTURE DIRECTIONS IN
PREHISTORIC POPULATION

Concern over human population dynamics in archaeology is relatively young in the Middle Atlantic and other regions. In fact, one could even go so far as to say that that the subject is still in its youth. The development of consistent typologies and a clear culture history narrative was (and still is) essential to empirically addressing prehistoric human population dynamics. Population studies in Middle Atlantic prehistory require more empirical study to evaluate the strength of inductive arguments that generally outline a "population explosion," relatively speaking, that was impetus for trends as increased residential sedentism, increased stylistic variety, and plant domestication. The data is available, and so it is a matter of applying the data. Settlement demography studies that synthesize large bodies of data for Viginia and Pennsylvania have been conducted by Wholey (2003, 2016) and Carr. These studies model population shifts throughout the Archaic Period. While they disagree on some of the details, particularly what happens during the Transitional Period, both agree that the story essentially follows a similar narrative. More studies like this could be facilitated with greater access to databases, such as the Pennsylvania Cultural Resources GIS. More sophisticated modeling could be achieved through delination of spatial territories defined through the distribution of stylstitic elements, resources niches, and such. Critical to these studies is consensus on regional artifact typologies, at least the basics, and clearly defined site types. I believe it is safe to suggest that GIS-supported methodologies will become increasingly important in data coordination and analysis at multiple scales of resolution.

The floor-area and area-density approaches implemented by Means and Gallivan for the Monongehala and Powhatan and Monacan regions provide good models for developing site-specific and even culturally bound population gauges for a time in later prehistory. The trick of discovering the most appropriate way to shift methodologies from one settlement system to another (that is, from mostly logistic to mostly settled), and from one scale of resolution to another is a difficult challenge, but an important bridge and key to creating our own (Middle Atlantic) understanding of processes related to social complexity and technological innovation. Human population and population dynamics factor significantly in discussions of emergent social complexity in area confronted with evident socio-political collapse. The topic does not receive as much serious consideration in most of the Eastern Woodlands, including the Middle Atlantic.

Global Change Archaeology—Population Ecology for the Future

In the late 1800s, Malthus predicted that population would eventually grow to the point where it exceeded food and land resources. Malthusian projections were brought back into the forefront during the 1960s and 1970s by publications such as the *Population Bomb* (Erlich 1968), which warned of mass human starvation due to overpopulation, and advocated immediate action to limit population growth. In the 2009 publication *Population Bomb Revisited*, Paul and Ann Erlich continue to stress the role of population growth in the onset of famine, plague, and water shortages. *Population 7 Billion* (Kunzig 2011) iterates that global population has just exceeded seven billion people and is projected to reach nine billion within the next thirty or so years. The article asks "Can the earth take the strain?" Researchers scramble from all disciplines to derive projections, develop scenarios, and propose mechanisms to avoid global overpopulation and collapse. Yet population growth and resource usage is not occurring at a steady rate or even in a standardized fashion across the globe. So while large-scale models are of significant value, efforts to model the interface between population, environment, and decision making at the local scale should be undertaken. Since its earliest concerns with human population numbers and growth estimates, Middle Atlantic archaeology has demonstrated the value of regional work in populations studies (e.g., Kroeber 1934; Feest, 1973; Casselbery 1974; Turner 1978; Becker 1989; Means 2006; Wholey 2013).

Archaeologists are increasingly willing, eager even, to engage in "global change" topics associated with population growth, climate change, sustainability, and resources management and planning. Global change archaeology, emerging from the ecological anthropology and environmental archaeology frameworks of the 1960s and 1970s, and the political and historical ecology frameworks of the 1990s, reflects a growing consciousness and concern for social, cultural, and environmental issues (Hardesty 2007). Modeling complex adaptive systems from the archaeological record is a key in global change archaeology, as is interdisciplinary collaboration. The archaeological record encompasses a large body of empirical evidence documenting environmental changes, human landscapes modification, and human resources utilization. The archaeological record also provides a long view to recognize patterning in human decision making, including cultural norms regarding family size, settlement size, and resources utilization, that impact overall population density and rates of population growth (Kohler 2004). In some areas and time periods, environmental change led to long-term negative consequences for regional human populations, whereas in other cases, changes favored intensification of production and increased population sizes (Kirch 2005). Thus, prehistory may offer lessons about what the future may hold

Today the term *sustainability* has become something of a catch-all term for modeling long-term survival. For humanity, this means the long-term maintenance and well-being of economic, social, and ecological dimensions. Archaeologists have recently been asserting their role in sustainability studies. In a recent article entitled *A Framework for Archaeology and Sustainability*, Joseph Tainter (2002) examines what he calls the "costliness of complexity" for the Mississippians of Cahokia and the lowland Maya and points out that problem-solving, or how societies chose to address what they deem as problematic, is an important framework for understanding historical trajectories related to sustainability or collapse. In his article "The Archaeology of Overshoot and Collapse" (Tainter 2006), he further emphasizes that, given the prominence of the conversation on population and sustainability, it is important to assess the evidence in archaeology for population overshoot or, I would add, successful initiatives to circumvent overshoot. Minnis (2001) states that "the past can serve the future. By definition, sustainability is long term, so it may be useful to consider this topic from an archaeological perspective." The lowland Classic Maya and Rapa Nui of Easter Island are often offered as case studies for how we, as scientists and humanitarians, may model and better understand the relationships between populations, resource stress, overshoot, and collapse. Middle Atlantic prehistorians have a unique perspective to bring into the conversation. As noted by Espenshade (Chapter 3 and Dent Chapter 17), Middle Atlantic archaeology is like few other places due to the tremendous ecological and cultural diversity present within a relatively small, compressed region. Middle Atlantic archaeologists must thus be very attuned to temporal and spatial scales of resolution in their specific work, while also undertaking a comparative perspective (e.g., Carr Chapter 11; Wholey 2013, 2016). As such, Middle Atlantic archaeology is positioned to construct a broad understanding of collective human agency in localized population dynamics that involve changes in group size and group mobility strategies and shifts in preferential settlement locales and habitats that is not focused on population overshoot and collapse, but rather on population resilience and responsiveness to changing external and internal circumstances.

REFERENCES CITED

Becker, Marshall J.
   1989   Lenape Population at the Time of European Contact: Estimating Native Numbers in the Lower Delaware Valley. *Proceedings of the American Philosophical Society* 133(2):112–22.

Birdsell, Joseph
   1957   Some Population Problems Involving Pleistocene Man. In *Population Studies: Animal Ecology and Demography*. Cold Springs Harbor Laboratory of Quantitative Biology 22: 47–69.
   1958   On Population Structure in Generalized Hunting and Collecting Populations. *Evolution* 12:189–205.

Boserup, Esther
    1965 *The Conditions of Agricultural Growth: The Economics of Agrarian Change under Population Pressure.* Chicago: Aldine. London: Allen & Unwin.

Caldwell, Joseph
    1958 Trend and Tradition in the Prehistory of the Eastern United States. *American Anthropologist* 60(6):1–88.

Casselberry, Samuel
    1974 A Further Refinement of Formulae for Determining Population from Floor Area. *World Archaeology* 6(1):117–122.

Haines, Michale R., and Richard H. Steckel
    2000 *A Population History of North America.* Cambridge: Cambridge University Press.

Hardesty, Donald L.
    2007 Perspectives on Global-Change Archaeology. *American Anthropologist* 109(1):1–7.

Feest, Christian
    1973 Seventeenth Century Virginia Algonquian Population Estimates. *Quarterly Bulletin of the Archaeological Society of Virginia* 28(2):66–79.

Jennings, Francis
    1984 *The Ambiguous Iroquois Empire.* New York: W. W. Norton and Company, Ltd.

Kingsland, Sharon
    1995 *Modeling Nature: Episodes in the History of Population Ecology.* Chicago: University of Chicago Press.

Kirch, Patrick V.
    2005 Archaeology and Global Change: The Holocene Record. *Annual Review of Environment and Resources* 30:409–40.

Kohler, Timothy
    2004 Population and Resources in Prehistory. In *The Archaeology of Global Change: Human Impacts on Their Environment,* edited by Charles L. Redman, S. R. James, P. R. Fish, and J. D. Rogers, pp. 257–70. Smithsonian Books, Washington, DC.

Kroeber, Alfred L.
    1934 Native American Population. *American Anthropologist, New Series* 36 (1):1–25.

Lee, Richard B., and Irven DeVore
    1968 *Man the Hunter.* Wenner-Grenn Foundation for Anthropological Research, New York.

Means, Bernard
    2006 The Social Implications of a New Method for Estimating the Number of Residents within Monongahela Houses from Their Floor Areas. *Journal of Middle Atlantic Archaeology* 22:31–50.

Minnis, Paul, and Wayne J. Elisens (editors)
  2001   *Biodiversity and Native America.* Norman: University of Oklahoma Press.

Narroll, Raul
  1962   Floor area and settlement population. *American Antiquity* 27:587–88.

Potter, Stephan R.
  1993   *Commoners, Tribute and Chiefs: The Development of Algonquian Culture in the Potomac Valley.* University of Virginia Press.

Reinhardt, Theodore R.
  1979   Middle and Late Archaic Cultures in the Lower James River Area. *Bulletin of the Archaeological Society of Virginia* 34(2):57–82.

Sanchez, Luis
  2010   Darwin, artificial selection, and poverty: Contemporary implications of a forgotten argument. *Politics and the Life Sciences* 29(1):61–71.

Tainter, Joseph
  2002   A Framework for Archaeology and Sustainability. In *Encyclopedia of Life Support Systems.* EOLSS Publishers, Oxford. [online] http://www.eolss.net.
  2006   Archaeology of Overshoot and Collapse. *Annual Review of Anthropology* 35:59–74.

Turner, Randolph
  1978   Population Distribution in the Virginia Coastal Plain, 8000 B.C. to A.D. 1600. *Archaeology of Eastern North America* 6:60–71.

Ubelaker, Douglas
  1976   The Sources and Methodology for Mooney's Estimates of North American Indian Populations. In *The Native Populations of the Americas in 1492,* edited by W. M. Denevan, pp. 243–89. University of Wisconsin Press.

Wholey, Heather
  2009   A Population Approach to the Middle Atlantic Archaic. *North American Archaeologist* 30(1):1–21.
  2013   Archaic Hunter Gatherer Population Ecology: The Middle Atlantic Transect Approach. *Journal of Middle Atlantic Archaeology* 29:75–86.
  2016   Transitional Period Settlement Population in Eastern Pennsylvania. In *The Nature and Pace of Change in Transitional Period Culture: 3000 to 4000 BP,* edited by R. Michael Stewart, Kurt W. Carr, and Paul A. Raber, pp. 111–20. Pennsylvania State University Press.

15

A Postcolonial
Perspective on Contact
Period Archaeology

Jay F. Custer

The "director's cut" version of the 1992 cinematic interpretation of James Fenimore Cooper's *The Last of the Mohicans* ends with Chingachgook, the "Last Mohican," delivering a soliloquy lamenting the death of his son and the impending demise of his people. He observes that Indian people will soon "be no more, or be not us." Genocide by its legal definition, the destruction of a human group *as a group* (Andreopoulos 1994), will have occurred. And when Chingachgook's adopted Euroamerican son objects to his father's view of the future, Chingachgook makes a longer statement about the inevitability of the replacement of one "race" by another.

The scene is a powerful ideological statement. The *inevitable* demise of Indian people is described by an Indian himself. It is classic mythology defined by Barthes (1972:129) as mental representations that make an action produced by human choices appear to be "natural" and inevitable. No one is responsible for the attempted extermination of Indian people. It all just happened on its own long ago. Vast immutable historical forces caused the events, not decisions by individual human beings. Indians "vanished," a favorite term used by Euroamericans to characterize the demise of Indian people (Dippie 1991) because "vanishing" is "something you do rather than something that is done to you" (Wilson 1998:xxii). To believe that Indian people "vanished" acts to "palliate national injustice as the inevitable adjunct of a conclusion that was unavoidable" (Welsh 1890:261). And today's Indian people, the survivors of the "be no more" part of the genocide, are now "no more us." Survival negates identity (Wilson 1998:xxiii). These mythologies are integral components of widely believed Euroamerican ideologies and mythologies about Indian people within contemporary American culture (Churchill 1994, 1996, 1998; Heike 2013; Hughes 2003; Mihesuah 1997; Slotkin 1973, 1985, 1992). They provide "an escape from some of the less pleasant implications of existence in an imperfect world" (Langer 1998:186), a world shaped by the Native American genocide perpetrated by Euroamericans (Churchill 1997).

ARCHAEOLOGY AND POSTCOLONIAL STUDIES

I contend that archaeological studies of the "Contact Period" in the Middle Atlantic act to validate and perpetuate the general mythologies of American culture and the hegemony and self-conferred epistemological advantages of Euroamerican archaeologists. Middle Atlantic Contact Period archaeology has always been a colonial enterprise practiced in the shadow of settler colonialism—a system of domination whereby an outside populace of European origin asserts its political, social, and economic domination over indigenous subaltern people and seeks to dispossess and eliminate them in order to take physical possession of their land and resources (Churchill 1997:421–22; Horvath 1972; Maddison 2013; Osterhammel 1995). Assertion of the colonizers' dominance lingers into the present with devastating consequences for the colonized population (Burger 2013; Churchill 1998; Cook-Lynn 2007; Fanon 1963; Four Arrows 2006; Freire 1970; Fuchs and Otto 2013; Herrero and Baelo-Allure 2011; Regi 2013; Said 1979; Schwarz 2011; Steinman 2012; Wilson and Yellow Bird 2005; Ziff and Rao 1977). In North America, the colonial domination is continued by the creation of "internal colonies" of Native Americans, a "Fourth World" located within the nation state that arose after their dispossession (Churchill 1996:184, n. 21, 509–46; Den Ouden 2005; Lee 2006; Manuel and Posluns 1974).

The observation that archaeology and anthropology find their origins, practices, and justifications within colonialism is neither new nor original (Asad 1973; Liebmann and Rizvi 2008; Lyndon and Rizvi 2010; Mallette 2012; McNiven and Russell 2005; Said 1993; Trigger 2006:166–210). Some anthropologists and archaeologists even pay symbolic lip service to this observation and superficially acknowledge the biases of method and interpretation that result from this relationship, and the recurrent "colonialist tropes," the socially constructed ethnocentric and self-serving conventional and essentialist representations of racial, ethnic, and cultural identity of the subaltern colonized, lurking within and haunting anthropological and archaeological research (McNiven and Russell 2005:2–4).

Russell Handsman (1987) provides an elegant discussion of the impact of colonialism on Contact Period archaeology in the Middle Atlantic region with particular reference to the Susquehannock Indian people of the Lower Susquehanna Valley. He expresses initial surprise that he could not find the term "colonialism" in his notes from a 1968 undergraduate class that discussed the Susquehannocks. He also observes that continued silence on the topic in the literature during the following nineteen years was "rather remarkable," especially because acknowledgment and confrontation of the theoretical issues associated with colonialism cannot be separated from the "empirical project" of Susquehannock archaeology and history: "Confronting colonialism is not what this tradition of Susquehannock studies has been about" (Handsman 1987:1). The silence was also remarkable because consideration of postcolonial issues had been taking place in anthropology and archaeology for some time (Ashcroft, Griffiths, and Tiffin 1995; Desai and Nair 2005; Loomba 1998; Wolf 1982) with "postcolonial thinking," consisting of methods of analysis that seek to identify and understand the long-term and ongoing intellectual and cultural legacies of the historical processes of colonialism. Postcolonial analysis considers the colonial subjugation of subaltern colonized peoples with respect to the politics of knowledge; the creation of cultural imagery of the colonizer, the colonized, and the colonial process itself; and the operation of social and political power within the creation of our ideas about the colonial process in the past and the present. Current archaeology is clearly a component of such "knowledge production."

Review of the Contact Period archaeological literature for the Middle Atlantic from 1987 to 2013 updates Handsman's observation. Confronting colonialism in Contact Period archaeology is not what Middle Atlantic archaeology has *ever* been about. The "rather remarkable" silence has lasted for forty-five years. Examples of the recent silence are many (Blanton and King 2004, with a few exceptions noted below; Custer 1984:172–79, 1986, 1989:332–41, 1996:301–318; Grummet 1995; Kent 1984; Potter 1993; Rountree 1989, 1990; Rountree and Davidson 1997; Rountree and Turner 2002; Waselkov, Wood, and Hatley 2006). Confrontations of colonialism are few (Custer 2005a, 2005b; Gallivan 2004, 2011; Gleach 1997; Handsman and Richmond 1995; King and Chaney 2004; McCartney 2004; Stewart 2014).

The absence of a confrontation with colonialism in Middle Atlantic archaeology is a result of active and concealed resistance by archaeologists. It is not a case of true ignorance of the basic issues of power and control inherent in postcolonial discussions of archaeological ethics, epistemologies, and hermeneutics. Instead, archaeologists are guilty of "willful ignorance," which in the language of St. Thomas Aquinas is the gravest of sins because it occurs "when a man wishes of set purpose to be ignorant of certain things so that he may sin the more freely" (*Summa Theologica* I–II, q. 76, a. 1, a. 3 in Fredoso 2009). I believe that most archaeologists are unwilling to confront fundamental issues of the current power relationships between archaeologists and Native American people because archaeology's unequal power geometry immediately becomes apparent in postcolonial discourse, or during any kind of useful reflexive consideration of regional archaeology (Custer 2005a). Most archaeologists working in the Middle Atlantic, and elsewhere, do not want to hear about any issues which would upset their intellectual hegemony, much less discuss these issues in any meaningful way, in spite of their feeble protests that they are very sensitive to such concerns (e.g., see reactions to Custer 2005a in Vol. 26, No. 1, of *North American Archaeologist*, also Custer 2005b).

Conscious and subconscious choices by archaeologists to remain ignorant of postcolonial issues pertinent to their work derive from fact that postcolonial analyses call into question cherished illusions of archaeologists as unbiased scientists:

> Most archaeologists take comfort in being impartial observers using scientific techniques, which, they believe reasonably protects them from anything but a passive involvement with their discoveries. For them, archaeology is the process of delivering the past into the present; they are the messengers, and the artifact is the message . . . [but archaeologists really are] the progenitors as well as the midwives at the birthing process we call excavation (MacGillivray 2000:7).

A discussion of moviemaking as the creation of Barthes's mythologies is applicable to archaeology. Robert Ray (1985:26–69) describes the many methods Hollywood moviemakers use to hide the enormous numbers of decisions that constitute movie production. Concealing choices allows moviegoers to suspend their disbelief and experience movies as something "real and natural." Ray also notes that Hollywood movies play an incredibly important role in communicating a wide range of American cultural mythologies, such as Chingachgook's observation that Indian people will "be no more, or be not us" with its implication of an inevitability devoid of choice. Ray (1985:55) states:

> The ideological power of Classic Hollywood's procedure is obvious: under its sponsorship, even the most manufactured narratives came to seem spontaneous and "real." A spectator prevented from detecting style's role in a mythology's articulation could only accede to that mythology's "truth." When that mythology also denied the necessity for choice, the result was

a doubling effect that made the American Cinema one of the most potent ideological tools ever constructed.

Archaeologists wield a similar and powerful ideological tool when explaining the significance of our findings to the general public. We present messages of inevitability of cultural processes and reinforce their veracity by ignoring and concealing the relationship of our findings to lingering issues of colonial power and privilege, and the relationship of our myth-making to our *own* power and privilege that stems from *our* self-serving definition of *ourselves* as the people best suited to deliver these messages. We make our messages of inevitability seem "natural," as if we have allowed them to emerge from the archaeological record all by themselves. Acknowledgment of complicity in colonialism would break the spell and destroy the symbolic doubling. Because we really do know this, Middle Atlantic archaeology is "scandalous" (Castenada 1996:63). Maintenance of obtuse ignorance is not exculpatory.

AN ARCHAEOLOGY OF COLONIALISM

The absence of postcolonial critiques of Contact Period archaeology in the Middle Atlantic damages archaeologists' ability to assess the effectiveness of our work creating relevant and useful knowledge about the past. Colonial perspectives act similarly to Stephen J. Gould's (1992:6) characterization of general scientific theory: "Theories act as straitjackets to channel observations toward their support and to forestall data that might refute them. Such theories cannot be rejected from within, for we will not conceptualize the potentially refuting observations." The current colonial perspective has always limited our ability to appreciate the complexity of the Contact Period archaeological record and to recognize Contact Period archaeological sites that do not necessarily meet criteria of "site authenticity" developed within colonialist archaeological ideologies.

Handsman describes two ways to consider the role of colonialism within Contact Period archaeology. One is "an archaeology *in* colonialism," which "presents itself as an 'impartial exploration' of the gradual transformation and disappearance of things native." It "confronts nothing and accepts everything . . . it makes what happened seem inevitable." It can "legitimize histories of oppression, invasion, and extinction" (Handsman 1987:1–2). "Archaeology in colonialism" characterizes the Contact Period archaeology of the Middle Atlantic region since the 1930s. In contrast, Handsman (1987:1–2) describes an "archaeology *of* colonialism," which "assumes the existence of social relations of inequality, of the processes of transformation and struggle, and despairs over what happened to native societies. It is a procedure of interpretive condemnation."

This chapter begins the process of "interpretive condemnation" proposed by Handsman and examines how archaeologists' colonial truths "are so well used" (Handsman 1987:6) in archaeological studies of the Susquehannock Indian people. This detailed postcolonial review of past studies is intended to be an example of "looking forward," especially when addressing the topic of colonial knowledge production. Application of a critical perspective allows identification of colonial themes and tropes that continue to affect our study of the Middle Atlantic archaeological record. After they are identified, we can move beyond them in future analyses.

THE EVOLVING TYRANNY OF
SUSQUEHANNOCK ARCHAEOLOGY

The Contact Period is an appropriate place to begin a postcolonial analysis of Middle Atlantic archaeology because its archaeology *is* the archaeology of the developing colonial system. It is the time when the European colonial system first impacts Native American societies and Europeans begin to create descriptions of Indian people to serve their own needs (Hoxie 2008). It is the crucible of colonial knowledge production when colonialisms' effects are most blatantly apparent, the time when relativization of our research is most needed and most strongly denied (Geertz 1984; Gellner 1985; Herskovitz 1972; Hunt 2007; Spiro 1986).

Archaeological studies of the Susquehannock Indian people are a significant focal point for postcolonial analysis in the central Middle Atlantic region. The colonial documentary record of the Susquehannocks is rich. Their sites are large. Susquehannock archaeological assemblages, especially those of grave goods, are spectacular. The results of archaeological studies of the Susquehannocks have been widely disseminated (Cadzow 1936; Kent 1984; Witthoft and Kinsey 1959). Susquehannock archaeology is based to an exceptionally large degree on the excavation of burials, which attract a prurient fascination in the minds of both archaeologists and the general public (Kinsey 1977:90–121). And, the best known professional practitioners of classic Susquehannock archaeology (Donald Cadzow, John Witthoft, Fred Kinsey, and Barry Kent) are among the most significant figures in the history of Middle Atlantic archaeology.

Susquehannock archaeology has also had a profound influence on the understanding, interpretation, and imagining of the Contact Period and the development of archaeological constructs of Native American society in the central Middle Atlantic region. Paraphrasing Wobst's (1978:303) commentary on "the tyranny of the ethnographic record" in archaeology, the cultural reconstructions resulting from archaeological interpretations of the Susquehannocks "consumed" by local archaeologists are tyranni- cal because they "can be made to fit any data." Lauria (2004:22) notes that an illustration of a Susquehannock warrior "looms" over John Smith's 1612 map of Virginia. The image and its associated symbolic hegemony of the Susquehannocks is also a metaphor for Susquehannock *archaeol- ogy*. Its interpretations *loom* over other studies of the Contact Period in the central Middle Atlantic asserting their own unchallenged epistemo- logical and hermeneutic hegemony. And, even though the most "recent" comprehensive synthetic treatment of Susquehannock archaeology (Kent 1984) is more than thirty years old, it has no real competitors of similar scope. Therefore, consideration of the developmental context of the ideas shaping and emerging from Susquehannock archaeology is necessary to evaluate the usefulness of these ideas, to better understand how these ideas exert their influence on other Contact Period archaeological studies in the Middle Atlantic, and to find a way to move forward and emerge from their looming shadow.

DONALD CADZOW AND THE BIRTH OF SUSQUEHANNOCK ARCHAEOLOGY

Susquehannock archaeology is one of the first publicly funded archaeo- logical endeavors in the Middle Atlantic. Donald Cadzow was among the very first researchers to hold an official government archaeological or anthropological title in the region (Custer 1996:61–63). His first excavation projects in 1931–1932 focused on burials and other pit features at numer- ous Susquehannock sites located in and adjacent to the town of Washing- ton Boro on the shores of the Susquehanna River in western Lancaster County (Cadzow 1936). The Susquehannocks were already well known from colonial archival records that had been summarized in numerous contexts, including county histories (Ellis and Evans 1883; Mombert 1869) and compilations of various archival sources (Eshleman 1908). Cadzow's goal was to link the Susquehannocks to petroglyphs found in the lower Susquehanna Valley (Cadzow 1934; 1936:7). His research is an example of the direct historical approach (Lyman and O'Brien 2001), which begins with the historically documented Susquehannocks, and then works back- ward in time using historical descriptions to guide his interpretations of the archaeological record.

European grave goods were abundant at most of the excavated sites, which were attributed to the Susquehannocks, including three large vil- lages (Schultz, Washington Boro, and Strickler) that became type sites

Table 16.1.　Ten-Stage/Phase Susquehannock Chronology

Stage	Date (ACE)
Common roots with the Iroquois	?–1450
Proto-Susquehannock	1450–1525
Early Schultz and migration	1525–1575
Schultz	1575–1600
Washington Boro	1600–1625
Transitional: Billmyer and Roberts	1625–1645
Strickler	1645–1665
Leibhart	1665–1680
"The void"	1680–1690
Conestoga	1690–1763

Source: Kent (1984:18, Table 1)

for the sub-divisions of standard Susquehannock cultural chronologies (Tables 16.1 and 16.2). Results of Cadzow's (1936:43–61) excavations at the Shenks Ferry Site, located seven miles south of the main cluster of Susquehannock sites (see Table 16.1), were different. European grave goods were very rare and positioning of bodies in graves differed from that of Susquehannock burials. Cadzow (1936:204–205) classified the Susquehannock sites' inhabitants as "Iroquoian" and the Shenks Ferry Site's inhabitants as "Algonquian." During the 1930s, these classificatory terms carried chronological, linguistic, cultural/ethnic, and racial meanings. Algonquian groups predated Iroquoian groups (Cadzow 1936:7, 9–14, 201–205). The "Iroquoian" Susquehannocks were viewed as very different from their immediate local "Algonquian" predecessors.

Cadzow's explanations of the differences between "Iroquoian Susquehannocks" and earlier "Algonquian" groups led to three general interpretive themes that have continued to haunt central Middle Atlantic Contact Period archaeological studies with little change for more than eighty years: (1) a migration involving violence and genocidal extirpation of local indigenous populations brought "non-local" Iroquoian Susquehannock people into the Lower Susquehanna Valley; (2) significant acculturation of the Susquehannocks, with attendant disappearance of traditional technologies and material culture, occurred due to access to European

Table 16.2.　Three-Stage/Phase Susquehannock Chronology

Stage	Date (ACE)
Schultz	1575–1600
Washington Boro	1600–1625
Strickler	1640–1675

Source: Kinsey (1977:100)

trade goods; and (3) the Susquehannocks ultimately "vanished" soon after 1760 with the process of their decline beginning in the 1670s.

Intrusive Iroquoian Susquehannocks

The idea of a Susquehannock migration into the Lower Susquehanna Valley derived from Cadzow's classification of them as an "Iroquoian" society, which implied a cultural affinity and origin of the Susquehannocks somewhere *outside* of the Lower Susquehanna Valley. Cadzow (1936:204–05) cited material culture similarities between the artifacts found at Susquehannock sites and those of northern Iroquoian (Iroquois), *and* southern Iroquoian groups (Cherokee). However, he mainly discusses Susquehannock ceramics' affinities with northern Iroquoian wares. The presence of collared vessel rims was an important attribute for identifying a northern Iroquoian affiliation for the Susquehannocks (Cadzow 1936:59–60) because earlier studies (Parker 1916, 1922; Wren 1914) had identified them as a distinctive attribute of northern Iroquoian ceramics (Cadzow 1936:76, 109; Niemczycki 1984:1–20). Most of the complete shell-tempered vessels from the Susquehannock sites illustrated in Cadzow's report do indeed have collared rims (forty-seven out of fifty-three: 89 percent). Only one of the grit-tempered Algonquian pots found by Cadzow (1936:60, 76) had a collared rim, and its presence indicated to him that "Iroquoian contact" with Algonquian people had occurred while both groups were contemporaneous occupants of the Susquehanna Valley (Cadzow 1936:60, 204).

An important corollary of the identification of the Susquehannocks as "Iroquoian" was Cadzow's use of material culture, particularly pottery, to document that identification. In doing so he applied normative ideas concerning the classification of artifacts that were well developed in American archaeology at that time (Custer 2001:75–81; Lauria 2012:57–63; Lyman, O'Brien, and Dunnell 1997; Wren 1914:63–68). Normative reasoning assumed that ideas about how ceramics should look were shared by members of individual cultures. These ideas limited the potential stylistic variation of ceramic attributes among people who shared a particular cultural origin. Limited ceramic stylistic variation within a group meant that archaeologists could identify cultural affiliations by defining different types of ceramics. Therefore, ceramic styles are definitively linked to cultures and particular sets of people, or "tribes."

Archaeologists struggled to develop methods to classify artifacts into "types" that could be linked to "cultural aggregates" (Lyman, O'Brien, and Dunnell 1997:159–206). The work of Rouse (1939, 1953, and 1965) provides a good example of the sophistication of such studies. Unfortunately, such sophisticated thinking is absent from Cadzow's work (Griffin

1937). He uses the equation "pots and potsherds equal people" as a basic assumption that need not be tested in any way to guide his ceramic classifications and analyses of cultural affiliations. This simplistic equation continues to haunt Susquehannock archaeology (Kent 1984:109–44).

Perceptions of Iroquois origins and migrations have changed over time, but Cadzow's characterization of the Susquehannocks as a non-local population who moved into the Lower Susquehanna Valley from some other location remains the dominant model of Susquehannock origins along with assertions, begun by Cadzow, that this population movement was a violent invasion. He uses the words "conquest," "invasion," and "migration" indiscriminately (Cadzow 1936:134, 205), and scenarios of genocidal violence are conjured up with some specificity. The Susquehannocks "had to drive the Algonquian occupants out of the region. It may have been the Lenape who were forced eastward and again it might have been other groups who were *exterminated*" (Cadzow 1936:134, my emphasis). And, Iroquoian people, including the Susquehannocks, "intended to have peace regardless of the fact that they often had to *annihilate* entire tribes in order to obtain it" (Cadzow 1936:12, my emphasis).

There is no direct physical evidence from Cadzow's excavations to support his conjuring of a violent genocidal Susquehannock invasion with the exception of a series of alleged cranial injuries sustained by one person buried at the Shenks Ferry site (Cadzow 1936:49, Burial 6). But Cadzow asserts that the purported traumatic injury was *not* the cause of death. Given that he was not an expert in the forensic analysis of human skeletal remains—the field of such forensic analyses was very much in its infancy in Cadzow's day (Krogman 1962)—and such forensic analysis often yields ambiguous results, this example of potential violence is problematic at best. However, the statement "Cadzow had no physical data to support the notion of a violent invasion" should be rephrased "Cadzow had no relevant data at all." He constantly remarks that skeletal preservation was poor (for example, Cadzow 1936:73–74, 99, 157–60), and similar comments are made by those who have more recently studied Susquehannock human remains and do not report any instances of traumatic injuries that could be attributed to warfare, torture, or cannibalism (Boza Arlotti 1997:26, 58, 62, 69, 171–72; Humpf and Hatch 1994; Kent 1984:198–99).

Cadzow also used the historical record to support assertions concerning "war-like" Iroquoians, including the Susquehannocks (Cadzow 1936:22–38). But most of the sources he cites concern events that occurred in the middle part of the seventeenth century after many decades of European contact, and are not necessarily relevant to the early time period of Susquehannock entry into the Susquehanna Valley. These accounts are presented in a very definitive manner and include vivid and lurid descriptions of torture and ritual cannibalism. Cadzow, along with most other scholars of his day, did not consider the fact that all of these accounts were produced by Europeans who were *not* unbiased observers of Native American societies. Meaningful critical perspectives are never applied to these accounts. The result is a series of rarely challenged tropes of war-like, torture-obsessed, cannibalistic Iroquoian people. For example, Kroeber (1938:148) observes that Iroquoian groups were not interested in

> systematic, decisive war leading to occasional great destructions but also to conquest, settlement, and periods of consolidation and prosperity. . . . It was warfare that was insane, unending, continuously attritional, from our point of view; and yet it was so integrated into the whole fabric of eastern culture, so dominantly emphasized within it, that escape from it was well-high impossible.

Or in the more recent words of Fenton (1978:315), Iroquoian warfare "locked its participants in a career from which the exits were capture, torture, and death or gradation to the status of ancients." Therefore, Cadzow was operating within anthropological research traditions of his time. From a postcolonial perspective it is easy to view these characterizations as projections of European settler colonialism upon the Susquehannocks, which dehumanizes them and justified European application of the same process of extirpation to the Susquehannocks. Furthermore, Cadzow's approach is part of a very common methodological trend within anthropology, archaeology, and ethnohistory which resolves any ambiguities in the data to the detriment of American Indian people (see discussions in Deloria 1970, 1997a, 1997b, 2001).

Acculturated Susquehannocks

Because the presence of European trade goods was the major attribute used by Cadzow to distinguish Susquehannock sites from those of their predecessors, the trade goods themselves are symbolic of perceived cultural differences between Iroquoian and Algonquian societies, differences that were caused by pronounced acculturation via contact with Europeans. Traditional technologies were very quickly and irrevocably replaced by European trade goods, a process which destroyed the "authenticity" of the Susquehannocks. With regard to ceramics Cadzow notes, "That the potter's art deteriorated with white contact is shown by the difference in the ware and forms recovered. . . . It was only *natural* that upon obtaining more durable containers of metal from white men the Indians would use them in preference to the fragile earthenware" (Cadzow 1936:114, my emphasis). Use of the word "natural" conveys the sense that acculturation, as reflected in material culture, was an *inevitable* process that operated beyond the realm of human choice, a classic mythological belief in Barthes's sense of the term. To paraphrase the cinematic Chingachgook's words, the Susquehannocks were "no more us."An odd feature of past Susquehannock studies is the absence of description and analysis of Susquehannock grave offerings as individual cultural assemblages from limited points in time. There is virtually no discussion of the co-occurrence of these artifact classes as cultural assemblages whereby the processes of acculturation could be evaluated. But when Susquehannock grave offering assemblages *are* viewed as cultural assemblages (e.g., Boza Arlotti 1997; Custer 1985; Lauria 2012; Srauss 2000), it is clear that indigenous technologies persisted throughout the Susquehannock sequence, albeit in somewhat smaller quantities as the process of interaction with Europeans developed.

Assumptions of acculturation are linked to the ideas of "war-like Susquehannocks." Historical sources document Susquehannock participation in the fur trade with the Swedes, Dutch, and English (Jennings 1966, 1968) and European grave offerings are an additional indication of that involvement. The presence of these items, and presumed inexorable process of acculturation and abandonment of indigenous technologies, lead to the belief that competition for access to the fur trade and a lust for European goods were major sources of intertribal warfare. The assumed linkage is symbolized by this chapter title in Kinsey's (1977:90) book intended for the non-professional audience: "The Susquehannock Indians: Trade and Warfare." The same page also includes a picture of a disembodied head from a Susquehannock grave, which had been on display in the North Museum at Franklin and Marshall College for many years (Witthoft, Kinsey, and Holzinger 1959:114, Figure 16). And, the same head is depicted yet another time in the same book for good measure (Kinsey 1977:115). In sum, the concept of the Susquehannocks' loss of authenticity due to rapid acculturation first evident in Cadzow's work remains an important, and convenient, belief of archaeologists studying the Contact Period in the central Middle Atlantic.

Vanished Susquehannocks

Cadzow's (1936:15) idea that the Susquehannocks "declined into obscurity" was not new (Bean 1884:47–49; Donehoo 1925:28; Ellis and Evans 1883:13–14; Eshleman 1908; Farrand 1904; Parkman 1963; Wren 1914). But Cadzow (1938:205) specifically notes that the Susquehanocks' "battles with their relatives to the north resulted in their final extermination." And he adds a racial theme; when the Susquehannocks "met with superior races it caused their downfall" due to "their lack of constancy [which] seemed to prevent them from organizing with any degree of permanence" (Cadzow 1936:11). The colonial message is clear. Indians' inherent characteristics caused them to vanish in an inevitable process.

The circumstances of the Susquehannocks' decline remain unclear and are subject to debate (Jennings 1968, 1978; Tooker 1984), but the result is presented as certain. There are no more Susquehannocks. A small remnant, identified as "Conestogas," did return to the Lower Susquehanna Valley in the eighteenth century, where they were massacred in the city of Lancaster in 1763 by vengeful Euroamericans, the "Paxton Boys," a "gang of border scoundrels" according to Skinner (1938:45). This appellation functions to characterize the perpetrators as a "bad" minority of Euroamericans who did a "bad" thing atypical of other "good" Euroamericans. The 1763 massacre is seen as the end of any authentic Indian presence in the Lower Susquehanna Valley and the specific end of the Susquehannock people (Richter 2005), a message perpetuated in numerous genres including statements in historical and archaeological studies (Bragdon 2001:33; Jennings 1978; Merrell 1999), books for the general public (Carmer 1955; Footner 1944; Kinsey 1977; Stranahan 1993), novels (Michener 1978), and school texts, which in spite of their age are still in use (Graeff 1953; Murphy and Murphy 1937; Wallower 1965). The cinematic Chingachgook's prophecy that Indian people would "be no more" is seen as true.

Cadzow's approach to knowing and imaging the Susquehannocks used the colonial historical record and archaeology as its prime information sources placed Euroamerican historians and anthropologists in the position of the most knowledgable "experts," and determined the methods of Contact period archaeology in the central Middle Atlantic. Because colonial domination of knowledge production is just as important as the knowledge created (Castenada 1996:60–65; Elie 2012), it is easy to see the ideology of "the vanishing Susquehannocks" as the result of Handsman's "archaeology in colonialism." Some researchers would eventually bring a critical perspective to the interpretation of the Susquehannock historical record (Jennings 1966, 1968), but that perspective has continued to remain absent from more current historical studies of the Susquehannocks (Hunter 1959; Kent 1984; Kinsey 1977).

SUSQUEHANNOCK MISCELLANY AND "WITTHOFTIAN INSIGHT"

The 1959 publication of *Susquehannock Miscellany* by the Pennsylvania and Historical Museum Commission (Witthoft and Kinsey 1959) was an official continuation of Pennsylvania's publicly funded program of Susquehannock research begun by Cadzow. John Witthoft was Cadzow's successor as state anthropologist and Fred Kinsey was Witthoft's assistant (Custer 1996:64–67). Approximately 60 percent of *Suquehannock Miscellany* is devoted to descriptions of Susquehannock site excavations and artifacts which clarified the contexts of the materials excavated by Cadzow. Fred Kinsey's (1959) description and chronological classification of Susquehannock pottery is a significant example. He studied more than nine hundred complete vessels and decorated rim sherds (Kinsey 1959:95) and followed a methodology firmly based in the cultural historical normative paradigm that dominated 1950s archaeology (Willey and Sabloff 1980:93–107). Site proveniences were significant attributes in Kinsey's analysis. Distributions of ceramic types were plotted against the dimensions of time and space (Kinsey 1959:95, Figure 11). Kinsey's study and contemporary studies of Iroquoian ceramics by Richard S. MacNeish (1952a, 1952b, 1976, 1980) were among the most definitive culture historical analyses of Iroquoian ceramics and provide the basis for later regional ceramic studies.

The remaining 40 percent of *Susquehannock Miscellany* includes John Witthoft's article "Ancestry of the Susquehannocks," a detailed elaboration of Cadzow's theme of "violently intrusive Susquehannocks." When *Susquehannock Miscellany* was published in 1959, the earlier elaborate Iroquoian migration scenarios had been replaced by cultural histories stressing an *in situ* development of the northern Iroquois within the Northeast (MacNeish 1952a; 1952b; Niemczycki 1984). Witthoft unequivocally embraced this idea, stating "the weight of recent evidence shows the Susquehannocks to have been of northern [Iroquoian] origin." By this time Witthoft had also proposed the name "Shenks Ferry" for the people who were the Susquehannocks' immediate predecessors in the Lower Susquehanna Valley. They were completely unrelated to the Susquehannocks, and the victims of the violent Susquehannock invasion (Witthoft and Farver 1952).

Witthoft (1959:20–22, 26) describes his study as an example of the direct historical approach and noted the importance of ceramic design analysis as a research tool: "our statements of cultural relationship, continuity, and change are made largely in terms of the ceramic history" (Witthoft 1959:36). This history could also allegedly be described with decade-level precision based on the presence of historically dated European trade goods (Witthoft 1959:29), an illusion of chronological precision that continues in the current Susquehannock chronologies (Tables 16.1 and 16.2). There is no sense of potential chronological ambiguities based on the varied historical economic and cultural processes that brought the trade goods to the Middle Atlantic region from numerous different European nations.

Studies of ceramics as indicators of "cultural aggregates" and past social interactions are a hallmark of culture historical studies (Lyman, O'Brien, and Dunnell 1997; Willey 1953), and are a component of current local archaeological research (Brett and Custer 2011). But Witthoft introduces a "hyper-normative" viewpoint that transformed Cadzow's "pots equal people" equation into "the presence of individual ceramic *attributes* equals the presence of people." He viewed ceramics as examples of *primitive* art with its "subconscious aspects, its relationship to motor habit, and its resistance to conscious designing and new learning" (Witthoft 1959:22). Ceramic production was so deeply buried in "primitive peoples'" subconscious motor habits that variation was minimal and could not be changed even when the "primitive people" made a conscious effort to do so (see also Vaillant 1939). Invoking the axiom that Susquehannock pottery is *always* shell tempered and Shenks Ferry pottery *always* grit-tempered, Witthoft stated that "Susquehannock pots" which are "perfect in every stylistic detail," except for the fact that they are made from grit-tempered clay, "were probably made by a Susquehannock potter from clay prepared and mixed by a Shenks Ferry person" (Witthoft 1959:23). Similarly, shell-tempered Shenks Ferry pottery vessels resulted when "the Shenks Ferry student of Susquehannock style used clay prepared and mixed with crushed shell by a Susquehannock potter" (Witthoft 1959:23). Furthermore, Shenks Ferry vessels with "Iroquoian" collars

> represent the deliberate attempt of Shenk's Ferry potters to mimic Susquehannock pottery, a conscious modification of craft skills which were almost entirely subconscious. Because of the unconscious and motor-habit nature of techniques involved in primitive ceramic industries, these people made pots which were a curious compromise, vaguely correct in their Susquehannock-like appearance but wrong in every detail (Witthoft 1959:23).

Thus, the co-occurrence of Shenks Ferry and Susquehannock pottery at a single site, regardless of the context of that co-occurrence, evinced *"face-to-face contact* between Susquehannock and Shenk's Ferry people" (Witthoft 1959:22, my emphasis).

Witthoft's conclusions concerning ceramics and social interactions, and their implications for archaeological constructions of Susquehannock culture, are important for three reasons. First, his methods and assumptions became significant components of later studies of the cultural meanings of the distributions and attributes of Susquehannock ceramics, particularly with regard to understanding Susquehannock origins (Kent 1984:111–24). Second, the notion of "face-to-face" contact between Shenks Ferry and Susquehannock groups, as presumably documented by their ceramics, is a significant precondition for ideas about Susquehannock "invasions" of the Lower Susquehanna Valley and the subsequent captivity, domination, and extirpation of Shenks Ferry groups at the hands of the Susquehannocks. Third, if the mere presence of Susquehannock ceramics, regardless of context, unequivocally indicates the presence of Susquehannock people at a site, then such sites can become fixed geographic points to document the Susquehannock invasion and its attendant violence, especially if the Susquehannock ceramics are derived from the early components of the ceramic chronology. Or if the ceramics are dated to later parts of the chronology, they become markers of a Susquehannock presence *outside* the core area of their main occupation area in the Lower Susquehanna Valley as they exerted their hegemony throughout the region. These sites then become new arenas for the enactment of Cadzow's tropes of Susquehannock violence, acculturation, and subsequent loss of indigenous "authenticity." Expanding the geographic range of the Susquehannocks also extends the area of applicability for archaeological interpretations based on Susquehannock studies, especially into areas of the Delaware River Valley. This extension leads to the notion that Contact Period sites throughout the central Middle Atlantic region *must* look like Susquehannock sites and show the same alleged patterns of acculturation; they should have an increasing abundance of European trade goods over time and few, if any, items of indigenous manufacture.

Witthoft uses Susquehannock ceramic distribution data to identify their homeland in the north branch valley of the Susquehanna River on the New York/Pennsylvania border near Athens, Pennsylvania (Witthoft 1959:27–32, 37–38; Lucy 1950, 1952, 1959). He then tracks their movement down the Susquehanna Valley by identifying "proto-Susquehannock" or Schultz Incised pottery at numerous sites between Athens and Harrisburg. This movement occurred because the Susquehannocks were "pushed southward from the upper Susquehanna Valley by the growing militarism of their kindred tribes in New York" (Witthoft 1959:59). They then swept away the indigenous populations, and "depopulated" the Susquehanna Valley (Witthoft 1959:27).

In the Lower Susquehanna Valley, the co-occurrence of Shenks Ferry and Susquehannock ceramics is interpreted by Witthoft as evidence of "joint occupation" of residential sites, which "represents the first stage in Susquehannock occupation of the lower valley" and "marks the termination of the Shenks Ferry culture as a separate entity" (Witthoft 1959:24) even though Shenks Ferry *people* may have survived among the Susquehannocks as captive "recognizable aliens" (Witthoft and Farver 1952:5). Slightly later, the Susquehannocks gathered at the Schultz site "to establish a large village which included many captives or adoptees" (Witthoft 1959:24; Witthoft and Farver 1952).) The intra-site surface distributions of the ceramics at Schultz indicate "a double village made up of two communities, one of Susquehannocks on the first hillock nearest the river and one of captive peoples on the second hillock back from the river" (Witthoft 1959:24). Subsequent large-scale excavations at the site (Smith and Graybill 1977) showed that it actually consists of two overlapping, and therefore non-contemporaneous, Shenks Ferry and Susquehannock village occupations which Witthoft conflated into a single occupation.

Witthoft should not be faulted for the fact that new data showed his interpretation to be incorrect. All archaeological interpretations are hostage to revisions due to the acquisition of new information. But it is important to realize how easily he adopted an interpretation involving a large and captive Shenks Ferry population headed toward their demise.

The trope of violent, war-like Iroquoian people, including the Susquehannocks, is a significant component of Witthoft's imaginings of their invasion of the Susquehanna Valley. He includes a digressive discourse on the psychosocial role and origins of warfare, torture, and alleged cannibalism in Iroquoian culture (see also Witthoft 1953), which shows the influences of "culture and personality" studies of that period (Benedict 1934; Harris 1968:393–463; Linton 1945; Wallace 1951, 1961). However, his approach is much more speculative than other regional culture and personality studies (Hallowell 1946; Holzinger 1961; Wallace 1951).

Witthoft's (1959:32) discussion begins with an assumption of innate Iroquoian violence: "The history of the Susquehannocks as a recognizable tribal entity began in violence about 1550, as it was to end with slaughter in 1675." He sees the roots of Iroquoian violence in the development of agriculture prior to European Contact with its attendant increase in the economic importance of women and a consequent diminution of the economic utility of men as hunters, which left them with little to do to fill their time. "Man, as a hunter, was the tool of vengeance; in times when his primary economic significance was fading, he made too good a hunter of men in his attempts to affirm his manly roles in society" (Witthoft 1959:33). Significant gender biases and essentialism are obviously part of his scenario, which nonetheless follows established trends in anthropological thinking about Iroquois matriliny and which often erroneously equate the existence of matrilineages with allegations of "matriarchy," an error discussed by Trigger (1978).

"Primitive" senses of causality in Iroquoian culture led to reliance on witchcraft accusations to account for unexplained events, particularly deaths from disease: "Death fed hostility, and hostility fed death in ever speeding cycles, and the people were driven into innumerable social fragments by hatred, fear, and suspicion" (Witthoft 1959:34). Consequently, the League of the Iroquois developed as a supra-local mechanism to suppress intra-societal violence and direct it outward. It was "a mechanism for focusing the hostility and ferocity of its people against other nations" with the ability to "graft other motivations (such as greed) upon underlying revenge motives" (Witthoft 1959:34). Therefore, the Susquehannocks and their Iroquoian kin "had a remarkable capability for repression of domestic hostility and an equally remarkable ability to exploit this hostility for the killing of aliens. . . . If the Iroquois brought peace to other areas, it was the peace of death" (Witthoft 1959:35).

European contact only exacerbated the situation. New European diseases increased the frequency of "unexplained deaths" and "raised the level of psychoses" within Iroquoian culture, and thus the lust for violence and revenge (Witthoft 1959:35). With the introduction of European weapons, especially firearms, and growing motivations to amass large amounts of trade goods, "skulking became massacre" (Witthoft 1959:35). Within this context of institutionalized violence, the Susquehannocks were "pushed southwards" to the Lower Susquehanna Valley and then "held their identity for a time as a suburban center for organized violence and hostility secondary to the League" (Witthoft 1959:35).

Within Witthoft's cultural reconstruction of organized violence, women exacerbated that violence and added torture and cannibalism to a lurid mix of warfare, massacre, and genocide, which was "determined by the hostility mechanism of Iroquoian culture" (Witthoft 1959:35). Again seemingly inspired by a gendered essentialism and a simplified version of culture and personality studies, Witthoft (1959:35–36) states that warfare, torture, and cannibalism were

> a mechanism of the whole society, involving the virago behavior of women as much as the displaced efforts of the hunter. Women mourning and crying for vengeance recruited and organized the warriors in a society where men seem to have had few dominant roles. . . . Women were at least as much involved in the orgies of war as men, and perhaps more so, for they ran less risk in their thirst for blood. When men brought home the prisoner of war, ritually bound in a packstrap as game animals were bound, the women claimed the captive as they claimed meat brought from the hunt. Women judged the captive, and, quite generally these primitive Xantippes, the traditional butchers of game, took the condemned captive apart.

The reference to Xantippe, the wife of Socrates whose bad temper made her name synonymous with the "female conjugal scold" (*Merriam Webster Dictionary*), reveals even more assumptions of gendered essentialism within matrilineal societies.

Concerning cannibalism, Witthoft (1959:36) states, "Early sources describe their behavior, and there is some testimony to it in the graves and village sites. At Washington Boro and at the newly discovered Sheep Rock site in Huntingdon County, the Susquehannock middens contain green-broken and boiled out pieces of human skulls and long bones, fragments of corpses which the women had cooked into soup in their kettles." Numerous researchers question the cultural context, objectivity, and veracity of historical accounts of Iroquoian cannibalism (Arens 1979). Other historians take the European accounts at face value (Abler 1980), creating an issue loaded with colonial ideological significance (Churchill 2000; Den Ouden 2007; Walton 2004). Nevertheless, any archival descriptions of cannibalism among the Iroquois are suspect. As for archaeological data, the previously noted poor skeletal preservation among the Susquehannock burials precludes the possibility of noting the presence or absence of definitive signs of traumatic injuries to the human remains in burials. There simply are no unequivocal data. Data on the alleged presence of human remains in trash midden deposits at the Washington Boro Village and the Sheep Rock Shelter are either ambiguous or non-existent (Guilday and Parmalee 1965; Guilday, Parmalee, and Tanner 1962; Webster 1985). Thus, there are no unambiguous direct data of *any* kind to support an ascription of cannibalism to the Susquehannocks.

The importance of *Susquehannock Miscellany* is evident from its reviews. William Fenton, the premier scholar of Iroquoian studies at that time, noted that he was "at a loss to pick among several brilliant passages to illustrate Witthoftian insight," and Witthoft's work "captures imagery worthy of larger canvas" (Fenton 1960:257–58). Other reviewers were equally laudatory (Dragoo 1960; Ritchie 1960; Weslager 1960). In sum, *Susquehannock Miscellany* sets the stage for subsequent studies of Susquehannock archaeology and reinforced Cadzow's colonialist themes.

"BIG TIME ARCHAEOLOGY" AND *SUSQUEHANNA'S INDIANS*

Extensive excavations took place in the Washington Boro area after the publication of *Susquehannock Miscellany*, the largest of which were undertaken by a consortium of Franklin and Marshall College, the Pennsylvania Historical and Museum Commission, and Pennsylvania State University under the direction of Fred Kinsey, Barry Kent, and Ira Smith. The impetus for these large-scale excavations was the threat of imminent destruction of Susquehannock sites by construction of public power generation facilities (Custer 1996:83; Kinsey 1977:81). Ultimately, there was no construction.

Shenks Ferry Studies

Fred Kinsey's work within the consortium was excavation of a Shenks Ferry village, the Murray Site (Kinsey and Graybill 1971), located less than one mile south of the Susquehannock Strickler site. The Murray site was a stockaded village approximately four acres in size containing an estimated total of fifty-two houses and housing an estimated population of approximately five hundred people (Kinsey and Graybill 1971:22–30). The village did not contain any signs of a Susquehannock occupation or European trade items, and was thus considered to be a "pure" Shenks

Ferry site abandoned just prior to, or during the initial stages of, the Susquehannock invasion of the Washington Boro area.

The Murray site research report included a description of the Shenks Ferry ceramic chronology (Heisey 1971) still used today with little modification. Heisey (1971:61–63) documents the addition of excurvate collars on the most recent vessels in the chronological sequence, an attribute missing from earlier Shenks Ferry ceramics, and confirms Cadzow's and Witthoft's observations. However, Heisey argued that collars on Shenks Ferry vessels were *not* imitations of Susquehannock ceramics as stated by Witthoft. Instead, the collars on Shenks Ferry vessels were part of a stylistic trend found throughout the Northeast. Therefore, the presence of a grit-tempered, collared ceramic vessel in the Lower Susquehanna Valley need not unequivocally indicate that Susquehannock people were supervising Shenks Ferry captive potters. This conclusion provides an important breach in the wall of Witthoft's monolithic hyper-normative approach to understanding the meanings of Shenks Ferry and Susquehannock ceramics for social interactions between the two groups.

Application of Heisey's ceramic chronology and a single radiocarbon date with a calibrated mid-point of ca. A.D. 1420 (Kinsey and Graybill 1971:39; Custer 1996:274, Table 25) placed the Murray site at the end of the Shenks Ferry chronology prior to the post-Susquehannock invasion era. Nevertheless, warfare, violence, and a shadowy presence of the dastardly Susquehannocks haunt interpretations of the Murray site. A "mass burial" consisting of the disarticulated remains of "sixteen or seventeen" adults, "possibly male," is described as an internment of "recovered dead from an incident of warfare" (Kinsey and Graybill 1971:13) even though no detailed biological anthropological study of the feature's human remains was ever undertaken or published. In a later publication, Graybill (1989) suggested that the remains might be better interpreted as the victims of an epidemic disease.

In support of the warfare interpretation of this burial, Kinsey and Graybill (1971:13) also note that "a slender non-Shenks Ferry type flint triangular point, *possibly Susquehannock*," was found within the "mass grave." This assertion extends the hyper-normative approach from the realm of ceramics into that of projectile point styles in support of characterizations of the war-like Susquehannocks. Originally stated by Heisey and Witmer (1964:19–20; see also Kinsey and Graybill 1971:21–22) based on impressionistic and anecdotal study of very small and selective samples (sometimes less than fifteen specimens), the assertion of ethnic/tribal differences in triangular projectile point forms has been shown to be erroneous when large samples are considered and analyzed using comparative statistical techniques (Custer 1983; n.d.).

Kinsey and Graybill (1971:13) also note the presence of an "extra" skull with a triangular point embedded in the mandible in a double burial located under one of the house floors, a common location for Shenks Ferry burials. This skull is identified as a "trophy skull" placed in the burial "apparently as an offering or as a ceremonial gesture" (Kinsey and Graybill 1971:13) and included in a list of indicators of a "culture under stress" from the Susquehannocks (Kinsey and Graybill 1971:39). The arrowpoint embedded in the mandible certainly indicates an act of violence, or very careless archery, but interpretation beyond that observation is highly problematic. Rather than a trophy, the skull's burial with other bodies could be a sign of reverence for a respected family member who died a heroic death at some point in the past. The speculative possibilities are endless, and remain *idle speculations* that most likely can never be tested in any meaningful way. They are of little to no use in understanding the archaeological record although they do reveal much about the colonialist biases of the archaeologists making the interpretations.

The presence of a double stockade with alleged "bastions or watch towers" and offset gateways at the Murray site is also presented as evidence of warfare with the Susquehannocks (Kinsey and Graybill 1971:22–24). The stockade posts are between two and five inches in diameter and are spaced between nine and twelve inches apart (Kinsey 1977:82; Kinsey and Graybill 1971:22). Even if the resulting structure were reinforced by interwoven laths, the effect would be more like that of a very large basket, albeit a double one, rather than the stout and impregnable "Fort Apache-like" fortification as implied by the term "stockade" or "palisade" and imagined and depicted as typical of local villages on the cover of the January 1934 issue of *Pennsylvania Archaeologist* (Custer 1996:72). The Murray site "stockade" would have deterred casual entrance to the village. But it is hard to imagine such a structure barring a determined assault, especially one that used fire, of the type that one might expect from Witthoft's inherently violent Susquehannock invaders intent on murder, mayhem, and enslavement and extermination of their enemies. Equivocal archaeological data are again marshalled to support the trope of war-like invasive Susquehannocks, even if there is no clear evidence that they were ever even present at the site.

Barry Kent's Susquehannock Synthesis

Consortium excavations of Susquehannock sites focused on the Schultz and Strickler sites which were threatened with nearly complete destruction by proposed development. Large-scale horizontal salvage excavations were undertaken to investigate Susquehannock settlement patterns at the household and community level, and many burials were also excavated.

Unfortunately, no detailed reports on the excavations were ever produced, although some journal articles with summary descriptions were published (Smith and Graybill 1977). Instead of standard site reports, Barry Kent (1984) provides short summary descriptions of the excavations of the Washington Boro area sites and other local Contact Period sites, detailed descriptions of the artifacts themselves, and a synthesis of the past and newly available historic and archaeological data pertaining to the Susquehannocks. His book, and Francis Jennings's (1978) article on the Susquehannocks in Volume 15 of the Smithsonian Institution's *Handbook of North American Indians*, constitute and remain the current definitive description of Susquehannock culture. Very limited "Addendum" updates of newly available data were included at the beginning of the 1992 and 2001 reprinted editions of Kent's book, but taken together, the updates are less than seven pages long, including references.

Kent's descriptions of the site excavations are exceptionally terse, especially regarding issues of archaeological contexts and associations of the artifacts within features and burials. One reason for this approach is his stated intention to write for a general audience (Kent 1984:iii). Detailed contextual data would not interest them. But another more revealing reason for the absence of the contextual data derives from Kent's continued embrace of simplistic hyper-normative assumptions. His belief in this approach, especially with regard to ceramics, echoes Witthoft: "In almost every society, individual artistic expressions on ceramics are executed within certain customary boundaries. That is to say, in almost any given society and during a particular time period, the majority of the ceramics which are produced will exhibit certain *uniform* characteristics" (Kent 1984:110). This axiomatic belief in limited stylistic variability at a given point in time always trumps any data concerning artifacts' contextual settings if artifact associations indicating contradictions to the normative assumptions are encountered (see discussion in Lauria 2012:52–55, 74–79). Artifacts "speak for themselves" within the hyper-normative paradigm. There is no need for any real considerations of context and association. Consequently, there are 184 pages of artifact descriptions and only 52 pages of very general "Evidence from Excavations" pertaining to the large scale excavations of numerous sites in the Washington Boro area in Kent's book. And artifacts are described by classes ("Native" ceramics, glass, metal) with virtually no consideration of their contextual associations, variability, or potential meanings within Susquehannock cultural systems.

The most important, and least adequately described, data in Kent's book pertain to Susquehannock household and community settlement patterns. Prior to his work, the only Susquehannock household data came from Kinsey's (1957) re-excavations at the Oscar Leibhart site where a postmold pattern of a structure measuring twenty-four feet wide and ninety-two feet long was found. The size matches well with ethnohistorically reported Iroquoian longhouses (Engelbrecht 2003:68–78; Fenton 1978; Nabokov and Easton 1989:76–91). Excavations of large segments of the Schultz and Strickler sites revealed the whole or partial remains of thirty more similarly sized structures (Kent 1984:325, 350, Figs. 94, 98; Casselberry 1971; Smith and Graybill 1977). Of special interest is Kent's (1984:354, Figure 99) juxtaposition of a reconstruction of the framework structure of a house from the Strickler site with a very similar 1751 plan drawing of an Onondaga longhouse by John Bartram. Because longhouse structures are the homes of matrilineages among the Iroquois (Fenton 1978; Engelbrecht 2003:68–72), it can reasonably be assumed that Susquehannock longhouses, coupled with their northern Iroquoian origin, indicate a similar matrilineally based Susquehannock social organization system.

Consortium excavations at the Susquehannock sites also focused on delineation of the size of Susquehannock communities. Substantial stockades, much more elaborate than those at Shenks Ferry villages, surrounded most of the Susquehannock communities and specific efforts were made to define their spatial limits (e.g., Kent 1984:350, Fig. 98). Combination of community size and household size and density yielded population estimates (Kent 1984:325–26, 360–65), which are listed in Table 16.3 along with additional estimates derived from very different methods (Casselberry 1971:180). The similarity of the estimates in spite of the use of different methods is striking, as is the large size of the populations and their increase over time, even in the face of increased opportunities for the transfer of epidemic diseases via more intensive European Contact. Unfortunately, this anomalous growth of the Susquehannock population has received little explanatory attention.

When Kent's book is considered within the context of the work of Cadzow, Witthoft, and Kinsey, it provides very few new *insights or perspectives* concerning Susquehannock culture and the process of its changes during the Contact Period. In fact, his stated goal is *not* to write a new history of the Susquehannock Indians (Kent1984:3). Instead, his data are primarily used to flesh out the bones of pre-existing colonial cultural constructions,

Table 16.3.   Susquehannock Village Population Estimates

Site	Date	Village Size	Population Estimate
Schultz	1575–1600	3 acres	1300 (1000–1500)*
Washington Boro	1600–1625	6.5 acres	1700
Strickler	1650–1666	12.5 acres	2900

Sources: Kent 1984:364, Table 22, for all except *Casselberry 1971:180

and he follows the same basic themes of interpretation initiated by Cadzow and continued by Witthoft. Lauria (2012:10) correctly observes that
Susquehannock archaeology has been "theoretically stagnant."

For example, Kent's analysis of "Native ceramics" focuses primarily on
the identification of the cultural and geographic origins of the Susquehannocks and tracing cultural historical links to other local archaeological
cultures of both the Contact and pre-Contact Late Woodland Periods
(Kent 1984:14–15). The normative approach is clearly dominant. "Pots still
equal people" and similar pottery styles are called "cousins" in a telling
metaphor (Kent 1984:116). Kent's discussion of ceramics and Susquehannock culture history often utilizes the words "borrowing," "contact," and
"influence" (Kent 1984:118–45), but it is unclear just what kinds of social
and cultural interactions were involved. He does link the "influences"
and "borrowing" to the trope of warfare "which usually acts to intensify
such exchanges" (Kent1984:129). He also sees the co-occurrence of Shenks
Ferry and Susquehannock ceramics as clear-cut evidence of "cohabitation
of sites" (Kent 1984:129, 131).

Kent uses similar approaches to expand Witthoft's characterizations of
a "proto-Susquehannock" cultural presence in the Upper Susquehanna
Valley, a "homeland" where the Susquehannocks' ancestors, with their
distinctive ceramics, lived before their invasion of the Lower Susquehanna Valley (Kent 1984:302–07). Identification of this homeland adds
crucial validation of the idea of a Susquehannock invasion because it
specifies its starting point in a region with convenient access to the target area and its populations. And Kent embraces the trope of a violent
Susquehannock invasion of the Susquehanna River Valley which elimi-
nates all of its indigenous populations, including the Shenks Ferry people
(Kent 1984:18–19), based on the same ambiguous archaeological evidence
described by Kinsey.

Using vaguely described similarities of ceramics from uncertain archaeological contexts at a series of sites located along a fifteen-mile segment of
the upper Susquehanna Valley, Kent identifies the Susquehannock homeland, assumes contemporaneity of all of the sites, estimates the number
of houses at each site (many of which have never been excavated), infers
a total population for the area, doubles the number to account for contemporaneous sites that must have been destroyed (or not yet discovered
and excavated), and thereby computes a regional population of a thousand people, which just so happens to match the inferred population of
the Schultz site, the first site occupied by the Susquehannocks after they
banded together and completed their murderous rampage down the
Susquehanna Valley. Kent (1984:306) does call the population numbers
"unsubstantiated," but nonetheless asserts the validity of the processes of
culture historical reasoning that produced the estimates.

Kent's use of the hyper-normative approach to ceramics leads to the development of the concept of a "unitary" Susquehannock cultural entity which occupies one, or at least only a few, home villages at any given point in time (see Lauria 2012:48–49 for a similar critique). Some earlier short summaries of data on the Susquehannocks (Swanton 1952:57 citing Hodge 1910) discuss early historic accounts suggesting that there were up to twenty contemporaneously occupied Susquehannock villages at various locales, that the Susquehannocks were "a confederacy rather than a single tribe," and that some villages usually ascribed to a single unitary Susquehannock culture were actually inhabited by independent, or semi-independent, cultural units within some kind of diffuse Susquehannock social grouping (also see Sorg 2004). Kent (1984:33–34) dismisses historical accounts upon which these interpretations are based, but they seem to be a no less reliable source than the ceramic data, especially as interpreted by him within the hyper-normative paradigm.

Kent's and Kinsey's Susquehannock chronologies (Tables 16.1 and 16.2) imply the presence of a limited number of Susquehannock communities at any given time with Kent's system geared toward a single village occupied in each "stage." In fact, Francis Jennings (1978:363) cites a personal communication from Kent stating that "only one village was occupied by the Susquehannock at any one time." On the other hand, Kent occasionally inconsistently states that there *could* be multiple contemporaneously occupied Susquehannock villages at various times and unspecified places (Kent 1984:19–23). He also invokes confusing and complicated scenarios where subsets of the Susquehannocks return to older sites to bury their dead in order to account for inconsistencies in dating of occupation sites and allegedly contemporaneous cemeteries (Kent 1984:22). It is equally likely that these inconsistencies may instead be the result of a false sense of precision in date ranges and a complicated overlapping of occupations at sites that is not necessarily apparent from current spatial data on site boundaries. The quality of the spatial data used to define Susquehannock sites' limits and locations of related cemeteries really is quite varied and ranges from excellent (Strickler site—Kent 1984:350, Figure 98), to very poor (Oscar Leibhart site—Kent 1984:369, Figure 103).

Belief in the notion of a unitary Susquehannock society is yet another consequence of use of a hyper-normative approach. If the presence of Susquehannock pottery at a site *must* indicate the presence of Susquehannock people, then each newly found site with Susquehannock pottery *must* be another location occupied in a serial sequence by the unitary Susquehannock society. Another phase of the chronology must be invented, or the population of new sites must be related to the contemporaneously occupied known sites in terms of "daughter villages" which were homes of the portions of the Susquehannock population who exceeded the spatial, social, and ecological limits of the main village sites (Kinsey 1977:109).

Discoveries of Susquehannock sites outside of the general Washington Boro area provide significant challenges to the notion of a unitary Susquehannock society. Pre-1610 Susquehannock sites in the Upper Potomac Valley near Romney, West Virginia, more than 190 miles from Washington Boro (MacCord 1952) were well known. Kent (1984:317) does his best to explain these Susquehannock sites "so far from their homeland" as the result of "trading, hunting, and *war* parties" (emphasis added), using well known existing interpretive themes. But more recent data from the region (Brashler 1987; Wall 2001; Wall and Lapham 2003) indicate a much more substantial Susquehannock presence there involving people who used Susquehannock pottery and buried their dead following Susquehannock mortuary customs at several sites. This more substantial occupation cannot be accommodated by Kent's speculations. He acknowledges these new data in both his 1992 and 2001 addenda to his book and tries to accommodate them as additional villages in the unitary sequence of serially occupied villages. His explanation requires a Susquehannock detour to the Potomac Valley during their migration prior to their settlement in the Lower Susquehanna Valley, and creates a tediously complicated scenario of Exodus-like Susquehannock wanderings. Equally convoluted explanations are offered for a newly identified Susquehannock village at Lemoyne (thirty-eight miles northwest of Washington Boro—Wyatt, et al. 2011); the Hershey Site (four miles southeast of Washington Boro—Howard 2003; Schulenberg, Weets, and van Rossum 2003); a historically identified, but not yet located Susquehannock village along the Schuylkill River near Pottstown (sixty-two miles northeast of Washington Boro—Hunter 1983); and a series of sites with Susquehannock pottery in the Delaware Valley including the Overpeck site near Kintnersville (one hundred miles northeast of Washington Boro—Forks of the Delaware chapter 14 1980; Kent 1984:314–15).

The notion of a unitary Susquehannock society has an attraction for archaeologists and the general public due to its ideological implications. If there were a single Susquehannock society, it can be tracked through the archaeological and historical records to its demise as a viable sociocultural entity in the mid-1670s via either an apocalyptic battle in the Lower Susquehanna Valley (Tooker 1984), or a nefarious plot by New York's governor, Thomas Dongan (Jennings 1968). The murders of the "last of the Susquehannocks," the Conestoga Indians, by the Paxton Boys in Lancaster in 1763 (Kent 1984:67–69) complete the saga. The Susquehannocks had come to "be no more" with the exception of remnant refugees who received asylum among the Lenape and Seneca (Jennings 1984), subsequently lost their Susquehannock cultural identity, and came to "be not us." Therefore, there can be no extant "real" Susquehannock Indian presence in southeastern Pennsylvania, or anywhere else for that matter. And, consequently, there is no one with a valid claim to land, artifacts, or human remains (Anonymous 1941; Custer 1995). In fact, verification of a Susquehannock Indian identity is a significant issue in current Native American Grave Protection and Repatriation Act (NAGPRA) claims by members of the Seneca nation who assert a Susquehannock identity (Beisaw 2010; Colewell-Chanthaphohn and Powell 2012). But if Susquehannocks were living in varied locations, some of whom escaped the fate of the Washington Boro–area populations (see Custer 1995; Robinson 1987), "real" descendants of the Susquehannocks can be present today and present valid repatriation claims.

The familiar colonial trope of Susquehannock Indian people rapidly succumbing to the allure of European trade goods, abandoning their traditional indigenous technologies, and becoming highly acculturated—thereby losing their authenticity—is prevalent in Kent's work, as it was in earlier studies (e.g., Kent 1984:63, 138, 140, 145, 157, 192–93, 248–53, 257). And, as stated previously, this viewpoint can be contradicted using the same excavation data that was used to generate it. Kent's insistence on the demise of indigenous technologies, especially those of flintknapping and pottery-making, is of special importance because this viewpoint is commonly used by archaeologists to deny the identification of Contact Period occupations at some sites, especially those post-dating 1680, based on the presence of artifacts produced by these allegedly "lost" technologies. This logic, and the notion that a Contact Period site cannot exist if it was not mentioned somewhere in the colonial archival record, and does not have beads, is used to discount numerous Contact Period sites in the Delaware Valley.

Rarely are these objections stated in written form. They are usually voiced as oral comments in papers presented at professional meetings, or in informal conversations among archaeologists. Examples of sites from the Delaware Valley whose Contact Period occupations have been discounted in this manner include historically documented Lenape towns and settlements (Playwicki—Stewart 1999; Minguannan/Opasiskunk—Witthoft 1955; Wilkins and Thomas 1997; and Mitsawokett—Heite and Blume 2003), and other sites with no archival documentation (7NC-E-42—Custer and Watson 1985; 7NC-E-60—Custer, Doms, Allegretti, and Walker 1998). 7NC-E-60 was ascribed to an African American occupation by a Contact Period "expert." Without having ever seen the site's ceramics, which are classic Minguannan sherds produced by Native Americans, he identified them as examples of "Colono-ware," a form of African American ceramics that look nothing like Minguannan ceramics (see Catts 1988 for examples of *bona fide* Colono-ware ceramics from Delaware).

The data cited by Kent in support of the view of lost indigenous technologies is often the result of negative evidence: "No excavated Indian sites of the post-1755 era in the Susquehanna Valley have produced arrowheads" (Kent 1984:193). Therefore, "guns had very nearly replaced the bow and arrow as a weapon and hunting tool for all of the Susquehanna's 18th century Indians" (Kent 1984:257). The problem here is that Kent equates "absence of evidence" with "evidence of absence." Use of this reasoning is a common problem in archaeology. But refutation of such interpretations is easy: just find a counter example. However, if the interpretation is used axiomatically, there can be no contradictions, and such axiomatic use is clearly demonstrated by the examples noted above. The situation is identical to that noted for application of the hypernormative approach and its own axiomatic assumptions. We can never find stone tools and indigenous ceramics at late Contact Period sites because we already *know* they cannot exist.

Susquehanna's Indians ends with a statement of the inevitability of the "competition and extinction" of human societies, which we "might well equate with the Darwinian concept of survival of the fittest" (Kent 1984:411). Susquehannock culture is "officially and completely a thing of the past, relegated, as it were, to a few largely forgotten passages of contemporary accounts" (Kent 1984:408). "Be no more, or be not us" came to pass through a completely natural and inevitable process. The colonial mission of knowledge production was complete.

CONCLUDING REMARKS

Archaeological studies of the Susquehannock Indians do not end with *Susquehanna's Indians*, although it might be easy to think so because even though newer studies are mentioned in the two addenda to Kent's book, no consequent changes were made in the main text and it continues to be cited as the definitive work on the subject. But newer studies *do* question some of the colonial tropes even if they do not take a postcolonial stance. In fact, there were enough new studies for the Pennsylvania Archaeological Council's 2012 annual symposium to be focused on "Recent Research on the Susquehannocks" and publication of the papers is in progress.

Some newer studies of the Susquehannock people are linked to NAGPRA repatriation requests by the Seneca (Colewell-Chanthaphohn and Powell 2012) and Onondaga (Beisaw 2010) for Susquehannock human remains and artifacts. Detailed analyses of burial contexts of human remains, artifacts, historic records, and past archaeological studies were part of both studies. The archaeological constructs of Susquehannock identity and traditional views of the ultimate fate of the Susquehannock people are critically examined and found to be inadequate. The hyper-normative model that characterized Susquehannock studies is questioned using an approach applied in similar critical studies of the Owasco archaeological cultural construct (Hart and Brumbach 2003). Both studies (Colewell-Chanthaphohn and Powell 2012:210–11; Beisaw 2010:244–45, 252–53) note that contests for power and control between Euroamerican museum staffs and Indian people are evident and affect the presence and use of information concerning Susquehannock Indians—a classical issue of the politics of colonial knowledge production and presentation. Of special relevance is Beisaw's (2010:244–45) remark: "By shifting our emphasis from the trait lists of culture history and the linearity of the direct historical approach to a theoretical framework that allows for the complexity of individual group identity, anthropologists can better fulfill their obligations to the NAGPRA process."

Three recent analyses of Susquehannock ceramics exhibit the shift in emphasis advocated by Beisaw, break the grip of the "pots equal people" equation, and build upon important criticisms of standard archaeological interpretations of Susquehannock culture history offered by Swartz (1985). Jasmin Gollup (2011) provides an important and sobering overview of the contexts of the ceramics used to document and support the existence of a "proto-Susquehannock" social group who lived in small hamlets in the upper Susquehanna Valley and then amalgamated to begin their rampage down the Susquehanna River Valley en route to Washington Boro. The available archaeological data generally have little or no context, the ceramic descriptions and classifications are unclear, and the constituent sites, although numerous, contain multiple Late Woodland occupations with a perplexing hodge-podge of co-occurring ceramic varieties. Gollup wisely does not presume to try to make sense of the situation using the presently available data. Others would have been wise to make the same decision.

Lisa Lauria (2012) and Alisa Strauss (2000) also provide new and complementary perspectives on Susquehannock ceramics using collections from classic Susquehannock sites in the Washington Boro area. Strauss studied attributes of Susquehannock pottery vessel form and function. Lauria studied vessel surface treatment and design element attributes related to the social contexts of Susquehannock vessel use and production. Both studies show that attribute analysis yields additional insights to Susquehannock culture that are not available from Kinsey's (1959) traditional culture historical typologies. Both studies also apply rigorous analytical methods to a large sample of vessels and sherds; Lauria (2012:49) studied 1885 sherds and vessels.

Lauria's study is of special interest because it demonstrates the problems that have arisen within Susquehannock studies by conflating a historically defined ethnic group with an "archaeological taxon" created by archaeologists. "These are separate but frequently conflated categories, neither of which should be understood as equal to any prehistoric reality" (Lauria 2012:43–44). She introduces the idea of colonialism's creation of knowledge by noting that this conflation acts "to reify" the colonial construction of Susquehannock culture, but does not pursue the notion any further. Lauria provides numerous interesting and important new insights to Susquehannock studies, including her novel perspective on the trope of acculturation and alleged cultural degeneration. In an enlightening argument well supported by her own data and that of Strauss, Lauria (2012:55–57, 65–68) states that a model of "cultural entanglement" of the Susquehannocks and European society and its trade goods is more useful than the standard model of degenerative acculturation and cultural loss. Her data, and that of Strauss, indicate that Susquehannock potters adapted their production methods and products to accommodate change in order to maintain their traditional social organizations, promote internal social equality, and strengthen kinship links within and among matrilineages. Ceramics were transformed for new functions and symbolic uses (Lauria 2012:6) and the Susquehannocks did not abandon or "lose" their traditional technologies (White 2001). This viewpoint clearly subverts much of the colonial discourse that pervades traditional Susquehannock studies.

All of the studies noted above suggest future research problems including more detailed contextual analysis of ceramic variation and explicit consideration of the effects of Susquehannock lineage organizations on material culture. My suggestions for future studies are: (1) abandon the notion of a Susquehannock "invasion," view the Susquehannock movement into the Lower Susquehanna Valley as a "migration," and then apply the concepts of archaeological studies of migrations as complex and variable social and cultural events (Anthony 1990; Rouse 1986); (2) follow Lauria's research methods and abandon the idea that the presence of Susquehannock pottery at sites outside the core area of Susquehannock habitation *must* indicate the presence of Susquehannock people, and examine the regional distributions of attributes such as vessel collars, plats of incised linear decorations, effigy faces, and design grammars (Custer 1987; Denny 2001; Griffith and Custer 1985); and (3) explore the possibilities and implications of a "non-unitary" Susquehannock social entity consisting of numerous contemporaneous affiliated communities.

In conclusion, I hope this chapter promotes the idea that archaeologists working in the Middle Atlantic must come to terms with the colonial legacy of all of our research for *all* time periods. Susquehannock studies are simply the easiest place to start. Perhaps this detection, and consequent realization of its effects, will create an atmosphere where we will recognize the complexity of the archaeological record that is currently obscured by colonial approaches.

ACKNOWLEDGMENTS

I thank Russ Handsman for generously allowing me to make use of his unpublished manuscript and Lisa Lauria, Andrew Wyatt, and Jasmin Gollup for providing copies of their research manuscripts. Last, but never least, I thank my wife, Sharon, for enduring my absorption with the writing of this chapter.

REFERENCES CITED

Abler, Thomas S.
  1980   Iroquois Cannibalism: Fact Not Fiction. *Ethnohistory* 27(4):309–16.

Andreopoulos, George
  1994   *Genocide: Conceptual and Historical Dimensions*. University of Pennsylvania Press, Philadelphia.

Anonymous
  1941   Veto Susquehannock Bill: No Susquehannocks Left. *Pennsylvania Archaeologist* 11(4):86–87.

Anthony, David W.
  1990   Migration in Archaeology: The Baby in the Bathwater. *American Anthropologist* 92:895–914.

Arens, William
  1979   *The Man-Eating Myth: Anthropology and Anthropophagy*. Oxford University Press, New York.

Asad, Talal (editor)
  1973   *Anthropology and the Colonial Encounter*. Ithaca Press, London.

Ashcroft, Bill, Gareth Griffiths, and Helen Tiffin
  1995   *The Post-Colonial Studies Reader*. Routledge, New York.

Barthes, Roland
  1972   *Mythologies*. Translated by Annette Lavers. Noonday Press, New York.

Bean, Theodore W.
  1884   *History of Montgomery County, Pennsylvania*. Everts and Peck, Philadelphia, PA.

Beisaw, April M.
  2010   Memory, Identity, and NAGPRA in the Northeastern United States. *American Anthropologist* 112(2):244–56.

Benedict, Ruth
  1934   *Patterns of Culture*. Houghton-Mifflin, New York.

Blanton, Dennis R., and Julia A. King
  2004 *Indians and European Contact in Context: The Mid-Atlantic Region.* University Press of Florida, Gainesville.

Boza Arlotti, Ana Maria
  1997 Evolution of the Social Organization of the Susquehannock Society during the Contact Period in South Central Pennsylvania. PhD dissertation, University of Pittsburgh.

Bragdon, Kathleen J.
  2001 *The Columbia Guide to American Indians of the Northeast.* Columbia University Press, New York.

Brashler, Janet
  1987 A Middle 16th Century Susquehannock Village in Hampshire County, West Virginia. *West Virginia Archaeologist* 39(2):1–30.

Brett, Perry, and Jay F. Custer
  2011 Description and Analysis of Decorated Riggins Late Woodland Ceramic Sherds from the Ware Site, Salem County, New Jersey. *Journal of Middle Atlantic Archaeology* 27:29–53.

Burger, Julian
  2013 Indigenous Peoples in the Commonwealth Countries: The Legacy of the Past and Present-day Struggles for Self-determination. *The Round Table* 102(4):333–42.

Cadzow, Donald A.
  1934 Petroglyphs (Rock Carvings) in the Susquehanna River near Safe Harbor, Pennsylvania. Safe Harbor Report No. 1, Pennsylvania Historical and Museum Commission, Harrisburg.
  1936 Archaeological Studies of the Susquehannock Indians of Pennsylvania. Safe Harbor Report No. 2, Pennsylvania Historical and Museum Commission, Harrisburg.

Carmer, Carl
  1955 *The Susquehanna.* Rivers of America Series, Holt, Rinehart, and Winston, New York.

Casselberry, Samuel E.
  1971 The Schultz-Funk Site (36LA7): Its Role in the Culture History of the Susquehannock and Shenks Ferry Indians. PhD dissertation, Pennsylvania State University, University Park.

Castenada, Quetzil E.
  1996 *In the Museum of Maya Culture: Touring Chichen Itza.* University of Minnesota Press, Minneapolis.

Catts, Wade P.
  1988 Slaves, Free Blacks, and French Negroes: An Archaeological and Historical Perspective of Wilmington's Forgotten Folk. MA thesis, University of Delaware, Newark.

Churchill, Ward
   1994   *Indians Are Us: Culture and Genocide in Native North America.* Common
          Courage Press, Monroe, ME.
   1996   *From a Native Son: Selected Essays on Indigenism, 1985–1995.* South End
          Press, Boston, MA.
   1997   *A Little Matter of Genocide: Holocaust and Denial in the Americas 1492 to the
          Present.* City Light Books, San Francisco.
   1998   *Fantasies of the Master Race: Literature, Cinema, and the Colonization of Ameri-
          can Indians.* City Light Books, San Francisco.
   2000   Review of "Man Corn" by Christy Turner and Jacqueline Turner. *North
          American Archaeologist* 21(3):268–88.

Colewell-Chanthaphohn, Chip, and Jami Powell
   2012   Repatriation and Constructs of Identity. *Journal of Anthropological Research*
          68:191–222.

Cook-Lynn, Elizabeth
   2007   *New Indians, Old Wars.* University of Illinois Press, Urbana.

Custer, Jay F.
   1983   Quantitative Analysis of Shenks Ferry and Susquehannock Projectile
          Points: Testing the Interethnic Variability of Stone Tools. University of
          Delaware Center for Archaeological Research Report No. 1, Newark.
   1984   *Delaware Prehistoric Archaeology: An Ecological Approach.* University of Dela-
          ware Press, Newark.
   1985   Analysis of Grave Good Assemblages from the Strickler Site, A Contact
          Period Susquehannock Site in Lancaster County, Pennsylvania. *Journal of
          Middle Atlantic Archaeology* 1:33–43.
   1987   Late Woodland Ceramics and Social Boundaries in Southeastern Penn-
          sylvania and Northern Delaware. *Archaeology of Eastern North America*
          15:13–28.
   1989   *Prehistoric Cultures of the Delmarva Peninsula: An Archaeological Study.* Uni-
          versity of Delaware Press, Newark.
   1995   Pennsylvania Profile No. 12: An Unusual Indian Land Claim from Lan-
          caster County. *Pennsylvania Archaeologist* 65(2):41–48.
   1996   Prehistoric Cultures of Eastern Pennsylvania. Pennsylvania Historical
          and Museum Commission Anthropological Series No. 7. Harrisburg.
   2001   Classification Guide for Arrowheads and Spearpoints of Eastern Penn-
          sylvania and the Central Middle Atlantic. Pennsylvania Historical and
          Museum Commission, Harrisburg.
   2005a Ethics and the Hyperreality of the Archaeological Thought World. *North
          American Archaeologist* 26(1):2–28.
   2005b The Perils of Apostasy. *North American Archaeologist* 26(1):199–37.
   n.d.   Analysis of Late Woodland and Contact Period Triangular Projectile
          Points from the Central Middle Atlantic Region. (In preparation.)

Custer, Jay F. (editor)
   1986   *Late Woodland Cultures of the Middle Atlantic Region.* University of Dela-
          ware Press, Newark.

Custer, Jay F., Keith R. Doms, Adrienne Allegretti, and Kristen Walker
  1998 Preliminary Report on Excavations at 7NC-E-60, New Castle County, Delaware. *Bulletin of the Archaeological Society of Delaware* 35:3–27.

Custer, Jay F., and Scott C. Watson
  1985 Archaeological Investigations at 7NC-E-42, A Contact Period Site in New Castle County, Delaware. *Journal of Middle Atlantic Archaeology* 1:97–116.

Deloria, Vine
  1970 *Custer Died for Your Sins.* University of Oklahoma Press, Norman.
  1997a *Red Earth, White Lies: Native Americans and the Myth of Scientific Fact.* Fulcrum Publishers, Golden, CO.
  1997b Conclusion: Anthros, Indians, and Planetary Reality. In *Indians and Anthropologists: Vine Deloria and the Critique of Anthropology,* edited by Thomas Biolsi and Larry J. Zimmerman, pp. 209–22. University of Arizona Press, Tucson.
  2001 Research, Redskins, and Reality. In *American Nations:Encounters in Indian Country,* edited by Frederick E. Hoxie, Peter Mancall, and James H. Merrell, pp. 458–67. Routledge, New York.

Denny, Peter
  2001 Symmetry Analysis of Ceramic Designs and Iroquoian-Algonquian Interactions. In *A Collection of Papers Presented at the 33rd Annual Meeting of the Canadian Archaeological Association,* edited by Jean-Luc Pilon et al., pp. 128–45. Ontario Archaeological Society, Toronto.

Den Ouden, Amy E.
  2005 *Beyond Conquest: Native Peoples and the Struggle for History in New England.* University of Nebraska Press, Lincoln.
  2007 Locating the Cannibals: Conquest, North American Ethnohistory, and the Threat of Objectivity. *History and Anthropology* 18(2):101–33.

Desai, Gaurav, and Supriya Nair
  2005 *Postcolonialisms: An Anthology of Cultural Theory and Criticism.* Rutgers University Press, New Brunswick, NJ.

Dippie, Brian
  1991 *The Vanishing American: White Attitudes and U.S. Indian Policy.* University of Kansas Press, Lawrence.

Donehoo, George P.
  1925 *Harrisburg and Dauphin County: A Sketch of the History for the Past Twenty-Five Years, 1900–1925.* National Historical Association, Dayton, OH.

Dragoo, Don W.
  1960 Review of "Susquehannock Miscellany" by John Witthoft and W. Fred Kinsey. *American Antiquity* 26(1):131–32.

Elie, Serge D.
  2012 The Production of Social Science Knowledge beyond Occidentalism: The Quest for a Post-exotic Anthropology. *Third World Quarterly.* 33(7):1211–29.

Ellis, F., and S. Evans
  1883   *History of Lancaster County.* Everts and Peck, Philadelphia, PA.

Engelbrecht, William
  2003   *Iroquoia: The Development of a Native World.* Syracuse University Press, Syracuse, NY.

Eshleman, H. Frank
  1908   *Lancaster County Indians: Annals of the Susquehannocks and other Indian Tribes of the Susquehanna Territory from about the Year 1500 to 1763, the Date of Their Extinction.* New Era Press, Lancaster. (Reprinted by Wennawoods Publishing, Lewisburg, Pennsylvania, 2000.)

Fanon, Frantz
  1963   *The Wretched of the Earth.* Grove Press, New York.

Farrand, Livingston
  1904   *The American Nation: A History, Volume II, Basis of American History, 1500–1900.* Harper and Brothers, New York.

Fenton, William. N.
  1960   Review of "Susquehannock Miscellany" by John Witthoft and W. Fred Kinsey. *The Pennsylvania Magazine of History and Biography* 84(2):257–58.
  1978   Northern Iroquoian Culture Patterns. In *Handbook of North American Indians, Vol. 15: Northeast,* edited by Bruce Trigger, pp. 296–321. Smithsonian Institution, Washington, DC.

Footner, Hulbert
  1944   *Rivers of the Eastern Shore: Seventeen Maryland Rivers.* Rivers of America Series, Holt, Rinehart, and Winston, New York.

Forks of the Delaware Chapter 14
  1980   The Overpeck Site (36BU5). *Pennsylvania Archaeologist* 50(3):1–46.

Four Arrows (Wahinkpe Topa, aka Don Trent Jacobs) (editor)
  2006   *Unlearning the Language of Conquest: Scholars Expose Anti-Indianism in America.* University of Texas Press, Austin.

Fredoso, Alfredo J. (translator)
  2009   *The Summa Theologica of Saint Thomas Aquinas.* St. Augustine's Press, South Bend, IN.

Freire, Paulo
  1970   *Pedagogy of the Oppressed.* Continuum Press, New York.

Fuchs, Eckhardt, and Marcus Otto (eds.)
  2013   Postcolonial Memory Politics in Educational Media. *Special Issue of Journal of Educational Media, Memory, and Society* 5(1).

Gallivan, Martin
  2004   Reconnecting the Contact Period and Late Prehistory: Household and Community Dynamics in the James River Basin. In *Indians and European*

Contact in Context: The Mid-Atlantic Region, edited by Dennis R. Blanton and Julia A. King, pp. 22–46. University Press of Florida, Gainesville.
2011 The Archaeology of Native Societies in the Chesapeake: New Investigations and Interpretations. *Journal of Archaeological Research* 19(3):261–325.

Geertz, Clifford
1984 Distinguished Lecture: Anti Anti-Relativism. *American Anthropologist* 86(2):263–78.

Gellner, Ernest
1985 *Relativism and the Social Sciences.* Cambridge University Press, New York.

Gleach, Frederic
1997 *Powhatan's World and Colonial Virginia: A Conflict of Cultures.* University of Nebraska Press, Lincoln.

Gollup, Jasmine
2011 An Overview and Analysis of "Proto-Susquehannock" Sites in the Upper Susquehanna Valley. MA thesis, Cornell University, Ithaca, NY.

Gould, S. J.
1992 Dinosaurs in the Haystack. *Natural History* March 1992:2–13.

Graeff, Arthur D.
1953 *The Keystone State: Geography, History, Government.* John C. Winston, Philadelphia, PA.

Graybill, Jeffrey R.
1989 The Shenks Ferry Complex Revisited. In *New Approaches to Other Paths,* edited by W. Fred Kinsey and Roger Moeller, pp. 51–60. Archaeological Services, Bethlehem, CT.

Griffin, James B.
1937 Review of "Archaeological Studies of the Susquehannock Indians of Pennsylvania" by Donald A. Cadzow. *American Antiquity* 3(1):96–99.

Griffith, Daniel R., and Jay F. Custer
1985 Late Woodland Ceramics of Delaware: Implications for the Late Prehistoric Archaeology of Northeastern North America. *Pennsylvania Archaeologist* 55(1):5–20.

Grummet, Robert
1995 *Historic Contact: Indian People and Colonists in Today's Northeastern United States in the Sixteenth through Eighteenth Centuries.* University of Oklahoma Press, Norman.

Guilday, John E., and Paul Parmalee
1965 Animal Remains from the Sheep Rock Shelter (36Hu1), Huntingdon County, Pennsylvania. *Pennsylvania Archaeologist* 35(1):34–49.

Guilday, John E., Paul W. Parmalee, and Donald P. Tanner
1962 Aboriginal Butchering Techniques at the Eschelman Site (36LA12), Lancaster County, Pennsylvania. *Pennsylvania Archaeologist* 32(2):59–83.

Hallowell, A. Irving
   1946   Intelligence of Northeastern Indians. Reprinted in American Museum
           Sourcebooks in Anthropology, Q3 – *Culture and Personality: Readings in
           Psychological Anthropology,* edited by Robert Hunt, pp. 49–55. American
           Museum of Natural History, New York. (Originally included in *Culture
           and Experience,* University of Pennsylvania Press, Philadelphia.)

Handsman, Russell G.
   1987   The Sociopolitics of Susquehannock Archaeology. Paper presented at the
           1987 Middle Atlantic Archaeological Conference, Franklin and Marshall
           College, Lancaster, Pennsylvania. (Manuscript on file at the University
           of Delaware Center for Archaeological Research.)

Handsman, Russell G., and Trudy L. Richmond
   1995   Confronting Colonialism: The Mahican and Schaghicoke Peoples and
           Us. In *Making Alternative Histories: The Practice of Archaeology and History,*
           edited by Peter R. Schmidt and Thomas C. Patterson, pp. 87–118. School
           of American Research, Santa Fe, NM.

Harris, Marvin
   1968   *The Rise of Anthropological Theory.* Thomas Crowell, New York.

Hart, John P., and Hetty Jo Brumbach
   2003   The Death of Owasco. *American Antiquity* 68(4): 737–52.

Heike, Paul
   2013   *The Myths that Made America: An Introduction to American Studies.* Colum-
           bia University Press, New York.

Heisey, Henry
   1971   An Interpretation of Shenks Ferry Ceramics. *Pennsylvania Archaeologist*
           41(4):44–68.

Heisey, Henry, and J. Paul Witmer
   1964   The Shenks Ferry People: A Site and Some Generalities. *Pennsylvania
           Archaeologist* 34(1):8–34.

Heite, Edward F., and Cara L. Blume
   2003   Mitsawokett to Bloomsbury: Archaeology and History of an Unrecog-
           nized Indigenous Community in Central Delaware, Delaware Depart-
           ment of Transportation Archaeological Series No. 154. Dover.

Herrero, Dolores, and Sonia Baelo-Allue (eds.)
   2011   The Splintered Glass: Facets of Trauma in the Post-Colony and Beyond.
           Cross/Cultures 136, Rodopi, NY.

Herskovitz, Mellville J.
   1972   *Cultural Relativism: Perspectives in Cultural Pluralism.* Vintage Books, New
           York.

Hodge, Frederick W.
   1910   Handbook of Indians North of Mexico. Bureau of American Ethnology
           30, Parts 1 and 2. Smithsonian Institution, Washington, DC.

Holzinger, Charles H.
   1961   Some Observation on the Persistence of Aboriginal Cherokee Personal-
          ity Traits. In Symposium on Cherokee and Iroquois Culture, Bureau of
          American Ethnology Bulletin 180, edited by William N. Fenton and John
          Gulick, pp. 227–38. Smithsonian Institution, Washington, DC.

Horvath, Ronald J.
   1972   A Definition of Colonialism. *Current Anthropology* 13(1):45–57.

Howard, R. Smoker
   2003   The Chronological Placement of the Hershey Site on a Dynamic Sociocul-
          tural Landscape. *Pennsylvania Archaeologist* 73(2):19–33.

Hoxie, Frederick E.
   2008   Retrieving the Red Continent: Settler Colonialism and the History of
          American Indians in the US. *Ethnic and Racial Studies* 31(6):1153–67.

Hughes, Richard T.
   2003   *Myths America Lives By*. University of Illinois Press, Urbana.

Humpf, Dorothy A., and James W. Hatch
   1994   Susquehannock Demography: A New Perspective on the Contact Period
          in Pennsylvania. In Proceedings of the 1992 People to People Conference:
          Selected Papers, Research Division, Rochester Museum and Science Ser-
          vice, Research Records No. 23, pp. 65–76. Rochester, NY.

Hunt, Robert C.
   2007   *Beyond Relativism: Rethinking Comparability in Cultural Anthropology*.
          AltaMira Press, Lanham, MD.

Hunter, Charles E.
   1983   A Susquehanna Indian Town on the Schuylkill. *Pennsylvania Archaeolo-
          gist* 53(3):17–19.

Hunter, William A.
   1959   The Historic Role of the Susquehannocks. In *Susquehannock Miscellany*,
          edited by John Witthoft and W. Fred Kinsey, pp. 8–18. Pennsylvania
          Historical and Museum Commission, Harrisburg.

Jennings, Francis
   1966   The Indian Trade of the Susquehanna Valley. *Proceedings of the American
          Philosophical Society* 110(6):406–24.
   1968   Glory, Death, and Transfiguration: The Susquehannock Indians in the
          Seventeenth Century. *Proceedings of the American Philosophical Society*
          112(1):15–53.
   1978   Susquehannocks. In *Handbook of North American Indians, Vol. 15: North-
          east*, edited by Bruce Trigger, pp. 362–67. Smithsonian Institution, Wash-
          ington, DC.
   1984   *The Ambiguous Iroquois Empire: The Covenant Chain Confederation of Indian
          Tribes with English Colonies*. W. W. Norton, NY.

Kent, Barry C.
   1984   Susquehanna's Indians. Pennsylvania Historical and Museum Commission Anthropological Series No. 6. Harrisburg.

King, Julia A., and Edward E. Chaney
   2004   Did the Chesapeake English Have a Contact Period? In *Indians and European Contact in Context: The Mid-Atlantic Region*, edited by Dennis R. Blanton and Julia A. King, pp. 193–221. University Press of Florida, Gainesville.

Kinsey, W. Fred
   1957   A Susquehannock Longhouse. *American Antiquity* 20(3):180–81.
   1959   Historic Susquehannock Pottery. In *Susquehannock Miscellany*, edited by John Witthoft and W. Fred Kinsey, pp. 61–98. Pennsylvania Historical and Museum Commission, Harrisburg.
   1977   *Lower Susquehanna Prehistoric Indians*. Science Press, Ephrata, PA.

Kinsey, W. Fred, and Jeffrey Graybill
   1971   The Murry Site and its Role in Lancaster and Funk Phases of Shenks Ferry Culture. *Pennsylvania Archaeologist* 41(4):7–43.

Kroeber, Alfred L.
   1938   *Cultural and Natural Areas of Native North America*. University of California Press, Berkeley.

Krogman, Wilton M.
   1962   *The Human Skeleton in Forensic Medicine*. Charles C. Thomas, New York.

Langer, Lawrence
   1998   *Pre-empting the Holocaust*. Yale University Press, New Haven, CT.

Lauria, Lisa M.
   2004   Mythical Giants of the Chesapeake: An Evaluation of the Archaeological Construction of "Susquehannock." *Journal of Middle Atlantic Archaeology* 20:21–28.
   2012   Defining Susquehannock: People and Ceramics in the Lower Susquehanna River Valley. AD 1575 to 1690. PhD dissertation, University of Virginia, Charlottesville.

Lee, Richard B.
   2006   Twenty-first Century Indigenism. *Anthropological Theory* 6(4):455–79.
      Liebmann, Matthew, and Uzma Rizvi
   2008   *Archaeology and the Postcolonial Critique*. AltaMira Press, Rowman & Littlefield, Lanham, MD.

Linton, Ralph
   1945   The Cultural Background of Personality. Century Psychology Series, Appleton-Century-Crofts, New York.

Loomba, Ania
   1998   *Colonialism/Postcolonialism: The New Critical Idiom*. Routledge, New York.

Lucy, Charles L.
  1950   Notes on a Small Andaste Burial Site and Andaste Archaeology. *Pennsylvania Archaeologist* 20:55–62.
  1952   An Upper Susquehanna Mixed Site. *Pennsylvania Archaeologist* 22:95–97.
  1959   Pottery Types of the Upper Susquehanna. *Pennsylvania Archaeologist* 29:28–37.

Lyman, R. Lee, and Michael J. O'Brien
  2001   The Direct Historical Approach, Analogical Reasoning, and Theory in Americanist Archaeology. *Journal of Archaeological Method and Theory* 8(4):303–42.

Lyman, R. Lee, Michael J. O'Brien, and Robert C. Dunnell
  1997   *The Rise and Fall of Culture History.* Plenum Press, New York.

Lyndon, Jane, and Uzma Z. Rizvi (editors)
  2010   *Handbook of Postcolonial Archaeology.* Left Coast Press, Walnut Creek, CA.

Maddison, Sarah
  2013   Indigenous Identity, "Authenticity" and the Structural Violence of Settler Colonialism. *Identities: Global Studies in Culture and Power* 20(3):288–303.

MacCord, Howard
  1952   The Susquehannock Indians in West Virginia. *West Virginia History* 13(4):239–53.

MacGillivray, Joseph A.
  2000   *Minotaur: Sir Arthur Evans and the Archaeology of the Minoan Myth.* Hill and Wang, New York.

MacNeish, Richard S.
  1952a Iroquois Pottery Types. *National Museum of Canada Bulletin* 124. Ottawa.
  1952b The Archaeology of the Northeastern United States. In *Archaeology of Eastern United States,* edited by James B. Griffin, pp. 46–58. University of Chicago Press, Chicago.
  1976   The *In Situ* Iroquois Revisited and Rethought. In *Culture Change and Continuity: Essays in Honor of James Bennett Griffin,* edited by Charles E. Cleland, pp. 79–98. Academic Press, New York.
  1980   Iroquois Pottery Types 32 Years Later. Proceedings of the 1979 Iroquois Pottery Conference, Research Records No. 13, Rochester Museum and Science Center, pp. 1–8. Rochester, NY.

Manuel, George, and Michael Posluns
  1974   *The Fourth World: An Indian Reality.* Free Press, New York.

McCartney, Martha W.
  2004   Last Refuge: Tribal Reserves in Eastern Virginia. In *Indians and European Contact in Context: The Mid-Atlantic Region,* edited by Dennis R. Blanton and Julia A. King, pp. 222–43. University Press of Florida, Gainesville.

McNiven, Ian J., and Lynette Russell
  2005 *Appropriated Pasts: Indigenous Peoples and the Colonial Culture of Archaeology.* AltaMira Press, Rowman & Littlefield, Lanham, MD.

Merrell, James H.
  1999 *Into the American Woods: Negotiators on the Pennsylvania Frontier.* W. W. Norton and Company, New York.

Michener, James A.
  1978 *Chesapeake.* Random House, New York.

Mihesuah, Devon Abbott
  1997 *American Indians: Stereotypes and Realities.* Clarity Press, Atlanta, GA.

Mombert, R.
  1869 *An Authentic History of Lancaster County.* J. E. Barr and Company, Lancaster, PA.

Murphy, Raymond E., and Marion Murphy
  1937 *Pennsylvania: A Regional Geography.* Pennsylvania Book Service, Harrisburg, PA.

Nabokov, Peter, and Robert Easton
  1989 *Native American Architecture.* Oxford University Press, New York.

Niemczycki, Mary Ann Palmer
  1984 The Origin and Development of the Seneca and Cayuga Tribes of New York State. Research Division, Rochester Museum and Science Service, Research Records No. 17. Rochester, NY.

Osterhammel, Jurgen
  1995 *Colonialism: A Theoretical Overview.* Markus Wiener Publishers, Princeton, NJ.

Parker, Arthur C.
  1916 The Origin of the Iroquois as Suggested by Their Archaeology. *American Anthropologist* 18:479–507.

Parkman, Francis
  1963 *The Jesuits in North America.* Little, Brown, Boston, MA.

Potter, Stephen R.
  1993 *Commoners, Tribute, and Chiefs: The Development of Algonquian Culture in the Potomac Valley.* University of Virginia Press, Charlottesville.

Ray, Robert B.
  1985 *A Certain Tendency of the Hollywood Cinema, 1930–1980.* Princeton University Press, Princeton, NJ.

Richter, Daniel K.
  2005 *Native Americans' Pennsylvania.* Pennsylvania Historical Association, University Park, PA.

Ritchie, William A.
  1960   Review of "Susquehannock Miscellany" by John Witthoft and W. Fred
         Kinsey. *American Anthropologist* 62(4):727–28.

Regi, Tamas
  2013   The Concept of the Primitive in Texts and Images. *Journeys* 14(1):40–67.

Robinson, W. S.
  1987   *Early American Indian Documents, Volume 6.* University Press of America,
         Lanham, MD.

Rountree, Helen C.
  1989   *The Powhatan Indians of Virginia: Their Traditional Culture.* University of
         Oklahoma Press, Norman.
  1990   *Pocahontas's People: The Powhatan Indians of Virginia through Four Centu-
         ries.* University of Oklahoma Press, Norman.

Rountree, Helen C., and Thomas E. Davidson
  1997   *Eastern Shore Indians of Virginia and Maryland.* University of Virginia
         Press, Charlottesville.

Rountree, Helen C., and E. Randolph Turner
  2002   *Before and After Jamestown: Virginia's Powhatans and Their Predecessors.*
         University Press of Florida, Gainesville.

Rouse, Irving B.
  1939   Prehistory in Haiti: A Study in Method. *Yale University Publications in
         Anthropology* No. 21. New Haven, CT.
  1953   The Strategy of Culture History. In *Anthropology Today*, edited by A. L.
         Kroeber, pp. 75–76. University of Chicago Press, Chicago.
  1965   The Place of "Peoples" in Prehistoric Research. *Journal of the Royal An-
         thropological Institute* 95:1–15.
  1986   *Migrations in Prehistory: Inferring Population Movement from Cultural Re-
         mains.* Yale University Press, New Haven, CT.

Said, Edward
  1979   *Orientalism.* Vintage Books, New York.
  1993   *Culture and Imperialism.* Vintage Books, New York.

Schulenberg, Janet, Jaimin Weets, and Peter van Rossum
  2003   The Hershey Site: An Update. *Pennsylvania Archaeologist* 73(2):2–18.

Skinner, Alanson B.
  1938   The Andaste. In A *Report of the Susquehanna River Expedition*, edited by
         Warren K. Moorehead, pp. 45–67. Andover Press, Andover, MA.

Slotkin, Richard
  1973   *Regeneration through Violence: The Mythology of the American Frontier,
         1600–1860.* HarperCollins, New York.
  1985   *The Fatal Environment: The Myth of the Frontier in the Age of Industrializa-
         tion, 1800–1890.* Atheneum, NY.

1992 *Gunfighter Nation: The Myth of the Frontier in Twentieth-Century America.* HarperCollins, New York.

Smith, Ira F., and Jeffrey Graybill
1977 A Report on the Shenks Ferry and Susquehannock Components at the Funk Site, Lancaster County, Pennsylvania. *Man in the Northeast* 13:45–64. (Journal has been retitled *Northeast Anthropology* and is often indexed under the new title.)

Sorg, David J.
2004 Lost Tribes of the Susquehanna. *Pennsylvania Archaeologist* 74(2):63–72.

Spiro, Melford E.
1986 Cultural Relativism and the Future of Anthropology. *Cultural Anthropology* 1(3):259–86.

Steinman, Erich
2012 Settler Colonial Power and the American Indian Sovereignty Movement: Forms of Domination, Strategies of Transformation. *American Journal of Sociology* 117(4):1073–1130.

Stewart, R. Michael
1999 The Indian Town of Playwicki. *Journal of Middle Atlantic Archaeology* 15:35–54.
2014 American Indian Archaeology of the Historic Period in the Delaware Valley. In *Historical Archaeology of the Delaware Valley*, edited by Richard Veit and David Orr, pp. 1–48. University of Tennessee Press, Knoxville.

Stranahan, Susan Q.
1993 *Susquehanna, River of Dreams.* Johns Hopkins University Press, Baltimore, MD.

Strauss, Alisa N.
2000 Iroquoian Food Techniques and Technologies: An Examination of Susquehannock Vessel Form and Function. PhD dissertation, Pennsylvania State University, State College.

Swanton, John R.
1952 Indian Tribes of North America. *Bureau of American Ethnology Bulletin* 145. Smithsonian Institution, Washington, DC.

Swartz, Deborah
1985 A Reevaluation of the Late Woodland Cultural Relationships in the Susquehanna Valley in Pennsylvania. *Man in the Northeast* 29:29–54. (Journal has been retitled *Northeast Anthropology* and is often indexed under the new title.)

Tooker, Elizabeth
1984 The Demise of the Susquehannocks: A 17th Century Mystery. *Pennsylvania Archaeologist* 54(3–4):1–10.

Trigger, Bruce G.
  1978   Iroquois Matriliny. *Pennsylvania Archaeologist* 48(1–2):55–65.
  2006   *A History of Archaeological Thought* (2d ed.). Cambridge University Press, New York.

Vaillant, George C.
  1939   *Indian Arts in North America.* Harper, New York.

Wall, Robert D.
  2001   Late Woodland Ceramics and Native Populations of the Upper Potomac Valley. *Journal of Middle Atlantic Archaeology* 17:15–37.

Wall, Robert, and Heather Lapham
  2003   Material Culture of the Contact Period in the Upper Potomac Valley: Chronological and Cultural Implications. *Archaeology of Eastern North America* 31:151–77.

Wallace, Anthony F. C.
  1951   Some Psychological Determinants of Culture Change in an Iroquois Community. In Symposium on Local Diversity in Iroquois Culture, Bureau of American Ethnology Bulletin 149, edited by William N. Fenton, pp. 55–76. Smithsonian Institution, Washington, DC.
  1961   *Culture and Personality.* Random House, New York.

Wallower, Lucille
  1965   *Indians of Pennsylvania.* Penns Valley Publisher, State College, PA.

Walton, Priscilla L.
  2004   *Our Cannibals, Ourselves.* University of Illinois Press, Urbana.

Waselkov, Gregory A., Peter H. Wood, and Tom Hatley (editors)
  2006   *Powhatan's Mantle: Indians in the Colonial Southeast* (rev. and expanded ed.). University of Nebraska Press, Lincoln.

Webster, Gary
  1985   Susquehannock Animal Economy. *North American Archaeologist* 6:41–62.

Welsh, Herbert
  1890   The Indian Question Past and Present. *New England Magazine* N.S. 3:260–69.

Weslager, C. A.
  1960   Review of "Susquehannock Miscellany" by John Witthoft and W. Fred Kinsey. *Pennsylvania History*, 27(2):234–35.

White, Sharon
  2001   To Secure a Lasting Peace: A Diachronic Analysis of Seventeenth-Century Susquehannock Political and Economic Strategies. PhD dissertation, Pennsylvania State University, University Park.

Wilkins, Elwood S., and Ronald A. Thomas
  1997   A Summary of Excavation at 36CH3, White Clay Creek Valley, Chester County, Pennsylvania. *Bulletin of the Archaeological Society of Delaware* 34:1–25.

Willey, Gordon R.
   1953   A Pattern of Diffusion-Acculturation. *Southwestern Journal of Anthropology* 9(4):369–84.

Willey, Gordon R., and Jeremy A. Sabloff
   1980   *A History of American Archaeology* (2d ed.). W. H. Freeman, San Francisco.

Wilson, James
   1998   *The Earth Shall Weep: A History of Native America.* Atlantic Monthly Press, New York.

Wilson, Waziyatawin Angela, and Michael Yellow Bird (eds.)
   2005   *For Indigenous Eyes Only: A Decolonization Reader.* School of American Research, Santa Fe, NM.

Witthoft, John
   1953   The American Indian as Hunter, Reprints in Anthropology from the Pennsylvania Historical and Museum Commission, No. 6. Harrisburg. (Reprinted from *Pennsylvania Game News* 24[2, 3, 4].)
   1955   Notes and Reviews. *Pennsylvania Archaeologist* 25(1):76–79.
   1959   The Ancestry of the Susquehannocks. In *Susquehannock Miscellany,* edited by John Witthoft and W. Fred Kinsey, pp. 19–60. Pennsylvania Historical and Museum Commission, Harrisburg.

Witthoft, John, and Samuel S. Farver
   1952   Two Shenks Ferry Sites in Lebanon County, Pennsylvania. *Pennsylvania Archaeologist* 22(1):3–32.

Witthoft, John, and W. Fred Kinsey (eds.)
   1959   *Susquehannock Miscellany.* Pennsylvania Historical and Museum Commission, Harrisburg.

Witthoft, John, W. Fred Kinsey, and Charles H. Holzinger
   1959   A Susquehannock Cemetery: The Ibaugh Site. In *Susquehannock Miscellany,* edited by John Witthoft and W. Fred Kinsey, pp. 99–119. Pennsylvania Historical and Museum Commission, Harrisburg.

Wobst, H. Martin
   1978   The Archaeo-Ethnology of Hunter-Gatherers or the Tyranny of the Ethnographic Record in Archaeology. *American Antiquity* 43(2):303–09.

Wolf, Eric R.
   1982   *Europe and the People without History.* University of California Press, Berkeley.

Wren, Christopher
   1914   *A Study of North Appalachian Indian Pottery.* (E. B. Yordy Company, Wilkes-Barre, Pennsylvania. Republished from Vol. XIII, *Proceedings of the Wyoming Historical and Geological Society.*)

Wyatt, Andrew, et al.
   2011   Phase III Archaeological Data Recovery Investigations at 36CU194, Proposed Norfolk Southern Railway Company Rail Connector Project,

Memorial Park, Borough of Lemoyne, Cumberland County, Pennsylvania. McCormick Taylor Inc., Harrisburg, Pennsylvania. Report on file at the Pennsylvania Historical and Museum Commission (ER# 05-2703-041).

Ziff, Bruce, and Pratima V. Rao (eds.)
1997 *Borrowed Power: Essays on Cultural Appropriation.* Rutgers University Press, New Brunswick, NJ.

16

✛

In Defense of Region

Middle Atlantica

Richard J. Dent

Almost all archaeology is regional. The articles that precede this chapter in the present volume can be read as clear evidence that the Middle Atlantic region is an authentic and practical research area in North American archaeology. There have, however, been whisperings over the years regarding the legitimacy of that notion. Some prefer to view the continent's Atlantic Coast as instead falling within just two established regions, the Southeast and Northeast. For example, the *Handbook of American Indians*, which has been dribbling out over the decades, divides what many consider to be the Middle Atlantic between the *Northeast* (1978) and yet to be released *Southeast* (forthcoming) volumes. Gordon Willey, in his landmark *Archaeology of North America* (1966) synthesis, chose not to recognize the Middle Atlantic, including it within much broader Eastern North America. More recently, Brian Fagan (1991) ignored most of regional archaeology altogether, instead focusing more on lifeways and then discussing just a handful of traditionally recognized regional areas. My purpose in this chapter is to make a further case for the legitimacy of the Middle Atlantic as an archaeological research focus in its own right. I want to begin to argue that such a region can be defended and that it has a long tradition of archaeologists treating it as a useful research focus. As caution, I am not so interested in arguing final exact boundaries. Boundaries in archaeological regions are always fuzzy and cases can be made for lines to be drawn differently. That will always be the case.

THE IDEA OF CULTURE AREAS

Anthropology, including archaeology, has had a long history of defining culture areas as a means of organizing and comparing data. In most cases the tact has been to establish culture areas as reflections of natural environmental zones that somehow influence cultural traditions. Clark Wissler (1928) argued for ten such areas within North America. Otis T. Mason had done so even before (1896). Perhaps the most well-known early effort was made by Alfred Kroeber (1939) with the publication of his *Culture and Natural Areas of Native North America*. In it he looked at the environmental relations of the native cultures of North America. This followed his previous attempt to do something similar for California. Others would follow.

In almost all instances there was an underlying assumption that culture reflected environment. The natural circumstances in which a native group found themselves were a key to defining culture areas. To Kroeber (1939:14) vegetation was the most useful determinate of cultural classification. And by extension, vegetation could be related to climate and associated fauna. Native traditions effectively became adaptations to all of the above, thus often establishing similar cultural traditions and technological adaptations within any given area. That area with a shared way of life then had an analytical utility to scholars. By extension, once culture areas were established, it was possible to examine historic relations through time within the area and between other areas. Echoing what I said earlier, anthropologists quickly realized that the weakest feature of any such mapping of cultural wholes quickly becomes conspicuous: the boundaries (Kroeber 1939:5). But that too is interesting. To foreshadow arguments to follow, it is interesting to note that Kroeber did define a "Middle Atlantic Slope area" (Kroeber 1939:101) within North America. William Henry Holmes (1897, 1903), Karl Schmidt (1952), and Robert Stephenson (1963) also argued early on for a Middle Atlantic archaeological area. Louis Brennan (2013) provides one of the few recent efforts to defend the Middle Atlantic as culture area.

Many attribute one of the first archaeological definitions of the Middle Atlantic region to the early research of William Henry Holmes (1897, 1903). That may be so, but probably only in the most general sense and as a coincidence of other research interests. Nonetheless, Holmes's Potomac-Chesapeake Tidewater Province did begin to approximate what we today call the Middle Atlantic (Holmes 1897; map as illustrated in Meltzer and Dunnell 1992:20), though slightly more constrained, especially along its western boundary. The province was instead bounded by the Fall Zone to the west, but did run north-south from New York State to North Carolina. All that aside, Holmes did much to draw attention to the fact that the region, however, it was defined, had an archaeological record and one that presented answers to questions that were vexing our interpretation of North American prehistory in his era. He also was to be applauded for going beyond the site or sites that were his immediate concern.

Karl Schmitt's (1952) posthumous article, in James B. Griffin's Green Bible (same date) makes one of the earlier explicit arguments for a Middle Atlantic Region. To Schmitt (1952:59) that region was contained within Virginia, Maryland, Pennsylvania, New Jersey, and Delaware: again, a bit more regionally constrained than at present. Nevertheless, he unambiguously refers to this as the Middle Atlantic area (Schmitt 1959:59), and goes on to say that it contained both Archaic and Woodland period remains. It did not allow for a Paleoindian period in that such an era was not yet completely recognized east of the Mississippi (see Dent 1995:50-52). The Archaic was seen as representing small scattered populations of hunters and gatherers, and the Woodland commenced with the introduction of pottery and eventually agriculture. It is important to note that he recognized so-called foreign influences from the Ohio Valley and New York State as well as from the South during the Woodland. In some ways, the importance of outside influences foreshadowed Brennan's (2013) more recent arguments for the definition of the region.

Robert Stephenson, at the end of his and Alice Ferguson's monograph on the Accokeek Creek site (1963:200–5), turned to the issue of the definition of what they called the "Middle Atlantic Seaboard Culture Province." It many ways it was defined on what they saw as a regional "cultural simplicity" affected by isolation from other groups in the Ohio and Mississippi valleys as well as those of the Southeast, in general. Within it they defined five foci, in the sense of the old Midwest Taxonomic System. Those foci again spanned from the Archaic into the Woodland period. They were also not shy about establishing boundaries. The foothills of the Blue Ridge Mountains were defined as its western boundary. That is an expansion from earlier approximations. It ran north-south from the Rappahannock River Valley to the south and ended to the north at the Palisades of the Hudson River. The Atlantic Ocean, of course, formed its eastern boundary (Stephenson and Ferguson 1963:202). All of Long Island was included within the area. In many ways that demarcation still approximates the ideas of many today recognizing a Middle Atlantic area. Some would argue the boundaries of the Middle Atlantic extend a bit further south (perhaps just into North Carolina) and likewise stretched somewhat further northward. I expect north-south extremes will always be open to debate given a lack of clear physiographic landmarks to define the extent of either.

In more recent time, the 1980s, Louis Brennan (through the efforts of Jack Hranicky that paper was finally published in 2013) again took up the issue of defining what Brennan called the "Middle Atlantic Region Cultural Province." Brennan (2013:24) saw the Middle Atlantic as an arterial system throughout which transferred certain cultural diagnostics. It is defined according to physiographic and environmental factors (Brennan 2013:24). It is interesting to note that Brennan believed no singular or salient cultural development ever took place within it (Brennan 2013:33). While that may or may not be true, I think the Middle Atlantic to Brennan was a place where ways of life, often developed elsewhere, were recast for new purposes and a new place—a legitimate culture area nonetheless. Brennan, like Stephenson and Ferguson (1963) before, was not shy in setting boundaries. The Blue Ridge to the west and the Atlantic Ocean to the east remained outer boundaries. While he does not much comment on a southern limit, he appears to accept the Rappahannock River Valley. Brennan does, however, based on his own research, argue the northern limits of the Middle Atlantic are to be set near the Hudson's Haverstraw Bay about 35 miles upstream from Manhattan Island.

MIDDLE ATLANTIC AS A NATURAL AREA

Past attempts to define study areas most often link those areas to definable natural or ecological zones. The acceptance of the Middle Atlantic as an archaeological region in part probably hinges on researchers seeing the region as a definable natural or ecological region within North America. I do not intend what follows to represent anywhere near an exhaustive recounting of the evidence in that regard, but instead a quick review of the arguments that can be made for the Middle Atlantic Region as ecologically distinct from its sister regions to the north (the Northeast) and south (the Southeast). I also presume that differences between the Middle Atlantic as well as the Northeast and Southeast of today mirror differences in the past. More exhaustive studies of localized long-term ecological change in parts of the Middle Atlantic can be found in Dent (1985), Dent (1995:69–96), and Carbone (1976). And there are other good examples.

Few contemporary researchers appear to dispute that the Blue Ridge Mountains represent the western boundary of the Middle Atlantic region. Those mountains represent the first significant elevation encountered as one moves back from the Coastal Plain and the Piedmont zones of the region. They represent a significant physical obstacle. The Blue Ridge sits on basement rock formed from magma overlain by granitic rock, sandstones, and sedimentary limestones. Some of the latter deposits have been subjected to further metamorphic transformative forces. Most believe the Blue Ridge was formed about 400 million years ago, and were later pushed even higher by tectonic activity around 350 million years ago. A good number of the chain's peaks exceed 5,000 feet in elevation.

For obvious reasons there is no doubt that the eastern edge of the Middle Atlantic is formed by the Atlantic Ocean. Given the Pleistocene marine regression followed by the Holocene transgression, it is safe to assume this was a shifting boundary over the last 10,000 years. Some early occupations are thus submarine, and one can make a case for the Island of Bermuda as being part of the Middle Atlantic. Given that post-Pleistocene marine transgression, a dominant landscape feature of the region consists of estuaries along the lower courses of its major rivers. Perhaps the Chesapeake Bay represents the premier such feature, but the Delaware Bay and the lower Hudson are likewise embayed. One ecologically defining feature of the Middle Atlantic region is certainly its rich estuaries and the prolific marine resources drawn to such protected habitat. If those creatures could adapt to the generally harsh conditions of estuaries they were able to establish themselves in great numbers. That fact was not lost on prehistoric and historic populations.

The southern boundary of the Middle Atlantic is less clear-cut. Vegetationally, the Southeastern Evergreen forest formation extends up to the west bank of the lower Chesapeake Bay (Braun 1950: Map of Forest Regions and Associations in Eastern North America). Likewise, the Oak-Pine Forest Association (Atlantic Slope Section) blankets much of the Middle Atlantic Inner Coastal Plain and Piedmont physiographic zones (Braun 1950: Map of Forest Regions and Associations in Eastern North America). It does transition into the Gulf Slope association, but not until reaching Georgia, further south than most would want to extend the Middle Atlantic. For these reasons, the southern boundary of the region will mainly be defined by archaeological or cultural similarities and thus will always be subject to debate.

A northern boundary is subject to the same difficulties, perhaps even trickier to define. Here two new forest associations extend down into the top of the Middle Atlantic. These include Braun's (1950; Map of Forest Regions and Associations in Eastern North America) Oak-Chestnut Forest Region, with two subdivisions. Those include her Piedmont and Glaciated sections. Using the latter, it would be possible to make a case for the Middle Atlantic extending to the north up into coastal as well as western Massachusetts. The former would take it up onto Cape Cod and even a bit northward. Again, the northern boundary of the Middle Atlantic will be a matter of identifying shared lifeways. Brennan's (2013) boundary of the Hudson River's embayed section, about 35 miles north of Manhattan Island also makes sense.

As stated earlier, I still do not want to become bogged down in setting exact boundaries. Regional boundaries are always fuzzy and subject to debate. Even established regions, like the Southwest, present boundary issues. The Pecos Pueblo is clearly an artifact of the Southwest culture area, but its location at the edge of that region, outside Santa Fe, New Mexico, was situated near the western end of the Raton Pass traversing the Eastern Front of the Rockies. There it served as a trading center with Great Plains groups. That mixing of lifeways was significant. Likewise, I have a series of historic photographs showing the Great Plains Sundance being conducted at the Taos Pueblo in the early 1900s. That too violates regional purity. Again, boundaries are always subject to debate and change.

That said, if a key variable in regional formation consists of ecology, what defines the Middle Atlantic are 1) the great Evergreen and Oak-Pine associations with the incursion of an Oak-Chestnut association at the northern edge and perhaps at higher elevations; and 2) the presence of great estuaries on its Coastal Plain and the rich resources they offered. The Middle Atlantic is a varied natural area given its latitude, and is also unique given the salt/freshwater mix of its embayed rivers. The Middle Atlantic is an ecotone, and that fact fairly well defines it. The region is not defined by natural sameness—it is primarily defined by ecological diversity.

A COMMUNITY OF MIDDLE ATLANTIC SCHOLARS

Another way to define and strengthen a regional definition is through sustained interest in an area by a community of scholars. While the present volume represents the first known book directly focusing on the Middle Atlantic, its chapters are the culmination of many years of research and represent a long-term focus on Middle Atlantic prehistory and history. Amateur collecting activities can be traced back in all parts of the region into the early eighteenth century (Dent 1995:26–27). The Tradescant Collection at the Ashmolean Museum in Oxford, England, contained objects from the region, including the famous Powhatan's Mantle, as early as circa 1638 (see Dent 1995:26–30).

With the establishment of the Anthropological Society of Washington in 1879 scholars of that era regularly met to present evidence for and debate the region's past. Many other institutions, particularly natural history societies, throughout the Middle Atlantic, began to do the same. An early stimulus was certainly the question of the timing of the earliest Native American inhabitants to enter North America. As discussed earlier, the region was thrust into the limelight with the research conclusions of William Henry Holmes (1897) at the Piney Branch Quarry site in Washington, DC. That research was, of course, Holmes's answer to the question of at what date early pioneer populations arrived in North America, specifically in the Middle Atlantic. Charles Abbott's claims for extreme antiquity, based on his research near Trenton, New Jersey, were called into question in the process.

In 1934/1935, the Eastern States Archaeological Federation was established, and while covering a much broader area, stimulated interest in the Middle Atlantic. Soon state organizations followed, with all states within the Middle Atlantic promoting research in the region through state societies. By the late 1960s, universities and other organizations sent archaeologists out over the Middle Atlantic. After student papers focusing on Middle Atlantic investigations were rejected by the Society for American Archaeology, a regional conference was established by William Gardner and Charlie McNett, respectively, from Catholic and American Universities in Washington, DC. The Middle Atlantic Archaeological Conference has now been meeting annually since 1972, and thanks to the efforts of Roger Moeller it has published an annual journal since 1985. It is not an exaggeration to say that the Middle Atlantic Archaeological Conference has done its upmost to solidify the region as a legitimate archaeological focus of research. Special acknowledgment is due the late William Gardner, the lion of Middle Atlantic archaeology (see Gardner (2013:75–86) for an amusing romp through his career and the ecology and archaeology of the Middle Atlantic region). The corps of students who passed through those programs, and other institutions of higher learning in the region, likewise did much to promote archaeology of the Middle Atlantic. It is important to note that the arrival of cultural resources management in the region in the 1970s was instrumental in placing the Middle Atlantic on the archaeological radar screen.

And the expansion of Middle Atlantic archaeological venues continued. Middle Atlantic archaeologists were soon in demand at many historic sites. Research programs at historic sites such as Williamsburg, Mt. Vernon, Historic Saint Mary's City, Monticello, Alexandria Archaeology, and the Association for the Preservation of Virginia Antiquities (Jamestown) have done much to increase our knowledge of the Middle Atlantic historic past. I should also note that the establishment of urban archaeology programs were a Middle Atlantic first. Many of these were started by women who had been denied access because of their gender to well-known research sites elsewhere in North America. Alexandria Archaeology, started by Pam Cressey, has become a model for such programs in the Middle Atlantic and elsewhere. As all this expansion took place, one saw an even greater interest at universities with archaeologists interested in the Middle Atlantic joining the faculties in increasing numbers. At present the Middle Atlantic Archaeological Conference draws more than 300 participants each year, all with a passion for regional prehistory and history. That fact alone is evidence of the viability of the Middle Atlantic as a region.

DIFFERENCES WITH OTHER
ARCHAEOLOGICAL REGIONS

Near the beginning of this chapter I cited Brennan's (2013:33) assertion that the Middle Atlantic was a place where ways of life, often developed elsewhere, were recast for new purposes and a new context; no single or salient cultural development ever took place within it. I think that is an overstatement. I want to take a moment to look at some of the elements of the Middle Atlantic archaeological record that are unique to the region and serve to separate it from others, both near and far.

First, the region is not ecological homogeneous as are many others. The Plains area is just that, covered with high and short grass prairies. Deserts dominate the Southwest. Closer to home, both the Southeast and Northeast are likewise more ecologically uniform. The former is dominated by the Southeastern Evergreen Forest, and the latter by the Hemlock White Pine Northern Hardwoods association (Braun 1950). The Middle Atlantic is instead more diverse, a large ecotone where associations to the south and north coalesce. It likewise is a zone of transition where large continental river systems are embayed as they meet the Atlantic Ocean.

The Middle Atlantic is characterized by generally acidic soils that quickly remove biodegradable materials from the archaeological record. Its archaeological record is more ephemeral, and recovering evidence of subsistence systems represents a greater challenge. Flotation was quickly adopted in the region. The same can be said for prehistoric community structure; it becomes a matter of chasing the stains of posts used in the domestic and village architecture of the Woodland period. In many ways, its prehistory is somewhat more ephemeral than other regions.

Brennan's (2013) contention aside, there are a number of developments that can be traced to the Middle Atlantic. Early on, the region joined the debate over Pre-Paleoindian with the discovery of the Cactus Hill and Miles Point sites. Two of the region's most famous Paleoindian sites, Thunderbird and Shawnee Minisink, were instrumental in calling into question the notion that Paleoindians were primarily hunters of Pleistocene megafauna. The latter produced direct evidence of seed gathering and fishing by site inhabitants (Dent 2007). Shawnee Minisink is also one of the most consistently radiocarbon dated Paleoindian sites in North America.

I also think the region has a unique story to tell in terms of the development of chiefdoms along the Atlantic Coast. Binford (1964) was the first to note a correlation between Falls Zone resources and increasing cultural complexity. To Binford, the focus was anadromous fish runs. Since that early research others have advanced a number of hypotheses regarding the origins of chiefdoms – the impact of European settlement, population pressure, trade, internal social competition, increased contact with outside native groups, and the like (see Dent 1995:276–77). I personally now believe that the documented population movements in the region late in prehistory were enough to make people empower leaders for cultural stability. Many new groups were formed out of old groups and leadership was crucial. While chiefdoms existed in other nearby regions, the process of creating ranked society started early in the Middle Atlantic. I have been successful, along with my partners in the Archeological Society of Maryland and the Maryland Historical Trust, in investigating a series of villages along the Middle Potomac River that offer evidence of the long-term development of ranked society from circa AD 1250 to the Contact era (Dent 2005, 2009, 2010).

As a corollary to the development of chiefdoms in the region, mortuary practices began to change. Ossuary burial represents one such change. Again, some groups in the Northeast, for example the Huron, practiced ossuary burial, but the practice appears early and sustained in the Middle Atlantic (Dent 1995:255–59). Dennis Curry (1999) has reviewed the practice in Maryland, and Christine Jirikowic (1990) presents a thoughtful explanation of its purpose. Ossuary burial was not region-wide in the Middle Atlantic, but the region is unique to the degree to which it was practiced, from the Eastern Shore to the Potomac drainage.

The Middle Atlantic was home to the first permanent English colony (Jamestown, Virginia) in North America and others soon followed in Maryland, Delaware, Pennsylvania, New Jersey, and New York. It has a unique and early record of cultural interaction and a large corpus of seventeenth century documents describing those encounters. As such, historical archaeologists represent a large portion of Middle Atlantic archaeologists. The Middle Atlantic region thus saw a number of unique developments during this era. Soon after early settlement, European inhabitants rediscovered post-in-the-ground architecture (Carson et al. 1981) and used it as a distinctive and widespread construction technique. With the somewhat later arrival of Georgian architecture, some regional modifications were made to it. The earliest Georgian or Palladian house I know of in the Middle Atlantic was Oxon Hill Manor, built in 1710. In many instances, traditional Georgian architecture was modified for local circumstances. False plates began to appear given hot humid summers, and stacks were moved to exterior walls for the same reason. The five-part Georgian mansion developed here, a central block flanked by hyphens and wings. The region was also an early adopter of Baroque street plans in more urban areas such as St. Mary's City and Annapolis. And there are undoubtedly many other nuances that characterize the historic archaeology of the Middle Atlantic.

To close this brief review, like all other regions, there are elements of the archaeological record that make the Middle Atlantic unique, and other elements that link it to the Northeast and Southeast. Whatever arguments can be made in either case, I feel there are enough specific Middle Atlantic traits to consider it a distinct region.

CONCLUSION

I hope that I have begun to at least make a start in convincing doubters that the Middle Atlantic is an area of North American worthy of regional status. I am sure that others could add even more in that regard, and perhaps it is best to view this chapter and indeed this book as the beginning of a larger dialogue toward that end. The Middle Atlantic is a diverse and varied ecological entity, characterized by several major ecological associations, along with the continent's largest and richest estuaries. The Middle Atlantic is further blessed by a large and creative group of scholars that offer interpretations of its past, at many individual sites and between sites in the region. The Middle Atlantic is a diverse region, in both ecological character and archaeological understanding and is a significant research area of merit within North American prehistory.

REFERENCES CITED

Braun, E. L.
 1950   *Deciduous Forest of Eastern North America.* The Free Press, New York.

Brennan, L. A. (Jack Hranicky)
 2013   A Paper by Louis Brennan. *Journal of Middle Atlantic Archaeology* 29:23–34.

Carbone, V.
 1976   *Environment and Prehistory in the Shenandoah Valley.* Doctoral Dissertation, Catholic University. University Microfilms, Ann Arbor.

Carson, C. and N. F. Barka, W. M. Kelso, G. W. Stone, D. Upton
 1981   Impermanent Architecture in the Southern American Colonies. *Winterthur Portfolio* 16:135-196

Curry, D. C.
 1999   *Feast of the Dead: Aboriginal Ossuaries in Maryland.* The Maryland Historical Trust Press, Crownsville.

Dent, R. J.
 1985   Amerinds and the Environment: Myth, Reality, and the Upper Delaware Valley. In *Shawnee Minisink: A Stratified Paleoindian-Archaic Site in the Upper Delaware Valley,* ed. by C. W. Mcnett, pp. 122–63. Academic Press, New York.

1995   *Chesapeake Prehistory: Old Traditions, New Directions*. Plenum Press, New York.
2005   The Winslow Site: Household and Community Archaeology in the Middle Potomac Valley. *Maryland Archeology* 41: 1–51.
2007   Seed Collecting and Fishing at the Shawnee Minisink Site: Everyday Life in the Late Pleistocene. In *Foragers of the Terminal Pleistocene in North America*, eds. Renee B. Walker and Boyce N. Driskell, University of Nebraska Press, pps. 116–31, plus ill. and references.
2009   Excavations at the Hughes Village Site: Life on the Middle Potomac River Bottomland. *Maryland Archeology* 45:1–28.
2010   Claggett Retreat: Formative Settled Life in the Middle Potomac Valley. *Maryland Archeology* 46:1–37.

Fagan, B. M.
1991   *Ancient North America*. Thames & Hudson, New York.

Fogelson, Raymond and William Sturtevant
2004   *Handbook of North American Indians, Southeast, Volume 14*. Smithsonian Institution, Washington, DC.

Gardner, W. M.
2013   How You Gonna Keep'em Looking at Potsherds After They've Heard Julian Steward: One Man's Journey into Cultural Ecology Or I'm in the Forest But I Can't See the !%&(o/o) Trees: A Play in Three Acts. *Journal of Middle Atlantic Archaeology* 29:75–86.

Griffin J. B.
1952   *Archeology of Eastern United States*. University of Chicago Press, Chicago.

Holmes, W. H.
1897   *Stone Implements of the Potomac-Chesapeake Tidewater Province*. Fifteenth Annual Report, Bureau of Ethnology, 1893–1894.
1903   *Aboriginal Pottery of the Eastern United States*. Twentieth Annual Report, Bureau of Ethnology, 1898–1899.

Jirikowic, C. A.
1990   The Political Implications of a Cultural Practice: A New Perspective on Ossuary Burial in the Potomac Valley. *North American Archaeologist*: 11:353–374.

Kroeber, A. L.
1939   Culture and Natural Areas of Native North America. *University of California Publications in Archaeology and Ethnology* 38.

Mason, O. T.
1896   Influence of Environment on Human Industries and Art. *Handbook of American Indians*. Smithsonian Institution, Washington, DC.

Meltzer, D. J. and R. O. Dunnell
1992   *The Archaeology of William Henry Holmes*. Smithsonian Institution Press, Washington, DC.

Schmitt, K.
    1952   Archaeological Chronology of the Middle Atlantic States. In *Archeology of Eastern United States,* ed. by James B. Griffin, pps. 59–70. University of Chicago Press, Chicago.

Stephenson, R. L. and A. L. L. Ferguson
    1963   *The Accokeek Creek Site: A Middle Atlantic Seaboard Culture Sequence.* Anthropological Papers, Museum of Anthropology, University of Michigan, No. 20.

Trigger, B. G.
    1978   *Handbook of North American Indians, Northeast, Volume 15.* Smithsonian Institution, Washington, DC.

Willey, G. R.
    1966   *An Introduction to American Archaeology, Volume 1, North and Middle America.* Prentice Hall, New Jersey.

Wissler, C.
    1928   The Culture Area Concept as a Research Lead. *American Journal of Sociology* 33:894–900.

Appendix
Sites Discussed in the Volume

Abbott Farm National Historic Landmark

Accelerator Mass Spectrometry (AMS)

Accokeek Creek site

Barton site

Black Creek site

Brodhead site

Cactus Hill site

Crab Orchard site

Faucett site

Keyser Farm site

Maycock's Point site

Meadowcroft Rockshelter

Miles Point site

Murray site

Overpeck site

Paleo Crossing Site

Paw Paw Cove site

Pennella Site

Peters-Albrecht site

Piney Branch Quarry site

Pig Point site

Plenge site

Schultz site

Shawnee Minisink site

Shenks Ferry site

Shoop site

Slaughter Creek site

Strickler site

Thunderbird site

Townsend site

Trigg site

Werowocomoco

Williamson site

Zimmermann site

Index